D1243828

CUP OF COFFEE

THE VERY SHORT CAREERS OF EIGHTEEN MAJOR LEAGUE PITCHERS

CUP OF COFFEE

THE VERY SHORT CAREERS OF EIGHTEEN MAJOR LEAGUE PITCHERS

ROB TRUCKS

smallmouth
press

New York , NY

Smallmouth Press
P.O. Box 661
New York, NY 10185-0661
www.smallmouthpress.com

SECOND PRINTING

2 3 4 5 6 7 8 9 .07 06   07 04 03 03 01 00

Library of Congress Cataloging-in-Publication Data
Trucks, Rob
major league baseball, interviews
Cup of Coffee / Rob Trucks.

ISBN 1-58848-039-9

Book Design by Christopher Chambers

Printed in the United States of America

For my mother

"All I knew at the time was that I was there, and it was a time when the greats were there. If I never made it another day, I could say, I had a cup of coffee with the big boys."

—Kirby Higbe, *The High Hard One*

FOREWORD

"Once a major leaguer, always a major leaguer."

That's the motto of the Major League Baseball Alumni Association. Anyone who ever participated—officially—in a major league ballgame is entitled to membership. It is the ultimate sports fraternity.

Most ex-big leaguers are not famous, except perhaps in their own minds. Most have had only a brief time in baseball's limelight. In the parlance of pro ball, they've had their cup of coffee and gotten on with their lives.

Rob Trucks's book *Cup of Coffee* honors eighteen former big league pitchers whose entire careers lasted fewer than fifty innings. None would claim fame, some may even be a bit bitter about their professional days, but all of them had an experience they'll never forget. Hell, I can feel their pain. It took me seven years to get a major league contract and I pitched just thirty-three innings before I was sent back to the minors for another year and a half.

I could've been a candidate for *Cup of Coffee*. My brief time in the majors created a thirst for more—eight seasons more as it turned out. I wish these eighteen pitchers whose career stories fill Rob Trucks's *Cup of Coffee* could've had many more memories to relish.

Perhaps this book will give them a taste of fame.

JIM BROSNAN
author of *The Long Season*

PREFACE

On this date fifty-one years ago, one of the most famous "cup of coffee" players in baseball history made his debut.

It was a Sunday afternoon. Over 18,000 fans were in attendance at Sportsman's Park to witness a doubleheader between the next-to-last-place Detroit Tigers and the hometown, and last-place, St Louis Browns. The day's promotion was a birthday celebration for Falstaff Brewery, the Browns' primary radio sponsor. Adults entering the park that afternoon received a box of ice cream, a slice of birthday cake, and a can of Falstaff beer courtesy of St Louis owner Bill Veeck.

Bill Veeck is in the Hall of Fame. He is credited with introducing exploding scoreboards and Bat Day to professional baseball. Veeck was the first owner to put players' names on the backs of their uniforms. He signed the American League's first African-American player, Larry Doby, in 1947, and in 1948 brought Negro League legend Satchel Paige to the majors as a member of the Cleveland Indians. Veeck proposed interleague play more than forty years before it occurred, advocated the abolition of the reserve clause in the 1950s, and helped plant the original ivy on Wrigley Field's outfield wall.

But despite this list of accomplishments, Bill Veeck is best remembered for bringing about the events that occurred in Sportsman's Park that Sunday afternoon in 1951. In his autobiography, *Veeck As In Wreck,* the owner wrote, "I would still be remembered, in the end, as the man who sent a midget up to bat."

In the second game of the doubleheader (the Browns lost the first game), St Louis sent three-foot-seven, sixty-five-pound Eddie Gaedel to lead off the bottom of the first inning. Gaedel's uniform, borrowed from the Browns' bat boy, was renumbered to 1/8. After home plate umpire Eddie Hurley checked to see that Gaedel had indeed signed a contract to play and was officially a member of the St Louis roster, Detroit catcher Bob Swift, on his knees, received four balls from pitcher Bob Cain and Gaedel trotted to first base with a walk.

That was Eddie Gaedel's cup of coffee. He was replaced by a pinchrunner, Jim Delsing, and never played in another major league game. The following day American League president Will Harridge banned Gaedel from baseball. In fact, Harridge went so far as to insist that Gaedel's name be stricken from the official baseball record, and that decision stood for an entire year. Eddie Gaedel's career stat line now reads 0 at bats, 1 walk, and a career on-base percentage of 1.000.

Baseball is the only professional sport that allows roster expansion for the final month of each season, so September 1 is also an important date. Every September 1, regardless of what day of the week the date falls on, each major league baseball team is allowed to expand its active roster from twenty-four to forty players. A larger roster allows greater opportunity for younger players, and it is worth noting that more than a third of the pitchers interviewed for this collection made their major league debut during the final month of the season. It is now nearly impossible for me to watch a baseball game in September without focusing on the players newly arrived from the minor leagues.

Wilfredo Rodriguez made his major league debut on September 21, 2001 and, if he does not return to the majors, can be classified as a cup-of-coffee pitcher. In baseball, the term "cup of coffee" designates a short stay, as in, "he was only in the majors long enough for a cup of coffee," and every player interviewed for this collection finished with less than fifty major league innings pitched in his career. To date, Wilfredo Rodriguez has pitched a total of three innings in the major leagues, including the pitch that became Barry Bonds's seventieth home run of 2001, the home run that tied Mark McGwire's single-season record just two weeks after Rodriguez first joined the Houston Astros.

Another recent addition to the list of cup-of-coffee pitchers also made his debut after the September 1 roster expansion, but with a considerably better result. Jim Morris first appeared in a major league uniform on September 18, 1999. He was thirty-five years old and a former high school science teacher. Pitching for the Tampa Bay Devil Rays in his home state of Texas, Morris faced one batter, Rangers shortstop Royce Clayton, and registered a strikeout. He appeared in four more games that year, and sixteen the following season, to finish his major league career with a total of fifteen innings pitched.

Morris's journey through sacrifice and struggle in order to achieve his boyhood dream of reaching the major leagues was made into a feature film, fittingly enough, by the Disney corporation. It's called *The Rookie*.

The first major league short-timer to obtain status as a literary figure, however, is Archibald "Moonlight" Graham, who, unlike Morris, achieved his fame posthumously. Graham is a central character in W.P. Kinsella's novel *Shoeless Joe*, later adapted as the film *Field Of Dreams*. In Kinsella's novel, the protagonist, Ray Kinsella, kidnaps writer J.D. Salinger and takes him to a Boston Red Sox game in an attempt to "ease his pain." While at Fenway Kinsella sees Graham's major league career stat line appear on the scoreboard:

Archibald "Moonlight" Graham
5'10" 170 lbs.
Born Nov. 9, 1879, Fayetteville, NC
Died Aug. 25, 1965, Chisholm, MN

	G	AB	H	2B	3B	HR	R	RBI	BB	SB	BA	SA	G by POS
1905 NY N	1	0	0	0	0	0	0	0	0	0	0	0	OF-1

Later that evening Salinger also admits to seeing the apparition, and the pair head toward Chisholm, Minnesota.

"Do *you* know who Moonlight Graham is?" Salinger asks.

"Only what you know," Kinsella responds. "A baseball player who was patted on the head by a dream. A man who played one inning of baseball for the New York Giants during the 1905 season. He never came to bat. He was just a substitute fielder for one inning."

"How can he be important?"

"That's what we have to find out," Kinsella says.

Virgil "Fire" Trucks is my great-uncle, my grandfather's brother. He is one of four men in major league history to pitch two no-hitters in a single season. He made the American League All-Star team in 1949 and

1954, led the league in shutouts both those seasons, and led the league in strikeouts in 1949. He was the winning pitcher in a 1945 World Series game and played seventeen years in the majors, including half a season for Bill Veeck's St Louis Browns in 1953. About a year ago I opened my copy of *The Baseball Encyclopedia* in order to refamiliarize myself with my great-uncle's career, but I was distracted. What captured my attention instead were the statistical lines of six other pitchers found on pages 2192 and 2193.

Bill Tozer pitched ten and two-thirds innings for the Cincinnati Reds in 1908 and never pitched in the majors again. Fred Trautman pitched three innings for the Federal League's Newark franchise in 1915 and never pitched in the majors again. Allan Travers? Eight innings for the 1912 Detroit Tigers. Harry Trekell? Thirty innings for the 1913 Cardinals. Hal Trosky pitched three innings for the 1958 White Sox and Bun Troy was a teammate of Allan Travers, pitching just six and two-thirds innings for the 1912 Detroit team.

There's something real and unfeigned about statistics, and I found myself returning to the Pitcher Register in *The Baseball Encyclopedia* over and over in the following months. I read the entries for Virgil, Bob Gibson, Vida Blue, and other familiar names, but I also came across some new ones—Roger Slagle, Bill Pierro, Ted Wieand—pitchers who had cup-of-coffee careers in the majors. These were men whose entire major league experience is represented in *The Baseball Encyclopedia* by a single line showing two innings pitched, twenty-nine innings pitched, six and a third innings pitched, and so on.

These men were good enough to play major league baseball but fell far short of reaching the Hall of Fame, and I began to see them as a kind of bridge between baseball fans like myself and players like Hank Aaron, Mickey Mantle, and Nolan Ryan, whose talents, honestly, are difficult to comprehend. I might dream that I've hit a home run in a major league game or that I've struck out a fearsome batter in a crucial situation, but I can't fathom hitting 755 home runs or striking out over five thousand batters, fearsome or not.

I thought that these men, like the real Jim Morris and the fictionalized character of Archibald "Moonlight" Graham, might have stories to tell.

I began my travels in October of 2001. I rented a car and drove across New Jersey to meet Ted Wieand at his home in Slatington, Pennsylvania. I took the subway to Brooklyn to speak with Bill Pierro in the house where he was raised. I flew to Atlanta and talked with Larry Yellen in his home just north of the city and ate breakfast with Cecil Butler at the

13

IHOP in Dallas, Georgia. I stayed with relatives in Birmingham, Alabama, when I met Reverend William Greason at Bethel Baptist Church. I took day trips to meet Arnold Umbach at his law office in Opelika, Sheldon Burnside on his back patio in Montgomery, Sean Whiteside in his den in Haleyville, and Stacy Jones on his front porch in Attalla. I stayed with friends in Nashville, Tennessee, and from there drove to White House to talk with Roger Slagle in his living room. In Arlington, Texas, I spent two nights at the home of cup-of-coffee pitcher Mel Behney so I could talk with Ray Peters in his study in nearby Flower Mound. From there I drove to Fulshear to talk and smoke cigarettes under an All Saints' moon with Joe Stanka, whose wife, Jean, would not allow me to leave until I had had my fill of local barbecue. Jim Foor and I ate and talked at a Thai restaurant in Houston.

I followed my spouse on business trips. In Minneapolis I met Mike Jurewicz at a Perkins' Family Restaurant. On Super Bowl Sunday I drove from Bradenton to Naples, Florida, to meet Fred Bruckbauer, one of two men since World War II with a major league ERA of infinity. Mr Bruckbauer and his wife, Kathy, invited me to their home that Sunday morning because they had been invited to a Super Bowl party later that day. As I was leaving that afternoon I tried, accidentally and unsuccessfully, to walk through their sliding glass door. The next morning, sore nose and all, I spoke with Fred Rath at his office in Tampa, and the following day Steve Ratzer and I spent an afternoon at a picnic table in front of the Wal-Mart in Lakeland, Florida.

Though each of these pitchers reached the major leagues, the road taken was, in every case, different. Though most were good all-around athletes as adolescents, four of these men never played an inning of high school baseball. While several of these men can be considered "bonus babies," the signing bonuses of others collectively wouldn't add up to a single house payment. Some remain fans of the team they played for, others have switched allegiances, while still others claim they are not baseball fans at all.

Some players left baseball due to injury or illness, some succumbed to family- or self-inflicted pressure. Some believe that they simply weren't good enough to last, while others believe they were in the wrong uniform at the wrong time. Some spent years in the minor leagues after pitching in the majors, waiting for another chance. Others threw their last professional pitch in a major league uniform and somehow walked away.

In *The Rookie,* Jim Morris's son asks his father if injuries are the reason he didn't make it to the major leagues.

"It's never *one* thing," Morris responds.

And this much is true. It's never just one thing that keeps a genuine talent from reaching the major leagues. It's never just one thing that causes a player's stay to be such a short one. Eighteen men—eighteen individual and unique stories—are represented in this collection, so I know that there are at least eighteen things that determine a career.

I feel fortunate for the opportunity to have met and talked with these men and to share their stories here.

Rob Trucks
August 19, 2002
New York City

Boston at Pittsburgh
Monday, July 17, 1950

Boston	ab	h	o	a	Pittsburgh	ab	h	o	a
Hartsfield, 2b	5	2	0	0	Rojek, ss	5	3	2	1
Marshall, cf	5	2	3	0	Beard, cf	4	0	3	0
§Mauch	0	0	0	0	Hopp, 1b	4	0	5	0
Olmo, cf	0	0	1	0	Kiner, lf	4	2	1	0
Torgeson, 1b	4	2	5	2	Bell, rf	4	1	3	0
Elliott, 3b	5	2	0	1	O'Connell, 3b	4	0	3	1
Gordon, lf	4	1	3	0	Murtaugh, 2b	4	1	3	2
Holmes, rf	4	0	0	0	Turner, c	4	1	7	0
Crandall, c	4	1	12	1	Pierro, p	4	2	0	0
Kerr, ss	5	0	1	2	Borowy, p	0	0	0	0
Sain, p	0	0	1	1					
*Reiser	1	0	0	0	Totals	37	10	27	4
Johnson, p	0	0	0	0					
†Cooper	0	0	0	0					
‡Sisti	1	0	0	0					
Hogue, p	0	0	1	0					
Totals	38	10	27	7					

Boston	0	0	2	0	0	0	1	0	5—8
Pittsburgh	2	1	2	1	0	0	0	0	0—6

Boston	IP.	R.	H.	SO.	BB.
Sain	6	6	8	6	4
Johnson (W. 2-0)	2	0	2	1	0
Hogue	1	0	0	1	0
Pittsburgh	IP.	R.	H.	SO.	SO.
Pierro	8a	6	8	5	5
Borowy (L. 1-3)	1	2	2	1	2

a-None out in ninth

*-Fouled out for Sain in seventh. †-Walked for Johnson in ninth. ‡-Ran for Cooper in ninth and batted in ninth. §-Ran for Marshall in ninth. R-Hartsfield 2, Marsh, Mauch, Torgeson, Gordon, Sain, Sisti, Hopp, Kiner 2, Bell, Turner, Pierro, E—Marshall, Crandell, O'Connell, RBI–Kiner 2, Turner, Murtaugh, Hopp, Marshall 3, Torgeson, Gordon. 2B-Crandall, Marshall 2, Torgeson. 3B—Gordon. HR—Kiner, Turner. LOB—Boston 10, Pittsburgh 8. WP-Pierro 2. PB-Turner. U-Stewart, Gore and Conlan. T—2:40. A—21, 450.

BILL PIERRO

Bill Pierro pitched twenty-nine innings over twelve games (including three starts) for the Pittsburgh Pirates in 1950. In that span he gave up thirty-three hits, walked twenty-eight, and struck out twelve. He lost both his major league decisions and finished with an ERA of 10.55. He was interviewed November 12, 2001 at his home in Brooklyn, New York.

Where were you raised?

Right here in this house. How's that?

That's pretty specific.

My mother, at the time, used to board children from the Angel Guardian Home, a Catholic home. You know, orphans. And it just happens she got me when I was about six weeks old. Somebody abandoned me in the back of a bar out in Long Island somewhere. I was about six weeks old. The cops rushed me to the home and my mother took me and boarded me until I was six years old and several couples wanted to adopt me. And my mother went to the mother superior and said, I've had him six years already. What would be my chances? And Mother Superior said, You first Of course. And my mother said, Wrap him up. We'll take him. Greatest family in the world.

Did you grow up in a large family?

No, no. They had their own two daughters, then they decided to adopt me. I was the only son. And it was right in the middle of the Depression—1932—when I was six years old. They didn't need me there, another mouth to feed. But they loved me that much. That's all I can tell you about that.

When did you first start playing baseball?

When I was thirteen or fourteen. In the neighborhood. We played stickball and baseball besides. And then when I went into the Marines I was on a couple of Marine teams, you know.

Did you play high school baseball?

No. I couldn't make the high school team.

Really?

I was probably the best of all of them but the coach said, You're too skinny. You're too skinny, which was ridiculous. They had no idea how hard I could throw a ball or anything.

Did you play other sports?

No, I couldn't make any of the high school teams. The guys that knew me and had played ball with me said, Jeez, we can't understand how the hell you didn't make it. We told the coach, you know, Give him a chance. Let him show you something. He said, No, he's too skinny.

Were you a baseball fan when you were growing up?

Oh, sure. Bob Feller. At that time I was really a Cleveland fan.

How do you get to be a Cleveland fan growing up in Brooklyn?

I just liked Bob Feller. He was my idol. And I always said, Gee, I wish I could be a Bob Feller some day. See, in them days they didn't have the speed gun that could tell you how hard Bob Feller was throwing. I would say Bob Feller had to be around ninety-eight, of course, and a lot of other guys, too, but they never had the speed gun when I was playing ball. We had no such thing as a speed gun or a pitch count. I mean, today—give me a break. If you're a strikeout pitcher you get, on the average, maybe ten a game. To strike out a guy you have to throw at least four pitches, on the average. So if you strike out ten guys, there's forty pitches right there besides the rest of the ballgame. I hear these guys today, Oh, the pitcher threw 120 pitches. Give me a break. God knows how many times, when I struck out seventeen and eighteen and nineteen guys in a game, how many times I threw two hundred pitches. Extra-inning games and all. They didn't have the splitter. They didn't have the sinker, which is what we called the drop. That's all. Just the drop. The knuckle-curve? No such thing. The split-finger? No such thing. Maybe somebody had that stuff but it wasn't known. Nobody called it that. Mainly my two pitches were the fastball and the sidearm curveball.

Did you throw the fastball sidearm, too?

Right. I was a sidearmer. They used to say, Jesus, he throws like Ewell Blackwell. And when you're a sidearmer and you happen to be in the nineties, the batters aren't too crazy about facing you.

It's hard for the right-handers to stay in.

Sure, because you're coming from third base.

Did your fastball have movement on it?

Yeah, that's what they said.

Were you just flinging it up there, or were you placing your pitches?

No, I just said, Here's my fastball. Hit it if you can. To me there was no inside, outside. High, yes. Because I knew my sidearm ball had a good rise to it.

You said you were with the Marines but didn't play high school ball. I'm assuming that since you were with the Marines instead of the Army that you enlisted.

Yeah, I went in when I was seventeen. I wanted to be a hero.

Did you graduate from high school?

No. I got up one day, my last time in high school, and it was English and I said, Mrs. Coughlan, can I be excused from class today? And she says, Why, William? You know, that's how the teachers talk. I said, I've got something to do. She said, What have you got to do that's so important? I said, I'd rather not say. She said, You better say, because if I don't know what it is, you're not leaving. I says, I want to go to Church Street. What for? she says. I said, I want to join the Marines. She says, Sit down. You're only a baby. She goes and stands in front of the door. She says, You're not going anywhere. I said, Mrs. Coughlan, please get out of the way or I'll pick you up and put you aside. She knew I meant it, so she stepped aside and she says, I hope they don't take you. Why don't you wait for the draft? I didn't even answer her. When the Marines accepted me I got what was called a war diploma, meaning you enlisted while you were in high school, and they honored that as a diploma. It was my last term.

That's in 1943. You said you played some ball while you were in the Marines. Where was that?

Quantico, Virginia, at the Marine base. Cherry Point, North Carolina. San Diego, California. And overseas—the Marshall Islands and Guam and all over.

Is this organized ball?

No, this is just Marine teams playing Navy teams and Army teams just amongst ourselves over there.

How long were you in the Marines?

I was in the Marines almost three years. I got discharged in June of 1946.

So you're twenty years old and you haven't played organized baseball. How does someone who's twenty years old and wasn't on his high school team become a professional baseball player?

When I got discharged I wasn't even thinking of it. And all of the guys around here—it sounds like bragging, I know—said, Jesus, Bill, whether it's baseball or stickball, you're some ballplayer. And I said, Aw, come on. And they said, No, no. Why don't you look into it? So I dawdled around and during the winter I said, Maybe I'll try it next year. So I happened to know some people right around the corner whose daughter was going out with Elbie Fletcher, who was the first baseman for Pittsburgh then, and I asked them to get me a tryout. First I had tried for a tryout at Ebbets Field. And they said, No, you're too small and you're too skinny. And I said, Yeah, I've heard that shit before. I was confident. They got me the tryout with the Pittsburgh Pirates through Elbie Fletcher. I went in to take the tryout and they signed me up before I left the ballpark.

Did you have any idea how rare that was at the time?

No. I know now. Nobody ever makes it out of these tryouts. But they gave me the tryout. Al Lopez was with the Pittsburgh Pirates at the time and Pittsburgh was in Brooklyn playing the Dodgers. And I said to Al Lopez, You better put a sponge in your glove. I throw pretty hard. He says, Yeah, yeah. Sure. So I warmed up and he said, Turn it loose, and I threw him about three pitches and he doesn't say it to me, he says it to one of the other ballplayers, he says, Jesus Christ, get me my sponge. And I was signed immediately.

So you were signed in Brooklyn at Ebbets Field, but for the Pirates.

The Dodger scouts were there, too, and they said, Jeez, what's the matter with you? You live in Brooklyn, and I said, Hey, I asked for a tryout a few weeks ago and you guys turned me away right from the door. You told me I was too skinny and too small, so you had your chance.

Where do the Pirates send you?

To Bartlesville, Oklahoma, which was the KOM League—the Kansas, Oklahoma, and Missouri League. Class D ball.

And this is 1947.

Right. I had just turned twenty-one in April.

So you go out to play in the KOM League and it's really the first organized baseball you've played. How did you do?

23

I won eight and I lost seven. The second year I was 17–8 and I set the strikeout record in that league that year. I got three hundred strikeouts. And the shutout record. I got six shutouts that season, and I struck out twenty-one in one game against the Independence Yankees. That was Independence, Kansas.

So you play two full years of Class D ball with Bartlesville.

Yeah.

I'm kind of surprised, if you've got the kind of stuff to strike out twenty-one in a game, that they don't move you up a level or two.

It wasn't so easy to get to the big leagues in them days. Today it's much easier. Number one, you've got about fourteen more teams, which means you've got fourteen more chances to make it. Cities like Milwaukee, Minneapolis, and Kansas City had Triple-A teams. Today they have big league teams. So on the average it took you five to seven years to get to the big leagues. But after the two years in D ball they sent me to Class B in the Big State League in Waco, Texas. And I won eighteen there and I lost eleven. Right after that the manager says, You're going to have a surprise when your contract comes. I said, What is it, buddy? What's it going to be? He said, You'll see. He didn't want to tell me. He was recommending me for Triple-A ball. From B to Triple-A.

That's a huge jump.

In them days, yes. Forget it. In other words, I'm skipping A and Double-A and going from B ball right to Triple-A. I get up to Indianapolis and who's my manager? Al Lopez. When I walk in the clubhouse he looks at me and says, I knew you'd be here. I was so happy. Then I had a pretty good season there. I won nine and lost two. Had a couple of shutouts. A one-hitter against Kansas City. I beat Louisville 1–0. I beat Toledo 2–1 in eleven innings. I could go the nine or ten or eleven innings. These guys today make me laugh. We were disgraced if we couldn't finish the game.

You're moving up the ladder. Did the money improve?

Oh, of course. Class B was $250 a month. Triple-A, all of a sudden, was $800 a month. I thought, Jeez, what am I going to do with all this money? Class D was $135 a month.

Could you live on that?

You could live but you had to struggle like hell. But it was a wonderful experience.

You were 9–2 at Indianapolis when they called you up.

Right. They called me up to the big leagues the last month of the season. Danny O'Connell and I were sent up.

The Pirates had a pretty bad team that year.

They always had a bad team.

You said that earlier in your career, when you were just flinging it in there, that you weren't always sure where it was going.

I didn't go for the inside or the outside. Like I said, I knew I had a good fastball and I just said, Here it comes, even if it's right down the middle. If I could just throw a strike I was happy, because I had a reputation for being a little wild.

What if you needed to plunk somebody? Did you just aim further in?

I never did that. I never threw at anybody because I figured if I hit somebody with my fastball I'm going to kill them. They were scared enough.

What if one of your guys got hit? Were you never in that situation?

No, I was in that situation but I didn't retaliate.

Can you still get along with your teammates if one of them gets hit but you don't hit their guy back?

Yeah. They all said to me, Why don't you knock him on his ass? I said, I can't do that. If I hit somebody in the head with my fastball I'll kill them. I know I will and I'm not going to be responsible for something like that. That's the way I felt.

When you get called up to the big leagues, is that the greatest day of your life?

25

Yes. Oh, sure. Definitely. I said, I'm here. I'm here. It's every ballplayer's dream. And every ballplayer wants to get into an All-Star game or a World Series one day, and that's why I was very happy to see the Yankees get their ass knocked off this year. They have enough. Give somebody else a chance to wear the ring.

Are the Pirates in Pittsburgh when you join the club? Do you and O'Connell make the trip together from Indianapolis?

Yeah, me and O'Connell went right to Pittsburgh.

What differences do you notice between the big leagues and Triple-A?

I got to be honest with you, I didn't notice much difference because, in those days, Triple-A was just a depot for somebody who broke a leg up there and you were called up. They knew you were ready to get to the big leagues.

Do they start off using you as a reliever since you're a rookie?

No. I was a starter right off the bat. My first game was against Johnny Sain and I had him beat in the ninth inning. I think I had him beat 3–1. But I walked a couple of guys, Billy Meyer got nervous, walked out and said, Give me the goddamn ball. I said, Okay, okay. That was my first game in the big leagues and even today I'm a little bitter towards Billy Meyer because I said to myself, If I was a manager I would say, I heard a lot about this kid in the minor leagues. We're in last place. We're never going to go anywhere. Let me see what kind of balls this guy's got, now that he's in trouble. Now, that was my opinion and it still is today. We've got nothing to lose. I've heard a lot about him. Let me see if he can get out of this. And I feel I could have.

Do you remember who they brought in behind you?

Hank Borowy, and they knocked the shit out of him.

Do you watch the rest of the game from the bench or are you so mad you go to the clubhouse?

No, I watched the rest of the game, until Borowy started getting his brains knocked out and I couldn't take it anymore.

You batted nine times in the majors and got two hits. Did you get a hit off of Sain?

I guess so, but you know what my batting average was for my whole career? Minor leagues and all? .059. I was a lousy hitter.

Danny Murtaugh also played on the 1950 Pirates team. Could you tell back then that Murtaugh was a manager in training?

Sure. Everybody liked him. He knew his baseball. Murtaugh was nice. He was good to me. All of them were good to me. Ralph Kiner was good to me. A very, very nice guy. Billy Meyer was the only nasty one.

Do you go to spring training with the Pirates in 1951?

Yeah. We left San Bernardino, California, where we had spring training, and on the way to Pittsburgh, by train, they had to pull me off in Cincinnati because I passed out. This was the onset of encephalitis. I was there for three or four days in the hospital, then I continued alone to Pittsburgh.

You passed out on the train?

Yeah, they rushed me to the hospital from the train in Cincinnati. And I was there for about three or four days and they released me and they figured everything was all right, and I got to Pittsburgh and I passed out in the hotel room. It was opening day and I didn't show up and Billy Meyer is cussing, That son-of-a-bitch from Brooklyn. That crazy bastard. Where the hell is he? And they had no idea I was in a coma in the hotel room. They found me about three days later. The maid found me. They called the ballclub and they rushed me to the hospital, Presbyterian Hospital in Pittsburgh.

But you had been out for three days?

Two or three days. I was out. I was in a coma. I was lucky I lived. It didn't scare me because I didn't know any better. When I finally woke up again, I asked the doctor, What happened? The doctor says, You have encephalitis. I said, Syphilis? He says, No, no, no. Encephalitis. I say, What the hell is that? He says, It's a brain disease. It's like polio or meningitis. One of those. It's the same family. I say, So how am I doing? And he says, I don't know yet. You haven't walked or anything yet and we're not ready to even let you try. You're still pretty weak. I said, Don't worry about it. I'll be out there next year. He said, I sure hope so, Bill. So while I was in the hospital, it so happened that I was situated right above the ballpark, and I'm looking out the window at a night game, you know? I can see everything, because I was way the hell up in the hospital. And the doctor comes walking in and he says, Hi Bill. What're you doing? Watching the game? I said, Yeah. He's standing behind me, talking to me, and I say, Hey Doc. No bullshitting. Truthfully, do you think I'll be playing ball next year? And he grabbed my shoulder, and I knew right then and there. The way he grabbed it, you know. He says, Look, Bill. How tough are you? Then I knew for sure. I said, I'm all right. Go ahead and let me know. He said, I don't think you'll ever put a ball suit on again. I couldn't believe it. I said, Bullshit. I'll be out there. But he was right.

So the last uniform you wore was a Pirate uniform. Did they ever find out how you contracted the encephalitis?

Yeah. You see, it happens to be an incubative disease. At that time they didn't know exactly. It could be a blow to the head, it could be food poisoning—which I had in the Marines—and it can also be a mosquito bite, which I had in the Marines, on Guam, when I was out in the Pacific. So they didn't know for sure.

First off, they didn't have the medicine that they have today. I might've made it if they'd had the medicine. Encephalitis can take four to fourteen years and you can be infected all the time but show no symptoms at all. Anywhere from four to fourteen years until it manifests in your brain and knocks you on your ass, which is exactly what happened. I figure I got bit by a mosquito in Guam in 1945 and this hit me in 1951. So there's your four to fourteen years. Six years. It caught up with me. All the years before I felt great. I was never sick in my life. I was like a piece of steel, for crying out loud.

What do you do when the doctor tells you that you're not going to play again?

I couldn't believe it. I figured, No way. Next spring I'm going to be in spring training. I was twenty-five years old and never sick a day in my life.

You're in the hospital for a while.

I was there almost a month.

Where do you go when you get out of the hospital? Do you come home to Brooklyn?

I came home, yeah. My father drove to Pittsburgh and picked me up, drove me home. And the whole winter I kept saying, I'm going to make it. I'm going to make it. I went out and took walks on cold winter nights alone and all, then I suddenly realized I couldn't run. I tried to run to keep a little warmer but I couldn't do it. A couple of nights later I went out again and tried to run. Same thing. I couldn't move. I said, Oh boy. Maybe he's right, the doctor. I still didn't give up. Not until spring training, then I knew for sure. I'd been through a couple of more doctors over the winter and they all said the same thing, You're never going to play ball again.

Could you even listen to baseball games on the radio that season?

I wanted nothing to do with it. I felt this way—if I can't play this game, then to hell with it. I don't want to know about it. And I'm still like that. All I watch is the playoffs and the World Series every year. The regular games all during the season, I never watch. I was a little bitter, I guess, but I did feel if I can't play the game, then what's the sense in watching it.

I understand.

A lot of people don't. They say, You were a ballplayer. You don't even watch the games?

Did you keep anything from your playing days?

Nope. In fact, I'm going to write to Pittsburgh one of these days. I want to write and ask them if they could please send me a jersey with my number, 13, on it.

That's a pretty low number for a rookie. Did you get to pick your number?

Yeah. The clubhouse guy said, What number do you want? At first I said, 69. He said, You crazy bastard. The fans will kill you. I was only kidding, I said. But I would like 13. He says, You're asking for trouble. That's a bad number, a hard-luck number. I said, That don't bother me. I don't believe in that crap and I still don't. I still don't. I believe this— what's going to be is going to be. Because the man upstairs, from the day

29

you're born until the day you die, is in control. This is what I firmly believe. What's going to be is going to be. And the more you worry about something and hope it doesn't happen, then sure as hell it happens. As soon as you become paranoid, that's when it happens.

So what did you do when you knew that baseball was over?

I became a grease monkey. I worked on General Motors cars—Buick, Chevrolet, and Pontiac—as a grease monkey. Then I gave that up and drove a taxicab for ten years. Then in 1969 I took the test to be a furniture finisher with the city. The Department of Public Works. And I passed the test and they hired me. I was civil service and I said, Thank God. They can't fire me. I'm civil service. Sure enough, in 1974 they closed the whole damn building down and we all lost our jobs. That was the only way you could lose your job. Then they turned around and they opened it up about a month later under the CETA program. Doing the same work we were doing. In the meantime, we'd lost our jobs. I said, Jesus, how ironic. I like to see people helped and these people need help, but, Jesus, you took my job away, then you turn around and open a building and you're doing exactly the same jobs again. I didn't think that was right. I really didn't think that was right.

Do you have any regrets? Obviously you wish you hadn't gotten sick.

Of course. That's the only regret. And the other regret was that game I pitched—my first game in the big leagues—that Pittsburgh was in last place with about another three weeks to go in the season. Billy Meyer should've said, Let's see what kind of balls this kid has. He should've left me in. Even if they knocked my brains in. I wouldn't mind if they were fighting for second or third place but that team wasn't going nowhere.

Did the Pirates give you any money when you signed?

Yeah, yeah. Big deal. I even hate to say it. A $250 bonus. My only contract with Pittsburgh, that I signed in 1951, was for $6,000 a year, which, in 1951, was more than a hundred dollars a week. Back then if you were making $70, $75 a week, you were making big money. I can only say, I didn't really care about the money, because I knew from what the sportswriters wrote about me and what opposing batters said about me that I was going to make it. And I did. So that's what kept me going. To hell with the money. I'm going to make it someday and I'll make it all up. That's what I said. But unfortunately I got sick and that's the end of that.

That is a terrible blow. On the other hand, it's better that you got sick in 1951 instead of 1950 and never making it all.

I've often said that—What if this happened to me in Triple-A? With all the write-ups saying I'm going to make it, it's not enough for me. I've got to be there and see it. Then I'll be satisfied. I don't care what the sportswriters and opposing ballplayers said about me. I have to see it for myself and then I'll be satisfied. And I did. And many times—you're right—I often said, What if this happened to me in Triple-A? I'd be wondering for the rest of my life. Would I have made it?

St. Louis at Chicago (NL)
Monday, May 31, 1954

St. Louis	ab	h	o	a	Chicago	ab	h	o	a
Moon, cf	4	1	0	0	Baumholtz, c	5	1	3	0
Schoen'st, 2b	4	2	3	4	Fondy, 1b	5	0	7	1
Musial, rf	3	1	2	0	Kiner, lf	5	3	0	0
Jablonski, 3b	3	1	0	1	Sauer, rf	2	2	1	0
Repulski, lf	3	1	2	0	Jackson, 3b	3	2	0	2
Alston, 1b	3	0	9	1	Banks, ss	3	1	2	2
Grammas, ss	3	0	1	3	Serena, 2b	3	2	1	1
Sarni, c	3	2	3	0	Cooper, c	4	1	6	1
Greason, p	1	0	0	1	Minner, p	4	2	1	1
*Yvars	1	0	0	0					
Deal, p	1	0	0	0	Totals	34	14	21	8
Totals	29	8	21	11					

```
St. Louis                      2  0  2  0  0  0  0—4
Chicago ..........................  2  0  3  7  0  2  0—14
     Stopped by rain.
```

St. Louis	IP.	H.	R.	ER.	BB.	SO.
Greason (L. 0-1)......................	3	6	5	5	1	3
Deal	4	8	9	9	2	1
Chicago	IP.	H.	R.	ER.	BB.	SO.
Minner (W. 5-2)	7	8	4	4	0	6

*-Hit into force play for Greason in fourth.
R—Moon, Musial 2, Jablonski, Kiner 3, Sauer 3, Jackson 2, Banks 3, Serena, Cooper, Minner. E—None. RBI—Musial, Repulski, Sauer 3, Jablonski 2, Banks 2, Minner 2, Jackson 4, Serena 3. 2B—Repulski, Kiner. 3B—Kiner, Serena. HR—Sauer 2, Jablonski, Banks, Minner, Jackson, Serena. SF—Jackson. LOB—St. Louis 4, Chicago 4. HP—Deal (Banks). U—Boggess, Stewart and Pinelli. T—1:53. Attendance—34,263.
Rain prevented second game.

BILL GREASON

Reverend William Greason reached the major leagues with the St Louis Cardinals in 1954 at the age of twenty-nine after several years in professional baseball, including a stint on the 1948 Birmingham Black Barons, where he was a teammate of Willie Mays. With the Cardinals Greason pitched in three games, starting two, for a total of four innings. He gave up eight hits, including four home runs, walked four, struck out two, and had a career ERA of 13.50. He was interviewed October 19, 2001 in the Pastor's study at Bethel Baptist Church in Birmingham, Alabama.

Where were you raised and when did you start playing baseball?

I was born and raised in Atlanta, Georgia. I was born in 1924. I went to school there—junior high school and high school—and after that I went into the service, the Marines, in 1943. I stayed through 1946 and played a little semipro ball for a year and came to the Birmingham Black Barons in 1948. I played with them until I had to go back into the Marines when the Korean War broke out. That was in 1951 and I stayed a year and got out in 1952.

But you played baseball before semipro, right?

When I came out of the service in 1946 I played a couple of games with the Atlanta Black Crackers, and the next year I went up to Nashville and played with the Nashville Black Vols. In 1948 I went to spring training with the Asheville Blues. I don't know whether they sold me or traded me, but that's who I started out with in 1948, and then the Barons came through spring training for an exhibition game and I pitched against them. And after the game they wanted me to go with them. I don't know what kind of deal they made. They don't tell you anything at the time and we didn't know anything. They just traded or sold us or did whatever they wanted. But I went with the Barons in 1948, and that was the year Willie Mays and I and two more guys, Jim Zapp and Joe Scott—we were all four rookies—started with them, and that year we won the National Negro League Championship. We defeated Kansas City in the playoffs. I pitched the deciding game. We played the Homestead Grays in the Negro World Series and I won the only game we won against them. Of course, it was in relief. Piper Davis used his supposed-to-be mainstays to start, but I went in in relief and we won that game. Of course, they beat us four games to one. Then I went back in the Marines in 1951 and I stayed a year, and while I was there I played with the Marines baseball team at Camp Lejeune, and they had some scouts there— they had one from the St Louis Browns—and he found out I was getting out in 1952, because we didn't have to stay but a year, and when I got out, Oklahoma City invited me to come out for a tryout, and I did, and I went to some prison in Oklahoma and I pitched against them and immediately afterwards they signed me. They offered me $2,000 to sign. Well, coming out of the Marines, you know, I thought that was pretty good. But once I got there, the man said, I'll tell you what I'll do. I'll give you $1,000 now. If you stay thirty days I'll give you $500 more, and if you stay until the end of the season I'll give you the other $500. I never did get all of my money. Oklahoma City had some of the largest crowds they ever witnessed there because there was just two of us in that league. Dave Hoskins and I, at that time, were the only two blacks in the league. We filled the parks wherever we went because Dave was a good pitcher, too. That year I won nine and lost one.

34

Was that Triple-A?

No, that was Double-A. I won nine and lost one and so the next year he signed me and I think I won seventeen and lost fourteen with a 3.48 ERA. I played in Oklahoma City, Houston, Rochester, and Columbus, and I played five or six years in the winter league with Santurce. Pedro Zorrilla was the owner of the team in Puerto Rico and he invited me to come over and I had some good years there. And in 1954, when the Giants won the World Series—Willie Mays and his crowd—Willie Mays came to Puerto Rico and played with Santurce and we had a team. We had Don Zimmer, Ruben Gomez, Sam Jones, George Crowe played first base, Ron Sanford at second, Buzz Clarkson at third, Roberto Clemente in left, Willie Mays in center, and Bob Thurmond in right field. We had a powerhouse. We swept everything. We went to Caracas, Venezuela, and swept the Series over there. They had teams over there from Panama, Cuba, Venezuela, Puerto Rico, and we won everything over there. I played a year in Mexico, too. I went back to Rochester and played with them for two or three years and then in 1959, I believe, they sold me to Charleston, West Virginia, but we couldn't get together on a contract so they gave me my release and I came on home.

You played with the St Louis Cardinals in 1954. How did you get there?   35

I was in Columbus. The Columbus Redbirds were in the American Association and Rochester was in the International League. I had some good years at Rochester. They called me up from Columbus. I had pitched against Herb Score and he beat me in a game 2-1 and right after that I got a call to go to St Louis, but I didn't want to go. For one thing, Eddie Stanky was the manager. He spoke to me one time. I stayed up there about seven weeks in the middle of the season. I didn't want to go. We had a good team in Columbus, and St Louis was losing. Johnny Keane was the manager in Columbus at that time and he told me to go on. I went up and I stayed about seven weeks and they sent me back. Eddie Stanky was something else.

Was he any better than he was seven years before when he caused problems for Jackie Robinson?

I couldn't tell because he didn't speak to me. He only spoke to me one time. I hadn't touched the ball for two or three weeks. I just sat on the bench. I'd go out and run and that was about it. Finally I started a couple of games, one against the Chicago Cubs, and they knocked me out early.

I think they were leading 4–3. And I started a game against Philadelphia and they got me out in the first or second inning. And I threw one inning of relief against the Giants and that was it. Of course, I hadn't touched a ball in over two weeks and I was a starter when I left Columbus. But one night in Philadelphia I was pitching batting practice and I was a little wild and Stanky came out cursing and I cursed back. He said, Get the damn ball over the plate, and I said, What the hell do you think I'm trying to do? And he just turned and walked away and that was the only time we ever spoke. It didn't bother me. I went back. I was happy to get out of there. They wouldn't let me go to spring training because I started playing winter ball. They said, If you give up winter ball, you can go. But I said, Who's going to take care of me during the winter?

Did you make better money playing winter ball than what the Cardinals were paying you?

I wish you could see the contract I got with the Cardinals. I made more in the minor leagues than I did with the Cardinals. They gave me a $900 contract when I went up there. I said, What is this? They said, You got to prove yourself. I said, You brought me up here. That ought to prove something. So I went ahead and signed it, but I was glad to leave.

St Louis was a losing team and Eddie Stanky's the manager. Looking back now, was there anything positive about your time in St Louis? You're glad you pitched in the major leagues, aren't you?

I reached my goal. I wanted to see what it was like even though I wasn't happy about going up there. I wanted to start in spring training because, at that time, I figured it wouldn't have been hard for me to get a starting spot on the roster. But when I look at it, after I gave up playing and entered the ministry, it was for a reason. I have no regrets. I don't regret anything I didn't accomplish. I made it. I started in Double-A when they had all that A and B and C ball. In 1948, when I came to the Barons, I was twenty-four.

You were twenty-nine by the time you made the majors, and that's pretty old for a rookie.

To make it at that age is tough. I figure if I had got a shot earlier, then I wouldn't have had any trouble. I don't have any regrets. I don't have any regrets about not staying up there. God had this worked out for me. When I stopped playing baseball I came back here and I worked for one of the leading stores downtown, Pizitz, for about fourteen years, and then I became a member of the church, was baptized, and went to school at Birmingham Baptist Bible College, went there for three years, graduated, and went to Samford University at night for six years. Then I graduated from there and I went back to Birmingham Baptist Bible College for another year. In fact, for ten straight years I was in school.

Were you particularly religious when you were playing baseball?

No, I wasn't, but I was brought up in a religious atmosphere. My mom and dad were church people and they believed in raising children right. There were five of us in that family. But we were brought up in a religious atmosphere and even though I played baseball and was not particularly religious, there were limits to where I would go. I did what every other man would do, you know, but I never messed with no drugs. I saw a lot of it. I even had a roommate who smoked pot. Even in the Marines in Camp Lejeune there was an ex-boxer, my bunkmate, and he found some marijuana out in the boondocks and he'd come in real late at night, but he finally got put in the brig. He socked a guard one night. But I was around it. I saw plenty of coke. And in Puerto Rico I saw plenty of that stuff, too, but I never even tried it. I did try to drink alcohol, beer. You know, in the clubhouse after the game they would have at least two cases of beer in there. I drank beer sometimes and I tried to drink some Scotch, but I couldn't do nothing with it. So when I made up my mind to leave it all alone, it wasn't hard.

37

Were you the only African-American on the 1954 Cardinals?

No, Tom Alston was the first baseman. He was the first one there.

So he was pretty much by himself before you were brought up. That's got to be tough.

Yeah, and he was really hurting because he had so much pressure on him. They wanted him to be the big guy on the team, him and Stan Musial. They were looking for them to be the big men and, of course, Tom wasn't doing anything.

He must've been happy to see you when you got brought up.

We became roommates, but Tom was really under a lot of stress and it didn't change much after I arrived because they were still looking for him to be productive and he just didn't do it that year.

Did you have anything to do with Red Schoendienst when you were with St Louis? He managed for quite a few years after he retired as a player. Did you see anything in him then that might indicate that he'd end up being a manager?

No, no. When you're on a losing team and you're trying to succeed in what you're doing, you don't look at other guys too much. One of the greatest ballplayers that I know that could've managed in the major leagues was the guy that managed the Black Barons, Piper Davis. He had everything. He was a student. He was smart, stern, and yet he could be nice to you. He knew how to approach you. He was the greatest manager I ever played for. Him and Johnny Keane, who finally managed the Yankees. I played for him on the Columbus Redbirds. They were about the best guys I played for.

What about players? Was Piper Davis one of the best?

Oh yeah.

Was Piper Davis better than Mays?

Piper was better than Mays when Mays started. Mays was just a rookie in 1948 but after that he developed. I would put Piper Davis up with any second baseman, any second baseman. The Red Sox bought him. They sent him, I think, to Scranton, but they never would bring him up. The Boston Red Sox and the New York Yankees, after my first year in Oklahoma City, they offered the owner $100,000 cash and players for me. That was the first year when I won nine and lost one, but he wouldn't sell me. He said, I'm going to wait until next year when I can get more. And I didn't cost him anything. But all of this worked for my good. I don't regret that. Mr Humphries, who was the owner at the time, he was a nice fellow. He took me into the clubhouse and told the fellows, Even though this fellow is black, I don't want you to look at him as being the first black ballplayer. He's a ballplayer. I bought him because I feel that he could help our team. And those fellows I played with in Oklahoma City were some of the best fellows I ever played with, and they were a white team. They were great fellows. I enjoyed playing. Of course, you got a lot of abuse. Even when we were playing with the Black Barons in different parks and all, folks would give you a hard time. They'd call you everything but nobody paid that much attention. We even called each other nigger. We'd been called that before but when other people said it, it was in a derogatory manner. But we didn't pay any attention. In that

Texas League, there was just two of us so it was tough, but I'd just smile and go on and pitch and did a good job. I didn't let it upset me. I'd look right at the person and smile, nod my head, and keep going. Why should I pay attention to that? I know who I am. I don't have to pay attention to what folks say. So that's the way it was with us, but we had already learned that, growing up in the South. In my hometown of Atlanta, we had to go across town to school and there were signs up—WHITE and BLACK. The South has always been, to me, more real than people up north. We used to go into restaurants and the waitresses would walk by you, not paying you any attention. And we'd ask them, Can we get some service? And they'd say, Do you see that sign up there? Because they'd have these signs that said, We reserve the right to refuse service. That was the thing that upset a lot of the fellows. We had a couple of light-skinned fellows, too. Jim Zapp—sometimes it was pretty hard to tell if he was white or black, so we'd have him go in stores for us sometimes. We'd pull our bus up to get gas and we'd ask if we could use the rest room and the man would say, We don't have no rest room for niggers, and so Piper would say, If we can't use the rest room then we can't buy no gas, so pretty soon people started letting us use it. We just took whatever was thrown at us and went right on.

When you were little, were you good at all sports?

I don't know. My abilities came naturally. When I was growing up we were poor and we didn't have basketball courts or football fields. We didn't really have anyplace to play like kids do nowadays. We could go to the playground, but that was the only place we had to play sports. They had what they call paddle tennis and they had softball, and that's about all we had. Like I said, mine just came naturally. We played stickball. That's how I learned to throw a curveball.

But you knew you were good, didn't you?

I thought I was. But my favorite sport at the time was football. We had a semipro team in Atlanta, the Atlanta All-Stars. We played two years over there. Of course, we didn't make any money. But I would work and play football.

What position did you play?

Quarterback and halfback at that time. I was a triple threat. I was a good football player for my size. At that time, the biggest guy you had to deal with was no more than 220 or 230 pounds. And they weren't fast They were strong but they weren't like these guys are now who pump that iron. I went out my last year in high school and we used to scrimmage every now and then against Clark College. They were in the SWAC and I was in one or two games over there. I could throw it and kick it and run it and catch it.

What did you throw when you were pitching?

A fastball and about three different curveballs.

So you had a drop-off-the-table curveball.

And a three-quarter and a sidearm. And I could change speeds on you.

So if I asked you what your throwing motion was, the answer would be, All of them.

All of them. Overhand, three-quarters, and sidearm, but most of them were overhand.

40 *Did you ever throw any junk?*

My last year or two I played around with it. I had a change-up that was out of sight. It was hard to pick up because I threw everything with the same motion. It was hard to pick the spin up on my change-up. The motion was the same because I knew how to release it. It was quite effective.

Do you watch much baseball now?

Every now and then, if I don't have something else to do. If I have some work to do then I say to heck with baseball. My sport is football. My wife watches sometimes with me and she talks about how hard they hit. And they do. I wouldn't dare get out there now.

Do the kids at your church know that you played Negro League ball with Willie Mays and made it to the majors?

Oh yeah. I went to California a couple of years ago when they dedicated the statue of Willie out in front of the new stadium in San Francisco. They invited me out, so I went out and stayed two or three days. I brought back a jacket and a couple of caps that they gave me. Orlando Cepeda was supposed to send me a team jacket but he never did. I had a nice time out there. I was on the program and said a few words for them when they dedicated the statue and I just told them I was happy that they recognized Willie while he was still living because I would've hated to come back and say a few words for someone who was dead. I've had a good life, a blessed life. This ministry has been a joy to me. This has been a great life for me. I've enjoyed it. I've always tried to help people. That's been my purpose in life. We were poor coming up. My parents didn't go to school. My dad was a laborer with five children. Mom stayed at home and tried to raise us and we were able to go to school and come out. My oldest brother went to college after he came out of the service and my youngest brother also attended college. He received a degree in electrical engineering. Both of them worked in the postal service for over thirty years. The oldest one was in there for about fifty. And the younger, after he'd put in thirty-something years, he became an electrician. And my sister is in real estate. None of us had the privilege to go to college to start with because we didn't have any money, but all of us turned out pretty good. We lived in the alleys. And I was determined, not only to get out of the alley, but to get the alley out of me. That was the main thing, to get the alley out of me. I did pretty good. I was determined to make something of myself. We were challenged by our teachers in school. They would bring up three or four blacks who succeeded and tell us, You're not anything. You won't do anything. But it was motivation. We would get angry and say, We'll show them. So with me, playing baseball and being in the ministry, I've had a great life. I've been blessed.

41

Cincinnati at Milwaukee
Saturday, September 27, 1958

Cincinnati	ab	h	o	a		Milwaukee	ab	h	o	a
Grammas, 2b	4	1	1	1		Haas, cf	4	1	2	0
eBailey	0	0	0	0		Schoen'st, 2b	1	1	0	0
Lynch, rf	4	2	3	0		Mantilla, 2b	2	0	3	1
Pinson, cf	4	1	3	0		Mathews, 3b	4	0	0	3
Robinson, 3b	5	0	1	0		Aaron, rf	2	0	1	0
Fridley, lf	4	1	1	0		DeMerit, rf	2	1	0	0
Dropo, 1b	4	0	2	0		Covington, lf	2	0	0	0
Dotterer, c	4	2	10	1		Taylor, lf	2	1	2	0
McMillan, ss	4	1	3	2		Torre, 1b	4	2	15	0
Hook, p	1	0	0	0		Crandall, c	3	0	4	0
bBurgess, p	1	0	0	0		Rice, c	1	0	0	0
Wieand, p	0	0	0	0		Wise, ss	1	1	0	5
Pena, p	0	0	0	0		Spahn, p	2	1	0	3
cBell	1	1	0	0		aBruton	1	0	0	0
Acker, p	0	0	0	0		Buhl, p	1	1	0	0
dColes	1	0	0	0						
						Totals	32	9	27	12
Totals	37	9	24	4						

Cincinnati	0	0	0	0	0	1	0	0	0—1
Milwaukee	0	0	4	1	0	1	0	0	X—6

Cincinnati	IP.	H.	R.	ER.	BB.	SO.
Hook (L. 0-1)	3	3	4	4	2	5
Wieand	2*	4	2	2	0	2
Pena	1	0	0	0	2	2
Acker	2	2	0	0	1	1
Milwaukee	IP.	H.	R.	ER.	BB.	SO.
Spahn (W. 22-11)	6	5	1	1	2	3
Buhl	3	4	0	0	1	1

*-Pitched to two batters in sixth.

a-Struck out for Spahn in sixth. b-Struck out for Hook in fourth. c-Singled for Pena in seventh. d-Struck out for Acker in ninth. e-Walked for Grammas in ninth. R—Fridley, Haas, Schoendienst, Taylor, Torre, Wise, Spahn. E—Grammas, Wise. RBI—Dotterer, Schoendienst 2, Torre, Crandall, Spahn 2. 2B—Pinson, Fridley, Dotterer, Taylor. HR—Spahn, Schoendienst, Torre. LOB—Cincinnati 12, Milwaukee 7. U—Smith, Dascoli, Donatelli and Crawford. T—2:39. A—19,670.

TED WIEAND

In 1958 Ted Wieand pitched two innings for the Cincinnati Reds in Milwaukee's County Stadium. Two years later he pitched four and one-third more innings for the Reds for a career total of six and one-third innings. In that span he walked five, struck out five, and gave up eight hits, including three home runs. One of those home runs contributed to a 1960 loss to Pittsburgh, his only career decision. He finished with a major league career ERA of 9.95. He was interviewed October 7, 2001 at his home in Slatington, Pennsylvania.

Your parents named you Franklin Delano Roosevelt Wieand. Do you have any choice about your politics, or do you pretty much have to be a Democrat?

I just about have to be a Democrat in my family. I was born in 1933 and my dad was out of work, and Franklin Roosevelt took over in 1933 and started the WPA, and my dad got a job in the WPA and named me after Franklin Roosevelt.

When did you start playing baseball?

When I was thirteen, I think. The American Legion started a team in Lehigh Township.

Did you grow up in Slatington?

In the country, over in the country about four miles from here. Everybody liked to play. We had pickup games between ourselves and we all turned out for this team and it did terribly. We didn't win a game for the first three years, but finally, when we grew up a little bit, we started winning.

Were you a pitcher from the start?

Yes, yes.

Did you ever play any other position seriously?

No.

44

Did you play other sports?

No. Baseball was it.

Did you have a favorite team when you were growing up?

Well, Allentown had a Cardinals farm team at that time so I naturally went to the Cardinals. That's who I signed with.

How did that happen? How do you go from being a high school pitcher in Slatington, Pennsylvania, to signing a professional contract?

Well, when I graduated from high school I was invited to try out for a lot of ballclubs. I was in Boston for three days with the Red Sox. I went to Yankee Stadium. I met with the Cleveland Indians. I went to Philadelphia for the Phillies and the A's. The St Louis Browns.

Are you getting letters? Phone calls?

Letters and invitations to come to these places to work out, and that's what we did. And, of course, I went down to Allentown many times and they had the scouts come and watch me and eventually they signed me.

Did you have several offers?

I had several offers.

And what made the difference? Was it because they were the Cardinals, or did they offer the most money?

Well, because they were the Cardinals. The money wasn't that much. It wasn't that much money but they told me I would play for Allentown my first year, that I would be able to stay home, and that was a big thing for me.

Even though the money wasn't that much, did you do anything special when you signed?

Yeah, I bought a car.

What kind of car did you buy?

I bought a Ford Victoria hardtop.

Was being a pro baseball player what you wanted to be when you grew up?

Well, yeah, after I started getting good at it. I didn't want to go to college. I wish I would've, but I didn't want to. And baseball just came natural to me.

Was signing the professional contract the best day of your life to that point?

Yeah, up to that point.

That was 1952 and you make the majors in 1958, but you got traded before you made the majors. You're traded during the winter meetings in 1957.

I got traded to Cincinnati.

That ended up being a pretty good trade for the Cardinals. They got Curt Flood for Willard Schmidt, Marty Kutyna and yourself. How did you find out you'd been traded?

They called me. It was a telephone call. It was fine with me. I wasn't getting anywhere with St Louis. The first year I played B ball and the second year I played B ball. The third year I played A ball and the fourth year I played A ball. The fifth year I played Double-A and the sixth year I played Double-A. So I wasn't really getting anywhere in the St Louis organization. I was in Columbus, Georgia, and I was twenty-one years old and I think I was the oldest pitcher on the staff. They really had a good farm system. They had somewhere around twenty teams in their farm system. They had a lot of good young pitchers ahead of me. And I thought that I could make the Cincinnati ballclub.

Did you start the season in Cincinnati?

I went to spring training with them, but I don't think I got in until the end of the season. For two years I got called up at the end of the season. In 1959 I was in Cuba. We won the Junior World Series when I was with Havana and that year I was Minor League Pitcher of the Year. I never had any complaints with baseball. I got all over the United States and Canada and Cuba and Puerto Rico and I never had any complaints about baseball, but I could never understand being voted Minor League Pitcher of the Year and never getting the chance to start a ballgame in the major leagues.

So were you a starter in the minors?

I did both. In fact, in Columbus, Ohio, I won a doubleheader on the Fourth of July. I started the first game and relieved the second game.

In 1958 you played in one game and pitched for two innings. Do you remember your debut?

It was against Milwaukee in County Stadium. I pitched to Warren Spahn and got him out. And he was a good hitter. I don't remember who it was but somebody hit a line drive right back at me and got me and they had to take me out of the game.

You gave up three home runs in your career.

One was in Pittsburgh. I came in to pitch in the ninth inning. Our pitcher had got hit hard in the first inning and Freddie Hutchinson took him out and put Orlando Pena in, and he pitched eight innings and didn't give up a run and we went ahead in the game by five runs or something. So Hutchinson said, That's enough for you, and he put in Bill Henry because Bill Henry was the star of the bullpen. Well, before Bill Henry got anybody out we were only one run ahead and I'm in the ballgame. I got the first two guys out and then Mazeroski hit a ground ball in the infield that nobody could get to and he beat it out. I get two balls and no strikes on the next guy, Bob Skinner, Pittsburgh's left fielder, and Ed Bailey was catching and he called time-out and he said, I want this one right under his chin. And I said, Okay, and I threw it right there. He took one step back and one-handed the ball, and that thing took off like a rocket. It hit the steel post and I thought it would knock the roof down. Man, did he hit that ball. In Philadelphia I came in and I'm throwing pitches and throwing pitches and the umpire's calling them balls and calling them balls, so Hutchinson tells me that I got to make them hit it. The batter had just been brought up, too. I'd pitched against him all year in the minors and he hadn't had a hit off of me, but I laid one in there and he hit it out. So Freddie Hutchinson came out and he was mad. He was out there talking to us and the umpire came out and said, You gotta break it up, Freddie, and Freddie said, You can't see a pitch. How can you see me standing on the mound? Our catcher, Ed Bailey, was complaining. Everybody was complaining, but the umpire wouldn't call a strike and the guy hit a grand slam and then I was back to Cuba.

What surprised you most about the major leagues?

It was tough. There were only sixteen teams. Today, I don't know. Everybody says baseball's better today, but I don't know if it is.

Did you feel different when you were in the big leagues?

Well, it was certainly better than the minor leagues. When I was with the Yankees you had to wear a jacket. And when you're on the road, you ate where they told you to eat—in the hotel. They didn't want you to eat just anywhere. The Yankees were first-class, no two ways about it. When I walked onto the field in Yankee Stadium, that made my career.

Now, when was that?

1961. I was sold to the Yankees.

So you were on the Yankees' roster but never got to pitch for them.

Right. I was with the Yankees for the first five weeks of the season maybe. When Ralph Houk sent me down he called me in and he said, It's not your fault. He said, We've had so many rainouts, and the guys I'm pitching—Whitey Ford and Ralph Terry—they've got to pitch because they're going to win me the pennant. And I could see that. I was low man on the totem pole and just didn't get to play. But it was an experience. The biggest thrill was during infield practice. If you ever watch, when the balls are hit to the outfielders there's always a pitcher that cuts the ball off, and I was cutting off for Roger Maris.

Were any of the players particularly welcoming when you came up in 1958?

Well, Jay Hook and Claude Osteen were up there. We three were friends and stuck together pretty good. Smokey Burgess was in the bullpen so we got to know him. I never ran into anyone that didn't like us, even though we were rookies. But the best situation that I had was with the Yankees. I lockered right next to Whitey Ford during spring training and he was a gentleman, really a nice guy.

What was your best pitch?

Oh, fastball. Definitely. I threw sinker-slider as well.

What would be your weakness as a pitcher?

Curveball, I guess. I did not have a good curveball. That could have been one of the reasons they didn't keep me. If you watch baseball, even today, how many people have a good curveball?

Not many, because if they've got a good curveball they can't get it called for a strike. Doc Gooden used to have an awesome curveball.

Camilo Pascual for the Washington Senators had a good curveball. He had a good fastball, too. During the fifties he was one of the most dominant pitchers. He was really good.

When Houk sent you down, was that the last time you were in the majors?

Yes, he sent me to Richmond and the first night I pitched I was in San Juan, Puerto Rico, and I hadn't pitched in a game in about six weeks. And I was throwing BBs. I was throwing hard, and all of a sudden my arm popped. And that was the end. I played after that but I couldn't do anything. I couldn't do anything in Richmond so they sent me to Amarillo, Texas, and I couldn't do anything there.

When did you know you had pitched your last game in the big leagues? When your arm popped with Richmond?

48

No. Even then I thought maybe it would be all right. I didn't pitch much the rest of the year and I thought resting it over the winter would make it better, so I went to spring training that next year but I couldn't get the ball to home plate.

When you say it popped, what exactly does that mean?

What happened is, the nerve goes through your elbow through a slot, and the nerve came out of the slot and it rides on the bone. The Yankees sent me to a doctor in New York and he said, I can operate on that, but there's a fifty-fifty chance that you'll lose the feeling in your hand. We had three kids at the time and it was hard for my wife to come back and forth to where I was playing, so I just said, No. That's it.

So after spring training in 1962 you go to talk to the doctor in New York and he tells you it's surgery or the career's over, and your wife's in eastern Pennsylvania. Do you call her on the phone to talk about it or do you just drive home?

No, I just drove home.

Do you think she knew when you walked in?

I don't think it bothered her too much. I think she was glad in a way.

If you've got three kids and you're twenty-eight years old and playing in Havana, Cincinnati, Richmond, Amarillo, and New York, how do you keep a marriage together?

Well, most of the time she came with me. She'd never want to do it again, but she flew to Seattle with three kids. It was something like ten and a half or eleven hours on the plane and when she got there she said, Don't you ever do that to me again. The second year we weren't married yet. The third year I played in Allentown, and the fourth year we were married and she went along to Columbus, Georgia, with me. The two years in Houston she was with me and from Houston we went to Seattle. Then the next year we went to Cuba and she was with me in Cuba. The next year I started in Cuba but that's when Castro took over and they started shooting. I brought them home then and the club sent me to Seattle, but she stayed home. Three weeks later they moved the Cuban ballclub to New Jersey, but I was stuck on the West Coast. She traveled with me but it was hard.

That's pretty unusual for a minor leaguer to be married and have his wife in town, isn't it? In a way you have to be scared every time the manager says, Can I talk to you for a minute? If you've got a family with you, it's a little more involved than just getting on the bus.

Yeah. She came to Cincinnati when I was there, even though it was just for a month. The only time she didn't come with me was when I went back to Seattle.

Did you keep anything from your playing days?

I had some balls from games that I won, but I had three sons so those balls ended up at the playground across the street. I have an autographed ball from the Yankees but it was during spring training and there were so many rookies there I don't have very many of the good ballplayers' autographs. When I was there I thought, They're just guys like me. They're just regular guys.

There's a painting on the wall of you in your Reds uniform. Did you have that done later?

50

They did that the same year I was with the Reds, in spring training. A guy came around and painted everyone who wanted it done.

You're on a 1960 Topps baseball card. How important is having your own baseball card?

To me it was real important.

If I asked how important was having a baseball card on a scale of one to ten.

That's a ten.

I was going to ask you if you watch much baseball on television, but when I came in you had on the Yankees–Tampa Bay game. It's the last day of the season, the Yankees clinched the playoffs a couple of weeks ago, and this is an almost meaningless game, so I'm guessing the answer is yes.

Yes. I watch the Yankees and my wife watches the Braves. She's a Braves fan.

Do you talk to the television when you're watching a game?

Oh yeah. All the time. Mostly it's, You dumb thing. You can't throw a strike. You're making two million dollars and you can't throw a strike.

When you first mentioned Yankee Stadium, a big smile came over your face. Do you ever go to any games?

I don't go to games because, well, we're both sixty-eight years old, and to drive into town like that is just not my cup of tea. And you can see it better on television. You don't have to leave the house. But I like the Yankees. They were first-class. And when you walk on the field at Yankee Stadium you know you've arrived.

Is there any particular pitcher you like to watch?

I think Clemens and Mussina are from the old school. They come in a little tight every once in a while and I think that's the way it should be done. I don't think you should hit anybody in the head, but you have to move them off the plate. These guys going up there today, they lift that front leg so high, you know that the only thing they care about is home runs. They took the game away from the pitchers, as far as I'm concerned. As soon as you throw at somebody you're out of the game.

So who's the best pitcher since World War II?

Bob Gibson. Definitely Gibson. He won two Cy Youngs, and should've won more. Another guy that I really like—he won the Cy Young once—is John Smoltz. He's a hard thrower and he'll come at you. And Maddux and Glavine. They're pitchers. Whitey Ford. 21–3. Always won the big games.

Do you have any regrets about your baseball career?

Just that I would've liked to have started two or three games in the majors to see if I could make it. And I never got a win.

Detroit at Chicago (AL)
Wednesday, September 2, 1959

SECOND GAME

Detroit	ab	h	o	a	Chicago	ab	h	o	a
Yost, 3b	2	0	1	3	Aparicio, ss	4	3	2	1
Osborne, 1b	5	2	9	0	Fox, 2b	5	2	1	4
Kuenn, rf	4	1	1	0	Landis, cf	3	0	7	0
Kaline, cf	3	0	2	0	Kl'zewski, 1b	4	3	4	0
Groth, cf	0	0	1	0	Torgeson, 1b	1	0	3	0
eHarris, lf	1	0	0	0	Lollar, c	3	1	6	1
Burnside, p	0	0	0	1	Goodman, 3b	3	1	1	1
Maxwell, lf	3	0	1	0	Esposito, 3b	2	0	0	0
Bolling, 2b	4	2	3	3	Smith, lf	4	2	2	0
Wilson, c	5	0	3	0	McAnany, rf	4	1	0	0
Bridges, ss	2	0	2	1	Latman, p	1	0	1	0
aLepcio, ss	0	0	0	0	Stanka, p	3	1	0	0
Morgan, p	0	0	0	0	Staley	0	0	0	0
Narleski, p	0	0	0	0					
bChrisley	1	1	1	0	Totals	37	14	27	7
Totals	33	6	24	10					

Detroit	2	0	0	0	1	0	0	0	1—4	
Chicago	0	0	0	0	11	0	0	0	X—11	

Detroit	IP.	H.	R.	ER.	BB.	SO.
Foytack (L. 13-12)	4.2	8	6	6	2	0
Morgan	0*	5	5	5	0	2
Narleski	2.1	1	0	0	1	2
Burnside	1	0	0	0	1	0
Chicago	IP.	H.	R.	ER.	BB.	SO.
Latman	4.1	5	3	3	5	3
Stanka (W. 1-0)	3.1	1	1	1	4	2
Staley	1.1	0	0	0	0	0

*-Pitched to six batters in fifth.

a-Walked for Bridges in eighth. b-Singled for Narleski in eighth. c-Grounded out for Groth in eighth. R—Osborne, Kuenn, Yost, Lepcio, Aparicio 2, Fox, Landis, Kluszewski, Lollar, Goodman, Smith 2, McAnany, Stanka. E—Wilson, Osborne. RBI—Osborne, Bolling 3, Fox 4, Kluszewski, Lollar, Goodman, Smith 2, McAnany, Stanka. 2B—Bolling. 3B—Fox. HR—Smith. SB—Aparicio. DP—Yost, Bolling and Osborne. LOB—Detroit 12, Chicago 7. HP—Latman (Kaline), Morgan (Aparicio). U—Stewart, Umont, Berry and Hurley. T—2:42. A—43,285.

JOE STANKA

Joe Stanka made two appearances for the Chicago White Sox in 1959. He finished with one win and no losses and an ERA of 3.38. He gave up just two hits while striking out three and walking four over his five and one-third innings of relief work. He also managed one hit in three at bats for a lifetime .333 average. He was interviewed November 1, 2001 at his home in Fulshear, Texas.

Where did you grow up and when did you first start playing baseball?

I was raised in Oklahoma—born in Hammon—and I guess the first baseball was probably in junior high school. I always went to small schools in Oklahoma. I lived in small towns. And I guess I played in every game that we played but we didn't play very many.

Were you a pitcher in junior high school?

First base, pitcher, outfield. We had trouble keeping nine on the field, but I did a little pitching. I went to the same high school with Joe Ford. He signed with the Cardinals. He did most of the pitching. Joe hurt his arm. I don't know whether he ever made the majors. He's still scouting. The point is, he did most of the pitching. And that went up through my junior year in high school. My dad was a railroader and we moved my senior year. He got a job in Waynoka, Oklahoma, where I graduated from high school, and that was the first year that they had had a baseball team in years. I did do all the pitching there. And then after I graduated, before I went to Oklahoma A&M—Oklahoma State now—we had a town team. And Enid, Oklahoma, has the national semipro tournament every year. Our town team went there and at this time I had probably participated in thirty or forty, maybe fifty, outside baseball games. Pitching or outfield more than first base. And a Dodger bird dog saw me pitch and he came over and wanted to know if I'd be interested in playing professional baseball. I said no, because I was an all-state basketball player and I had a scholarship at Oklahoma A&M. Baseball was something to do on Sunday. I gave no thought to it other that that. And he said, Well, if you ever change your mind, let me know, and I'll get ahold of a scout. I'm sure we can get you some bonus. And that was the last I thought about it until I went to school. First of all, they told me I had to study. They hadn't told me that when they offered me the scholarship. I was never a student. And what I really wanted is the woman in there in the kitchen now. So everything considered, I quit college and went back to work on the railroad. We got married and had a baby boy and the doctor wanted his money, which was $300. It sounds ridiculous now. The hospital and the doctor's bill was $300. And the railroad had just gone on strike, and the guys told me, It's going to be a long one. I remembered that the Dodger bird dog said he could get me a bonus. So there was a guy that had been on that town team that had gotten a bonus with the Dodgers a couple of years before, and he said he got $300. I said, Well, why don't I play ball during the summer? Get the bonus, pay off the doctor bill, and when the season's over, go back to work on the railroad. And that's what I intended to do, but seventeen years later I was still playing baseball.

Did you meet your wife in high school?

Yes, in Waynoka.

Did she go to A&M as well?

No.

So your body's in Stillwater and your mind is somewhere else?

Right.

Do you even consider playing baseball at Oklahoma A&M? Would they have let you if you'd wanted to?

That's an interesting question. I thought about it—just something to do—and I said something to somebody there, one of the other students, and they said, Forget it. Oklahoma State had always had good baseball teams, and they said the coach wouldn't let anybody walk on there if he didn't recruit you. They said, He won't even let you try out. I don't know if that was a fact but that's what I was told, so it was the last I thought about it.

You played both basketball and baseball in high school.

Yeah.

Did you play any other sports?

Football.

You played everything and you were good at everything.

I played in the second football game as a senior in high school and it was the second football game I'd ever seen in my life. I had absolutely no idea what was going on. We laugh about it now, but they called this play forty-four on four. I had no idea what that meant. I turned to the guy next to me and asked, What am I supposed to do? About ten or fifteen years later, during the Wilkinson years—I'm not an Oklahoma State fan, I'm a Sooner fan—it dawned on me. Four back through the four hole on the four count. But it took me fifteen years to figure it out.

Did you consider going to OU?

I was offered an Oklahoma scholarship. Bruce Drake recruited me personally. But A&M, two years earlier, won the national championship and I'd always wanted to go to Oklahoma A&M.

Were you better at basketball than baseball when you were in high school? Did you even know that you were a good baseball player, since you've got Joe Ford in front of you, before you get to Waynoka?

I didn't think about it. Never thought about it. Never entered my mind.

But surely either when you arrived in Waynoka or when a bird-dog scout approaches you about pro ball, you've got to have an idea that you're good.

I wasn't interested enough to be curious.

Basketball was your sport.

Yeah.

So you didn't choose baseball. Baseball chose you with a $300 doctor bill.

Basically. I'll tell you how I got back in. I quit and got back in. I had a horrible, horrible first year. I went to Ponca City with the Dodgers—that was the Dodgers' Class D farm team—and somehow I missed the photo day and the manager said, Well, to heck with it. He was a young manager, too, and apologized to me later. He was getting ready to send somebody out—it was cut time—and he said, Well, we don't need him anyway, then, if he can't get here for a photo. So they optioned me from D ball to D ball, to Duncan in the Sooner State League. So I went to Duncan. I got there right before a game started—it was on the road—and I saw these two guys pitching. Now, I could throw pretty hard, and the Dodgers at that time, more so maybe even than now if possible, wanted that fire. That's all they looked at. They said, We can teach you anything else. We can't teach you fire. And I was sitting in the stands watching these two guys pitch, and I don't know how that ball ever got up there. They were just barely going. I said, Shoot. Not only will I not lose a game, they won't get a hit off of me. It wasn't that I had that much confidence, it's just that they were horrible. And I started a couple of days later and beat the league leaders. That's the only game I won that year down there. I ended up 1–9 with about an eight-something earned run average. The point being that I quit.

You were going to quit before they fired you.

Yeah, but I wasn't thinking that. It didn't dawn on me whether or not they would send me a contract. I was quitting anyway. So I went back to work on the railroad but in a different capacity. Before I had been on the repair track, and this time I went to work as a switchman. I had a regular job, which was very unusual for my seniority, but it was on the graveyard shift. And one night about two o'clock in the morning, the yardmaster was out. The yardmaster is the guy that controls that yard, or that area. And we got to talking about him and they said, Yeah, he's on call seven days a week, twenty-four hours a day. The guy says, You want to know something, Joe? We're getting overtime pretty much every day down here. We probably make more money than he does, working overtime. I said, Whoa. Wait a minute. I'm eighteen, nineteen years old and if I even get that far, that's as far as I can go? At eighteen, nineteen, if I can see the farthest I can go, I'm not going very far. So I went home that night and I told Jean, We're going back to play baseball. But if it hadn't been for that conversation, I might've stayed on the railroad. That's how intrigued I was with baseball.

So you call the bird-dog scout on the phone, he sets up a tryout, and it goes pretty well.

Well enough.

Do you get a $300 signing bonus?

I got a little over double that.

What did you do with the extra money after you paid the doctor?

I probably paid off some more bills.

By the time you sign to play professionally, are you strictly a pitcher?

Yes.

What are you throwing besides a fastball?

I was throwing a knuckle-curve, which was pretty good. But they said, You will not throw that again, ever. They said, It will tighten up your muscles. I understand somebody or a couple or three are throwing the knuckle-curve now but I quit throwing it, which pretty much left the fastball.

Where do you learn the knuckle-curve?

I have no idea. Probably somebody showed me, but I have no idea.

But you had it and, for a time, that was your second pitch.

Yeah. I had an in and an out and an out-curve and a drop. I didn't know how it worked with signals. I didn't know whether a curve was an in or an out or an out-curve or a downer.

You were a thrower then, rather than a pitcher.

Right. And I wasn't a pitcher for a long time.

Let me get the chronology straight. You sign in 1950 and go straight to Ponca City.

Yeah. Then in 1951 I went back to Ponca City.

Did you improve?

Yeah, I went 16–5, something like that.

58

What do you think makes them send you a contract for the second year if you go 1–9 in D ball?

Back at that time they were filling rosters, so it's not like now. Now they might not have sent me a contract, even throwing fire. The scouts that I know, they tell me that if they don't see a definite prospect, somebody out of college or a real high school phenom, they don't sign him. But there were so many clubs. Brooklyn had about thirty ballclubs at that time, including four Class D clubs.

Do you stay with Ponca City the whole year?

Yeah.

What do you do during the off-season? Does anybody try to work with you since you're a thrower and not a pitcher?

They let you go and didn't worry about you. But there was a big furniture store in Ponca City—I forget exactly how it came about—and they needed help in the winter, didn't need help in the summer. I needed a job in the winter and didn't need a job in the summer. I forget exactly how we got together, but I went back there every year for five or six years. As soon as baseball season was over I'd just show up, and when spring training came I'd disappear.

Where do you go for your third year?

In 1952 I had a Class A contract at Pueblo. Western League.

That's a good-size jump.

That was from D to A, a pretty good jump. At that time that was a big jump for Brooklyn.

You've been a professional for a couple of years so I assume that your interest in and knowledge of the game has grown so you're aware, at the time, that you've skipped over two levels of ball. This is an unusual, positive occurrence. Are you excited when you show up?

Yeah, I think they only had two Class A clubs. The other one was Elmira, New York. It was known that the prospects moving up went through Elmira. They had their prospects in Elmira and their second team in Pueblo, so when I got an Elmira contract, why, I was pretty pleased about it. But I hated spring training. Always did. All except my first year or two. And so when we got out of spring training I laid a story on Fresco Thompson. And so to help me out he switched me from Elmira to Pueblo. That way I could go on through and pick up my family in Waynoka. But it turned out good. I had a very so-so year that year in Pueblo but I always had good outings against Des Moines, which was a Cub farm team. And Wid Matthews was down there quite a bit because that was about their top farm club. Wid Matthews was the everything, except for Wrigley, for the Cubs at that time, and he liked what he saw in me and drafted me. I don't know what would've happened if I'd gone to Elmira, but I wasn't ready to be a Class A pitcher at that time. I was still a thrower. Still learning. I wouldn't have stayed with Elmira, but I did stay with Pueblo.

And sometimes when you've got a family, staying's a very important consideration.

Yeah, and that's one reason why I stayed there. Bill McCahan told me later, he said, I had to send somebody out and it was between one of you three pitchers, and the other two didn't have a family. Maybe he felt sorry for me, because at this time I was still just throwing the fastball.

Are you getting any instruction at all?

No. When they talk about the Dodgers really giving help, I laugh. Because I wasn't the only one. It's a known fact. All clubs are like this. They pick their boys and they're going to make it regardless. And if they don't pick you, you're not going to make it. I went to McCahan, because he was a pitcher for the Athletics, and I said, I need some help with the curveball. And he said, Joe, I never threw a curve in my life. I don't know how to help you.

What kind of coaching staff do they have for A ball squads in the Dodger organization in 1953? You have a manager.

Period.

No pitching coach, no batting coach.

A lot of them, in D ball, were playing managers. That's it. One guy. And he was usually a catcher or infielder starting out his managing career. That's changed a lot. Back at that time Bob Feller was the only one who worked out with weights. If they caught you working out with weights, they hung you. They fed you salt tablets like crazy, and all this stuff.

You go home at the end of the year.

Go to work in the furniture store. Spring training comes and there I go. I was ready to go. I was beginning, at that time, to look forward to baseball season. Baseball didn't actually become a job until about the sixth or seventh year. From then on it was what I did for a living. That's my job.

I know this is minor league and I know that the money's not much, but is it better than you're making at the furniture store?

Oh yeah. But not by much.

Do you set a standard of living, like try to live on what you make at the furniture store and save the small amount above that, that you get during the season? Or is it grilled cheese sandwiches during the off-season and sandwich meat during the season?

You probably know that in the minor leagues you get paid the day the season opens and you stop getting paid the day it closes. And so there's a period of time there that you're without money. From the second through about the sixth or seventh year, I'd borrow from Household Finance and I would pay them off during the season and get caught up by the end.

Where do you go after Pueblo?

I went to Los Angeles, the Cub farm team. That would've been in 1953. That was open classification at that time, and I was always shipped out somewhere—Des Moines or someplace—from there, until 1954. I had a good season in 1954 and I got a Cub contract.

Is it a positive thing when the Cubs draft you?

I was thrilled to death when I was drafted by the Triple-A, or open classification. I took it very positively. This was one step below the majors, and that was 1953 and 1954. In 1954 I was back in A ball at Macon, Georgia, in the Sally League, and I had a real good year there, particularly the last half of the year. Had an exceptional second half of the year. And I guess Matthews thought I might be taken by another club, but a major league club would've had to get me, so to protect me they gave me a Cub contract. I didn't make the Cubs. I've never seen Wrigley Field. I'd like to one of these days. Went back to Los Angeles, and in Los Angeles I had an eyeball-to-eyeball that year with the manager.

What was the source of the dispute?

Hurt feelings. These previous three years when spring training was over and it was cut time they'd say, Well, we got guys coming down from the big leagues. We've got to pitch them. And that's standard. It wasn't a "had to," but it was easier than saying, We're sending you out. So when I came with a Cub contract I said, Aha. Now it's different. As I remember, what happened with the manager was we had probably four games in San Diego and he had the four veteran pitchers slated. But the fourth one came up ill and I said, Well, that's me, then. But he started somebody else that had been in B ball, and I was real mad and hurt about that, I guess. When I finally got in I had a bad game and he took me out. Well, I'm thinking, It wasn't my fault. It was his, you know? And when he came out to take me out, I threw the ball down behind the mound and he said, Pick up the ball, kid. And I said, If you want it, you pick it up. He said, I said pick it up, and I said, If you want it, you pick it up. And the next day I was in Macon.

Let me ask you about the Cub contract. You can look at it now and see that they needed to put you on the forty-man roster in order to protect you. That's flattering, but when you get the contract is there a flicker of hope that you might actually make the club?

Yeah. Yeah. I figured I had a very good chance of making the club.

Are you a starter from the time the bird dog sees you all the way to Macon?

Every year I was a slow starter in the season. And every game I was a slow starter in the game. I think the White Sox kind of looked at me as a set-up man, more relief than a starting pitcher. I don't know. I wasn't there that long and we didn't have that good a rapport. They would've been real sorry because I was not a relief pitcher at all. You haven't talked to a slower starter.

You mentioned your lack of fondness for spring training earlier. Is it a mental thing that causes the slow starts, or is this more of a physical thing? That you're a big man and it takes some time to get it going?

A little of both. Besides, I'm lazy. I just hated the exercise. I hated the running and the calisthenics. Whatever there was about spring training, I hated it.

Do you gain weight while you're working at the furniture store in the off-season, or do you come to spring training pretty much in the same shape as when you left?

Pretty well the same.

Is that your thinking? I don't need to do this because I'm not out of shape?

No. I didn't think about it. I was skinny. I was skinny for a long time.

How do you do in Macon?

The first half of the year, so-so, and had a fantastic second half. By the way, I never ran a step after July the Fourth. Johnny Sain—if you re-member, he was regarded as one of the best pitching coaches around—he said that running was way overrated. In fact, I think he even stopped some of them from running so much. They didn't know. They thought they knew.

Where are you in 1956? Do you still belong to the Cubs?

I still belong to the Cubs until the Cubs bought Johnny Briggs from Sacramento. I was part of that trade.

What level ball is Sacramento?

It's open classification. The Coast League at that time, the fans and the owners out there, they wanted a third major league. And, of course, the powers that be in the major leagues didn't want that, which is why the major leagues agreed to expand out west. The Coast League wanted to be higher than Triple-A, so they came up with the open classification instead of calling it Four-A or something. It gave them a little more status.

You're there four years. Whether you're in A ball for four years or in open classification for four years, there's got to be a feeling of stagnancy, doesn't there? There have to be nights when you're wondering if you're ever going to move up again.

Hope springs eternal.

Does Sacramento have a working agreement with one of the major league clubs?

No, because that club tried to develop some young ballplayers and sell them.

So you can make the jump from Sacramento to any team in the majors. It's just a matter of who buys your contract.

I was very close to going to Kansas City. I went to Cleveland. I was sold to Cleveland on a conditional basis, but being a slow starter, they said, We don't like the conditions.

Who on the Sacramento ballclub had their contracts purchased and moved on to the majors?

There were quite a few, really, the next few years. Clayton Dalrymple, Ray Webster, Harry Bright, Al Heist, Cuno Barragan, Johnny McNamara, Marshall Bridges. Those come quickly to mind.

When those guys move up, are you happy for them, or is it more of a why-not-me feeling? Or is it a case-by-case basis depending on the player and the circumstance?

Most of those were never any competition to me anyway. Bridges had a lot better year than I did. Remember what Ruth said about making more money than the president? Bridges had a better year. My roommate for four years, Roger Osenbaugh, was sold conditionally to Pittsburgh but he didn't make it either.

Was he a pitcher?

Yes, he was a pitcher. And he had a better repertoire, so to speak. He and I were just real close friends. I didn't begrudge that any at all, of course. I was happy that he came back. Not to wish him ill at all, but he was a good roommate.

What kind of team is Sacramento?

Horrible. We were known as the Sad Sacs. Frankly, the hitting and the fielding wasn't very good and I was never an ERA man. I led the league in ERA one year, but most of the time I would have some real horrible games, particularly early in the season, which would ruin the ERA. I might have a lot of 2–1 games, a few 1–0 games, some 3–2 games, but I would also give up four runs in the first inning and not get anybody out.

Are you a pitcher yet, or are you still a thrower?

I would say probably the last two or three years in Sacramento I'm more of a pitcher, but I'm still working with the fastball. My control was not what the kid from Atlanta has. My slider would be there every now and then. It's mostly, Here's a fastball. If you can hit it, fine.

You don't belong to the Dodgers anymore and you haven't belonged to them since 1952. Did you ever throw the knuckle-curve again?

No.

Did you ever think about it?

No, I never did think about it. I did have a forkball that was pretty good from time to time, but never any coaching help. That's not an alibi. It's just a fact. There's a lot less training out there. Hopefully there's more now than there was then. I wasn't the only one.

You said that the coaching staff was manager only in the early days. What's the staff like in open classification?

The first year out in Sacramento we had it very good, kind of an overkill. We had the manager, Tommy Heath, and for whatever reason Jerry Priddy was brought in as a coach, and Ferris Fain and Chuck Stevens. All of those guys were coaching, more or less. They were all on that first year's team. Then I think most of those did not come back the second year, so basically we didn't have a coach after the first year.

After you sign the pro contract with the Dodgers in 1950, does anybody— teammate or manager or coach—does anybody ever teach you anything about pitching?

The only actual teaching or training or coaching goes back to McCahan. One of the big names who had pitched for the Athletics happened to be in Lincoln—this is the Western League—right after I had asked McCahan for some help. And I forget this guy's name but he was a scout for the A's and McCahan asked him to work with me for a little bit, and he worked with me about three days there—very little—and I left there throwing a pretty good curve. And that lasted about a week. That was the only time. Now, some of that's my fault. You do look back. I have no regrets about anything about baseball. I don't regret getting out of the Dodgers organization. I don't regret throwing the ball down, saying, You want it? You take it. Knowing what I know now, if I could do it then, I would keep insisting. But as a reason, not an excuse, when you have to fight for a job all the time, my arm was such that I couldn't throw between starts. I had nothing if I did, and my arm was sore. So I couldn't work out, practice. It wasn't where I could go to the bullpen if I needed help and have a coach help me. The only way to do it was if they'd have said, Look, I know you've got a bright future. We're looking to you for the future. If you don't get in a game this year, that's fine. You're on the team. You're going to be here, but we see that you can't pitch in between. You can't practice. You can't learn. You can't train. So we're going to train you as much as we can, even if you never get in a game all year, but you've got to have some breaking stuff. And you might work on that control while we're at it. That would've been the only thing. That's one of the reasons I don't have any regrets about insisting that I get some help some-where. Because I was always fighting for a job up until probably 1957.

65

The White Sox buy your contract in 1959. Is this an end-of-the-year move, or does it happen earlier?

Sacramento had a good start in 1959 and we led the league most of the year, and when they bought my contract, in the negotiations, Sacramento said, Well, we're fighting for the pennant. You can't have him until the end of the season. The White Sox agreed with that but then we took a tailspin so we were kind of out of it, so they said, Go ahead. But I still think I reported either the first or the second of September.

Did you get a percentage of your sales price?

Ten percent.

Was that a significant amount?

It was very welcome. It wasn't any real big deal but it was certainly big at the time.

Did you do anything special with the money or did you just sign it over to Household Finance?

Pretty well Household Finance. I think it was $3,500.

Is the team in Chicago when you join them?

Yeah.

So you walk into old Comiskey Park and they give you your uniform.

Well, there's where the trouble started. As I remember, I spent the night in Sacramento the night before. I either took a bus or flew to San Francisco, and flew from there to Chicago. When I got to the hotel there was a note from Hank Greenberg, who was the general manager at that time. He was the person that scouted and bought me. And the note said, As soon as you get to the hotel, get on out to the ballpark. I'm going to have you start tonight.

But you woke up in Sacramento that morning, and lost part of the day flying east, so this isn't early.

No, I got there about the time most guys were going out to the ballpark. He knew that. He said, As soon as you get to the hotel, drop your bags and come to the ballpark. And now remember, we're fighting for the pennant right then. At that time it was certainly not sewn up, so that was kind of a surprise. Anyway, I'm dead tired and I get out there and Lopez had a different idea than Greenberg anyway. Billy Pierce started, as I remember, and he got in trouble, and Lopez calls down for me to warm up. So I get up and I'm tired, and even though this was my tenth professional season, still it was my first time in a big league ballpark. I was probably somewhat nervous, and I pulled a groin muscle warming up. I never started a game that I wasn't a little nervous. I think anybody's lying if they say that they aren't. Anyway, Pierce got out of the inning and so I didn't get in that night.

The next night, whoever started got in trouble, Lopez called me, and I did get in. And I was fine then. I'm very thankful I didn't get in that first night. I don't know where that ball would've gone that first pitch or two, but that second night I was fine.

Who are you playing?

Detroit.

And when you go in, the White Sox are behind.

Yeah, and we had a big inning, which made me the winning pitcher. If you notice, I hit .333.

I'll get to that.

Make sure that you do. Do you want a highlighter?

How early in the game do you come in?

Probably the fourth or fifth inning.

And how long do you last?

About three innings. But by this time the groin muscle, which I'd never hurt before—I wasn't sure what my groin was before that—anyway, it was hurting real bad and my control got worse, so out I came. I'd had a sore arm off and on but never had any injuries before that. The next day I went to the trainer and had him check me out and he said, You've got a bad groin-muscle pull. I said, What do I do? He says, What do you want to do? I said, What I want to do is get back in the game as soon as possible. He said, Well, that means you have to totally stay off of it. Don't run. You don't even need to suit up but if you suit up, don't run. Stay off of it as best you can. And I said, Well, should I tell Lopez? He says, I'll take care of that, but he never did. And I don't know this until World Series time. The way I found out was, after we won the pennant, Bob Shaw told everybody in the clubhouse, If you've got tickets you want to sell, I can get you good money for them. And I said, Well, I'm not going to need all of mine so I'll see what I need and you can have the rest So a couple or three days later he was passing out some money to some of the guys that he sold tickets for, and I said, Did you get my tickets? And he said, You don't have any tickets. I said, Wait a minute. What do you mean I don't have any tickets? He says, They said you have no tickets. So I hit the steps about ten at a time to go talk to Greenberg and I said, I'm either on the team or I'm not on the team, and if I'm on the team I want tickets. And he said, I don't know anything about it. I'll get you the tickets, and he turned around and walked off. And I said, Oh, and another thing while we're at it. I took a cut to come up here from Sacramento. He said, No you didn't. I said, Yes, I did. And he said, Well, we have your contract. I said, Well, I'm making such and such now and I was making such and such in Sacramento. He said, That's not what they said. I said, Well, there was expense money. He said, Well, that's illegal, so that wouldn't have been transmitted. He said, I'll see that you get that, too. It was a relatively small amount, but at this time I'm a little mad because I hadn't pitched in about three weeks. I hadn't even been called on.

Are you in good enough health to pitch?

Yeah, I got over the groin pull. I was out about five or six days. My groin was okay and I'm back in uniform but he never called for me.
So Greenberg said, I'll get the money, and then he turned around again, but he said, But you've got a hell of a lot of guts talking to me about more money when you refuse to pitch. I said, I have no idea what you're talking about. What are you talking about? And he said, Well, Lopez called down for you to warm up and the bullpen coach said, He doesn't want to pitch. I said, That never happened. I don't know what you're talking about. And then we talked about it. Every once in a while I'll think about it, not that I'm sorry it happened. I'm glad it happened because that got us to Japan and that was better. But the trainer never told Lopez, so Lopez just totally disregarded me.

You pitch in two games for the White Sox. Your win comes against Detroit and that was your major league debut, but you get into one other game.

Yeah, I never tell anybody how I got that win. I think we scored twelve runs that inning.

You're not on the World Series roster. They have to go back to a twenty-five-man roster for the postseason and there's some kind of something going on between you and Lopez and Greenberg and the trainer. Does Greenberg end up getting you tickets for the Series?

Yeah. Me and another guy, a September boy also, a left-hander, ended up pitching batting practice for the Series. I pitched to the left-handers and he pitched to the right-handers, or vice versa.

So you wore your uniform to throw batting practice, go into the clubhouse, shower, and then go sit in the stands to watch the game?

On the ninetieth row of the Coliseum in Los Angeles. You know how many innings I saw of that? Not many. That year it was played at the Coliseum and they had ninety-thousand-plus at each of the three games. They won't do that again.

The White Sox lose, four games to two, but they beat Koufax both times he pitched. What do you do when the season's over?

We go to Caracas for winter ball. It was the second or third year that we'd gone. By this time, having won the American League pennant, Lopez is on the circuit all the time. And I'm reading *The Sporting News* down there and they get Pizarro and a couple or three other pitchers, and I'm not in good stead, so I said, That's it for me. There's no way that I'm going to make that team next year. I'm not even going to get a halfway decent chance, so that's when I left the White Sox.

Do you get an invite to spring training? They don't just release you. They own your contract, right?

I'll have to tell you about Japan to answer that question.

That's fine.

So I'm seeing this and early that year I had kind of mentally said, This is my tenth year. If I don't get sold to the big leagues this year, I'm out of here. I don't know what I'll do, but I know what I'm not going to do. I don't know whether I would've come back or not, but that's kind of what

I had figured. In spring training that year we were playing the Cardinals and they had just come from Japan. And we were talking with Gary Blaylock, and we were asking him about Japan, and he said, Any of you guys want to go, they're looking for Americans. If you decide you want to go, I've got a contact. And so I said, Let me have it. And not long after that I met this guy, the liaison, in San Francisco. Cappy Harada worked pretty close with the San Francisco Giants. And I met Cappy then and we talked about it and he said, If you decide you want to go to Japan, get in touch with me, and I said okay. So I totally forgot it, or I thought about it off and on. Actually I think I knew about being sold to the White Sox about midseason, and at that time I forgot about Japan. But then when all this happened, Japan came to mind again. And Cappy told me, I can get you a good bonus and a good contract, and that sounded real good to me. I came home and I knew that I had to do something, so I was prepared for whatever, but I got the contract from Greenberg and it was for the minimum salary. Minimum if I made the club. If I was sent out, which I knew I was going to be, I'd make less. I knew, especially with all that happened and me a slow starter and spring training—I couldn't get out Molly Putz in spring training—so I know I'm out of here and I know I'm San Diego bound. So I wrote back and said, This is not acceptable. I'm going on voluntary retirement. And I had asked this guy. I said, They're not going to give me my release, and he said, I think voluntary retirement will be all right. So this went back and forth a little bit. Greenberg said, What are you going to do? You can't make this chopping cotton in Oklahoma, and that didn't set very well with me either. I said, Whatever. I'm not playing for that. Put me on voluntary retirement. And he said, Well, probably you're going to change your mind. You know if we send this in, the rules state that you can't become active again until sixty days into the season. I said, That's all right. I'm through. So he said, For safety's sake, send it to me. If you don't show up for spring training, I'll send it in to the commissioner. Which he never did. But nothing was said about it until I went to Japan and had a good year. And then all hell broke loose.

How long after the Series is over is it before you talk to Cappy?

Well, it was in Venezuela, and I went to Venezuela pretty shortly after. It had to have been just a very few weeks after the Series. Of course, I'm reading *The Sporting News* every week, so probably three weeks, four max. The White Sox are acquiring these pitchers. There were fifteen or sixteen that were going to be on the roster. You can imagine what chance I had. So at that time I would say it was probably early December when

I contacted Japan. I really don't know if Japan hadn't worked out whether I would've gone back there to play ball or not. I don't think so.

Did they have spring training in Japan?

They had spring training that ends all spring training. They go in after the season is over, and after their Series is over, then they go on exhibition. All teams go for about a month. When they're not playing exhibitions they're in spring training and winter training. They only have about a month and a half of no baseball.

You don't speak Japanese when you go there?

Oh, no. No.

But they provide you with an interpreter.

Yeah.

And they're allowed how many non-Japanese players?

It goes up and down. Two or three. It was three at the time.

What team did you play for and what other non-Japanese players were on your team?

Nankai Hawks in Osaka. That year they had two *niseis,* which are foreign-born Japanese. Second generation. One was a *nisei.* One was Hawaiian. But they got rid of the Hawaiian before too long. They asked me to get them help with a player, and I recommended Buddy Peterson, who I'd played with and against in the Coast League.

It's got to be a little lonesome, even if your wife and family are over there, not to be able to talk to your teammates.

A few of them spoke a little English, and then, too, I always had to look before I sat down on the stool to see that the interpreter wasn't there. I had to make sure that he wasn't there. He was too close. He sat on the bench with us.

How do you communicate with your catcher?

You don't communicate with the catcher.

Do you throw what you want?

I learned that about my third year. As far as I was concerned, the catcher was asking me what I wanted to throw. It seemed to me that every time the catcher would call for a pitch that I wasn't sure about but I went ahead and did it, it turned out bad.

Is that true for the five-plus innings you threw for the White Sox? Do you remember who you threw to?

Sherm Lollar.

He knows these hitters and you don't. You're a rookie.

You have to remember, too, though, that Lollar's probably smart enough to say, This guy probably knows what he wants to throw. I don't know that. I can't tell you whether I shook him off. I would say that if he would call for anything but a fastball I would. Well, I had a pretty good forkball, and I was confident in that. He asked me, of course, what pitches I had and he warmed me up a little. I'm going to guess that I didn't shake him off, but not in deference to him.

How did you do in Japan?

I did very well.

Is dominating *too strong of a word?*

No, most of the time I wasn't dominating. My 1964 season, I was very dominant the last half of the season.

You played from 1961 until when?

Through 1966.

You're there for a while.

Seven years.

Did you make good money?

Yeah. Very good money. Not like they're making now, but at the time, considering the perks and considering that they paid the Japanese tax and I was deferred from being out of the States—I paid no income tax— I probably was making more than most major leaguers.

Did you come home in the off-season?

Every other year. We stayed over there every other year.

It sounds like a very pleasant experience.

I had the best job in baseball. To say that's one thing but I'm fixing to prove it. They have what they call the ace, and he starts every third or fourth game. At that time Mondays were off and Fridays were off for travel. And where here we've got a twenty-five-man roster and you don't mess with it, there they have a fifty-man roster. Every team has a farm team, twenty-five and twenty-five, but they have one sheet with everybody's name on it. And before every game they circle the twenty-five that are eligible for that game. Now, with that in mind, the first meeting that I had with the manager, he asked me how often I could pitch. I went over on a two-year contract, and at that time my goal was to play those two years, save tons of money—which I didn't—come back, and conquer the business world—which I didn't. Not only did I not come back after two years, when I did, I didn't conquer the business world. I only tried. It conquered me. And I said, Well, if you're asking me how often I will pitch, I'll pitch every day if you want me to. Now, if you're asking me how often I can do you a good job, every fourth day. Sometimes I have to wait until the fifth day. I didn't tell him this, but what I'm saying is, I've got a two-year contract, ironclad. If you ruin my arm, I don't care. I'm guaranteed two years. Well, he thought he'd change that, and he saw it didn't work, so it got to where I wasn't even eligible for some games, so I'd do the running and then I'd go to the Osano Hotel, which was the officer's billet where I bought cigarettes for ten cents a pack and I got Chivas Regal—a double shot—for twenty-five cents. Here I'm making tons of money, and a lot of times, say if we were going on a three-day road trip, he'd pitch me the last day at home and the first day back, and I didn't even go on the trip. So I had the best job in baseball.

You said that your best year over there was 1964. Was there a step down in 1965 and another step down in 1966? Is that why you quit when you did?

1966, my last year, was a horrible year. They did ask me to come back, pleaded, basically. In 1965 I had a good year, but he didn't pitch me that much either. We lost our oldest son over there. He was asphyxiated in 1965. And I quit. I hope you never have a problem like that. There is no pain that compares. And I resigned. At that time each team was only allowed two non-Japanese players, but the teams that had three were grandfathered. Now, once I resigned, that cut them to two, so once I decided to come back they couldn't take me, but another club wanted me. The guy on this club, the ace, became my best friend on that club. And he said, I will be managing this club in two years—that's already a given—and I'd like for you to come back. I'm going to manage the farm team next year and I want you to be my coach, and then coach on the big club two years from now. I said, No, I've had it. My legs are gone, my desire's gone. But anyway, that was with another club. That was near Tokyo. In 1964 I was Most Valuable Player in the league and Most Valuable Player in the Series. I had three shutouts in that series. I opened the series with a shutout. I lost the third or fourth game. I had a shutout in the sixth game. The next day the phone rang that morning, the morning of the seventh game. This is the next day and I'd pitched nine innings. The phone rang and I turned to Jean and I said, That's Fuji—that was our traveling secretary—wanting to know if I can relieve tonight. Well, he said, the manager wants me to start. Okay, I said, but you better have somebody warmed up. But I had a better game in the seventh than in the sixth, I thought. I don't know about the hits and the strikeouts or the walks. This is God given. I don't know why. You can't psych yourself into that. My arm was fine, all during the game, after the game, the next day. Not a pain. Why? I don't know why.

Was that the best year of your professional career?

I was 26–7.

Do you have any regret that you hit your peak on a Japanese stage instead of in the majors?

My only regret along that way is that I didn't go over there sooner. I'll tell you something else. I said I was optioned from D ball to D ball that first year, to the Duncan Utts.

The Duncan Utts?

That's the reaction I always get. I wouldn't trade that first year. I'd rather have been with the Duncan Utts that first year than the New York Yankees.

But what's an Utt?

That was the guy's last name. Otto Utt. We've had more fun with that. I'm not laughing at the guy's name, but when you say the Duncan Utts, I get the same reaction that you gave me. Really and truly, I'd rather have had that, now, than have been with the Dodgers that whole year.

What makes you decide to retire? Is it time to move the family back? Are the skills not what they used to be?

They're gone. The desire's gone and my physical condition's gone. I was just tired. I'd had enough. And this roommate I had for four years in Sacramento had gone into life insurance and mortgage insurance and he'd talked me into preparing to come with him, and so I had studied that and I think had even acquired my insurance license in the meantime. And I had no fear of it. I was going to come and just sell everybody in the United States an insurance policy, because I really believed in it. I still like life insurance, it just didn't like me. I had too much pride. I just couldn't stand the rejection. So we left and came back and I went into the life insurance business, but not with him. And that didn't work out, so when I handed my kit into the general agent I was telling a couple of friends good-bye and one of them said, Well, what are you going to do? And I said, I don't know. I think I'll go into business for myself at something. And he had me check into a franchise employment agency because a friend of his had bought and done real well. And I went over and talked to them. The home office just happened to be right around the corner and Houston was open. And I had heard Houston was the coming city, so against my wife's objection—Can't we talk it over, hon? No, it'll be gone—I plunked down the money for a Houston franchise and that didn't work out. But we stayed here in Houston. We came in September of 1967. We like Houston.

75

Did you keep any memorabilia from your playing days, whether from Japan or the States?

I have two balls. I was not a collector. I have the ball from the Detroit game and I have the ball from the seventh game of that Japan series. You know Louisville sends you bats for the World Series. I had those. I gave them to my son. I had a white bat and a black bat from the 1959 World Series. Very, very little memorabilia. I've got plaques from that 1964 season for Most Valuable Player in the league and Most Valuable Player in the Series. That's about it.

Do you watch much baseball now?

No. I see very few Astro games, but I'm interested in what they're doing. But I sleep whether they win or lose. When the Sooners lose now, which hasn't been often lately, I don't sleep as well.

Minnesota at Kansas City
Tuesday, April 25, 1961

Minnesota	ab	r	h	rbi	Kansas City	ab	r	h	rbi
Versalles, ss	5	0	3	1	Howser, ss	5	2	2	3
Green, cf	4	0	1	0	Hankins, rf	5	1	1	1
Mincher, 1b	5	0	0	0	Lumpe, 2b	4	3	1	0
Allison, rf	0	0	0	0	Klimch'ck, 3b	2	2	2	2
eWhisenant	1	0	0	0	bCarey, 3b	2	1	1	1
Lemon, lf	4	0	1	0	Siebern, lf	4	2	1	1
Battey, c	2	1	0	0	Thr'berry, 1b	4	2	1	0
Bertoia, 3b	3	1	1	0	Tuttle, cf	5	3	3	4
Gardner, 2b	3	0	1	0	Sullivan, c	4	3	4	5
Sadowski, p	1	0	0	0	Bass, p	4	1	0	0
Stange, p	0	0	0	0					
aValo	1	0	0	0	Totals	39	20	16	17
Br'ckbauer, p	0	0	0	0					
Stobbs, p	0	0	0	0					
cNaragon	1	0	0	0					
Giel, p	0	0	0	0					
Moore, p	0	0	0	0					
dHenry	1	0	0	0					
Pleis, p	0	0	0	0					
Totals	31	2	7	1					

Minnesota.............................	0	0	0	2	0	0	0	0	0—2
Kansas City............................	0	1	6	3	0	8	2	0	X—20

Minnesota	IP.	H.	R.	ER.	BB.	SO.
Sadowski (L. 0–1)....................	2.2	6	7	7	3	1
Stange	0.1	0	0	0	0	1
Bruckbauer	0*	3	3	3	1	0
Stobbs	2	0	0	0	1	1
Giel	0.1	5	8	7	2	0
Moore	1.2	2	2	2	3	2
Pleis	1	0	0	0	0	0
Kansas City	IP.	H.	R.	ER.	BB.	SO.
Bass (W. 1–0)	9	7	2	2	9	2

*Pitched to four batters in third.

b-Ran for Klimchock in fourth. c-Flied out for Stobbs in sixth. d-Struck out for Moore in eighth. e-Grounded out for Allison in ninth. 2B—Blair 3, Robinson, Adair, Lau, Blefary, Aparicio, White. 3B—Tuttle, Sullivan 2. SB—Versalles. SF—Howser. E—Lemon, Gardner. PO-A—Minnesota 24-12, Kansas City 27-16. DP—Mincher and Versalles; Howser, Lumpe and Throneberry 3. LOB—Minnesota 11, Kansas City 6. WP—Stange, Moore. U—Stewart, Linsalata, Berry and Umont. T—3:04. A—4,994.

FRED BRUCKBAUER

Fred Bruckbauer appeared in one major league game for the Minnesota Twins in their inaugural season of 1961. He pitched to four batters, yielding three hits and one base on balls. He is one of two men since World War II to finish his career with an ERA of infinity. He was interviewed February 3, 2002 at his home in Naples, Florida.

Tell me where you grew up and when you first started playing baseball.

I was born in New Ulm, Minnesota, and I was raised in Sleepy Eye, Minnesota. I guess I started playing baseball when I was four or five years old, and loved it and went on from there. I grew up in the right place. Southern Minnesota was a hotbed of baseball back in the early, mid-fifties. A lot of the towns around there would hire former Minneapolis Millers and St Paul Saints, Triple-A back then, who were nearing the end of their careers. The towns would bring these people out and it was a semipro league. Three games a week. And they'd find them a trade, a job in town, because they had probably put in fifteen, eighteen years in the minors and were not going to make the majors. And some of them were making some pretty decent money back then, times as they were. So they'd bring these people out and hire them and give them a trade in that town and they'd play baseball in the summer for these towns in southern Minnesota. There was the Western Minnesota League, or the Western Minny as they called it, and the Southern Minny. And it was a great time to grow up in the baseball field around there.

In high school I had the opportunity to pitch for the local team. As I mentioned, we played three games a week. Sleepy Eye was a town of thirty-two, thirty-three hundred, and many times we'd draw that many people to a ballgame. It was great. The fans were super. I loved it, and through high school did quite well playing with former major leaguers and many minor leaguers. I had the opportunity then to get a scholarship to the University of Minnesota, and, at that time, the University of Minnesota was doing very well in baseball. Back then, you could not play Big Ten ball when you were a freshman, but I had played at least that caliber in high school so there was no doubt in my mind that I was on my way.

My sophomore and junior years at the University of Minnesota were very good, and I still hold a few records at the University of Minnesota as a pitcher. I made all-American my junior year. Not both presses, but just one. Either AP or UPI, I don't remember which one. And I had the opportunity to go around and work out with different clubs and so forth with the possibility of signing a professional contract. Back then, agents were more or less unheard of, so my dad was my adviser. To kind of make a long story short, we were in, I believe, St Louis, and there was a fellow with the old Senators named Joe Haynes who I respected a lot, as well as their local scout in Minneapolis–St Paul, Angelo Giuliani. I trusted those people implicitly, along with Dick Siebert, who's now deceased, the Minnesota baseball coach. Great people.

Anyway, I think we were in St Louis with intentions of going on to other tryouts—Detroit, Baltimore, maybe Cleveland—working out with them and hopefully getting a professional offer. They called my dad and myself then in St Louis and said they'd really like me to bypass all this and come right to Washington, and I said, Gosh, I can't do that, because we'd made commitments and so forth. And Joe Haynes, I remember, said, I know all those people. I'll take care of it. We really need you here now. The major league team is out of town and the injured reserves are ready to go and the Triple-A prospects that they're going to call up are in town and we'd like for you to throw three innings against them. So we made that commitment and bypassed the others. I trusted him enough that he took care of our other commitments, which was a great move for us because we got into Washington, D.C., and met Calvin Griffith, the owner then, and I started the game that evening and I pitched the first three innings and I had a pretty good evening. I struck out eight and I broke the other guy's bat, so that really worked well. Of course, we knew we had a pretty good evening, so we hung out for a while and then left the ballpark that night about midnight with the contract that we wanted. In between then I did call my college baseball coach, Siebert, and said, I got this offer, and he said, Gosh, kid. I hate to lose you for your senior year, but take it. So we did.

Were you good at other sports?

In high school. Baseball, of course. Basketball. Football.

Were you equally good at all of them, or were you good at football, good at basketball, and really good at baseball?

Exactly.

What pitches were you throwing as a college pitcher?

I had one of the best curveballs, supposedly, around.

Was this over-the-top, twelve to six?

Yeah. A little bit after twelve to a little bit after six. And great change of speeds. I needed to work on my fastball movement, and that I did get developed.

Did you have good velocity?

Fair. I don't remember, on the old gun, exactly what it was but it was around ninety.

Often times it seems like scouts don't look for anything but speed from their prospects, but it sounds like you were already a pitcher when you signed.

Exactly, and I needed to be. When I was in high school, playing in the Western Minny and Southern Minny Leagues, those people, of course, a lot of them were in Triple-A, so you're not going to blow anything by them. So you needed to change speeds and be a pitcher instead of a thrower.

It sounds like you were fortunate to learn that lesson as early as you did.

It was out of necessity. Baseball's a good teacher for a pitcher. You either get the people out or you're gone. End of story.

You and your father are in D.C., it's midnight, you've had a good outing, and you have a contract in your hand. Is this the best day of your life up to that point?

To that point, yeah. It was very exciting. Especially with the evening I had.

You're grinning ear to ear.

You bet.

You get back to the hotel with the contract in your hand. What happens after that? Do you sign the contract that night? Do you just sit in the hotel and smile for a few hours?

That we did, and right before we left the ballpark we called my mom and, of course, my girlfriend, Kathy.

This is 1959, and the rule then was if you received $4,000 or more in bonus money, they had to bring you up and put you on the big league roster within two years.

That's correct.

Were you above?

Very much so. Supposedly I got the biggest bonus the Washington Senators ever paid. I think we reported that I got $30,000.

You're how old when you signed?

I'd just turned twenty-one.

Do you do anything special with the money?

Not really. Of course, a year later we bought a new car. You had to buy a new car.

What kind of car did you buy?

It was a dandy. We bought a Ford two-door hardtop. We still have the canceled check. We paid $3,200 for it. Cash.

Brand new.

Oh yeah. Brand new. In fact, the Ford dealer in town was a good friend of the family, so, of course, I had to buy a Ford. And I kind of had an idea of what we wanted, and Kathy and I were dating, of course, all through high school, so we said we wanted a two-door hardtop, a white one with everything on it.

Do you get to spend some time in Sleepy Eye, or do you have to go right back out?

No, right back out. I reported to Appleton, Wisconsin. That was in the Three I league—Illinois, Indiana, and Iowa. That was B ball back then, and Jack McKeon was the manager. Good guy. That was less than half the season. I was rookie of the year in the Three I League.

Obviously you did very well if you won rookie of the year. How's the competition? You've played in a successful college program in the Big Ten Conference and before that you'd pitched as a semipro against former minor leaguers. Is the level of competition in the Three I league comparable?

No, no. It's definitely a step up, because you have nine ballplayers there who can hit the ball. Generally in the other leagues there were some pretty weak sisters in the lineup.

If you got through the three through six hitters you were okay.

You were okay. And then you could kind of relax an inning. Of course, being a starting pitcher, I've always maintained, and a lot of them do, when you're healthy and have your good arm and your good fastball, your good curve, one out of four times you really don't have to think very much, but the other three times you better find out what you're doing and adjust or you're going to get hit.

Do you come home after the year in Appleton?

I played the short season in Appleton and after that I reported to the Senators in D.C.. I did not pitch for them but they called me up and I spent the rest of the season there.

So in 1959, you pitch for the University of Minnesota, sign a pro contract, play a few months in Appleton, and then get called up to the majors at the end of the year.

Right. At the end of the 1959 season I reported to the Senators and just was there in the bullpen, sitting in the dugout.

Do you know that you're not going to get to pitch?

No. No, I do not. Of course, then I think the Senators finished thirty games out, or twenty-five games out, in 1959.

In hindsight, do you think you're called up because of the contractual obligation surrounding your bonus?

No. In our discussions it was hopeful that I would make the Senators' pitching staff the next year.

You've had success at every level so far. Are you overwhelmed at all being a part of the major league club?

Not overwhelmed, because I knew I could do it.

So you go home after the major league season.

And Kathy and I got married during the off-season, in December.

Life is beautiful.

Couldn't be better.

Are you on the major league roster for spring training in 1960?

Correct.

Did you have a good spring?

Very good, up until I pitched against the old Milwaukee Braves. I started against the White Sox in spring training and had a good outing. Started against the Braves and I think I went six or seven innings and two-hit them or something. I did a little running, went back in the clubhouse, and I remember Griffith and Cookie Lavagetto, the manager at the time, coming in the clubhouse and I was just getting out of the shower and Lavagetto shook my hand and he said, Kid, you're going to be our fifth starter in D.C.. Great, you know? Everything was really beautiful, but after that my shoulder was really never the same. I don't remember hurting it. I don't remember doing anything, but my fastball was more or less gone.

In later years I went to the Mayo Clinic quite often. They're trying to find out what's wrong. I suppose it was rotator cuff, but they didn't know how to take care of it back then. Now it would be a simple process. Their final diagnosis, and this is a couple of years later, is if we do something with it we may ruin more than we know how to fix.

When do you know your shoulder's hurt?

The next outing. It just more or less went downhill after that. I had to learn to pitch much differently, going with a little bit of this, turning the ball over, more of the slider, and still using the off-speed. My curveball was not as snappy as it was without the velocity. So I really became kind of a junk pitcher.

They tell you that you're going to be the fifth starter and then your arm's hurt. Do you end up making the roster? Do you leave camp with the team?

I did not. They sent me to Charlotte and I opened the season there. I think I had a no-hitter for eight and one-third innings, or something like that, and after that it just deteriorated more.

Is this the Southern League?

No, this is A ball. They figured playing down south in the heat, I could get rid of whatever I had, but they had no idea.

If they reassign you at the beginning of the season and you leave with the rest of the minor leaguers, that doesn't leave a lot of time for diagnosis.

I went to a few doctors there and then started the cortisone shots. I spent all year in Charlotte, then towards the end of the year somebody thought maybe it was my tonsils or something. The doctor in Charlotte. They sent me to D.C. and took my tonsils out and I suited up there a few times but did not play. And then at the end of the season, I went home and I was very discouraged because I knew something was seriously wrong with my shoulder.

So you've been in a major league uniform, on the Senators' roster, in both September of 1959 and September of 1960 but you haven't thrown a pitch in a major league game. Is that discouraging?

Very. Knowing better, knowing that I didn't have my velocity and so forth, I was just saying a few prayers hoping it would get well. And so were they.

You mentioned starting the cortisone shots when you were with Charlotte. Do you remember your first cortisone shot?

Very much so. It was without novocaine and in the socket of my shoulder in kind of a dentist's chair. First they unscrew the tube and screw another one in and go around in there, like I said, without novocaine, and when I left the doctor's office I was perspiring quite heavily. It was tough. And then I went out to throw in a couple of days. The next day? No way. As I mentioned, things just deteriorated after that. Velocity and so forth.

When the doctor looks at you—and this is probably a doctor the Senators have chosen—and he tells you that you need a cortisone shot, do you just say, Yes, sir, or do you have second thoughts? Had any of the guys you'd played with had cortisone before? What's your experience with or knowledge of cortisone at that time?

Very little. It was a new drug at the time. It was supposed to be the wonder drug. And it was like, I sure hope it helps.

Was the cortisone an ongoing treatment? Did you get a shot once a week? Once a month? Or was it, I did this once and it didn't help so I'm not going to do it anymore?

No, I don't recall there being a schedule but I had lots of cortisone shots.

I don't think they would do that today but back then they thought it would help. It didn't.

So you go home at the end of 1960 and you're discouraged and hurting.

Very. So then in 1961 the Senators move to Minnesota, which was kind of in the plans way back then. Stressful winter. Report with the Twins to spring training, still in Orlando, and had a fair spring the way I didn't want to pitch. Without the good fastball. Went north with the Twins and my arm was still fair, and we were on the road for quite some time. The only game I was in was in Kansas City, and I think I threw to four hitters. That game they used eleven pitchers. Everybody got in. It was just one of those nights. I think I gave up a broken-bat single and a couple of bloops. No one hit the ball well. Anyway, it was bad. It seemed like after that, things got progressively just a little bit worse all the time, so they sent me to Syracuse in the International League.

You pitch on April twenty-fifth. How much longer do you stay with the team?

I probably spent another month in Minnesota and did not pitch.

Is there any excitement, even though this is a lopsided ballgame, about finally getting into a major league game?

No. I knew my arm wasn't good.

That almost sounds like dread.

Exactly.

This is your job and you have to do it.

Yeah. Knowing that during spring training and at other levels I can still get these people out a little bit, or for a while.

Do you feel like you don't belong?

There were times with the arm condition. When I started, I was on top. You can do no wrong. And now that's deteriorated, yes.

At this stage in your life, are you able to leave those frustrations at the park? I mean, this is more than a job. When you come home at night, are you still upset?

Very much so. Yeah. And that's where Kathy was just super with me.

But you're on the road when you finally get into a major league game and you pitch to four guys and they don't hit you well, but you don't get anybody out, either. How bad is that night? You're in Kansas City, you're away from family, you've finally pitched in the majors, but your arm's getting worse instead of better.

It was not a good evening, but, again, a telephone call back to Kathy and, of course, the Minneapolis–St Paul papers had been to our apartment already. They had interviewed her. So she said, They've been here already. Things will get better. So we just went on. Like I said, she was great.

At this point, you're really glad to be loved.

Amen. Nothing else is going well.

88 | *Is Lavagetto still the manager when you get sent down?*

Yes.

Is he the one that calls you into the office?

Yeah. He said, Fred, we have to make a little room here and we're going to send you to Syracuse and let's get that arm better.

And you're not surprised because you haven't been pitching.

Exactly. I've got to go do something and hopefully go work out this soreness, which didn't happen.

Is it soreness or is it pain? Is it dull? Is it sharp? Soreness sounds natural.

Oh, no, this is unnatural, without a doubt.

Does it hurt when you're not throwing?

No, but I cannot throw hard, even in Syracuse. We had kind of a makeshift ballclub there but I won quite a few games. I really don't remember how many, but it got to a point where after three innings of trying to throw hard again, with the old motion, I couldn't even feel my fingers. Of course, I made trips back to the Mayo Clinic. They tried. I tried, but it just wasn't to be. I probably spent as much time at the Mayo Clinic as I did with the major league teams.

Do you finish that year with Syracuse? It sounds like your numbers were okay.

I finished that year with Syracuse and I did okay, but not to my satisfaction.

Did they call you up in September?

No, I didn't go back to the Twins at the end of the year.

But this isn't particularly disappointing or surprising.

By that time I was kind of coming to the realization that I'd about had it.

How many more years do you play?

We reported to spring training with the Twins in 1962, and by that time things were bad.

Do you still have a major league contract that year or is it a split contract?

Major league. But that was part of my agreement when I got my bonus. They had to give me a major league contract for three years.

So when you go to spring training in 1962 you might've had a hope of making the Twins team, but it was a faint one.

Right. So they wanted to send me down again, full knowing that I'm probably coming home. I was in Orlando and then in the first cut they sent me to Fort Walton Beach, which I didn't report to. I just said I was coming home. Then they were going to send me back to Charlotte and I did go back there for a little bit of time, and then we quit. I came home.

This is in midseason.

Even before then.

Is this a release or a resignation?

It was a mutual deal. Except for Calvin Griffith. He said, You can't quit. I said, I need to quit and get on with my life. I've got a family now, and this isn't going to work. It's getting worse. It's not getting better.

You don't want to be talked into staying. A lot of people, if they really wanted to quit and go home, would wait until Calvin had gone home.

Calvin has quite a reputation but he and I got along quite well. So I figured it would've been the appropriate thing to tell him. He didn't agree with me but that was our decision and that was it.

Does the decision to quit follow several nights of talk between you and your wife?

Oh, yes. Many nights.

This isn't one bad outing and an impetuous reaction. You and your wife are in agreement that it's time to move on.

Without a doubt.

So you give up the security deposit in Charlotte and pack up the car.

And head back to Sleepy Eye.

What's the trip home like? Do you know what you're going to do now that baseball's over?

Go back to college and work on my master's degree. I taught a year at Mankato High and coached baseball.

If you're coaching high school, then baseball's still a part of your life, but at this stage do you bother to watch the Twins on television, or do you have to put it over on the side? Did you have any withdrawal symptoms?

Yeah, I mean, I could still go to a game and watch a game without a problem, but I was never a big fan or a spectator. I had to get involved. Even before expansion I probably couldn't tell you the eight teams in the American or the eight teams in the National League.

Do you watch baseball now?

Yes. I'm more or less an average fan. When the playoffs start and the World Series, yeah. And, of course, we still have some friends in the front office with the Twins. We're close here to Fort Myers and spring training, so every year we have a few of the ballplayers over to the house and have a little get-together.

When were you at your best? If you could've picked when you pitched in the majors because that was the pinnacle of your ability and talent and experience, when would that be?

Probably the first two thirds of spring training in 1960. I learned a few things playing in minor league ball and things were jelling. Things were humming. I could put the ball where I wanted to and had fun doing it.

You pitched against the Braves that spring training and they had Hank Aaron and Eddie Mathews among others. Did you ever face a batter and have a conscious moment of, This is Eddie Mathews, or This is Hank Aaron?

It's funny you mention those two. I still remember throwing against them. Yeah, Mathews was good. Even as a rookie, I remember I got him on a fastball and a nice change-up. I remember him grunting on the change-up. I assume he knew I was a rookie and I wouldn't throw him a change-up like that, but I did. Aaron was scary. I can still remember one of the times I threw against him in spring trainiing. I remember this time very well. Earl Battey was the catcher then and I had Aaron 3–2 and he called for a fastball and I shook it off twice, which would go to a curveball and, as I said, I did have a good one. I busted it off good and you just know that you got him. Even when you let it go. It was going to be right at the knees on the black part of the plate on the outside. You just know you got him. There isn't time to think all this but you know it, and all of a sudden the bat came around but he missed it for strike three.

Los Angeles at Milwaukee
Monday, April 23, 1962

Los Angeles	ab	r	h	rbi	Milwaukee	ab	r	h	rbi
Wills, ss	5	0	0	0	Bedell, cf	5	1	3	0
Gilliam, 2b	4	1	2	0	T. Aaron, lf	2	0	0	0
Moon, 1b	4	0	0	0	cH. Aaron	1	0	0	0
Snider, rf	3	2	2	1	Butler, p	0	0	0	0
T. Davis, lf	4	0	2	1	dMenke	1	0	0	0
Roseboro, c	4	1	2	1	Jones, rf	4	0	1	0
Carey, 3b	3	0	0	0	Mathews, 3b	4	1	1	0
W. Davis, cf	3	1	1	2	Adcock, 1b	4	0	0	0
Moeller, p	4	0	0	0	Bolling, 2b	3	0	1	0
					McMillan, ss	4	0	2	1
Totals	34	5	9	5	Uecker, c	2	0	0	0
					aKlimchock	1	0	0	0
					Krsnich, lf	1	0	0	0
					Burdette, p	2	0	1	0
					Willey, p	0	0	0	0
					bCrandall, c	2	0	0	0
					Totals	36	2	9	1

```
Los Angeles.............................  0  0  0  2  1  2  0  0  0—5
Milwaukee..............................  1  0  0  0  0  0  0  1  0—2
```

Los Angeles	IP.	H.	R.	ER.	BB.	SO.
Moeller (W. 1–1)...................	9	9	2	2	2	4

Milwaukee	IP.	H.	R.	ER.	BB.	SO.
Burdette (L. 0-3)	5.2	8	5	5	0	4
Willey	1.1	0	0	0	0	0
Butler	2	1	0	0	2	1

a-Struck out for Uecker in seventh. b-Forced runner for Willey in seventh. c-Flied
out for Aaron in seventh. d-Flied out for Butler in ninth. 2B—T. Davis, Bolling.
HR—W. Davis, Roseboro. SH—Carey, T. Aaron. E—Carey, Moon, Roseboro. PO-
A—Los Angeles 27-14, Milwaukee 27-10. DP—Bolling, McMillan and Adcock.
LOB—Los Angeles 5, Milwaukee 10. WP—Moeller 2. U—Steiner, Boggess, Landes
and Smith. T—3:04. A—7,656.

CECIL BUTLER

Cecil Butler made his major league debut for the Milwaukee Braves in 1962 against the Houston Colt .45s. He garnered his first win in that game and later in the year achieved a complete-game victory against the National League's other expansion team, the New York Mets. His major league career, ending in 1964, lasted eleven games and thirty-five and one-third innings. Butler gave up thirty-three hits and struck out twenty-four while walking nine. He held opposition batters to a .237 average and finished with a 3.31 ERA. He was interviewed October 20, 2001 at the International House of Pancakes in Dallas, Georgia.

How did you get started in professional baseball?

I signed my first contract with the Atlanta Crackers. I had signed a football scholarship with the University of Tennessee-Chattanooga when I finished high school.

What position did you play in football?

We played both ways back then. I was a quarterback but I also played defensive and offensive end.

I'm guessing with your height you played some basketball, too.

I had a world of basketball scholarship offers.

So you were a good all-around athlete.

I was pretty good. Fair.

I'm not trying to get you to brag on yourself, but if you've got college scholarship offers in two sports and sign a professional contract in a third, I'd think you being a good all-around athlete would be a pretty safe statement.

If I had it to do over again I'd have gotten more education, but what you did for a living didn't mean that much when I was growing up. The Lord's been good to me. I've been in the painting business since I got out of baseball and still pretty much work when I want to. Life's been good to me. I can't complain. I've been very lucky.

Were you better at baseball or was baseball your favorite?

We didn't even have baseball in high school here in Dallas. I started playing baseball out in the country, in the cow pasture, but I started playing with a men's team in Douglasville when I was about fifteen years old, pitching on Saturday and Sunday at times, in an amateur league in Atlanta.

When you're playing for this Douglasville team, what are you throwing besides a fastball?

That was about it. I tried to throw a curve.

Did you have a lot of movement on the fastball?

Yeah.

Did you know where it was going to move, or did you throw it center of the plate?

I could throw strikes but I hadn't learned, really, how to pitch. I was probably twenty-three years old before I had a good idea, because it's in and out and up and down. But if everybody could pitch that way, everybody would be great. If you watch now, it's the same as it's always been. Your good pitchers pitch like I'm talking about. They stay ahead. People like Maddux and Warren Spahn. If they get ahead of you, you better not take that pitch a little bit inside or a little bit outside. It works on the hitter's mind. It's like Lew Burdette was. He didn't always throw the spitter. When he beat the Yankees three times in the World Series, he was pitching.

So you signed with the Crackers.

The scout—we were sitting there before I signed—Mr Felix Garrett, the scout who signed me, said, Earl, this fellow's from the country and he needs a little money. I'm just sitting there. I didn't know they gave you money to sign. And he said, Well, how much do you want us to give him? And he said, Give him a couple thousand dollars. And Earl said, Well, we'll give him a thousand today and then when he makes the Double-A club we'll give him another thousand.

Did you do anything special with that thousand dollars? That was more money than you'd ever had before, right?

In 1957 when I went to spring training and started the season in Panama City, Florida, my mother and daddy didn't have an indoor toilet. My uncle was in construction with a big company in Atlanta so I called him and asked him how much it would cost to put a bathroom on Mother's house, a septic tank, the whole bit. And he said, Well, Cecil, it'd probably be six or seven hundred dollars. And I said, Well, when you can get started on it, do that for me. So that's where most of it went.

That's got to be a pretty good feeling to be able to do that for your folks.

It was. It probably made me feel better than signing the contract did, because when I got home, Mother was thrilled to death, and I was for her. I can remember toting water from the spring. The first year that I played I was making $225 a month. I think about Warren Spahn. I think his top salary was $85,000 a year and that was in the early sixties.

And he was one of the best left-handed pitchers ever.

He was one of the best I've ever seen. So in 1957 I played for Panama City in the Alabama-Florida League, and in 1958 I was in Waycross. In 1959 I was in Jacksonville and in 1960 I went to Austin, Texas, in the Texas League. I'd probably forgotten about that other thousand dollars. Well, that second month I was there, when I got my regular little check, there was another extra check in there for an extra thousand dollars.

What'd you do with that money?

I probably blew that. It wasn't important because, you know, you re-member certain things and I don't remember that. I didn't keep a lot of things that I should have. I've always been a giver. I mean, it don't take that much from me if everybody around me, my family and everybody, has what they need. My mother and father weren't takers. But when I was in Austin, I had learned to pitch and I was burning that league up that year.

Had you learned the curveball by then?

I didn't have a great curveball but I had better control and I probably had as good a slider as anybody in the Texas League. I tried to throw a forkball because of Dave Fracaro. He was from Wisconsin, and we were in the instructional league in Bradenton when the Braves trained down there, and he had huge, long fingers, and he had a great forkball. I'd never heard of one until I saw him. I tried and I tried but I didn't have any control. I could throw one but I couldn't get it to the point where I could throw it over the plate. I could throw a knuckleball. Phil Niekro and I played together at different times when we were coming up and when we were in Louisville, George Susce, an old-timer, he tried to get Phil to quit throwing a knuckleball. And Phil didn't have anything else. He didn't throw hard enough to break glass. I've thought about that over the years. That's a Hall of Famer who would've been out of baseball in a heartbeat if he'd done what the coach had told him.

Did you throw over the top or three-quarters?

I threw right over the top. You know, when we were playing they'd give you the ball and here it is. It wasn't any, You go five innings. I was 8-2 or 8-3 in Austin and they sent me up to Louisville in Triple-A, and I couldn't wait to get there and then I sat on the bench. I didn't pitch any. I didn't know what to do. I didn't like it. At that time Stan Lopata, a catcher for the Phillies, he was in Louisville, and Frank Torre was down out of the big leagues in Louisville. But I didn't get to pitch very much and I found out the following year that the Cubs were trying to buy my contract and that was one of the reasons why the Braves sent me to Louisville and sat my butt on the bench. People don't realize what a business it is. And your owner's got to make a living, too. Lou Perini owned the Braves then, and he was one of the biggest builders in the world. That's where he got his money. And then he sold out to that Reynolds group in Atlanta and they were some of the nicest people you'd ever want to meet. They'd come down to spring training and put on uniforms and bring their kids. They were just good people. The Braves have always been first-class.

Did you start the 1961 season in Louisville?

Yeah. I started to have some arm trouble there. And then in 1962, I went to spring training with the big club and stayed with them.

Do you know enough of these guys from the minors and spring training to almost feel comfortable, or do you feel like a raw rookie?

No, not really. You know, I'd been in spring training before. You'd have to be around people like Burdette especially, and Spahn, Mathews. They were just the nicest people you've ever met.

Burdette and Spahn weren't worried about a young kid coming up to take their job?

No. Burdette was actually there to help you. He took care of me when we broke camp and went to Milwaukee. If you were with him—if you went to eat or went to have a beer or what have you—you didn't have to worry about money, because the people in Milwaukee wouldn't accept your money. That's just the way they treated everybody. They started talking about, You won't need a car. I said, What do you mean I won't need a car? Well, Bud Selig, who's the commissioner now, he had a Chrysler dealership, and after the season started about thirty players and coaches went out there and got their picture taken and then you got a new car to drive. And all you had to do was put gas and oil in it. Now, mine was not a big luxury car, but still it was a new car. I'd never had a new car. If I hadn't had arm trouble I think I would've had a few years up there.

Well, you had a good first year. You pitched in nine games and one of those was a complete game. You had an ERA of 2.61 and opponents only batted .217 against you. Was it arm trouble that got you?

They sent me to the Mayo Clinic in Rochester and I saw three specialists. And they said they didn't see how any pitcher lasted any length of time because your arm is just not supposed to do all that, even if you're mechanically perfect. They did surgery and it just never was the same. Of course, I played a few more years, but it was never there anymore.

What did they cut on when they went into your arm?

I had two bone spurs and I had a bunch of chips that they cleaned out of my right elbow. It's crooked as a snake now.

So that did you in for that year.

In 1963 I played for Denver in the Pacific Coast League.

Were you able to throw from the start of the season? When did you have surgery?

Well, they more or less left it up to you. They didn't leave it up to the doctor. Dr Brewer, the orthopedist who did the surgery in Wisconsin, he didn't want me touching the baseball for seven or eight months, but I started feeling a little better. My arm was in a cast for six weeks. I went back and when they sawed that cast off I thought I was going to pass out. My arm looked like raw hamburger because I'd been scratching it with coat hangers and all. And I went through all that therapy and stuff and then during the winter here I went up to the high school up there and I took a sack full of baseballs and I'd throw them up against the stands in the wintertime.

Did you think you were ready when you went to spring training in 1963?

Yeah. And I was for a while. I started throwing good in Denver. We were in Spokane or Tacoma and I struck out sixteen one night. They called me back up in 1964 but it just wasn't there. I couldn't really reach back and throw it anymore. The last year I played was in the old stadium in Atlanta because they thought the Braves were coming down a year before they did, and we played in the International League down there. As a matter of fact, I was the first pitcher to hit a home run down there.

So your last year in baseball is 1965. Is it easy to quit after all that time?

No. No. It didn't really hit me until I got home. I was in the Texas League because they had sent me out there from Atlanta. My arm was just gone. They were probably helping me out. I knew the end was coming, I just didn't know which way. We were all sitting around the hotel one afternoon out there. We were in El Paso. And I told Carl Green, my roommate, I'm not going to the ballpark anymore. This is it. I guess the end of the season was less than a month away. But I went across the border and some teammates came across and got me that night and that was it. Of course, I talked to Billy Hicks, the manager, the next day in the hotel and he said, Well, I didn't want to tell you, Cecil, but I think they were getting ready to release you. And I said, Well, I just made it easier for them.

Is this the end of the season?

It was close to the end of the season. But I'd gotten to the point where I just couldn't throw it up there. I didn't like being beat all over.

Did you come back to Georgia?

Yeah. I left Austin and I went to Milwaukee, and then I went to Chicago, then I came to Indianapolis, came to Nashville, then I came on home. I had some fun on the way home.

Do you remember your major league debut in 1962?

I pitched four innings in Houston and won the first game there. Carlton Willey was pitching and then I came on in relief. And then I started against the Mets. That's when I beat them right there.

Was that the complete game?

Yeah. Casey Stengel was managing the Mets and he had an article in the paper the next day in New York about me curving their pants off, and I didn't even have a good curveball. Del Crandall was catching. I was watching a game on television the other night and saw all the stuff the pitcher and catcher go through and sometimes it doesn't mean a thing. Del Crandall was one of the better catchers there's ever been, and he was sitting back there and, of course, you go through all this stuff. But you just watched his mitt and how it was turned—whether it was turned forty-five degrees or flat or inside or up—and that was what you were throwing. It was easier on the infielders, the second baseman and the shortstop, that way.

Since you were a rookie, I assume you threw whatever Crandall asked for.

I didn't do no shaking off. I didn't do no shaking. I had some good catchers, I'd have to say that. Bob Uecker was a good receiver. He hit over .300 one year at Louisville but he was a comedian, or tried to be. He was a character.

Did you get to keep the ball from your first win in Houston?

No. I wish I'd have thought of it then. Some of the biggest thrills I ever got in baseball was Burdette and people like that introducing me to Sandy Koufax and Don Drysdale and Mickey Mantle, Roger Maris, people like that. I was probably like a little kid. My grandson, David Sam, loved baseball cards. And I saw—this was years ago—where Hank Aaron would be signing his book over at Commoner Mall one Saturday morning, so I called my daughter and told her what was happening and that I was going to take David Sam to go shopping. So I went and picked him up on Friday night and we got up early that Saturday morning and we were walking down the mall and went by this bookstore and I saw David Sam looking but I just kept walking, and he said, Papa, do you know who's over here? And I said, Who? And he said, Hank Aaron. He's autographing his book. And I said, Really? Well, we'll go back by. The store hadn't opened yet. So we went back and Hank was sitting behind the desk there and I spoke and he looked up and saw me and then he stood up and we shook hands and I said, David Sam, this is Hank Aaron. And his mouth just flew open.

Do you watch much baseball now?

I'm watching more than I did. That year that they struck put a bad taste in my mouth. I didn't care about it. I really didn't. But I watch them now. I was telling you that I live in the woods. Well, there's no cable where I live, so I had a man come over three or four years ago to put me in a satellite and he started looking around and he said, Cecil, how far does your land go? How far can you clear out? And I said, What do you mean? And he said, We can't put a satellite down here. I didn't realize that. I said, Well, I wouldn't give my trees for all the satellites there are. So I pick up about eight or ten channels. I never have been a television man. I don't like to take the time to watch it. But I watch the Braves games.

Are you a Braves fan?

Yeah, but down towards the end of the year there's a lot of teams—I don't know any of them but I pull for them because they've got players on the teams who've never been there. I was halfway pulling for the Athletics this year. Why, I don't know. I played with Joe Torre, and he's a fine person, but good God, how many rings can they wear?

Are there any particular pitchers you like to see throw?

Maddux. Somebody like Schilling. Randy Johnson. Bobby Bragan had a write-up in the Milwaukee paper after I started having arm trouble and it was an article on Cloninger, myself, Hank Fischer—quite a few of the younger players at the time—and he made the statement that when my arm was right, I was the hardest thrower in the Braves organization. So I like to see those power pitchers.

I didn't realize how good Maddux was until he came to Atlanta. I'd seen him on the Game of the Week on Saturdays a few times and I didn't realize how he could be as successful as he was with what he had, but I'd never seen him enough to understand the way he pitched until he got to Atlanta. I mean, he might throw a nine-inning game and never make a mistake. And that's just hard to do. When I pitched, I relied on throwing. I didn't learn to pitch until later on.

Al Kaline hit a line drive off of me in spring training one year. I can remember it like it was yesterday. I had two strikes on him, no balls. In my head, I said, I'll just blow him away. I got a little bit cocky. Well, I gave it my best and today I can still hear that ball come by my ear. It went off the center-field wall for a double. That's what I was talking about earlier. Giles, the Braves' second baseman, is going to be a good ballplayer. A young fellow like that. I've watched him enough to already know that fastballs don't intimidate him. And he can get around on it. They're going to have to get him out some other way than with fastballs because he can turn on a fastball.

If I asked you to write a scouting report on yourself before the arm trouble hit, what would be your strengths and weaknesses as a pitcher?

I would think my strengths would be my fastball and slider. I didn't really have that good of a change, and my curveball wasn't that good. There were times that my curveball was a lot better. Now, my slider would dip, and there wasn't that much difference between the speed of my slider and my fastball. After looking back, changing up is the biggest thing there is. You can't beat a change-up if you don't change your motion. That's the thing about Maddux. Everything he throws is with the same motion. Of course, everybody's more knowledgeable now. Everything gets better in this world. I've thought lately about that stuff that happened in New York and young people being the leaders of this country and, of course, at my age I've lived most of my life. You get to thinking. You see some bad kids but then you see young people who are some of the nicest people you could meet. We're still in good hands. Every week I get baseball cards to sign. The majority of people who get into baseball and autographs and all of that are some of the nicest people you'd ever want to meet.

Pittsburgh at Houston
Thursday, September 26, 1963

Pittsburgh	ab	r	h	rbi	Houston	ab	r	h	rbi
Schofield, ss	4	0	0	1	Vaughan, ss	4	0	0	0
Clemente, rf	6	0	0	0	eTemple	1	0	0	0
Stargell, 1b	6	0	2	0	Woodesh'k, p	0	0	0	0
Savage, cf	5	0	0	0	Farrell, p	0	0	0	0
Clendenon, 1b	5	1	1	0	McMahon, p	0	0	0	0
Bailey, 3b	5	2	2	0	fSmith	1	0	0	0
Alley, 2b	5	1	1	0	Morgan, 2b	5	2	2	0
Brand, c	3	0	1	1	Weekly, rf	0	0	0	0
Butters, p	3	0	1	1	aSpangler, rf	4	0	1	0
McBean, p	1	0	0	0	Warwick, 1b	5	0	1	0
gMota, p	0	0	0	0	Goss, cf	4	0	1	1
Face, p	0	0	0	0	Asprom'te, 3b	3	2	2	1
					Wynn, lf	4	1	2	3
Totals	43	4	8	3	Grote, c	2	0	0	0
					Bateman, c	0	0	0	0
					bStaub	0	0	0	0
					Yellen, p	2	0	0	0
					Umbricht, p	1	0	0	0
					cRunnels	0	0	0	0
					dFazio	0	0	0	0
					Lillis, ss	1	0	0	0
					Totals	37	5	9	5

Pittsburgh	0	1	0	1	0	2	0	0	0	0	0—4
Houston	1	0	0	0	0	2	0	1	0	0	1—5

Pittsburgh	IP.	H.	R.	ER.	BB.	SO.
Butters	7.2	6	4	4	7	8
McBean	2.1	1	0	0	2	2
Face (L. 3–9)....................	0.2	2	1	1	1	1
Houston	IP.	H.	R.	ER.	BB.	SO.
Yellen	5*	7	4	2	1	3
Umbricht	3	0	0	0	1	4
Woodeshick............	2	1	0	0	0	2
Farrell	0.1	0	0	0	1	0
McMahon (W. 1-5)............	0.2	0	0	0	0	1

*Pitched to three batters in sixth
a-Ran for Weekly in first. b-Intentionally walked for Grote in eighth. c-Walked for
Umbricht in eighth. d-Ran for Runnels in eighth. e-Grounded out for Vaughan in
eighth. f-Struck out for Woodeshick in tenth. g-Walked for McBean in eleventh.
2B—Bailey, Goss, Brand. 3B—Wynn. HR—Wynn. SB—Clendenon, Morgan.
SH—Bateman, Schofield, Spangler. SF—Goss, Schofield. E—Brand 2, Vaughan,
Morgan, Aspromonte, Woodeshick. PO-A—Pittsburgh 32-12 (two out when winning
run scored), Houston 33-14. DP—Butters, Brand and Clendenon. LOB—Pittsburgh
11, Houston 14. HP—Butters (Weekly). U—Jackowski, Crawford, Kibler and Sudol.
T—3:14. A—2,782.

LARRY YELLEN

Larry Yellen was drafted by the expansion Houston Colt
.45s in 1962 and pitched five innings as a starter in 1963.
In 1964 he pitched another twenty-one innings for a
career total of twenty-six innings in fourteen games. He
finished his major league career with a 6.23 ERA, giving
up thirty-four hits while striking out twelve and
walking eleven. He did not receive a decision. He was
interviewed on October 13, 2001 at his home in Duluth,
Georgia.

How do you start playing baseball growing up in Brooklyn?

I guess like any other kid starts playing baseball. You play catch, you take
a liking to it, your parents see that you take a liking to it, and they encourage you. I was the middle of three brothers. My older brother, Marty,
was not athletically inclined. My younger brother, Jay, was a little bit, but
not much. But you just keep on doing what you like to do whether it's

playing a piano or riding a bicycle or, sooner or later, driving a car. And as a kid I just liked to play catch and grab a bat and hit a baseball, and I was lucky enough to be encouraged by my parents and one of my uncles who was very close to me.

Did they see your desire to play, your enjoyment of the game, or did they see your talent as well?

They had to see my talent. That's a great question and not something we really discussed in later years but they had to see it. They had to see it when we were playing punchball in the streets of Brooklyn when I was eight, ten years old and playing with thirteen- and fifteen-year-old kids. They saw my athletic ability. They saw how I could catch a ball with one hand, if you will, while other people had trouble catching it with two hands. I was fast and I was quick. My reflexes were very, very good and I just had an innate instinct to play the game. And it wasn't just baseball. I was good at basketball and I was good at football. I just wasn't tall enough, that's all.

Were you better at baseball or did you enjoy baseball more? At what point in your life do you make a choice between sports?

I guess it was during my early high school years. I made the high school baseball team as a freshman, which was very rarely done.

What high school?

I went to Lafayette High School in Brooklyn, the same high school that Bob Aspromonte went to, and, of course, Sandy Koufax graduated four years before I did. I always told people that the only two things we had in common was the fact that we both graduated from the same high school and we were both Jewish. Other than that there was nothing in common. I think by the time I got into high school I basically knew that baseball was my first love. I didn't realize at the time it was going to be a career, but I guess all kids, well before that time, until they come to some realization, think that they're going to go on and become a professional athlete. At least I hope that's the way kids think these days, because why squelch that dream? I'm sure I had it.

Baseball was my art, and I considered it an art even back when I was younger. But again, when the baseball season wasn't around I did play football. It was touch football. It wasn't hard contact. My parents were very, very protective of me, especially in my freshman and sophomore years of high school when they knew that there might be something of a career for me in baseball, and they didn't want me to get hurt playing football. I was pretty good in basketball also, but at five eleven I wasn't tall enough to even consider it.

You mentioned baseball as an "art." I'm assuming that's as opposed to craft. Tell me about baseball as an art.

If I can give you the difference between an art and a craft as I understand it in regards to baseball, a craft anybody can learn. You make an art out of a craft by being better at it than most, I guess. That might go against the dictionary definition of the two words but I'm just giving you my feeling, or what my idea of it is. I looked at it as an art and I tried to perfect myself in a way that would make me stand out from the rest of the people that I competed against. I was good as a sophomore and I got better and better and better.

You mentioned your older brother wasn't athletically inclined. Where did your talent come from?

From my dad. My dad was athletically inclined. He could literally throw a ball left-handed and right-handed. I remember him throwing left-handed and right-handed and it seemed a lot better than I could do it. I was not ambidextrous but I got his athletic ability in one form or an-other. That's where it came from. The fact that he worked nights for thirty-two years while I was growing up didn't give him the opportunity nor the time to spend with me to play catch, so to speak, so my uncle Aaron, my mom's brother-in-law, spent a lot of time with me. I rarely got to see my dad except on weekends. I'd come home from school and he'd be leaving for work.

What did your dad do?

He was a foreman in a corrugated-box factory that his uncle owned in Newark, New Jersey.

In high school, when you make the team as a freshman, are you primarily a pitcher?

Only a pitcher.

So you're sitting out some games?

107

Yeah, but it didn't bother me. I played some shortstop earlier when I played sandlot baseball and when I played Little League baseball, but my arm was five years beyond anybody else's arm of an equal age so when I was eight I was throwing like a twelve- or a thirteen-year-old.

Did you have a favorite team growing up?

Are you kidding? There was only one, the Brooklyn Dodgers. They moved out in 1957 when I was fourteen years old, and it was like the world came to an end for all of us. I don't know if you've ever seen the television series *Brooklyn Bridge*. I get the chills talking about it to you right now. It was about a Jewish family and there was one episode about the Dodgers leaving and how they felt about it. It was like it happened yesterday when I was watching that episode. It was awesome.

Did you get to go to many games? Did you listen to games on the radio?

I remember the radio in the living room and we'd be sitting around the radio listening to *The Lone Ranger* and stuff like that, and we'd be listening to the Dodger games, too.

Did you have a favorite player?

I can't say I did. I just loved the Dodgers. I lived and died with the Dodgers.

They leave in 1957 when you're fourteen. What happens to your fandom at that point? Do you pick another team?

My heart went with them to Los Angeles, I guess, for a while. The Mets didn't come until 1962 and by then I was well on my way to believing I was going to spend twenty years in the major leagues and go into the Hall of Fame. Honestly, between 1957 and, let's say, 1960, I've got to believe that I continued rooting for the Dodgers out in Los Angeles. I've got to believe I did. Because there's no way in God's green acre that I rooted for the New York Yankees. I hated the bums.

What about now?

I'm a die-hard Braves fan.

How do you feel about the Yankees now?

I have absolutely no compassion, no feelings for the American League at all. None whatsoever.

So as long as Atlanta goes to the World Series and wins, you could care less who they play?

Correct. I was never a Yankee fan. Not even for thirty seconds.

Is there anything about the American League that's caused this disdain?

No, I think it was just playing in the National League and always believing the National League was superior to the American League, right or wrong.

You're pitching in high school and you're playing well. How do you take the step from being a high school pitcher to signing your first professional contract? Are you drafted?

Well, there's a little stumbling block in between. By the time I was a senior in high school I was good. I was voted MVP in New York State. I have a picture in our office upstairs of Rusty Staub presenting me with the award for MVP in New York State.

Can your head fit through the front door of your parents' house in Brooklyn at this point?

Yeah. It never really did go to my head. I was pretty down to earth. If I ever got out of line—and I don't remember ever getting out of line—I had the kind of family that would smack me and put me right back into line. Nevertheless, I've got the MVP in my pocket now and I'm a senior in high school and I've had a great year, but I've got an older brother who becomes a psychiatrist so he's gone to four years of med school, and I've got a younger brother who gets his Ph.D. in mathematics and who has written a book that's up on my library shelf now, and I'm the schnook in the middle, okay?

At any rate, it was difficult for me, it was impossible for me to convince my parents that I should play baseball right out of high school. I had several clubs that were interested. I wish I could tell you which ones they were but I can tell you that the Mets were not one of them. They had just signed Ed Kranepool and I was looking for some money. I thought I deserved some money, and they couldn't afford to do it because of the way the draft was set up at that time. If they didn't protect you one out of the first two years in their organization—put you on the major league roster—they could lose you in the draft.

Now I've graduated high school and my parents are forcing me to go to college, and there was no fighting with them. So I go to Hunter College, uptown in the Bronx. I still live in Brooklyn so I get on the train—I don't own a car—and I travel anywhere from an hour and fifteen minutes to an hour and thirty minutes each way up to the campus in the Bronx. And I don't crack a book because I'm ticked. I'm going to prove to my parents that they made me do the wrong thing. So I'm playing baseball for Hunter College but they have minimums for GPA and here my minimum has to be a 2 and I've got to go to the school psychologist and convince the school psychologist that it's going to be more detrimental to my future not playing baseball than playing baseball. And I convince him of that and he lets me play my sophomore year. And when I finally wind down to a 1.8 my parents throw up their arms in the air and say, Okay, go ahead. And I wind up signing with Houston after that.

Now, if you ask me what is the proudest moment of my life, it's receiving my degree in 1987 after going back to school, and not only getting my degree but graduating with a 3.87, summa cum laude. I got that at the State University of New York College at Fredonia, which is upstate New York about thirty miles southwest of Buffalo. My younger brother, Jay, was teaching up there and that's why I went up there. And when I got through in 1987—I know I'm jumping ahead here—I had to make a decision as to whether to go back down into the rat race of Manhattan or come down to Atlanta. My brother was about to give up his tenure at the State University to come down to Atlanta and if he was giving up his tenure, which, you know, teachers don't do, then I was coming down here, too.

So you aren't drafted but ballclubs are still keeping an eye on you at Hunter?

The draft was different from the way it is today. You got offers from several teams. There was no choosing a player. It was like, I guess, several different movie studios going up to an actor and saying, Here's a contract. We can offer you this. Then XYZ studio comes along and betters the contract. Well, the same thing happened in baseball at that time. It wasn't just one club. I think there were about four or five clubs that were interested in me.

Being with Houston in 1964 was probably to my detriment because I had a poor first half of 1963. I had an excellent second half. I could've used the whole of 1964 in the minor leagues and maybe—wishful thinking—gone up in 1965 and stayed in the big leagues. But because of the way the draft was set up, you had to stay one of the first two years in the big leagues. That's why I was there in 1964. It wasn't because I was great or belonged there.

But they couldn't take up every Double-A prospect that they signed so there's got to be something about bonus money that makes you prone to that rule.

They gave me $55,000.

That's a lot of money back then.

Yeah.

Now, when you get the $55,000, are you still able to get your head through the front door? Are you still a good kid?

Yeah. I wish my parents were here so they could tell you. I signed my contract in the summer of 1962. I got married after my first season in November of 1963. I wasn't a wealthy person but it was good money back then and I bought my first Pontiac. I paid cash for it.

What else did you do? You didn't spend $55,000 on a Pontiac.

Well, a little chunk of it went back to my parents to help my older brother through medical school.

You were a good kid.

No, don't give me more credit than I deserve, because I did have, later on, after I got out of playing baseball, some kind of resentment for not having the choice of determining the amount of my contribution.

But you were nineteen years old. Even if you felt pressure to help out, there are a lot of kids who would say, No, Mom, this is my money.

Well, that's interesting that you would say that, but you obviously didn't live during that period.

In 1963, Houston was trying to field the youngest club in major league history. I was going to be there and the article on the youngest team being fielded makes it into *The New York Times.* My parents read it and the next thing I know the phone's ringing and my mother's saying, How can you do this to me? How can you embarrass us this way?

Because you were scheduled to pitch on Yom Kippur?

Correct. I have two kids, Stacey and Michael—both very, very good athletes—but anyhow, Stacey reads the article and the thing that Stacey says to me is, Boy, your parents really had control over you back then. And I said, Sweetheart, it wasn't so much that they had control—which they did—but it had a lot to do with the respect I showed my parents also. Things have changed now. I have always encouraged my kids, especially my daughter, to be very, very independent, to state her mind, and she's got one of the biggest mouths in the South now because of it. The point is that times have changed. So when you say to me, Hey, it's your money, go back and research what the culture was like back then. I can see where you're coming from, and I totally agree with you, but it wasn't that easy.

There are some people who would think that that would be a good time to cut the family cord, when you're nineteen years old and have $55,000 in your pocket, so it could be that your parents raised you right.

My parents had a commitment. They've built something over the years.

Did you sign with Houston because they offered you the most money?

No. They did offer me the most money but I went with them because they were one of the two new expansion teams and it was a good place to grow. The other expansion team was the Mets, and, as I told you before, they'd already invested the money in Kranepool.

Did you sign early enough in the year to play for the Houston organization in 1962?

I went to the Rookie League in Arizona—Apache Junction, Arizona. That's where they used to have their spring training before they went to Cocoa Beach. They had a winter league there and I played in the winter league in Apache Junction. We had a barbershop, we had a bar, and we had a little place where you could go buy a quart of milk or something, and that was it.

Are you on the big club's roster for spring training in 1963? In 1963 you pitched in one game.

I went to the minor league camp in one of the Carolinas. I played in the Texas League but the Houston minor league camp was in North Carolina, I think. At any rate, I played with San Antonio in 1963 for the entire season. After the season was over with San Antonio, I was called up along with a few other people.

And they want you to start the game when they attempt to field the youngest team in major league history. They've got Rusty Staub who's nineteen, Joe Morgan who's nineteen, and Jim Wynn who's twenty-one. In 1964 the team gets older because you have Nellie Fox and Don Larsen, but Larry Dierker comes up and he's only seventeen.

Larry Dierker. When we were on the road in either Chicago or St Louis, there was a kid who was trying out. He could throw BBs. He had a great breaking ball, he threw a change-up, and the kid didn't look like he had even started shaving yet and his name was Larry Dierker. Unbelievable.

So 1963 they've got it set up towards the end of the year that they'll field the youngest starting lineup in major league history. You're scheduled to be the starting pitcher but it's Yom Kippur. When do you find out that you're supposed to start that game? And does it register in your mind that that's Yom Kippur?

It was no more than a week before, and it might've been just a few days before when I got the phone call from my parents.

Who realizes that the day you're scheduled to pitch is Yom Kippur?

My mother. I have no clue. I'm in a dreamworld. *The New York Times* picks up on the fact that we're going to field the youngest team in major league history and my parents read the article.

Does your mother call and tell you you can't make your major league debut?

No, my mother calls and she lays on a little of what we call Jewish guilt. How can you do this to us?

And what is your response to your mom?

My response to my mom is, I'm sorry. I didn't realize it and I'll take care of it. I was aggravated. I was upset. I remember that. But I also remember not having a choice. Again, this is what my daughter was talking about when she said, Boy, the control that parents had over their children was incredible. Because we're talking about 1963. I'm twenty years old.

You tell your mother you'll take care of it. Do you do something that day?

I went to the park and saw Paul Richards on the field—I think we were in Houston—and it was probably in the two and a half hours that we were there before the game started, you know, taking batting practice or whatever, and I said, Oh, by the way, I got a call from my mother and it totally skipped my mind that it was Yom Kippur and it's a violation of the Jewish faith and I'm not going to be able to pitch. I was mealymouthed. I was embarrassed.

You were giving away your major league debut.

Yeah, that was the first time I was going to pitch in a major league game.

What were you embarrassed about?

I was embarrassed that I'm going to my boss and saying, I can't do what you want me to do. That was embarrassing to me. And he turned around and apologized to me, profusely, for not realizing that it was Yom Kippur.

Why should he realize that it's Yom Kippur? I'm thinking that being a general manager of a professional ballclub at the end of the season—bringing up talent, evaluating, but primarily being geographically located in Houston, Texas—the Jewish calendar is not front and center in the guy's mind. Why should he know?

He might've been apologizing just to be a nice guy, or maybe he saw the embarrassment in me and wanted to soften the blow a little bit.

You're the only Jewish guy on the team, right?

I believe so. I don't believe I had a Jewish teammate.

Because it's not a matter of pitching, really. You don't even go to the park that day.

You don't drive. You don't do anything.

So when did you make your major league debut? Did they just move you back a day?

They moved it back a few days. It was against the Pirates in Houston.

You pitched five innings.

I pitched five innings and I remember Roberto Clemente. I don't remember Willie Stargell. The one to remember, though, was Roberto Clemente.

Were you scared? Were you nervous? Were you excited?

All of the above, probably. I wasn't walking to the mound like a twenty-year veteran. It was what I'd wanted all my life, since I was about three years old grabbing a baseball in my hand, and here I was at the age of twenty pitching in the major leagues. And, as it turns out, it was something that I would not only never forget but something not many people will allow me to forget.

What do you remember about the game? You know that you faced Clemente in your debut. Do you remember how you did against him?

Yeah. Bob Lillis was playing shortstop and Clemente hit a rocket, a one-hopper, that almost took Bob Lillis from shortstop and put him in the left-field stands. But Lillis wound up throwing him out, of course. But he hit a rocket off me. I wish I could remember some of the other guys.

You don't give up a home run until the second year. Do you remember who hit home runs off you?

Frank Howard hit a home run off me. I believe he was playing for Los Angeles. He hit a home run off me. I once walked Willie Mays with the bases loaded. He was taking pitches that were like an eighth of an inch off of the plate that he probably could've rocketed out of the county but he chose to walk with the bases loaded, and that embarrassed me. During spring training in 1965 I did get Mantle to hit into a double play. There was a big article written about that in one of the New York newspapers. It was like I'd gotten my three hundredth win or something. They made a big deal about getting Mantle to hit into a double play. But I faced Clemente, I faced Mays, I faced Mantle. I faced Henry Aaron, too. He was awesome also. Henry was just unbelievable. I remember facing both Henry Aaron and Eddie Mathews.

1964 was your last year in the big leagues. Did you go to spring training with Houston in 1965?

In spring training of 1965 I was with them, too, because I was supposed to break training with them just to pitch in the games to open up the Astrodome, against the Yankees and against Baltimore. And I couldn't go because I got sick—the flu or something—and as a result, instead of breaking and going with the team, they sent me to Triple-A in Oklahoma City.

So you never pitched in the Astrodome.

I never, ever got inside the Astrodome. The Astrodome was being built in 1964. I remember going on road trips—I was with the major league club in 1964—coming home, and seeing another part of the roof of the Astrodome was done because the Astrodome, if you recall, was right next to Colts Stadium.

Do you start the season with the club in 1964?

I start the season in 1964.

So you get sent down at some point.

Correct. Sometime after the All-Star game.

Do you remember that happening? Do you remember getting sent down?

I was sent down—I want to say—to Amarillo in the Texas League.

Does the manager tell you? Does the pitching coach tell you? Do they tell you that you're going to come back soon?

They're sending me down because I've been sitting around too long and they wanted me to get some work down there.

Did you believe them?

Yes. Of course. I believe I came back up at the end of the 1964 season, but after the minor league season was over. And in 1965, as I said, I went to Oklahoma City, did lousy there, went to Amarillo in the Texas League, didn't exactly turn that world on fire, and that was the end of my career.

When do you know that your last game in the majors is your last game in the majors?

It was during the 1965 season when I knew—not thought, but knew—that I was going to have a good year in Triple-A and be called up during the season. I guess it was around the time that I got sent down from Triple-A to Double-A.

Were you injured or anything?

No, the only injury I had in my whole life—including high school and sandlot—is the first third to half of the 1963 season I had a bad shoulder, which they had to give me cortisone shots for, and I couldn't pitch.

You start 1965 in Oklahoma City and you get sent down to Amarillo, and about the time you get sent down to Amarillo you're thinking, I may not get back.

That's right, but there's another element here. I'm married at the time, too. I was married in 1963. My wife is pregnant with our son and she has to stay in bed virtually all the time towards the end of her pregnancy. I'm not putting that on the same level as my poor performance during the year, and I'm not blaming it on that either, but between the two it was a rather simple decision for me to walk away from baseball at the end of the 1965 season.

And what do you do? What do you do when baseball's been the thing that you do better than anything else? What do you do after you take care of your wife?

Well, she actually was not with me. My son was born August thirtieth of 1965.

You finished the season?

Yes. I don't get to see him until he's a week old.

Where are they living at the time?

They're in Brooklyn and they were staying with her mother. Then I come back and we get an apartment and then we're off on our own then.

You come home to Brooklyn in September and your child's a week old. It sounds like you knew you weren't going back in 1966. What do you do with yourself and a wife of two years and a week-old son?

Well, I'm going to go out and I'm going to get a job and I'm going to support them, and, of course, my wife is going to stay home and she's going to take care of my kid because I'm a big guy and I'm going to make a lot of money and wives didn't work back then during those years. You kept them from working.

But you've just spent a little time in the majors and you don't have a serious injury. Why do you walk away so soon?

I think that it was something that occurred during the entire 1965 season. It was not just in my mind that I was up and then now I'm being sent down. Being supposed to start in the Astrodome during the exhibition season, starting in Triple-A, going from Triple-A to Double-A, not doing well at all in Triple-A obviously, not doing real well in Double-A where I had done well my first year in baseball. I guess it was a realization that, Well, maybe I wasn't going to make the Hall of Fame.

If you hadn't made the majors in 1963 and 1964, if you had only pitched minor league ball in 1963 and 1964, do you think you would've quit at the end of 1965? Was playing in the majors the accomplishment?

Heavens, no. No, it wasn't. If anything, playing in the majors, looking back at it, was to my detriment.

I think I'm asking that, but in a roundabout way. You probably got brought up too quickly, but would you have quit after 1965 if you had never been to the majors?

Everything else remaining the same? I still have the bad year in 1965? I don't see how I can honestly say that I would not have made the exact same decision. It would be easy for me to sit here and say to you, I know for sure being in the major leagues really screwed me because I needed to pitch every fifth day, as opposed to only pitching when we were ten runs ahead or ten runs behind. It would be very easy for me to say that my lack of participation in the game in 1964 is what ended my career. I think it had something to do with it, but it could also very well be the realization that I was not as good as I thought I was. That, at best, I was going to be a fringe major league pitcher.

But you were twenty-two years old when you quit. Did you ever have any thought about going back?

No. I was gone. In fact, Houston contacted me in the winter of 1965 after I told them I wasn't coming back and they offered me a modest contract to come back in 1966. It wasn't a bribe or anything, trust me, but my mind was made up and I wasn't going back. I just didn't feel like I was major league material anymore.

So you didn't want to do it if you weren't going to be good at it?

Oh, no question about that. No question about that. I'm not the type of personality that did things for the sake of doing it.

So what did you do?

I began a sales career that I'm still in right now. I never earned a whole bunch of money. I never starved. I struggled but I thought I did what I liked, and I'm as happy as can be right now.

You told me earlier that you were a Braves fan. Is that primarily through television? Do you ever go to any of the games?

I do go. My son has season tickets. They used to be four rows behind where Ted Turner and Jane Fonda sat.

Is there any particular pitcher you like to watch?

I love Maddux and Glavine, especially Maddux since he's right-handed. They're textbook pitchers. Whitey Ford pitched that way.

Did you keep anything from your major league career?

No, no. My parents kept a scrapbook and I gave it to my son Michael when he was growing up, plus he still has my glove. I have pictures up in my office of my signing my first professional contract and another with Rusty Staub presenting me with the MVP for New York State.

You have a baseball card. How important is that to you?

When I get requests in the mail, when the cards are sent to me, it'll moisten my eyes. I feel pretty good about it.

Pittsburgh at Milwaukee
Saturday, October 3, 1964

Pittsburgh	ab	r	h	rbi	Milwaukee	ab	r	h	rbi
Wissman, cf	4	0	1	0	Carty, lf	4	2	2	2
B. Bailey, 3b	5	1	1	0	Cline, cf	1	1	1	0
Clemente, rf	4	1	1	0	Aaron, rf	4	1	1	1
Clendenon, 1b	5	1	2	0	Blackaby, rf	1	0	0	0
Mazeroski, 2b	4	0	1	1	Klimchock, 3b	5	1	1	1
Mota, lf	5	0	3	1	E. Bailey, c	5	2	2	3
Alley, ss	3	1	1	1	Torre, 1b	4	0	1	1
May, c	3	0	1	1	Alou, 1b	0	0	0	0
Cardwell, p	0	0	0	0	Kolb, cf-lf	4	0	1	1
Schofield, ph	1	0	0	0	Woodward, 2b	4	2	2	0
Blass, p	1	0	0	0	Alomar, ss	4	1	2	1
Lynch, ph	1	0	1	0	Umbach, p	2	1	0	0
Virdon, pr	0	1	0	0					
					Totals	38	11	13	9
Totals	36	5	12	4					

Pittsburgh	0	0	0	0	1	0	0	2	2—5
Milwaukee	3	0	2	0	0	4	1	1	x—11

Pittsburgh	IP.	H.	R.	ER.	BB.	SO.
Cardwell (L. 1-2)	2	5	3	3	0	2
Blass	3*	5	6	4	0	0
Schwall...................	1	0	0	0	0	0
Bork...................	2	3	2	2	0	1
Milwaukee	IP.	H.	R.	ER.	BB.	SO.
Umbach (W. 1-0)	8.1	11	5	3	4	7
Spahn	0.2	1	0	0	0	0

*Pitched to four batters in sixth

E—Alley, Mazeroski, Blass, Alomar. DP—Pittsburgh 1, Milwaukee 2.
LOB—Pittsburgh 10, Milwaukee 5. 2B—Alley, Clendenon, Klimchock, Woodward.
3B—E. Bailey, Cline. HR—Carty (22). SH—Umbach, Clemente. SF—Alley.
HBP—by Cardwell (Umbach). WP—Cardwell, Blass. T—2:30. A—5,636.

ARNOLD UMBACH

Arnie Umbach pitched eight and one-third innings in
his major league debut for the Milwaukee Braves in 1964.
In the process he picked up his only major league win.
Umbach also pitched in twenty-two games in 1966 and
finished with a major league ERA of 3.10 over forty-nine
innings. He gave up forty hits while walking eighteen
and striking out twenty-three. He was interviewed October 17, 2001 at his law office in Opelika, Alabama.

Where were you raised and when did you start playing baseball?

I was born in Virginia. Dad was a football coach and he came to Auburn
as a football coach under the head coach, Carl Voyles. Dad was from
Oklahoma, and being from Oklahoma he had wrestled all his life and
was very interested in wrestling, so he started wrestling in the southeast
and when Voyles got fired he stayed as the wrestling coach and head of
the men's PE department, which they had back then. They don't anymore. So I've spent all my life in Alabama except for the first two years.

My dad also started Little League in Alabama because there wasn't any organized baseball for kids, so I started in Little League and we were fairly successful. We went to the Little League World Series in 1955. That's when I started playing baseball.

How did the team do?

We came in third. And none of us had hardly been out of the state so it was a big deal.

Were you a pitcher on that team?

Yes. A pitcher and a first baseman.

Your father, obviously, was a good all-around athlete. He's in the Alabama Sports Hall of Fame and the Wrestling Hall of Fame. Was wrestling his love or was that choice circumstantial?

He absolutely loved wrestling. That was his first sport. He knew nothing about baseball. He learned just so he could coach me, but he knew nothing about baseball. He learned but he never played.

Were you a good all-around athlete as well?

Well, I played football like everybody else, high school basketball, baseball.

Were you better at baseball or did you like it better?

I liked it better. I had several football scholarships offered but instead of playing football in college I signed out of high school to play baseball.

Did you ever wrestle?

Not much. My dad wouldn't let me wrestle. I had a younger brother who was an SEC champion, but there's a wrestling move called the switch that can be rather tough on your shoulder and my dad was afraid that I might get hurt. Apparently he realized that I had more talent in baseball than I had in wrestling. Not that I would've been any good at it.

A lot of parents out there would steer their child towards their sport.

I doubt he ever played any baseball in his life. I doubt he'd ever been on a baseball field.

Where did you go to high school?

I went to high school at Auburn until the tenth grade, and then went to a prep school called Baylor in Chattanooga.

When you're playing baseball at Baylor, are you playing any other positions?

The same thing. Playing first base.

Were you a good hitter as well?

Yeah, you know, I think you'll find most pitchers in high school are pretty good hitters.

Are you playing any other sports?

I played football and switched to soccer. At Baylor, it was played in the winter and the reason I did that was because I could do soccer and then go inside and start getting ready for baseball season during the winter. I didn't have to worry about switching from a large ball to a small ball.

123

What pitches are you throwing in high school?

Fastball, curveball, change-up.

Who teaches you the curveball?

Dad.

Even though he's never played baseball before, he does the research so he can teach you.

Right.

Is the fastball your best pitch?

Yeah.

Did you have good movement on it?

Yeah, that was probably one of the best things I had going.

Did you know where it was going to move, or did you throw it center of the plate?

I just tried to throw it for a strike. I didn't know how to pitch as far as up and in, in and out, and that kind of thing.

Do scouts start coming to watch you at Baylor?

Really what started that was there was an amateur baseball summer league for sixteen-, seventeen-, and eighteen-year-olds, and the finals were in Johnstown, Pennsylvania. And Alabama got up a team and I went with the team from Birmingham and I was sixteen and I struck out twenty-four batters in a game. And there were a lot of scouts, as you can imagine, up there, and I think that probably started it. They kind of started following up after that.

So you knew that you were good before you got to Baylor?

Yeah.

124

Are you a good kid? Does success give you a big head?

Yeah, I was a good kid. Dad took care of that. I was pretty much a straight arrow. I didn't drink a beer until I was twenty years old. Baylor was a military school and there were a lot of kids up there for discipline reasons, but I never got into any trouble.

You graduate in 1961 and you've got several scouts coming to Chattanooga.

The Braves, the Tigers, and the Yankees were the three that seemed more interested, and they would talk to Dad back in Auburn. They talked to me very little.

Did you have a favorite ball team growing up?

Yeah, it was probably the Yankees.

Do you like the Yankees because they're winners?

Yeah, that's what you read about. I had never seen a pro game until I saw the Chattanooga Lookouts play when I was a senior in high school.

Are these three teams making you offers just before your graduation or just after your graduation? Are you still in Chattanooga or are you back in Auburn?

Well, I didn't actually agree on anything until I got back to Auburn after graduation, and then I left immediately to start playing.

Are all three organizations offering about the same money?

No, the Yankees and the Braves were offering more. I wound up signing for $100,000. That was one of the highest bonuses paid at that time.

That's a huge sum for that time. Are both the Yankees and the Braves offering you $100,000?

No, I think the Yankees were offering $80,000, but I don't really remember because all of this went on with Dad.

If the signing bonus had been $10,000 instead of $100,000, would you have considered going to college and playing, or were you ready to be a professional?

I didn't have any idea the money was like that. I had signed a scholarship with Auburn and I had football offers from Ole Miss, Auburn, and Dartmouth, but Dad didn't want me to play football so I signed a baseball scholarship with Auburn in the spring. But I didn't know what I was going to do.

125

What made up your mind?

Well, the scouts did in a sense. At that age, the money wasn't the thing for me. Back then, colleges played twenty or twenty-five games and according to the scouts, some of them, maybe, were D ball or C ball, and it was just a waste of time. If you're going to play you need to go out there and play the whole year or you're going to get behind.

I have to ask you what you did with the money. I'm assuming that, with that much, most of it would go in the bank, but you have to buy something special for yourself, don't you?

Well, I bought a Chevrolet is the only thing I did with it. I wound up paying off the rest of my folks' house, spent $25,000 sending my brother to med school, and the rest of it went to undergraduate school and law school for me.

You were a good kid.

Well, I don't know about that. But being the good kid turned out to be a disadvantage. I was brought up in a family culture that the coach was always right and you did what the coach said. I hadn't been playing six months, and, you know, back then—I don't know how it is now—the minor league coaches are the major league coaches' drinking buddy back when they played together on such and such team. The only way for them to get to the major leagues is get a prospect and get him to the major leagues. And I hadn't been playing six months. You have a bad game, can't get a breaking ball over, and it was, Here, you need to change the grip. Do this. And you know, I should've had enough sense to say, Look guys. They gave me $100,000 so somebody figured out that I was doing something right so leave my ass alone. But I didn't do it, and I was so screwed up in a couple of years. And then, mentally, when you reach a certain level, everybody can only run so fast, throw so hard, and I was piecemealing going to school as much as I could when I wasn't playing winter ball, and when it got just right down to it I had something else to do. It wasn't as though if I lost this game I was going to the factory. And that made a difference. This is all hindsight, of course.

You sign the contract with the Braves in June of 1961. Is that the best day of your life to that point?

Yeah.

How long does it take you to pack and go after you sign?

The first thing they did was the Braves were playing in Chicago and they took me, my mother and dad, and my grandmother who was visiting from Oklahoma—she was in her seventies at the time—to Chicago and we got to watch a couple of games and I got to walk out on the field and warm up before the game, you know, and that kind of thing. That was obviously the first major league game that I'd ever seen. Then I went to Vancouver, which was a Triple-A team. I left from Chicago. The reason was because there was a guy named Billy Hitchcock from Opelika who was the manager at Vancouver. I know that's the reason because you don't send someone out of high school to Triple-A. And it helped having Billy there. Back then Triple-A had guys going up and down. You don't have that anymore. I mean, there were guys thirty-two years old playing Triple-A ball. And I'm eighteen. I didn't pitch much, and then I went to Yakima, which was B ball at that time, and each year kind of worked up. We were on the major league roster, the guys that got some money. We had major league contracts.

Do you know how early they had to call you up so you wouldn't be subject to the minor league draft?

I don't know what the rules were. I know we had to have major league contracts and I know the minimum salary was $7,500.

So you signed a split contract.

Yeah, what we would do is we would go—well, it was Bradenton then, then they moved to West Palm Beach—when the major league team broke camp, we would go to Waycross, Georgia. It was an old military installation and it was the Braves' minor league camp. And then, Triple-A would break first, then Double-A, and then on down like that.

Are you still throwing fastball, curveball, and change-up when you get to Yakima?

Yes.

Are you working on anything or are you throwing like you did at Baylor?

Just like that.

Where do you go after the season in Yakima?

I go to instructional league in Florida.

1964 is your first game in the majors. You started your major league debut and lasted eight and one third. You gave up eleven hits, five runs, three of them were earned. You walked four and struck out seven. Being a rookie, going eight and one third and not getting to pitch again, I've got to believe it was in September.

Yeah, it was in the fall. That was against Pittsburgh.

In County Stadium or Forbes Field?

It was at Forbes.

Do you remember any of the guys you threw against? Clemente was on that team.

Back then there were very few hitters who could hit the ball with any authority to the opposite field. The ones that went to the opposite field were Punch-and-Judy hitters, but Clemente could drive the ball. I didn't know how to pitch somebody like that so I stayed off the plate and that's where he hit. I had no clue how to pitch to Clemente. I just tried to keep it down.

After a couple years of minor league ball and a couple years of going to spring training and instructional league, theoretically there's some coaching in there. How different are you from the pitcher who graduated from Baylor three years before? What can you do in 1964 that you couldn't do in 1961?

I had a little better control, but what you don't get, or what I didn't get—it was my fault—is learning how to pitch. They would have team meetings, but they would tell everybody the same thing. You know, this guy's a first-ball, fastball hitter. Pitch this guy out and in. Well, maybe I could or could not. Maybe you can get him out that way but that doesn't mean I can do it. So I didn't learn much more about how to pitch because you didn't get that in the minor leagues. They had a roving pitching coach. There's a guy I'm thinking of who was a major league coach named Whitlow Wyatt. Just a really nice guy, but he was the kind that you had to seek out. But he was very available and all that kind of stuff. But I didn't have enough sense to join him at the hip and sit through every game with him and talk to him. And if I'd have been like Randy Johnson it wouldn't have made any difference.

Do you have any idea how fast you were throwing?

It was probably in the low nineties, but no, I don't have any idea.

How long were you up with the club in 1964 when you get your start?

I came up when they expanded the roster and stayed until the end of the year.

So you were up for a month but only pitched one game. The Braves finished fifth that year. Do you have any idea why you didn't pitch more? Did you ever ask?

Well, what was strange was when they got ten runs down I didn't get in.

Do we blame the manager, Bobby Bragan, for that?

You can. I don't know. It would've been nice if someone would've come up and said, Hey, if so and so gets in trouble before the fifth, you're in there. If it's after the fifth, you're not going in. I don't know if I was forced on him. I don't have any idea about the front office.

Are you back on the forty-man roster for 1965?

Yeah.

Do you get cut early?

Late. I got chances in spring training.

Did you pitch okay in spring training?

I don't remember, but obviously not good enough to impress anybody.

Where did you spend the next year?

In 1965 I was with the Crackers in Atlanta. That was the year before the Braves came. I think I was like 13–1 that year or 13–2, something like that, in Triple-A.

But you don't get called up.

And I was out of options the next year so they had to keep me. Well, they didn't have to.

But you didn't do anything or say anything to get on Bragan's bad side?

No. He was a strange guy, to me. But no, I don't ever remember talking to him.

Bragan starts the year as manager in 1966 and then Hitchcock takes over during the year.

I started the year with the team and then I wasn't there when Hitchcock took over. What happened was a guy named Paul Richards was the general manager. And he took everybody—the guys they would look at as fringe players and the minor leagues, too—and over the All-Star break we went to Austin, Texas, and we were forever out on the field. And we had these little drills. He was big into drills. You had to throw so many pitches on the outside, so many pitches on the inside, and back and forth and up and down. And that's how they evaluated you. Shortly after that he traded Mathews to Houston and I was one of the players to be named later.

When you came up in 1964, and you walked into the locker room in County Stadium, were you overwhelmed?

Absolutely. Absolutely. There were a lot of class guys and some of them that weren't. Torre was very helpful to me. I don't know why. He really tried to help pitchers. Like, when we went to play the Mets, I'll never forget, he took me out to where his mother lived and we were having an Italian meal. And his brother Frank helped me a lot. He was in Vancouver and was pretty much pissed off when I got there because he was on their 1957 World Series team and this was 1961. But really, the same kind of guy. As nice as he could be. Of course, I was excited going to Torre's parents' house, and when he said, Italian meal, I thought we were having spaghetti.

When Torre takes you over to the house, is it just you and him? He can't be taking the whole team over there.

No, just he and I and maybe Wade Blasingame. We were signed the same year. He and Torre were roommates.

Who did you room with?

Different people. Denis Menke was one. You take different people like Menke or Felipe Alou. People don't come any better than that. They would be helpful.

I understand that people are people and there's good and there's bad. Did they ever treat you like a rookie?

There were typical guys. Somebody like Lew Burdette. Aaron wasn't particularly friendly, probably because we were getting as much money as he was and he'd been playing for ten years. I'd probably have been pissed, too.

But you and Sandy Alomar get traded to Houston along with Eddie Mathews for Bob Bruce and Dave Nicholson.

Nicholson was one of these guys that was supposed to be the next Mickey Mantle. He looked the part and hit the ball a mile.

It's a winter trade. New Year's Eve 1966. But you don't spend the whole year with the Braves.

That must've been when I went to Oklahoma City. I think about June or July I went from Atlanta to Triple-A.

If you get sent to Oklahoma City in June or July, do you get brought back in September?

I don't think I did because I think I was out of options then, when they sent me down. I knew I wasn't going to be with the Braves anymore.

How did you find out you'd been traded?

I don't know whether they called me or if I just read about it. I don't really remember.

That should've been big news—Eddie Mathews getting traded from the Braves.

I couldn't have read about it because I don't ever remember seeing my name anywhere. I think I just got a letter or call saying, You're with Houston. Either that or Houston contacted me. There was a guy named John Mullen who was with the Braves as a general manager who went to Houston. He might've called me.

You go to spring training with Houston in 1967.

I don't think I went to the major league camp.

But you're 13–1 with the Crackers in 1965. You go to the majors in 1966 and have an ERA of 3.10. You're striking out more than you're walking. I don't know how you don't make the major league roster, especially for a team like

Houston, because they're still not very good.

They're awful. But I started having arm trouble. I started having shoulder problems about then, too. I had had a child, and he was about two or three. Auburn was on the quarter system and they were letting me leave early and come in late. And I didn't take any elective courses. And back then, in law school, they let you in without a degree. You had to go talk to the dean and convince him you wanted to go and all that kind of stuff. So I got this idea that I was going to try and pull that off. So I went and talked to the dean and they had agreed to do it so I had actually completed one year of law school before I got my undergraduate degree.

This is all during the winters?

I would come in after the quarter started, which wasn't any big deal, but I would have to leave to go to spring training roughly when winter quarter was about half over, and that was a struggle. I would take twenty-three hours a quarter, which you had to have permission to do. That was a pretty good load.

If you were a full-time student it would've been a pretty good load. If you're a professional baseball player trying to carry that many hours, it's damn near masochistic.

Yeah, it was. The winter quarter was the tough one because you had to trust the professor to follow the syllabus. And when you went in to take the exam, you had to do it on your own, basically.

Do the Braves know you're doing this?

Yeah.

Do they render an opinion?

Yeah.

And it wasn't, Boy, we are so impressed that you're a fine upstanding man working double time to get your education.

No. It probably hurt me. They would want me to go to Puerto Rico or the Dominican for winter ball and I didn't want to. I'd had enough baseball for one year and I didn't want to do that.

So this might be one of the reasons they don't keep you up. They think, It's hard enough being a major league player. If you're giving that your all, how can you possibly be doing this other?

Right. And everybody didn't get to go to winter ball.

So where does Houston send you for the 1967 season?

I went to Triple-A. That's when I had arm problems. I think that last year I pitched very few innings. I was in Oklahoma City twice, and that gets confusing. The only reason I remember is that's where all my relatives were. My mother and dad's parents were from Oklahoma so I can remember seeing all of them.

When did you know that your last game was your last game?

Well, I really didn't because I kept thinking my arm was going to come around.

So even when you're with Houston and they send you to Double-A you think you'll get back at some point.

133

Right. Right. They traded for me. They didn't give up anything, I'm sure. I was a throw-in, but still.

Does anything encouraging ever happen in Houston?

No, I don't go to spring training or anything. I don't ever remember going to Houston's major league camp.

Do you retire at the end of the year or do you get so frustrated that you just go home during the season?

I think I finished out the year but I remember hustling back to start law school. My arm was still hurt. I gave it a year and it didn't get any better, and, like I said, I had a family and it was time to get home. I was twenty-eight years old.

Do you watch much baseball now?

I watch a good bit of it. I probably enjoy it more now than I did.

Do you have a favorite team?

Yeah, the Braves.

Are there any particular pitchers that you like to watch?

Yeah. Like everybody else I like to watch Maddux. I like Smoltz. I don't relate to Glavine, him being left-handed and pitching outside like he does. I don't understand it.

Have you ever been to Cooperstown?

No, but I'd like to. It's just the distance.

If you went to Cooperstown, what would you want to see first?

Well, I would probably go check the pitchers out, obviously. I would like to see the guys I really admired watching, like Drysdale and Koufax and Gibson. You know, those kind of people. I would sit on the bench and couldn't believe that they could do what they could do.

Did you keep anything from your playing days?

I've got a bat and a few balls. That's one of the things I really regret, that I wasn't enough of a fan.

Is this your bat? Does it have your name on it?

Yeah. Yeah.

That's pretty cool, for a pitcher to have his own Louisville Slugger.

Yeah, it was. But I really regret not getting autographs. You'd sit there at the table and sign dozens of balls. They'd put dozens in front of you. You didn't know where they were going. And why I didn't ask for a few I don't know, but I regret it.

Is there any significance to the balls you do have?

No. I've just got a couple of autographed balls. I've got a team ball from one year that has Spahn and Burdette and Crandall. That group of folks. I've got an old Milwaukee Braves hat and a Vancouver traveling bag.

You talked about facing Clemente and not really knowing how to pitch him. Were there any other batters that really meant something to you?

I think, because I had been a Yankee fan, in spring training I remember pitching to Yogi Berra. He hit a fastball up around his eyes.

But you're standing on the mound thinking, That's Yogi Berra.

Oh hell yeah.

Do you have any regrets?

Yeah, if I'd have put more into it I would've matured a little quicker.

What could you have done?

I could've been more attuned to learning how to pitch. Talent got me to a certain level and then I sort of hit a wall. And I didn't know what to do. I was around some great pitchers and I would see them do it, but I never knew why or anything. I was too intimidated to ask them what they were thinking, what they were trying to do, and I didn't pick up on things until late, like switching pitching patterns during the game.

You gave up two home runs in the majors. Do you have any idea who hit them?

No.

Is that one of those things that's good to forget?

No, that's probably a good example of what I'm saying. I should've remembered who it was and what they hit and what the heck I did wrong. Whether it was just a poor pitch or the pattern was wrong, or he changed and I didn't. I should've remembered. I should've picked up on that.

135

Baltimore at New York (AL)
Tuesday, September 7, 1965

SECOND GAME

Baltimore	ab	r	h	rbi	New York	ab	r	h	rbi
Aparicio, ss	6	1	2	2	White, 2b	5	1	2	0
Snyder, lf	6	1	2	1	Barker, 1b	4	0	1	1
Powell, 1b	5	1	1	2	Pepitone, rf	5	0	1	0
Robinson, 3b	5	1	2	0	Tresh, lf	4	1	1	1
Blefary, rf	4	2	2	0	Boyer, 3b	4	0	1	0
Lau, c	4	0	2	3	Repoz, cf	4	1	1	2
Adair, 2b	5	1	1	0	Gibbs, c	4	1	2	0
Blair, cf	4	2	3	0	Linz, ss	1	0	0	0
Bunker, p	4	0	0	0	Clarke, ph-ss	3	1	1	0
Bowens, ph	1	0	1	1	Cullen, p	1	0	0	0
					A. Lopez, ph	1	0	0	0
Totals	44	9	16	9	Howard, ph	1	0	0	0
					Moore, ph	1	0	1	1
					Moschitto, ph	0	0	0	0
					Totals	38	5	11	5

Baltimore	0	1	1	4	0	0	1	0	2—9
New York	0	0	0	0	0	0	0	0	2—5

Baltimore	IP.	H.	R.	ER.	BB.	SO.
Bunker (W. 8–7)	8	7	3	3	1	2
Hall	1	4	2	2	0	2
New York	IP.	H.	R.	ER.	BB.	SO.
Cullen (L. 3–4)	3.1	9	5	5	3	1
Reniff	2.2	3	1	1	0	2
Jurewicz	1	2	1	1	0	1
Blanco...	2	2	2	1	2	2

E—Gibbs. LOB—Baltimore 13, New York 7. 2B—Blair 3, Robinson, Adair, Lau, Blefary, Aparicio, White. HR—Powell (12), Repoz (11). SB—Aparicio, Snyder. T—2:50. A—9,244.

MIKE JUREWICZ

Mike Jurewicz made his major league debut for the New York Yankees on September 7, 1965. He pitched a total of two and one-third innings in two appearances, yielding five hits and two runs. He also walked one and struck out two, and finished with a career ERA of 7.71. He was interviewed April 15, 2002 at Perkins Restaurant in Apple Valley, Minnesota.

Tell me where you grew up and how you started playing baseball.

Well, I was born in Buffalo, New York. I moved to Wisconsin just prior to my tenth birthday. I just played some park ball in New York. I was eight years old and just went to the park to play baseball like all kids do. I'd wake up in the morning and go play ball all day long and then I would go home. One day there was a coach there for the ten-year-old league and he saw me playing and he asked me if I would be interested in playing on his ten-year-old team. So even though I was only an eight-year-old, I ended up playing on a ten-year-old team, and actually was one of the better players on the team.

It was kind of ironic because when I moved out to Wisconsin they were just starting the Little League structure. The first year that they had Little League was my first year in Wisconsin. I lived in Beloit, Wisconsin, a southern town, right on the border, and I went out for the Little League team and actually made the Yankees. I played for the Yankees for three years, so it was almost an omen of things to come. They had a parade through town and they built a brand new ballpark, so to me, as a ten-year-old, it was like playing in the major leagues. It just didn't get any better than this. I was used to playing on skin infields, anywhere you could throw down four bases.

Were you a pitcher from the beginning?

Yeah. Being left-handed, I played in the outfield and first base, but I was also a pitcher for as long as I can remember. I always had a real strong arm, but I was always pretty small for my age. I never really grew until I got to high school. When I was in eighth grade I was five two and weighed about ninety pounds. When I graduated from high school I was six three and weighed 195 pounds, so I grew a foot and gained a hundred pounds in high school. But I always could throw hard and I think I had a strong arm because I was throwing things my whole life—a baseball, a football, or just throwing rocks trying to hit cans in a field.

I come from a family with eight boys and two girls and I'm eighth in the family, so I had to learn to compete with my older brothers or I didn't get to play. When I played basketball I knew I wasn't going to take any shots because I was the youngest one on the team, so I learned to play defense. I learned to dribble well and handle the ball so kids couldn't take it away from me. When I played baseball I knew I was going to get stuck in the outfield. They would go easy on me when they pitched to me, but they would always keep the competition one notch ahead so I would have to improve my skills if I wanted to be able to compete.

How important was having the handful of older brothers towards you becoming a professional athlete? Did any of your brothers play college ball, or professionally? Were you the best athlete in your family?

I grew up with the idea that you always respect your elders, whether your elders are two years older or fifty years older. You always address everybody as Mr and Mrs, so I just assumed, growing up, that anybody older than me was better than me. Even if I went out and got four hits in a game and this guy struck out four times, I still thought that he must be better because that was the way things are supposed to be. I just figured that he had a bad day and I had a good day. I always looked at my older brothers in the same way.

My oldest brother, Skip, was legendary. We lived in a suburb of Buffalo, New York. We grew up in a real small community so any accomplishments were always legendary in our area, and one of his legends is that he hit the longest ball ever hit in our town. He was a three-sport athlete. He played football, basketball, and baseball at Canisius High School. Everybody said that football was his best sport although he was a heck of a baseball player. He went to college on a football scholarship. Well, after his freshman year he and another buddy decided to enlist in the Navy, and off they went. And they were coming home for Christmas one year on a furlough, and there were four of them in the car and somebody drove them off the road and they hit a tree and one of them died. My brother barely survived, but it virtually ended his athletic career. I mean, they gave him the last rites and he had to wear a brace on his leg for the next ten years and that type of thing, but still he's the legend in the family. I just assumed he was the best athlete in the family.

All of my brothers excelled in sports and they all have their own stories. A few of them received college scholarships. Jim and Ron played football in college and Ron went through an exhibition season with the Bears. He made all but the last cut. Jack played basketball at Marquette. Tony and Fred had heart conditions and Fran had osteomyelitis as a baby, so those things hampered their careers but they still had outstanding high school careers. Even my sisters, Barbara and Alfreda, were very athletic and competitive in sports. My dad was also a great athlete but our real inspiration came from my mom, who was the greatest fan I have ever seen.

When I went to high school I was all-state in three sports, so if you took a survey and asked all my brothers and sisters, I guess I'd probably get my share of the votes as the best athlete in the family. Even as a freshman I played on the varsity baseball team, but again, I went to a small high school. There were only 275 kids in the high school during my first two years so I was able to compete pretty well with all the older guys. It was then that I started to realize that maybe I was better than some of these other kids that are older. My last two years of high school, we moved to Milwaukee and I went to a school with about twenty-five hundred kids so it was a big adjustment, but I was still able to compete with the older kids.

You made all-state in three sports. Are you as good in either of the other sports as you are at baseball?

Yeah, I think so. I was all-state in football and had scholarship offers to several schools and narrowed it down between Notre Dame and Wisconsin.

What position?

I was a wide receiver. I signed a scholarship tender to go play football, but when baseball season came around the scouts and recruiters all said I'd be making a mistake playing football. Even if I didn't get hurt, it'd hurt me just going through the weight-training program. I was told that I would bulk up the muscles and it would affect my pitching. If you want to be a pitcher you need long, loose muscles. In high school my baseball coach was also my football coach and he was also a bird-dog scout for the Braves and the Braves were in town at the time, and they tried real hard to sign me to a contract right out of high school. He advised me not to play football my senior year so I didn't go out at first, but after two days I just started getting antsy, you know. I said, There's no way I'm not going to play, so I went out and played and was all-state.

In basketball there was one ballplayer on our team that was better than I was. He was only a junior and he was our star ballplayer, but we both got all-state recognition. We played against guys like Rocky Bleier. He's from Appleton, Wisconsin, so we played against him in the state tournament in basketball. We had a tremendously talented senior class. We were ranked number one in the state in football, and we were number one in basketball and we won the state tournament in baseball, but, yeah, I think I was equally good in all three sports.

Is baseball even your favorite sport?

Yeah, baseball made the most sense to me because in baseball I was able to dominate. It was clear to me that baseball was my strongest sport even though other people may have disagreed. You can dominate in basketball if you're Michael Jordan, you know, but I've already mentioned there was one kid on our team that was better than me. In football you're not going to dominate unless you're a quarterback who throws five touchdowns a game or a running back who rushes for two hundred yards a game. As a wide receiver I'm reliant on my quarterback. If he doesn't get me the ball, then I'm an unknown on the football field.

So you like baseball better because you were a pitcher.

Well, I just had a real passion for baseball because it was the national pastime, you know. That was the one sport you played all day long. You got up at daybreak and you didn't quit until you couldn't see the ball anymore. I just played it all day long and I enjoyed it. You really didn't need anything to play. You just walked outside and there's your baseball field. With basketball you still have to have a hoop and a court. I played basketball all day during basketball season, but basketball is a winter sport so you're limited in the north as to how long you can play outdoors.

I don't know. I just think logically. I'm a real pragmatist, and it just seemed to me that if I was going to have a career anywhere, baseball was the best one to have. I looked at longevity and injuries and all those types of things. If I had to do it now, I'd probably play golf. I think I just grew up with the idea, like every kid does, that I wanted to be a major league baseball player someday, and nothing else got in the way of that passion. Whether I was all-world in football or basketball, I was going to play baseball when I grew up. To me there was never any question. I was always going to play baseball.

You signed right out of high school.

Yeah, in 1963. I was seventeen years old when I signed a baseball contract.

That's two years before the draft begins.

I had free rein. I was able to deal with all of the teams. Gosh, when they first started scouting me I think there were twenty teams in baseball and I was negotiating with eighteen of them. Again, the practical side of me said, Where's the best opportunity to get to the major leagues? And I narrowed it down between the Phillies and the Yankees. Cincinnati probably came at me the hardest, and Cincinnati and Philadelphia both offered more money, but I looked at the minor league systems and who was out there.

The Braves automatically assumed I would sign with them. They tried playing the hometown card, even though they already knew they were moving to Atlanta because they moved shortly thereafter. They had just signed Denver Lemaster and Danny Schneider out of Arizona State. They were both left-handed and they each got over a hundred grand. I think Danny got $125,000. And I said to them, I don't care about the money. I'll sign for free, but when push comes to shove and it comes down to putting me on a team and I'm competing with Danny Schneider, are you going to protect your $125,000 investment and go with him?

At seventeen years old you're that aware of how this all works?

Oh yeah. Absolutely. My goal was to play in the major leagues and I wanted to find the quickest route in getting there.

You know that the organization is going to try and cover its investment and it might work against you. If they've got $100,000 in this player, they're not going to let him flounder in the minors.

I actually said that to John McHale when I was in his office at Milwaukee County Stadium. He was general manager of the Braves at the time.

Did you have a favorite team growing up?

Sure. I was a huge Brooklyn Dodgers fan. I thought it was unfair of them to move out to Los Angeles. I thought it was a lousy trick. Just like now, the Twins have been talking about leaving town. The Minnesota North Stars left and went down to Dallas to play hockey, so I've always been sensitive to those kinds of issues. I was always a Brooklyn Dodgers fan.

What about after they moved to Los Angeles?

Once they moved to Los Angeles I was still a Dodger fan but I felt like there's got to be somebody else.

I quickly became a Milwaukee Braves fan when we moved to Wisconsin in 1955. I've always been a hometown fan. The toughest adjustment I ever had was moving from Wisconsin to Minnesota and becoming a Minnesota Viking fan, because we always hated them. We were Packer fans in the glory days and it took me forever to convert. I always hated Bud Grant but it turned out that he's actually a really good guy and a great coach. But he was the enemy. Even when I converted I couldn't figure out who I was rooting for when I was watching the Packers.

I was athlete of the year in my senior year and Vince Lombardi gave me the award. That was one of the highlights of my life. People say, Well, you played in Yankee Stadium and things like that, but I have a few highlights in my life. One was being there for Mickey Mantle Day in Yankee Stadium. Bobby Kennedy was there and John Lindsay, the mayor, and Frank Sinatra and all the celebrities were there. Everybody wanted to be a part of that special day, you know, and I was a part of it because I was a member of the team, so that was a highlight. Hitting a home run in my very first professional at bat. Pitching a no-hitter was a highlight. Ralph Houk, the Yankee GM, was in the stands. I remember them all, and as big as any was Vince Lombardi giving me the award. There's no bigger legend in coaching, in my mind, and no better coach. He may not have had all the people skills, but he sure knew how to motivate and he knew how to put a championship team on the field.

But you don't sign with Milwaukee, the hometown team, because they've signed Lemaster and Schneider?

Basically, yeah. My whole thought process was, I want to get into base-ball when I'm young, and if I'm not going to make it I want to get out while I'm young.

You are pragmatic.

Yes, I am. As much as I love baseball, and as strong of a passion as I had for it, I always felt I had a pretty good head on my shoulders and if baseball wasn't going to be in my life, then I wanted to get out and get on with it, so I went in with that attitude. It got me out of baseball quicker, probably, than I should've given up on it, but that was what I went with and that was how I ultimately made the decision.

That outlook would make me think that you should be signing with a team like the Mets or the Colts.

They were loaded with left-handers. They had left-handers on the Triple-A roster having great years.

So you're checking out the Triple-A rosters?

Well, I'm asking. Scouts are coming to me and I would say, Okay, I want to know who you've signed in the last year. I want to know what you've got in your farm system. Who are the left-handers? And they're not going to risk lying to me, because if I find out differently then they're immediately eliminated. Like I said, the two best opportunities were with Philadelphia and the Yankees. In fact, Philadelphia was probably a little better opportunity than the Yankees because the Yankees had Howie Kitt at the time. He was a big guy and he threw hard and they gave him some pretty good money, and he was having a fairly decent minor league career. He was kind of wild, but I compared him to Sam McDowell. He threw very hard and he had a pretty good curveball, but he was wild. The Phillies were devoid of everything, but when I narrowed it down to those two I couldn't get away from the Yankee mystique. Chances are they're going to be in a World Series at some point in my career, while the Phillies hadn't been there forever, since the old Whiz Kids.

You said the Phillies and Cincinnati both offered you more money.

They did. They certainly did. Cincinnati really worked the hardest. Cincinnati was fairly close. The Phillies were almost like, We'll come back and make you an even better offer, but they also respected the fact that the decision was made.

You know, that's everybody's dream—to play on a championship team. Dan Marino never won a Super Bowl. It's one of his regrets in life. John Elway was fortunate to do it at the end of his career, but for my money, Marino was a better quarterback than Elway. It's a shame, because here's a kid that goes to the Super Bowl as a rookie thinking, Okay, I'm going to be back fifteen more times before my career is over, and he never got the opportunity to win one. Just being there is one goal, and then once you're there your goal is to win, and I knew with the Yankees I would have an opportunity to do that.

Did they give you enough that you could be classified as a bonus baby?

Yeah, I was a bonus baby. Those were the days when they didn't have a lot of money. There were only a couple of guys in baseball making $100,000, and that was Mantle and Mays. I was clearly a bonus baby, but they always tell rookies, We can give you a big bonus, but your regular contract can only be so big. Every kid who signed a contract in those days signed for $500 a month. That's what I signed for, but I got my bonus and they gave me college money to put aside so I went to Marquette during the off-season.

What did you do with the bonus money? Did you buy a car?

No, because, believe it or not, when I signed I didn't even have a driver's license. I had older brothers that drove and I knew if I got a license I would have to be the chauffeur for my mom and my younger brothers. I also figured that even if I got a license I'd never be able to drive because I'm fourth in line to get the car, so I didn't get my license until my eighteenth birthday. I had already played a season of pro ball before I got my license.

So what did you do with the bonus money?

We grew up with pretty modest means. There were ten kids. My dad was a mechanical engineer, but in those days he was probably only making about $4,000 a year. My mom was a professional cook. She cooked in restaurants, but the reality was we were poor because of all of the kids. I gave a big chunk of the money to my mom. My brother was in college at the time. I gave him money to pay for his tuition. My sister had twins and she didn't have health insurance so I gave her some money to pay for the hospital bill. My attitude was, I just want to play baseball. Everything that I have is really a godsend. My talent is God given. It's not something that I went out and developed. I certainly built on what He gave me but the reality was that I was lucky. I was the luckiest kid alive because I realized my boyhood dream, you know, and when you don't have money it doesn't mean anything to you.

Did you do anything for yourself?

No. I didn't buy one single thing for myself. I didn't even buy a glove or a pair of baseball shoes, because when you sign a contract they sign you to these glove contracts and shoe contracts and bat contracts and that type of thing.

I'm trying to remember if I bought anything. I was used to hand-me-downs from my older brothers. Whenever I got new clothes they'd last forever. I'm a boy, so give me my jeans and my sweatshirt and I'll wear that every day. I really didn't have any shopping skills. If I wanted to go buy myself something, I wouldn't even know what I'd buy. I was very content. You grow up and whatever you have you're appreciative of. Even to go out and buy a new bike or something, I just had no urge to do any of that. I put some money away, but I never spent any of it. I think the first thing that I probably ever bought for myself was a car, because I was going to get married.

Is this a girlfriend from high school?

She was, actually, a high school sweetheart. Sports was my whole life, so I was sweet sixteen and never been kissed. I went all the way into my junior year without ever dating. We had a basketball party at the end of my junior year and everybody had to bring a date and that type of thing, and there were girls that I liked but I was too shy to ask them out. It took me six weeks, until the day before the party, to actually work up the courage to invite somebody. She was the sister of one of my best friends. I never would've been able to go out on my own and grab somebody off the street and say, Do you want to go out? In the end that sort of worked

145

against me as well, because ultimately the first girl I ever kissed, that I ever dated, was the girl that I married.

When did you sign the contract?

After graduation I went and played for a summer team for a couple of weeks, and then I signed around the middle of June. Obviously, once the baseball season was over the recruiting intensified, and the scouts knew that I had signed a scholarship to go play football in college, so the first task was to convince me not to play football. Notre Dame said that if I didn't want to go there on a football scholarship, they would give me a baseball scholarship. And that was another thought—it's hard to say no to a Notre Dame. You grow up with that thought, and I was born and raised a Catholic and I'm still a practicing Catholic today. I could've gone there during the glory days. Three kids off of our all-state team went to Notre Dame. Rocky Bleier went there and a guy named Tom Regner was there. I played against him in high school and he ended up being an All-Pro with the Houston Oilers. The three of us could have gone to Notre Dame together, you know, and it would've been a lot of fun.

146

Is signing the contract the best day of your life to that point, or is it just another step in the journey?

You know, it's hard to say. I have a brother who's two years older than I am and you would've thought he was the one signing the contract. He was so buzzed over the whole thing that I was almost more happy for him than I was for myself, but because sports were such a big part of my life and I was always able to play at such a high level, to me it was just like another step. As a little kid, you dream of playing in the big leagues, but you never believe that you're ever actually going to get the opportunity to do so. But then all these people are courting you, they're making you a believer, so now I'm thinking, Jeez, I can play. I can play college ball and I can play professional baseball.

How long is it after signing the contract before you leave for rookie ball?

Almost immediately. As soon as they could get me an airline ticket.

And where do you go?

Harlan, Kentucky. It was a nightmare. It's a coal-mining town. I'm sure it was a very nice town but it was night and day compared to what I was used to.

Is this comparable to Johnson City?

Johnson City is New York City compared to Harlan, Kentucky. I think there were about four thousand people in the town. It's a coal-mining town that's surrounded by mountains. The big showcase in town was the hotel, the New Harlan Hotel. That's where everybody stayed, and in the middle of the hotel lobby there's this humongous piece of coal. It was the single biggest piece of coal ever taken out of the mines, you know, so that was their claim to fame. People came from all over Kentucky to see this piece of coal. I stayed in the hotel for maybe two weeks, just long enough to find a roommate, and we went out and ended up staying in the basement of one of the local homes.

    The sportswriter was a lady named Mabel Collins, and she used to bring cookies and muffins and stuff to the ballpark. Well, the first game I ever pitched I threw a three-hitter and I struck out seventeen guys and Mabel comes to interview me and we talk about the game and this and that, and she starts asking about my family and all these other kinds of things, and the next day the headline on the sports page is MIKE JUREWICZ COMES FROM A FAMILY OF TEN. The article is about my family, and in the very last paragraph of the article it said, By the way, Mike pitched last night and had seventeen strikeouts. It was really funny.

    They want you to think about nothing but baseball and that's why they send you to Harlan, Kentucky, because you can't think about anything other than baseball.

Rookie league is where they weed people out.

One of the problems we had in rookie league was that year they signed about twenty-eight guys to the rookie league, and twenty of them were probably pitchers. So when you went there they said, What other positions did you play? As a pitcher you're always the star of the high school team and usually the best athlete, so where else did you play? And guys would say, Well, I caught. I played short. I played second. So the manager would put the guys in those positions. Some guys never pitched one day in their professional career and got released before the end of the summer. This was just mind-boggling to me. I'm thinking, What the heck is going on here? One of our catchers was a guy who signed because he was dating the scout's daughter, and the scout just wanted to set him up so he gave him a nice big bonus. The kid bought himself a new car, played that summer, and he was gone. He never came back the following spring, but he had a new car and a nice bonus.

But you're a bonus baby. You're not worried somebody's going to try and make you a left fielder, are you?

Well, I didn't really think about it that way because I guess I believed that I could probably make the majors as a first baseman or an outfielder if I didn't make it as a pitcher. I'm left-handed so I'm kind of restricted to those two positions.

You were that good of a hitter?

Baltimore actually wanted to sign me as a position player. They said, Forget about pitching. And it was kind of ironic because the first game that I batted there was a kid from Buffalo, New York, that was a left-handed bonus baby with the Orioles. He threw hard and had a good curveball, but that's the kid I hit the home run off of, so I'm thinking it's kind of weird, this whole twist of fate, that the Orioles actually wanted to sign me as a position player.

When I went to the rookie league, again, I'm the dutiful little soldier and I do as I am told. The advantage I had in arriving late I thought was a disadvantage at the time. Because I waited a few weeks to sign, the team was set. They never asked me where else I played. They just assumed I was a pitcher. My reputation preceded me. I threw, you know, ninety-eight miles an hour and had a big curveball and was a strikeout pitcher.

Do you throw anything other than a fastball and curveball at this time?

I threw a change-up as well, but mostly just fastball and curveball.

Are you a thrower when you get to rookie ball, or are you a pitcher?

I'm sure I was a thrower.

So even though you've got a change-up, you're not really thinking about placement and changing speeds. Not if you're throwing in the upper nineties.

They said, With the stuff you have, don't look for corners. I'm left-handed so the ball tails and it moves and it dips. They said, Throw to the middle of the plate and the movement will take care of the corners and everything else.

Could you control your movement?

When I signed a contract, I couldn't. It was pretty consistent that you had that little tail, that natural screwball that left-handers have, so for the most part I just threw the ball. As I moved up into pro ball I could get it to move different ways, where it would dip down or run in on the batters.

There's no pitching coach in rookie league, is there?

No, but fortunately Gary Blaylock was my manager and he had been a pitcher in the major leagues. He pitched for the Yankees for a little bit and for St Louis, so he was a big help to me. I knew I was going to be a pitcher. They all knew I was there to pitch, and plus, all the other positions were now filled. Once I started hitting the ball, then they said, Jeez, you are a good hitter. We're going to play you in the outfield for doubleheaders, just to give the other guys a rest, but your career is as a pitcher. I also used to pinch-hit my rookie year. I think I batted .385, but again the disadvantage of signing late was that I had to wait for my opportunity. I was there for two weeks, and even though my reputation preceded me, they were trying to win a pennant so they're going with the guys that they know can produce. So I had to wait for a while. It was probably ten days or a couple of weeks before I got that opportunity, but once I did, then I established myself pretty quickly.

Did you go to instructional league or anything like that at the end of the season?

No. They had talked about winter ball and things, but winter ball then was, you know, going to Venezuela or Mexico. They didn't really have the Gulf Coast leagues and those types of things, at least not my rookie year. Shortly thereafter, when they got into the draft and expansion, then they quickly set up instructional leagues in the winter.

Where are you for spring training of 1964?

That first year, my first spring training, I went right to Hollywood, Florida. I played in the rookie league and then I went to Hollywood, Florida, which was the regular minor league camp, not too far from Fort Lauder-

149

dale. The minor league complex was down there. It was just a big massive group of guys. They didn't necessarily say you're going to the A league, or Double-A or Triple-A or whatever. Triple-A was pretty much separated from everybody else. Double-A was also separated from everybody and A was just one classification when I signed. It wasn't like the old days where you had D ball and C ball and B ball and A ball. It was just one mass of guys that all played in the A leagues, so you alternated teams every day and you didn't really know where you were going.

The Florida State League was the highest classification of A ball that they had. They had Greensboro, North Carolina, and that was probably equivalent to a B league. Shelby, North Carolina, was a C or a D and so on. They had those types of teams, but you didn't know where you're going. Again, we all had the dream of playing in Fort Lauderdale, because it was a major league ballpark, as were all the parks in the Florida State League. It was all the spring training complexes for the major leagues. I did end up in Fort Lauderdale, but again, I wasn't conscious of Where am I going to play, or What am I going to do. My only goal was just to go down there and play ball and do the best I could and where the chips fell they fell, you know.

Are you in Fort Lauderdale all year?

Yes, which is what I wanted. I mean, I was happy to be there. The Florida State League was split into two halves and we won the first-half championship. The St Petersburg Dodgers won the second-half championship so we played each other, and in the playoffs Mike Kekich pitched against me. He pitched a no-hitter against us and I pitched a two-hitter and beat him one to nothing in the ballgame. He ended up walking a guy and we bunted him over and then there was a wild pitch and we end up scoring a run and we win one to nothing. That was another one of my thrills in life, but my best friend in baseball was Fritz Peterson. The ironic twist of fate is that Fritz Peterson and Mike Kekich ended up swapping wives.

Fritz Peterson was signed by the same scout just after they signed me. Fritz went to Northern Illinois so he was four years older. I graduated from high school the same time he graduated from college. And Art Stewart, the scout who signed us, told him, Look up Mike when you're down there. Fritz is left-handed and I'm left-handed, and when you get into baseball the one little bit of negative is the attitude that, This guy's in my way of getting to the big leagues, so there's a natural tendency to not like this guy because he's left-handed and I'm left-handed, but for some reason we just really hit it off. We were both left-handed, a little bit goofy, and wanted to have fun and we didn't take baseball as seriously as everyone else did.

Do you think the stereotype is true, that left-handers are a little bit off-center?

Well, I believe that people have left-handed brains and right-handed brains, but I think it was just more of a personality mesh as opposed to anything else. You know, it's hard to take life seriously when you've got older brothers that are constantly humbling you. You're never going to be a hotshot or a big star. As good as I was, when I signed a baseball contract I was still wondering why my older brothers never signed a contract. As far as I was concerned, they were all better ballplayers than I was, you know. I was always being humbled but I always enjoyed life and had fun.

Speaking of enjoying life and having fun, are you married in 1964?

No. I got married in 1965. I actually made a deal with my girlfriend that we would get married once I made the major leagues. I got called up in 1965, and that's the year I played and I went home and got married that winter.

When you find out that you're getting called up to the majors, are you thinking more about making the big leagues or getting married? Were the two events linked?

No, it never even entered my mind. Obviously, as great a day as the day you get married may be, this moment was here in the present. What happened was I was having a pretty good year and they sent Ralph Houk down to watch me pitch because he was the GM at the time. The game he came to I pitched against a Minnesota farm team. They were in Charlotte at the time as the Charlotte Bees, but they were a Minnesota farm team, and I pitched a no-hitter with him in the stands, knowing that he was in the stands. And they said, Well, if you can respond to that kind of pressure, you can play in the majors, and so that was obviously another one of my big thrills.

When I played in the rookie league I played against the Wytheville Twins and Charlie Manuel was on that team, so you cross paths with all these guys that end up in the big leagues, you know. Reggie Smith was also on that team. You don't really expect to be called up. You don't say, Well, I'm having a really good year, maybe I've got a chance of going to the big leagues. I mean, that's the furthest thought from your mind. Had

I played five or six years and I'm in Triple-A and an all-star in Triple-A, then maybe I start thinking about the majors.

In 1965 you're in Columbus, Georgia, the whole year?

Right.

And the Southern League is Double-A at that time?

Right. The old Sally League, and then they changed the name to the Southern League. It was, by far, the strongest Double-A league in all of professional baseball. They could have competed with Triple-A teams. You look at those teams that played then and there was a huge percentage of ballplayers that played in the majors. You know when I first signed they said one out of every 352 guys who sign gets a chance to play in the major leagues. In that league there were a ton of players that made it.

It's the end of the season in 1965. The manager calls you into his office and you have no idea why.

Right. I just figure it's an end-of-the-year thing, that he's going to say good-bye and stuff. It was actually after a ballgame because they knew before the actual season was over. They said, When the season does end, you'll be going to New York. Roy White and Rich Beck were on my team and they went with me, so we got to travel together. It was pretty special.

You fly out of Atlanta.

I guess it must've been. I think I probably flew without an airplane, you know. I don't even remember getting on an airplane.

Did you meet the team in New York or on the road?

We met them in New York. We were actually playing Baltimore in a doubleheader on a Sunday afternoon. It was the first time I ever walked into Yankee Stadium.

You haven't been to spring training with these guys, so you really don't know anybody with the team. When you get called up, Mickey Mantle is Mickey Mantle and Elston Howard is Elston Howard. These aren't people you know.

Right. Right. I'd never met any of them in my life. The first time I go there somebody has to tell me where the locker room is, and I walk in and there's my locker right between Mel Stottlemyre and Whitey Ford. All the pitchers were on one side. Mickey Mantle had the last locker before the training room because he spent most of his time in the training room, you know.

He plays several more years but he's gimpy by the end of 1965, isn't he?

Yeah, lots of injuries. They had Ace bandages that were reinforced with foam and they used to put that on him, after they taped his ankles, from his ankles to his hip. It almost looked like a cast. He'd play with those every day, but to me it was still Mickey Mantle—All-Star, Hall of Famer, all-world. In my mind, Mickey Mantle's the greatest baseball player who ever played the game. If he'd been able to avoid injuries, he'd have every offensive record there was to have.

How are you able to sit there and pull up your stirrups without thinking, That's Mickey Mantle and that's Whitey Ford and this is Yankee Stadium? Being a major league baseball player is one thing, but being nineteen years old in the Yankee Stadium clubhouse putting on the same uniform that Mickey Mantle's putting on is a few steps past, Hey, I'm a major leaguer.

153

Yeah, well, you've got to back it up one step. Out of spring training that year I figured I'm going to go play A ball, maybe end up back in Fort Lauderdale. I don't know where I'm going to end up. I certainly had hopes that maybe, if I got lucky, I could play in Double-A. When I went to spring training, that was where I got my first taste of the major leagues. That was when I went to the Triple-A camp, and it felt like the major leagues. Then I got sent to the Double-A camp and it appeared that I had a shot at making the Double-A team. It exceeded my real expectations because when I went down there there were all these guys, twenty-five and twenty-six years old, that had played and had had really good years the year before, guys that had played in Columbus the year before.

And you figured they'd get the shot first.

Yeah. And the interesting thing was that attitude, This guy is keeping me from a spot on the team, was real prevalent there. So I was a bad guy, because if I'm going to make the team I've got to knock off somebody who was on the team last year, or someone's buddy that they felt should be on the team instead of me.

But you don't realize that, at nineteen, you've got a better shot at getting on the team than somebody who is twenty-six with the exact same skills? I mean, being younger is working as a positive.

Right, right. I didn't know that at the time, but I'm pretty quick to realize that I'm not a very popular guy. At any rate, I really felt like an outcast, like I had done something wrong. I'm a bad guy because I'm depriving somebody else of a spot on the team. And I didn't know what to think of that or make of it. Do I go tell the people that I don't really want to play here?

It finally came down to the fact that I wanted to play major league baseball, and if this is the next step—and it was a giant step—there was no question in my mind that I could, at least, compete at this level. If they believed in me, certainly I can believe in myself, but it wasn't any fun. Breaking camp as a loner and going to Columbus, Georgia, and trying to find a place to live and not having any friends and that type of thing. Fortunately, once I pitched the first ballgame and had a great game, then everybody said, This guy can help us win a championship. Certainly the position players recognized that. The position players realized that I was not going to keep them from the major leagues. Also, we didn't have any other good left-handers on the team, so I wasn't keeping anybody out of the rotation. I was a good ballplayer, so I was pretty quickly accepted and it turned out to be a great year and a fun year. I developed a lot of good friendships there, but the point here is that when I'm on my way to Yankee Stadium I'm thinking, Okay, these guys are all going to hate me because now I'm up here in the big leagues and someday I'm going to knock one of them out of a job, you know. To my surprise, just the opposite was true. The attitude was, I've been here, I've had my career and I'm willing to help any way I can to help you stay here, so it was kind of refreshing and obviously a wonderful surprise.

One thing that was a huge disappointment was I was walking down the hallway in Yankee Stadium with goose bumps, you know, but once I got inside the locker room it was just like walking into any locker room with my teammates. And I'm thinking, Here are all these guys that I grew up idolizing and I'm going to get this huge rush from meeting them, but I didn't. It was just like meeting any other ballplayer. These are my teammates and I've got to get into my uniform. We've got to get out on the field. I don't have time to just sit there and bask in all of the excitement and things.

The clubhouse guys take me around the locker room introducing me to all the ballplayers, and I'm meeting everybody and it's not a big deal. It's like, Wait a second. I'm getting cheated here. There's something not

right here. They were cordial, but, again, it was just like talking to another teammate, you know. The one introduction I looked forward to
more than any other was meeting Mickey Mantle who, in those days,
had a fairly passive personality. He would get out of his car and he'd be
mobbed all the way to his locker, first by fans and then by reporters. It
was just ridiculous, you know, so he was the only guy that I did not get an
opportunity to meet before the game. But we were playing a doubleheader and I got a chance to pitch in the second game.

So you pitch the first day you're up there? The first day you're in uniform?

Yeah. I went in in relief and pitched against Boog Powell and Paul Blair
and those guys, but I come in after the game and I'm going to the shower.
I grab a towel to go take a shower, and, again, Mickey Mantle's is the last
locker before the shower and the training room. And as I walk past his
locker, he calls out my name, you know. He said, Hey, Mike, and I turned
around and said, Yeah. He said, My name's Mickey Mantle. I just want
to apologize for not introducing myself before the game. Well, now I've
got goose bumps and I can't hide them. This is the rush that I expected
to get from everybody. I mean, I can barely talk. The only thing that
comes to my mind is Mickey who? Who is this? Am I dreaming? I really
couldn't say anything. I just stood there frozen with this huge, huge emotional rush. It was everything that I expected from meeting all the other
guys so it kind of made up for the disappointment before the game. The
embarrassing thing is that I'm in my towel and I'm literally shaking,
trembling; but that was, obviously, one of the biggest highlights of my
career, you know. So we got to be good friends and when they had Mickey
Mantle Day I said, Could you just do me a favor and put my name in
your speech somewhere? I want to be immortalized, even if it's just
through your speech.

Roger Maris was on that team. Great guy. He was probably my most
favorite player. He just went way out of his way to make me feel like I
was part of the team. Again, Mickey was fairly passive and when you go
anywhere or you're on the road he's constantly hounded by people. But
Roger Maris would take the time to call you in your room and ask you to
go out and do this and do that or whatever. He was probably, from the
human-nature, personal standpoint, my favorite ballplayer. Tony Kubek
was there, and Joe Pepitone and Bobby Richardson and Clete Boyer and
Elston Howard. This was the last year of the old dynasty. Kubek and I
flew home together because he was from Wausau, Wisconsin. He loved
me because he was the only Polack on the team so when I came along I
absorbed the brunt of all the Polish jokes.

155

We went to Cleveland to play the Indians and they had a massive stadium and I'm in the locker room getting dressed, you know, and some old, old guy comes up and starts talking to me in Polish. I said, I'm sorry. I don't understand Polish. I really don't know what you're saying. And he's still going on and on and he's got a ball in his hand. He's trying to have a conversation with me and I don't understand one word he's saying. I don't even think, Well, who let this guy in the locker room, because that thought doesn't even enter my mind, you know. So this goes on for several minutes, and when you're a rookie they're always trying to play jokes on you. My first week, when I was in Yankee Stadium, a sports-writer called and left a message and said his name was Mr Lyon and when you called back it was the phone number for the zoo and that type of thing. Well, I never fell for any of these jokes, but they always figured they were going to get me somehow. So this guy's going on and on and all of a sudden he starts bawling and he starts screaming and yelling and people come over and say, What's going on here? What did you do? And then he starts speaking English. He says, All I wanted was an autograph for my grandson and this guy wouldn't give it to me. He won't even talk to me. I'm totally flustered and wondering how I'm going to get out of this situation, and it turned out that this was a practical joke. The old man was one of the clubhouse guys or something with Cleveland, but unfortunately I did buy into that one. That was their way of welcoming you to the club. Everybody started laughing. It was like, Okay, we finally got you, Mike. You didn't fall for all the other ones, but we got you this time.

How are you out on the mound that first day against Baltimore?

I threw hard. There was a lot of energy and a lot of adrenaline screaming through my body, so I probably could have thrown the first pitch completely out of the stadium.

Are you okay after that? Are you able to block out the fact that you're pitching in Yankee Stadium?

No, because there are three decks there, you know, and I was used to playing in minor league ballparks and those were always awesome to me, so when all of a sudden I'm in Yankee Stadium it just blows me away. It's not something you can easily put out of your mind. I sat on the bench. I didn't sit in the bullpen. I just sat on the bench soaking it all in.

You didn't think there was any chance of getting in that first day?

No. This was just a way of getting a feel for what major league baseball is all about. My dream was, Let me put a uniform on and just sit on the bench. I don't care if I ever play. Just let me do that. So then they said, Do you know how to get down to the bullpen? And I said, Well, I guess I just run across the field and hop over the fence in right field, because that's where the bullpen was at the time. And they said, No, no, no. You've got to go under the stands. They said, Whitey, why don't you take him down and show him how to get there. And as we're going out to the bullpen there are guys playing golf under the stands. They have a little miniature golf course set up. It was late in the season and we're no longer in the pennant race so everybody is pretty relaxed.

So I go down and warm up, and, again, the first pitch that I threw, even warming up, I'm trying to throw it as hard as I can because I've got so much adrenaline going. At any rate, there was a lot of adrenaline flowing and everything is kind of a blur. You just get caught up in the moment, but that quickly passes and then you just say, Okay, I'm throwing the ball to Elston Howard now. So I just followed his lead. He came out and did a great job of getting me to settle down and just relax and do what I do best, you know. At that point in my career I felt like I knew how to pitch and I know what I want to throw and what I don't want to throw, but obviously, in this case, it's, Whatever you say, Ellie, I'm going to do it.

But he knows what your pitches are.

Right. He said, Just throw hard. Try to stay within yourself. So I got through that experience okay. They had Charlie Lau catching for them that day and I struck him out. Paul Blair got a base hit off of me. I also pitched against Luis Aparicio and Boog Powell.

What's the other game you pitch?

Cleveland. I pitched in Cleveland. About the most memorable thing there was when I threw a 3–2 change-up to Rocky Colavito and I threw it right down the middle of the plate. I'm sure the pitch fooled him because he never took the bat off his shoulder. At that point in my career I had a good change-up, a real good change-up. I threw it right down the middle of the plate and the umpire called ball four. My brother, who lived in Buffalo, New York, at the time, was taping the game off the radio. They didn't have videotapes but they taped it off the radio, and Joe Garagiola and Jerry Coleman were the radio guys, and they said, Okay, there's a rookie not getting the call. That pitch was right down the heart of the plate.

157

So your one walk was Rocky Colavito.

Right, right. But I threw hard. What I was really waiting for was my opportunity to get a start. That was my dream, and they kept saying, You're going to get a start. You're going to get a start. The game that I pitched in Cleveland—and this was before they had DH's, so when it came your time to bat and you're losing, you're out of the game—I was going to start that game, but they decided to start Al Downing. It was in the newspaper that I would be starting so that was pretty exciting. Al had a bad shoulder and they were trying to find out if he could pitch or not, so they said, We're either going to start Al Downing or we're going to start you. In the paper it said, Starting for the Yankees, either Al Downing, with such and such a record, or Mike Jurewicz, o-o. He ended up starting the game and pitched a few innings and his arm hurt or whatever and they put me in there. I think he pitched two innings. So I got in, and then when I went into the dugout it was my turn to bat and we were losing so they put a pinch hitter in for me so I didn't even get to have an extended time on the mound there. They said, We'll end up getting you a start somewhere. Well, then what happened was I had a problem with my back. I never liked air conditioning. I never grew up with air conditioning and I never used to sleep with it because, for some reason, my back or my kidneys or whatever are real sensitive to drafts and things, and I don't wear pajamas when I sleep, but in the hotel room you've got a roommate so the air conditioning's on. Well, I caught a draft and I got a cold in my kidneys or whatever and I couldn't throw because my back was so painful and it kind of screwed up any opportunities to do a lot of pitching. Well, then we started getting to a point where they said, We want you to get a start, but Mel Stottlemyre's going for twenty wins and obviously that's a career opportunity, and it was Whitey Ford's last year and he was going for the most wins as a Yankee pitcher. They even put Whitey in in relief a couple times hoping he'd get a win. I think Stottlemyre missed winning his twentieth game two or three times and we were in Boston for the last weekend of the year and they didn't want a left-hander pitching in Boston, but at the same time this is my only opportunity. Well, to make a long story short, the second to last day of the season Whitey Ford gets his record and the last day of the season Mel Stottlemyre gets his twenty wins and I don't ever get a start. It was disappointing, but not real disappointing. I didn't even look at it as a disappointment. I looked at it as the biggest thrill of my life. I'm nineteen years old and I'm going to be pitching in the big leagues for twenty years, so I'll just come back next year and have the opportunity then, and we'll go from there.

So what happens the next year?

Well, I actually hurt my elbow, and couldn't really quite figure out what was wrong with it. I used to play a lot of basketball in the off-season, so I can only surmise what happened. I used to get undercut playing basketball. When that happens you come down on your elbows or whatever. Well, what happened was I cracked my elbow. I didn't realize it actually, but I had a broken elbow. The end of my elbow cracked and actually separated. It formed a pincer in my elbow and it would occasionally grab the nerve. So at times I could throw and have no problem at all, but then the nerve would work its way in there and I couldn't throw the ball fifty feet. They thought I was some kind of flake because I would go down there to throw and I would be throwing ninety-eight miles an hour, then I'd go out the next inning and I couldn't reach home plate. I'd say, There's something wrong with my elbow, and they'd think I was just some flaky left-hander, you know, that's looking for attention or something. Well, they took X rays and found out that my elbow had actually healed cracked. Then they performed the surgery and they had two choices—one is to rescrape the surfaces of the bone, put a little pin in there and just mend it back together; or the other option, which was to just break this piece off and reattach the tendons to what was left of my elbow. Well, they decided to do that. The surgery was a success but my doctor at home said, You ought to just lay off for a year. Don't even pick up a baseball. Let that thing really mend its way back on. But the Yankees' doctor said, You shouldn't need to do that. Lay off four months and you should be fine. They performed the surgery in September.

It's hurting to throw. How much do you pitch that year?

Once they finally understood what the problem was they just said, Throw when you can throw. So I'd go out some days and pitch an entire game and I'd go out other games and barely last an inning.

So your innings pitched are down, but you're with the team the entire year?

Just about. They actually sent me home and said, We're going to operate on you and we'll let you know when. Then they called me up and said, You know, the doctor said you can actually keep throwing. So rather than give up the season—you're not damaging it any more to throw— just go ahead and keep throwing and we'll operate when the season's over. So I went back and played the year out and threw when I could.

Are you back in Columbus in 1966?

No, I actually went to Toledo, Ohio, to play for the Mud Hens. They were the Triple-A team for the Yankees then.

So the surgery's in 1966.

I worked hard through the off-season so when I went back to spring training, I was fine. I felt okay and I was able to throw without pain, but I took it very slowly, maybe up to three-quarters speed. As soon as I got up to full speed and turned the ball loose, the tendon started to tear away from the bone. I think it might even have been the first game of the year. I was up there throwing—in fact, I think it was on Easter Sunday—and I threw a pitch, and when I let go of the ball I just heard a snap and felt a tremendous pain in my arm.

Do you remember what kind of pitch?

I think it was a fastball. I just came over the top and released the pitch. All I remember is when I threw it, I felt like I was throwing it over the top of a fence and my arm just came down on the fence. The pain just shot straight up. That, in effect, ended my career, because again the doctor said, Well, that's really unusual. That shouldn't have happened. They didn't feel like they needed to do surgery again. They said it just kind of tore a little bit, and, again, just let time heal it. Well, then I went through that whole nightmare of trying to rehabilitate, and then they wanted me to go to winter ball because I obviously lost an entire season. I said, I don't want to go to winter ball. My doctor's advising me against it and I'd rather just stay home and condition the rest of my body and come down to spring training and be strong and ready to go. In the meantime, I had gotten married and we had a baby on our very first anniversary, right to the day. I got married on December twenty-seventh, baby on December twenty-seventh. We go to spring training with a young baby and, all of a sudden, it was almost like I was blackballed or something. I'm a bad guy because I didn't cooperate and I didn't do what they wanted me to do. I'm doing things my way. You're just a ballplayer and we're the Yankees. We're telling you what you should do and you're not doing it, you know. So it was a real sense of not belonging. In the meantime they have the draft and they have more players available, good prospects, and their minor league system is producing some pretty good ballplayers. When I got hurt, that was Fritz Peterson's opportunity to pass me by as the next left-hander on the totem pole.

I didn't expect to go to the big league camp and I spent spring training at the Triple-A level. My arm was strong and I didn't give up an earned run that whole spring. I think I pitched about thirty innings. I had a great spring. I was throwing hard, as well as ever. A good long winter's rest is exactly what I needed, and I was pretty fired up. Then on the last day of spring training they decide to send me to Double-A, and I went in to talk to the head of the minor leagues—they had a farm director who was the head of all the minor leagues—and I said, This is crazy, you know. I can pitch at the Triple-A level. I know how professional baseball works now, and if you don't want me on your Triple-A team, option me out to another organization. One of the years that I was rehabilitating I actually got optioned out to the White Sox. I was loaned to the White Sox, you know, because they needed pitching, they knew me, and I was available. So I said, I want to play Triple-A somewhere. If I go to Double-A and do well, it's going to be expected because I've already proven myself at the Double-A level. If I do well, my next promotion would be to Triple-A, not to the big leagues. If I do poorly—and that could be the subjective opinion of my coach or manager—then my career is over. At any rate, I said, How about just finding me a place in Triple-A somewhere? And he said, We're sorry, but we've got to give guys opportunities that had good years last year. You, basically, had a nonyear. All the other major league clubs are in the same position we're in. It's the last day of spring training. I couldn't really argue with his logic because I could see that it would get me nowhere. Instead, I asked for my release and they gave it to me.

It's almost impossible to find a spot on the last day of spring training.

That's true. That's all too true. But I also knew that I was somebody who threw in the high nineties and I was left-handed, a rare commodity in baseball. When I went to the White Sox and pitched for them, they said, You know, all we ever thought about you was how hard you threw. We never realized what a great curveball you have. I always thought my curveball was my best pitch and throwing hard was just something I was blessed with. A curveball is something you've got to develop. So I just couldn't get the thought out of my mind that if I still had the same potential I always had and I'm only twenty-three years old, why would they let me go? Or even say, Just go to Double-A. Try to convince me to do that. Instead they just said, Here. Here's your release. If you think you can go hook on with somebody else somewhere, why don't you go do that? And my first thought was to get in touch with the Braves because they were up in West Palm Beach and I had pitched against them several times in the spring, so they knew, in my mind, that I was the real deal. That's an old term we all used. Then I sat down and thought about it. I had said I would get into this thing young and if things didn't work out I was going to get out of it young. Now I'm married and I've got a little girl with another one on the way and there's no guarantee I won't go out and hurt my arm again. I was pretty discouraged by the whole ordeal, so I went home without making any effort to do anything.

You're out of baseball at age twenty-three, and you're a left-handed pitcher who can still throw over ninety miles an hour?

Yeah. Well, I went home and a friend of mine convinced me to play amateur ball, which I did. I dominated there. I was pitching no-hitters and having a good time. I actually had an opportunity to sign after that but my wife really didn't support that move at all, and, again, with no guarantees and no promises and now she's pregnant with another baby on the way, I said, This is the right thing to do. Coming from a family of ten, I've always been family oriented and I love kids and I felt like I could survive in life without baseball. It wasn't big dollars yet, even then, so, you know, I just said I'm going to stay out.

You don't exactly survive without baseball. You don't take the risk of running back into professional ball, but you're still playing in the amateur league.

Well, if I would've had a little stronger support from my wife at the time. We're not married anymore, but I think if I would've had a little more encouragement there... I've always been one to never look back, but it's pretty hard not to look back when you see left-handers at such a premium, when you see guys with records of 10-19 that are signing $8 million contracts.

Left-handers who can throw more than ninety miles an hour often have blank checks put in front of them.

And I've had lots of people tell me that I'm crazy. Friends of mine that were umpires in the major leagues that even after retiring would scout or do some amateur umpiring would say, You can pitch in the major leagues today, you know. So that was tough. That was really tough.

You were trying to do the right thing.

I really believe that my commitment was to my family, and, again, having a wife that didn't encourage me to pursue my dreams and, also again, looking at it realistically from the standpoint of I could go back there and go through this whole cycle all over again, you know. I could hurt my arm again. There are any number of things that could happen. If I wanted to look back, I would say I was an idiot for not pursuing it, because I could've had a career in baseball. When I broke in, you know, I was considered the ace of the staff. I averaged more than a strikeout an inning. I used to get into pitching duels with the Nolan Ryans, Tom Seavers, and Jim Palmers of the world. We broke in at about the same time and had the same potential, and these are guys in the Hall of Fame. My ability was equal to theirs, so you can only think about what might've been. I don't look back to a point where I wake up every night in the middle of the night saying, What did I do? Or wake up every morning thinking about, What if I'd only gone back and played baseball? But if I have a conversation with you or someone like you who wants to rehash my career and what might have been, it's hard not to think about it.

When did you know that your last major league game was your last major league game? Had you been at home for a couple of years before you realized it was over?

I knew it when we moved up to Minnesota in 1976. We moved here on my daughter's birthday, July eighteenth, and the state tournament in Wisconsin started in the middle of July, so on the way up here I stopped in Madison and pitched a ballgame at the state tournament, and I pitched a no-hitter in that game.

This is amateur ball.

It was a high level of amateur ball. It was the best Wisconsin had to offer and we played the best teams from a four-state area. We also played in national tournaments and traveled to Nicaragua one year. I was playing for a team in Waukesha, Wisconsin. I actually lived in Waukesha at the time and a good friend of mine was the sponsor and the manager of the team, and he was the one that convinced me to go back and play. When I got to Minnesota, I did some pitching here. With the Twins here in town I got an opportunity to go to the Dome and work out with some of their coaches and scouts, and I actually had a chance to sign with the Twins.

But you're thirty-one years old.

Right. That was the thing. But they believed that, even at that age, I could still pitch another five or six years. I always kept myself in fairly good shape, and they felt that I could still have a career. Unfortunately, the ultimate decisions in the negotiations were made by Calvin Griffith. I wasn't looking for a lot of money or anything else that would require a significant financial investment on their part. I was looking for an opportunity to go down and train in the major league spring training camp because I believed that, as old as I was, I needed to make a quick jump if I was going to make it to the major leagues. The only way I could do that was to have the major league staff see me throw. Send me down immediately after that, but give me an opportunity to pitch for these guys. Then I'll go down to the minor league camp and pay my dues. And they really didn't want to give me that opportunity. I also had a good job at the time. Again, it's a risk. Now I'm older so it's even more of a risk, and who's going to take me seriously, so I passed on it. If they would've given me the opportunity to go to the major league camp, I would have done it, but without that opportunity I decided that it was just not worth it.

Does it hurt any to hear Jim Morris's story, him going back at thirty-six or thirty-seven after being out for ten years?

That didn't hurt at all. I'm super happy for the guy that he had his cup of coffee. In some respects I look at it as, well, this guy went back to live out his dream and he hurt his arm and he never really had much of a career, you know. I'm thinking that very same thing could have happened to me, so in some respects I look at it and see that there are no guarantees. Anything can happen, good or bad. It hurts only because I didn't take advantage of an opportunity that was there in front of me.

I've always been a huge believer in fate. When things cross my path and people say, Why are you doing that, it's because God put me in this moment for a reason. Again, it was one of those issues where now my kids are in school and I have to leave my family. I can't take them to spring training. They're established here. That made it the toughest thing, and that was the ultimate reason why I didn't go, because I was going to have to go without my family. That weighed pretty heavily into the thing. I was looking for a sign, and the sign, to me, was, We're not going to let you go to the big league camp. Give me a sign and that, to me, was the sign. It's a risk and a gamble. You're pursuing your dream, but you're doing it on your own and you've got a family that you're responsible for. My whole life before that, all I wanted was an opportunity to pitch. I did have dreams or fantasies of, Just let me pitch one game in the major leagues. That's all I care about. Let me get the start that I always dreamed about. Give me the game. Let me start. Let me finish. Don't pull me out after an inning, you know, and say, We need to pinch-hit for you, or any of that kind of stuff. Just let me do it. Give me that one opportunity. I don't care if I never play another game in the big leagues.

So there was a period in my life when I had that dream, and in terms of looking back, I didn't look back and say, Give me a career. I said, Give me one game, just to prove it to myself. I always believed that I could be, you know, a major league pitcher. Not only a major league pitcher but one of high ability, but I can only believe that. I know that I can't prove it to anybody unless somebody puts me on the mound and lets me do it. There was a period in my life where I said, Just give me that opportunity, so once I passed on the Twins opportunity I realized I was never going to pitch in the major leagues again. And yet I watch guys now when I go to ballgames and I'm thinking, Okay, even today, as an old guy, I've got a better curveball than that guy. I can throw as hard as that guy. I'm thinking, I could go out there. Maybe my arm's not strong enough to last for an entire season, but I still believe I could go out there and pitch at the major league level. I'm smart enough and good enough, but realistically people would think you're totally whacked out of your mind, you know. Maybe they'd give Satchel Paige an opportunity, or Minnie Minoso an opportunity. But I still play amateur ball, and I still play that at a high level. And people's jaws drop now and they say, Man, you're an old guy that still throws awfully hard. You've got an incredible curveball.

Bouton was with the Yankees when you were there. Did you read Ball Four?

No, but I read several reviews on it and talked to some other ballplayers about it. I just thought it was sacrilegious for him to write the book. You know, there is a fraternity among ballplayers and I think there are things that are sacred to the baseball community that need to be left alone. You know, you're privileged to be exposed to some of these things, and to exploit it by bringing it out, to me it's shameful and it's an affront to your friends and your teammates. He made a bad name for himself. He black-balled himself in the baseball community.

What about something like Bull Durham, *where the stories are similar but the characters are fictional? Is that okay?*

I loved *Bull Durham*. I liked *Bull Durham* because it was real. You know, you see *The Natural* and all these other baseball movies and say, Okay, this is fantasy. *Bull Durham*, when you saw that, it was real. They filmed it in real minor league parks. I was thinking, Oh, my God, I was there. This is how it really was. So I did like that movie because it was so realistic, but at the same time it was all fictional, so they weren't identifying anybody. Nobody said, Well, that pitcher was really this major leaguer or that catcher was this major leaguer. It was fictional people that played minor league baseball. But terms like "The Show." I'm going to The Show. Those were real terms. It was the real deal. I enjoyed *The Natural* and I enjoyed *Major League*. I enjoy those movies from an entertainment standpoint, but as far as, This is the way it really was, *Bull Durham* was the real deal, for sure.

Did you keep anything from your career? A game ball or a hat or a pair of shoes?

That is one of my biggest regrets that I do look back on, because when you leave at the end of the year guys will grab their uniform or shirt or pants or whatever. I'm leaving as a nineteen-year-old thinking, I'm going to be back here next year, or certainly at some point in my career, so I don't need to grab much. All I took was a baseball hat. And I still have the hat, but that's about the only thing I really took. Oddly enough, I still have my Little League uniform that says YANKEES across the front. I do have baseballs that are autographed. Joe DiMaggio would come to spring training to help out the outfielders and things, so I have a ball signed by him.

I have a few balls that I've handed out to friends and relatives with all of the Yankees on it. The big thing with autographs is, are they authentic? Clubhouse boys would sometimes sign balls for the ballplayers and I'm telling you, their autographs were better than the real guys'. They used to sign Whitey Ford's name and they used to sign Mickey Mantle's and Roger Maris's name, but most of the other guys signed their own balls. We had a contract and an obligation. We got paid for coming into the locker room every day and signing several dozen baseballs. But I personally went around and hand delivered the balls to Mickey, Whitey, Roger, and all the other guys because I wanted them all to be real, so I have a few of those. It's good to be able to look at a ball with my name on it, and to show it to some of the nonbelievers that you meet later in life.

Chicago at New York (AL)
Tuesday, September 10, 1968

SECOND GAME

Chicago	ab	r	h	rbi	New York	ab	r	h	rbi
Bradford, rf	4	0	1	0	Clarke, 2b	5	2	3	0
McCraw, 1b	4	0	0	0	Tresh, ss	3	2	1	0
Aparicio, ss	3	0	0	0	Robinson, cf-lf	2	1	0	0
Alomar, 2b	1	0	0	0	White, lf	1	0	0	1
Ward, 3b	3	0	1	0	Pepit'e, ph-cf	2	0	0	0
May, lf	4	0	1	0	Kosco, 1b	4	0	2	3
Josephson, c	4	0	0	0	Colavito, rf	4	0	0	0
Berry, cf	4	0	1	0	Smith, 3b	3	0	0	0
Mor'les, 2b-ss	2	0	1	0	Gibbs, c	4	0	1	0
Peters, p	0	0	0	0	Verbanic, p	3	0	0	0
Wynne, p	0	0	0	0					
Hopkins, ph	1	0	0	0	Totals	31	5	7	4
Rath, p	0	0	0	0					
Williams, ph	1	0	0	0					
Priddy, p	0	0	0	0					
Melton, ph	1	0	0	0					
Ribant, p	0	0	0	0					
Totals	32	0	5	0					

Chicago	0	0	0	0	0	0	0	0	0—0
New York	3	2	0	0	0	0	0	0	x—4

Chicago	IP.	H.	R.	ER.	BB.	SO.
Peters (L. 4-12)	0	3	3	3	2	0
Wynne	2	2	2	1	2	1
Rath	2	1	0	0	1	0
Priddy	2	0	0	0	1	1
Ribant	2	1	0	0	0	3
New York	IP.	H.	R.	ER.	BB.	SO.
Verbanic (W. 6-5)	9	5	0	0	2	3

E—Aparicio (16), May (1). 2B—Tresh (18, off Peters), Kosco (14, off Peters). SH—Verbanic (3, off Rath). IBB—Tresh (6, off Rath). SB—Clarke (17, 2B off Wynne/Josephson). U—Hank Soar, Nestor Chylak, Bill Kinnamon, Russ Goetz. T—2:29. A—10,198.

FRED RATH

Fred Rath pitched eleven and one-third innings in 1968 and eleven and two-thirds innings in 1969 for the Chicago White Sox. In those twenty-three major league innings he yielded nineteen hits and eleven walks while striking out seven. He finished with a record of 0–2 and an ERA of 4.70. He was interviewed February 4, 2002 at his office in Tampa, Florida

Tell me where you grew up and when you first started playing baseball.

Well, I was born and raised in Little Rock, Arkansas. I started playing baseball when I was about ten years old, I guess. I played Little League, Pony League, American Legion. I went to Baylor University, graduated from Baylor University, but I went there on a track scholarship. I didn't go there on a baseball scholarship. I played baseball my final year at Baylor, and that was in 1965, which was the first year of the draft. I was drafted by the Chicago White Sox after that year.

Now, when you say that you played your final year at Baylor, that makes it sound like you didn't play your freshman, sophomore, and junior years.

I didn't. I went there on a track scholarship.

Which is also a spring sport.

Which is a spring sport, so you couldn't play both. I had aspirations of trying to go to the Olympics, because when I was in high school I had the second highest high jump in the nation. At that time it was six feet, seven inches, which today wouldn't get you anything. But I really wanted to try and go to the Olympics, and the Olympics were in 1964. I hurt my leg my sophomore year so six ten was the highest that I was ever able to jump. I couldn't get into that seven-foot range, which is what you have to do.

When I wasn't able to go to the Olympics in 1964 I went to the track coach and said, I'd really like to play baseball my final year, and he gave me the permission but said that he did want me to compete in the Southwest Conference meet at the end of year, which I did, but I played baseball that whole time.

Arkansas did not have high school baseball at that time, so you played during the summer. I played with a group of college kids that were from Little Rock but playing at different colleges across the country. They had come home for the summer, and we formed a team and just traveled all over Arkansas playing ball.

So there was no conflict between baseball and track in high school because track was in the spring and baseball was in the summer.

Yeah, and in high school, track was a fairly big sport because it was the only spring sport. They didn't have baseball. That's how I got into that. So I played my last year at Baylor and I was on the all-Southwest Conference team and was really the first pitcher in Baylor's history to beat Texas and Texas A & M twice in the same year. And they were both powerhouse teams at the time. So I got drafted in the equivalent of what would be the third round today. They did it a little bit different then. I got my $8,000 bonus and took off to the pros.

You get drafted around the first week in June. Have you graduated? Do you have the degree in hand?

Yes, I've got a degree in hand in management. A bachelor's degree in business administration, major in management.

So you don't really have much negotiating room when the White Sox come to you with an offer.

No, you're absolutely right. It seemed to me that the number-one draft pick for the White Sox that year received thirty or forty thousand dollars.

Was $8,000 their first offer?

Pretty much, and it was pretty much take it or leave it. Like you say, there wasn't any negotiating room.

If I can back up to high school, I can't imagine that you would be better at another sport than you were at track, because six seven as a high school senior in 1961 is very impressive. Did you play football or basketball? Did you get attention from colleges in any sport besides track, or did you just say, I'm high jumping six seven and this is what I'm doing?

Well, you've got to back up before that to when I was in junior high. Junior high was the seventh, eighth, and ninth grade in Little Rock. Again, this goes back in history but Little Rock in 1957 and 1958 went through its integration problems. Arkansas was the first state chosen to integrate its schools because it was considered not to be a real southern and not to be a real northern state. My dad happened to be on the school board at the time so we were heavy in the midst of all this. And when I was in the ninth grade is when they started the integration of the high school, and there was a big debate—do you start in the first grade and go up or do you start at the high school and work your way down? And it was felt by the school board that it was better to start at the higher grades than the lower, thinking that the parents wouldn't be as involved and it would be easier for everybody to accept. So my ninth-grade year was the start of the integration, and I ran for president of my junior high school, and, because my dad was on the school board, the guy running against me said that if I was elected president then the school would be integrated. So he won.

When I was in junior high I was playing football, I was playing basketball, and I fooled around with track. My tenth-grade year, all the schools in Little Rock were shut down. The governor came in and just decided, We're not going to have school this year. I'm going to close it down. At that time, because I didn't have a tenth-grade year, I took correspondence courses. We would meet at a church—a whole group of us—and we'd work on our correspondence, just like we were going to school but we didn't have a teacher. And because kids didn't have any-place to go, we started a track team there. We didn't have anything else, just a track team, and I ran track. When I went into my eleventh-grade year, I said, To heck with it, I'm not going to play football and I'm not going to play basketball. I'm going to concentrate on track and baseball. Those are the two things I want to do. It aggravated a lot of the coaches because they wanted me to play but I said no. So that's how I got into the track and into the baseball.

When I was in the ninth grade my brother and sister were going to the high school, and when we would take them by the school with my dad, you know, you had tanks on every corner. You had the 101st Air-borne Division lined up shoulder to shoulder around this massive, four-block-by-four-block facility. Shoulder to shoulder with bayonets every single day with crowds of twenty and thirty thousand people out there. It was quite something.

Did your parents ever think about moving?

No, no. We didn't move. It was an order by the Supreme Court that you integrate, so it had to happen. But there for a while, our whole family, along with some others on the school board, were kind of in no man's land because the blacks didn't like us and the whites didn't like us. I got chased home from school many times, and even when I was playing football in ninth grade we had to have practice over with by four-thirty every afternoon so the parents could pick you up or you could get home before it got dark. So it was a very interesting time but it all blew by. When I got into the eleventh grade it was pretty much done and every-thing was back to normal, because the kids started realizing, I don't have a school. I'm not getting an education here. And it was really the stu-dents, people like myself and my age, that were forcing the parents to back off. We need school. We've got to have a place to go to school.

When you start playing baseball, are you immediately a pitcher?

Actually, when I started playing I was a catcher. They had a rule back then that you could pitch whoever you wanted to pitch up to a certain point of time, but then after that day the first three or four guys that pitched were your pitchers from then on. And I happened to go on a vacation so I couldn't pitch because they used other people. So I caught. Pony League was really the first year that I started pitching, but I also caught. I kept catching. As a matter of fact, I caught all the way up through American Legion ball, as well as pitched, because I loved catching. I thought it was great. Then when I went into college, that was when I really went to pitching exclusively.

I understand accepting the track scholarship, but did you generate any interest from college coaches while you were playing American Legion ball?

No, because, again, the high school didn't have a program and nobody kept up with you, really, during the summer. I had offers from both the Braves and the Yankees to sign out of high school, but I wasn't sure baseball was what I wanted to do and I knew I wanted an education. Because I ran track in high school, and also ran the hurdles and did some other things, that's where all my scholarship offers came from. It was through track, not from baseball. Not many people knew me from baseball circles because there wasn't a program. So to go to college I needed to do it on the track scholarship.

When you pitch at Baylor your senior year, what kind of pitches are you throwing?

Mostly a fastball and a curve. I threw fairly hard but I was wild. It would be nothing for me to go out and walk seven or eight guys in a game. I'd work my way out of it, but it was mostly those two pitches.

173

But your senior year in college you're more of a thrower than a pitcher.

That's right.

Do you have movement on your fastball?

It was natural. I had more of a little natural sinkerball, just because of the location of where the arm was in the release, and had a fairly good curveball at that point in time.

Are you still in Waco at the time of the draft or are you in Arkansas?

No, I'm back in Arkansas.

Do the White Sox call to tell you you've been drafted? Does the scout come by the house with an offer? What's the procedure? Being the first year of the draft, this is a new process for them as well.

It is. There was a scout by the name of Paul Austin who was from El Dorado, Arkansas, and he had been scouting me. I had known Paul for a while, just through the summer leagues and stuff, and we talked quite a bit and he called me on the phone. Actually I was gone that day and he called my home and my mother called me and told me I'd been drafted by the White Sox. Then he and I got together right after that in a hotel room where he was staying in Little Rock, and a couple of days later I signed.

Did you go by yourself? Did your dad go with you?

No, I'm by myself at that point. It was just so much different back then. It was not as formal as it is today. There were no agents. Agents weren't even heard of. Even talking to the parents just wasn't kosher back then.

So he offers you eight thousand with a take-it-or-leave-it tone?

Well, he offered a little less and then got it to eight and he made a call to the White Sox and came back in and said, Well, the White Sox said take it or leave it. What else are you going to do? Go get your lunch bucket? I said, Okay. So I signed and then went down to Sarasota, which is where their training facilities were.

Did you fly or drive?

I drove down and stayed for July and August. They would bring all of their newly signed people in, and we played down there in a league. They didn't have the different types of leagues, short-season leagues, that they have now. Everybody kind of played down in their spring training facilities and occasionally you'd get a guy that maybe moved up to A ball if somebody got hurt or something.

For a while your dream is to make the Olympic team as a high jumper. Has becoming a professional baseball player replaced that dream or is this just something to do before you start your management career? How bad do you want this?

Well, that's an interesting question, because at the time I graduated from Baylor I had the military facing me. Back then you still had the draft and you had Vietnam going on and all that. And I'm kind of saying, Okay, what am I going to do? Should I go into the military right away and spend my two years? Well, I'm not real crazy about doing that, and then, by that time, the draft comes up and I said, Okay, I'll give this a whirl and see what happens. I didn't know how good I was. Maybe I could do something. Maybe not. It really was not to take a job because I was going to get drafted. There wasn't any question. As a matter of fact, when I was playing in the short season I got my draft notice. It was sent to Little Rock and I was able to say, Guys, I'm not in Little Rock anymore. Now I'm down in Sarasota. Back then the way it worked is they would redo it and send it again. Well, by the time it got down there I was back in Little Rock, so I said, Guys, I'm not in Sarasota anymore. Now I'm in Little Rock.

It finally caught up with me in Little Rock and I went in and, at that time, everything in the reserves was closed down except the Marine Corps. They still had some openings in the Marine Corps, so I enlisted in the Marine Reserve. They have six months when you initially go in and I got out of that around the middle of March the next year. Spring training had already been going on for a couple of weeks, and I went down and thought, Boy, I'm really going to be behind everybody, being in shape and all that, but as it turned out, because of everything I did in the Marine Corps, I was far ahead of everybody else in spring training.

Considering it's a six-month commitment, the timing almost couldn't be better. You get to do the short season, then the six months, and still be back for part of spring training.

Right. And so I went to spring training and they said, Okay, you're going to go to Appleton, Wisconsin, and I said, Where's that? I'd barely heard of Wisconsin, much less Appleton. So I went up there. What I liked about the reserve was they had what they called the thirty-day program. You could either go once a month on the weekends and then two weeks in the summer, or you could do thirty days. I said, This'll be great, because I could go in October, November, January. So my first two years in, that's what I did. I went in January. But then they cut it out, and that's really what started hurting me, because I'd be right in the middle of the season and have to leave for three weeks. You know, you don't think that's much, but when you're in a routine and you're going good, and then you're out for two weeks and you can't pick a ball up with everything you're doing there, and then you come back, it takes you a while before you can get going.

What year do you go to Appleton?

1966.

Is this single A?

Yes.

Are you with them the whole year?

Yeah, I'm there the whole year. That's really what turned my whole thinking on baseball around because I went 17–3, and had a 1.9 ERA.

And they don't send you to a higher league?

Oh, no. That didn't happen back in those days. You had to go through the system. You had to go A ball, Double-A, Triple-A. Nobody, back then, went from A ball to the majors. That didn't happen.

I didn't necessarily mean pulling you up to the majors, but if you're 17–3 and your ERA's below two, it seems like they would at least bring you up to Double-A to see how you would do.

Remember that the White Sox back in those days were called a good-pitching, no-hit team. They would win 1–0, 2–1. Their team ERA was well under three. But back then you didn't see anywhere near the movement you see today. You were there and that's just kind of where you were. But that season really kind of turned me around as far as, this is what I want to do and I love this game.

Is it the experience of that first year or is it the learning that you're good?

Well, it was more going against the guys, seeing that, hey, I can do this and I'm good at this. I don't know if they still do it today or not, but back then the White Sox played the Cubs every summer for one game, and I got called up to pitch in that game. It was an exhibition game so it wasn't being called to the majors, but both the Cubs and White Sox called up some of their players so now I've gotten the eye of the club. I pitched two innings up there and did real well against the major league players, so now I'm even a little more excited about it all. We finished the season up and we were fortunate that our team won the league, won the championship. And then at the end of the year the White Sox called me up. They didn't put me on the major league roster but they called me up to work with their pitching coach and I stayed with them for about three days, working out with them, pitching batting practice.

From there I went down to winter ball in Sarasota. At that time winter ball was a little different than it is now because that winter ball was considered to be for the more elite of the organization. If you got invited to winter ball, then you were well thought of within the organization. It was kind of a high Double-A or a low Triple-A league back then.

This is more the equivalent of instructional league rather than the winter ball played in the Dominican.

Well, it was equivalent to what was going on over in the Dominican, because it was a very high caliber. Very seldom did you ever see an A-ball player going down there.

But when you're in Sarasota following the season, are the major league coaches merely watching you or are they actually trying to provide some instruction?

The major league pitching coach, a guy named Ray Berres, was one of the instructors down there. He was working with us directly. Now, the major league manager, he was just down there for a short time kind of looking at what was going on.

Are you still a two-pitch pitcher?

Well, that's what they were working on, to change me, to get me to throw more pitches, and we developed what they called a runner. It's a fastball. It's not quite like a slider but it jumped out real quick, and I did a little more work on the curveball to make it a little quicker, sharper type break instead of the lazy break. And I made some changes in my motion, and the next year when I went to Double-A, I did not have a real good year because I was trying to get the changes made that they wanted. Then I went down to winter ball again and we worked on it some more, and then the next year I went back to Double-A and lost my first game before I won ten in a row.

What was Ray Berres's background?

Ray Berres was a catcher, but he had been pitching coach for them for years and years and years. Really, I thought the world of Ray, and I learned more about pitching from him than anybody. He really helped me. At the same time that all this was going on, you've got to understand that the White Sox were a team in turmoil. Al Lopez was the manager, but then when I started Eddie Stanky became the manager. Stanky was the manager at the start of the season, then Al Lopez came back in for a short period of time. I felt that if Al Lopez had come back and coached I probably would've had a longer time in the major leagues, because he

177

liked me. He liked what I did. But then you've got Les Moss coming in and then the next year you had Don Gutteridge come in, and at the same time you had a bunch of changes going on in the front office. I think one year we lost over a hundred games.

Four managers in two years is almost schizophrenic.

Well, you had a general manager at that time, Ed Short, who was not very well thought of. There was just a lot of turmoil.

In 1967 when you're working on those pitches, trying to get a better snap on the curveball, and you don't have a strong season, do you feel like the organization is patient with you?

Oh, no question. Right after the year in Appleton, they put me on the major league roster. They came to me, Ray Berres and some of the others, and said, Fred, we think you've got real potential but we need you to work on these things because if you're going to be a success, this is what it's going to take. So don't pay a lot of attention to what your record's going to be this year. It's more important that you learn how to do this. And it took me that year and then going down to winter ball and working with Ray some more. Then everything really started clicking.

You're on the roster in both 1967 and 1968, but they're doing this to protect you. Is there a glimmer of hope somewhere in your mind that you might actually leave spring training with the club, or are you completely aware that you're on the major league roster to ensure the White Sox hold on to you?

Well, in the first few years, that's what it was, them protecting me, because it was kind of a well-known fact within the White Sox organization that you have to prove yourself.

In 1968 I was doing real well. Like I said, I lost my first one and then I won ten straight. My ERA was down to about two point three, two point four, but then I had to go into the two weeks' military training, and when I came back I kind of struggled, trying to get my rhythm back, and that's when they called me up in 1968.

So your record's 10–2 on September first

Well, probably by that time I'm about 10–3. And they called me up, which was a surprise because, again, they didn't call too many people from Double-A up there. It was mostly from Triple-A.

Does the manager call you into his office?

No, I got a call from the general manager in my hotel room and he said, We're calling you up. Ed Short called me, said they were calling me up and I was to join the team in Washington, D.C.

How excited are you?

Oh, I'm extremely excited. They called me the day of our last game, so as soon as that game was over I was to catch a plane and go out there.

But you weren't in Evansville, because you said he called you in your hotel room.

We were on the road.

So you don't even get to go back to Evansville to get your belongings.

No, my wife had already packed up everything when we went on the road, and she went back up to her home. I met her when I was playing in Appleton, so she went up there and I was going to join her and then drive back down to Sarasota for winter ball. Then they called me up and I couldn't even get ahold of her for a day because she was on the road. I finally got hold of her and then she came down to Chicago and we lived in a hotel suite for those thirty days. When we'd go on the road she'd go back to Appleton.

So you go to D.C. Is anyone else from Evansville on that plane?

No, I'm the only one. There were a couple of other players called up but they were from the Triple-A team. I got in late that night, went to the hotel, got on a bus with some of them going to the park, and it was me sitting there with my mouth shut and just kind of observing. I think we only had one game with Washington before we flew up to New York to play the Yankees. And that's where I had my first appearance, at Yankee Stadium.

Making your major league debut in Yankee Stadium has got to be special.

Well, it was extremely special for me because it goes all the way back to my high school days. The summer before my senior year, Bill Dickey, the Yankee catcher and Hall of Famer and just a very nice guy, called me

179

when he was there and asked me if I would like to go throw batting practice to the Yankees. This was in 1960 and I was going up to New York for a Key Club convention. And I said, Well, sure, and he said, Okay, I'll call you back. I'll get it all arranged and you'll meet Casey and the guys. And so he did. He called me back and had everything arranged, but he said, Fred, the only problem is you can't throw batting practice because it will make you a pro, and you don't want to ruin your last year in high school. But go up there. You'll go down in the dressing room, you'll meet all the guys, you can sit out there during batting practice and talk to them and you can watch the game. And I said, Okay.

He told me where to go and I did just as he said. The guy there was expecting me and took me right down to Casey Stengel's office, and I was just kind of in awe the whole time. You have to realize that it's 1960 and I'm from Arkansas, never traveled much, never gone out much, and now I'm sitting in Casey Stengel's office in Yankee Stadium. I thought, Here are these athletes who are the epitome of what you want to be, and they're playing in Yankee Stadium. Everything's going to be plush. You had this certain image of purity, of what athletes were.

So I go up there and they take me into Casey Stengel's office and this is the smallest thing I've ever been in. It's made out of wood and it's got chicken wire around the top of it, and he's got his desk and I'm looking around going, What is this? And we sat there and we talked for about thirty minutes, just about nothing and anything. He asked me what I was doing, and he said, Come on, let me introduce you to the guys, so we go into the dressing room and it wasn't big either and here they all are. Now, this is before the game. Here they all are in their shorts, and they had their socks on, and they're all smoking and they're all drinking and they're gambling and I'm walking in. Now, I didn't drink at that time, I didn't smoke. I was one of these pure athletes thinking they're the same thing and I thought, What in the world is going on here? And here's Mickey Mantle and Yogi Berra and Elston Howard and Ryne Duren and Tony Kubek. I'm just in a daze. It was a real thrill for me. Then they took me out and I sat in the dugout while they took batting practice. So now to make my first appearance in Yankee Stadium was quite a thrill for me.

How did you know Bill Dickey?

Well, Bill Dickey knew my dad. Bill Dickey was from Little Rock, and he had kept up with me, unbeknownst to me, and had some conversations with my dad. He knew that I had some potential so he just called. At that point it was open. Everybody was a free agent, so you could really sign with anybody you wanted to.

So Dickey's doing this scouting on his own.

Yeah.

Are you a Yankee fan before you walk into Yankee Stadium in 1960?

Well, I was really more of a fan of the St Louis Cardinals because it was closer to home. My dad took us up there for a trip one time and that was pretty special. But who didn't know the Yankees? Who didn't know how good they were? And if you had said, Fred, where would you want to go, the Cardinals or the Yankees, I would've said, Of course, the Yankees. To see that stadium and that history and all that stuff.

Are you a Yankees fan when you leave that day?

More of one, but, you know, I don't get carried away. I never have been one to really be a booster of anyone. I'm not a big booster of Baylor. I'm not a big booster of the White Sox. I enjoy the game and how it's played.

You've been to spring training twice with the White Sox so you know some of the guys on the team. Do you still walk into this as a red-faced rookie, or are there people who remember you from spring training?

I knew all the players that were there and they knew who I was and they kind of knew what I had done for the year so it wasn't totally foreign to me, but at the same time I was up there to pitch this time. I mean, spring training is spring training. There's a little more looseness, but now you're in the season. Now it begins to mean something.

This can't be a very happy bunch of major league players. They lose nearly a hundred games that year, they've had three different managers, and when you're losing it's often not very fun.

You're absolutely right. Al Lopez was the manager and had brought back some kind of sense to the whole thing, because it wasn't a lot of fun. You could see the tension on everybody. They were doing bad. There were a lot of guys that had been there the year before, or two years before, when they were making a run for it. The problem was the White Sox traded away a lot of their younger players to make that one run to try to win it. I remember Ken Boyer came over with us. He was on the real downside. Rocky Colavito. And during spring training Rocky Colavito and I became good friends. Rocky and I looked a lot alike and when we were down in Sarasota I got to know people from stores and stuff because I lived there. And Rocky told this story about when he went into a drug-store one time and they said, Oh, Fred, how are you doing? And we laughed about that because it was probably the only time in his life he got mistaken for someone else. But we became good friends. So I knew them and they made me feel very comfortable. They didn't just stick me out there and say, Okay, survive on your own. It was a good group of guys up there—Gary Peters and Joel Horlen and Bruce Howard.

Is Berres still the pitching coach?

Berres is still the pitching coach at this time.

And you've got a rapport with him.

Right. He always liked me and helped me. It was very comfortable for me.

So you make your debut in relief at Yankee Stadium. Are the White Sox well behind when you come in?

Yeah, they are, but for me it didn't matter. This was my showcase and I needed to do something. I'm sitting out in the bullpen and it's still early in the game and it's still somewhat close and I'm sitting out there and they call a guy by the name of Bob Priddy to warm up. So he starts warming up and I'm sitting there and I'm watching him and I'm seeing what I thought was one of the most phenomenal pitchers that I've ever seen. I mean, he's absolutely throwing BBs. His ball is breaking like crazy. His curveball is off the table and I'm sitting there and I say, My gosh, because Priddy was terrible. And the guy next to me kind of laughed and said, Wait until he gets in between the white lines. He falls to pieces. Can't get it over the plate, his fastball straightens out, his curveball doesn't break. And I'm saying to myself, If this is what a major league pitcher is, I've got a long way to go. And sure enough, Priddy walks out there and just gets lit up. So then they call me to warm up and go into the game.

And you know Priddy's getting hit so you're thinking, This is it.

Yeah. It's a matter of whether it's this inning or the next, because he was getting hit. He got through that inning and started the next one and got into trouble right away so they called me in. Back then, when they took you in they took you in by a cart. It was a little different in that they would take you right along the third-base wall. I mean, right along the wall. And all these kids are running down there and they're throwing things at you and they're yelling at you and they're swinging at you, and I'm kind of nervous anyway, and this is going on and I'm saying, What in the world is happening here?

So I went to the dugout, dropped my jacket off, and started walking out to the mound, and Rocky Colavito happens to be the guy that I'm going to face first. And I walk by Rocky and he smiles at me and he says, Just relax, kid. You're going to be okay. And I said, I'm scared to death, Rocky, and he just started laughing.

When I came in, there was a runner on first and second. Colavito was up and I get behind three balls and one strike, mostly pitching on just sheer mechanics because everything's going so fast for me. So I threw the next pitch, which was clearly a ball, and Colavito swung at it and just looked out at me and smiled. So I threw the next pitch and he just half swung and we got a double play. Mantle was the next batter I faced and I got him to pop up, so I got out of the inning and that was my first inning of major league ball. Then they took me out and brought someone else in.

Getting Mickey Mantle out in Yankee Stadium in your major league debut has got to be worth an ear-to-ear grin.

Well, yeah, but you have to remember, this was Mantle's last year. He was hobbling. He was not the player that he was.

You get back to the hotel. Do you call your wife? Your dad? When do your feet touch the ground again?

After the game I had pretty much calmed down. I had an aunt and uncle that lived up in New Jersey and they had watched it on TV. They called me. I did call my wife and my dad but that was about it. Again, I can always look back and say my first appearance was in Yankee Stadium and that has always been a thrill for me.

You get in five games that year and you pitch real well. Your ERA is 1.59. I expect you end the season feeling pretty good about your prospects.

I felt real good about it. Everybody was real pleased. I went back down to winter ball again to work on some more things with Ray Berres. Everybody was real pleased, but at the same time I knew I was going to Triple-A. That's just the way things were. But I knew that if I got a good start in Triple-A then that kind of sets it up.

So you're not surprised or overly disappointed when you start the next season there instead of in Chicago.

No, I knew going into spring training that's what it was going to be. And I did real well in spring training. The first strike was during spring training that year so I started the first spring training game against Baltimore and got in three innings and did real well. But then, when all the players came back, they had such a short time they really had to use them. At the same time the White Sox were totally unorganized and our Triple-A team was just absolutely the pits. I didn't have a real good season statistically, but I still got called up at the end of the year. But it was a whole different team. It was made up of a bunch of guys that had come from other organizations who were on the downside of their careers, and everybody was laughing and joking and pulling gags, and here we were in last place losing a ton of games. I started a couple of games but it was just a fiasco.

One game I started was against Kansas City and there was a fly ball hit out to the left fielder and he misses it, and because he made such a bad play on it he pulls up with his leg and doesn't even get the ball, and it's an inside-the-park home run. And it's not an error because he doesn't get the ball, but he's laying there on the ground holding his leg and everybody's screaming, Get the ball. Get the ball. I mean, we didn't even throw it into the infield, so it was not a fun time.

But the guy's leg was okay after the game?

Oh, he gets up to bat the next inning. 1969 was not a fun year. Everybody had bad attitudes, and then in 1970 there was this big change and the whole team was kind of a different team. At this point I'm probably twenty-six years old and I'm still on the major league roster. Don Gutteridge is the manager now and I go down, after that season, to winter ball and at the end of winter ball Gutteridge came to me and said, I want you to go and play in Venezuela. And I said, Don, I can't do it. He said, What do you mean you can't do it? I said, Don, since 1966 I've played the season and I've played winter ball. I get two months off and then it all starts over again. I said, I went through that this year. You guys called me up and now I'm down here playing. We're in December and I'm tired and I need some rest He said, Well, it would do your career good to go. I said, Don, I can't do it. It's not going to do my career good because I'm tired. My arm is dead. And I killed myself.

Oh yeah. You put the gun in your mouth.

I didn't know it at the time but I went to spring training the next year and they're telling me, You're going on this trip, and then I wouldn't pitch. Then the same thing would happen the next day and I wouldn't pitch and I wouldn't pitch, and now it's been seven days where I hadn't thrown in a game. And now I have to go into the Marine Reserve for the weekend so I'm not there Friday, Saturday, or Sunday, and I walk in Monday morning and Don says, You're starting today. I said, What do you mean I'm starting? He said, You're starting. I said, Okay, but Don, I haven't pitched in ten, eleven days. He said, Well, you're starting today. And I said, Okay.

So we were playing the Dodgers and I went out and in the first inning it was boom, boom, boom. I struck out two of the three. I go out there the second inning and I couldn't get anybody out. I'm throwing as hard as I can throw and they're hitting them as far as they can hit them. I mean, there's lined shots all over the place. Steve Garvey is up. I throw one at his head and Steve barely moves. Then he proceeds to hit the next one out of the park. Nine runs later I finally get them out. Now, I haven't had the first visit from a coach, from anybody. I'm just out there getting buried. I still can't quite figure out what's going on and I do my running and I go in and a reporter from Chicago comes over to me and he says, You know what happened today, don't you? And I said, No, I really don't. He said, They buried you. They've already made up their mind. You're not going up and they needed to bury you. I was out of options, so they had to keep me and they didn't particularly want to lose me in the organization. He said, Fred, whether it took two innings, four innings, or five innings, you were going to get buried. And sure enough, I went right through waivers and that was kind of my career.

Nobody signed you? Nobody picked you up?

No, because, you know, you just had to see it. My poor wife sat through the whole thing. It was not pretty.

But that's just one outing.

But it's hard in spring training. People want to wait thirty or sixty days to see how their players are going to do, and that's kind of the worst time to go through waivers.

So they sent you through waivers at the end of spring training when you can't catch on with anybody.

Yeah, it was towards the end. So I'm still playing Triple-A with them. I'm not on the major league roster and then, towards the end of the year, I was playing pepper. I'd never had any leg or knee problems at all and I was playing pepper and went to get one and my whole knee went out, and I couldn't straighten it up. The cartilage had broken off and I had to have an operation at the end of the year. And that kind of did it. I said, Well, shoot, that's it. That was in 1970. I went home, really wasn't doing much because I was looking for a job. I had always told myself, Hey, I've got a degree. I'm going to play baseball for the six years that I'm in the Marine Corps, and at the end of that time, if I'm not up I'm out. Because I'm not going to stay in this game and beat my head against the wall forever. So I had one more year to go after the 1970 season, and I had more or less given up and was just doing a little work to get my knee rehabilitated. I wasn't throwing or anything. And then I get a call from the Hawaii team and they want to sign me. Well, shoot, I'll go over to Hawaii and play, so I signed with them.

The only problem was the manager there was Bill Adair, and Adair was my Triple-A manager my last year in Tucson and he and I didn't see eye to eye about a lot of things. So I go to spring training, which was down in Yuma, Arizona, and the last night of spring training Adair comes to me and says, We're trading you to Eugene, Oregon. They were the Phillies' Triple-A team. So I went there and they didn't have a spot for me. I sat around with them for about thirty days and then they finally sent me back to Evansville, which was Triple-A with Milwaukee. I finished the year up there, mostly throwing relief and spot starting, and it was good for me to have done that because it got it out of my system. I just said, Okay, enough of this monkey business.

Did you experience any withdrawal symptoms after it was over?

No, I just kind of said, Well, I gave it my best shot. Some people make it, some don't. I could sit back and say, Well, it's politics and all that, but it really isn't. It gets down to you're either good enough and you shine, or you're not. And all these guys that say, Well, it's politics, well, it really isn't. If I had been good enough, I would've been there with somebody. But it was just that last little bit that it takes that makes the difference between somebody that gets there long-term and somebody that almost gets there. And I recognized that.

The whole time I was there, I always felt like I gave everything I had. I worked hard. Because I had run track I did more running, as a pitcher, than anybody. I mean, I enjoyed running and none of that bothered me. So I never said, Well, I wish I'd done this different or I wish I'd done that, because at the time I really felt like I gave everything I had. So I walked away and said, That's life. Some people can make it and some can't.

I've got a son who's playing baseball now. And I look back at my days with Ray Berres, and with all of the mechanics and stuff that he taught me, I've been able to help my son. He's kind of like me. He had a week up with Colorado. He's still at Triple-A. He's with the Cubs this year. He's had some good years and struggled some, but this is going to be it for him. He's got to decide, I think, this year whether he can make that last little step and stay or not.

But he was probably able to go into it with more open eyes than most pitchers his age, because of your experience.

Well, I think he had more of a love for it at an earlier age than I did. It's kind of what he wanted to do. He went to college on a baseball scholarship and did real well in college, and that's what he wanted to do.

Because this is the one thing that he wanted, do you think it's going to be tougher for him to make the transition out?

I think it is. I think it is. You know, when he was playing and he was eleven and twelve years old he wanted to pitch and I wouldn't let him. I said, No, Fred. History is full of pitchers that are really good at this age, but they all lose it because when you're at that age you're nothing but an arm thrower. And as I look back, the fact that I couldn't pitch when I was eleven and twelve, I think, helped me. So I wouldn't let him pitch. He didn't start pitching until he was fourteen. And as he looks back now, he's always thanked me for that, because he saw all these kids. The only one that he played with that made it was Brad Radke. Brad pitched earlier but then Brad had a period of time in there when his arm was bad and he didn't pitch. He played shortstop. And then he started pitching again. But all the other kids that he played with, none of them ever got there. Fred really didn't start blossoming until he got into pro ball. His second year in pro ball he was a closer and really did well for a couple of years.

It sounds like you had one of the easier transitions out of baseball. You didn't experience the withdrawal some others have, but I would assume you watch a decent amount of baseball now just because it's your son's business.

Well, I'm not a huge fan. I've been over to the Devil Rays maybe two or three times. I hate that stadium. It's the worst stadium in the world. I like to watch it on TV. I will watch it on TV but I don't get carried away with it—but I don't get carried away with any sport. You see a lot of guys down here that are just die-hard fans of the college they went to, and I'm just not that way. But I do still enjoy it. I have enjoyed the time with my son in working with him and watching him progress, and doing a little coaching with other players.

Did you fly out when he got called up?

You know, he was with Colorado Springs and we went out there on a vacation and spent five days with him. We get on a plane, fly back to Florida, and he gets called up. The general manager calls him. They knew we were in town and he said, Are your parents still there? And Fred said, No, they've left. And he goes, Well, they're going to kill us.

They called him up and it was kind of funny. There was a message from him when we got home and I said, Something's happened. He didn't say what, but I just knew, knowing baseball, that something had happened but we didn't know what. So he calls us from the dressing room later that evening and told us he'd gotten called up and we were just devastated because the game was about to start. I did not, at the time, have the dish TV. Now he calls at about four o'clock our time. He had gotten there but he said, Don't worry about tonight. They told me I'm not doing anything tonight. I said, All right. So I went out and bought the dish and I called to get the baseball and they said, It'll take about a week. And I said, No, you don't understand. And so I got it turned on in the next hour and we watched that game, only he didn't get in.

So now it's Wednesday night and we get in front of the TV and we turn it on and there's no game. I called them up and I said, I just bought this thing, and they said, Oh, Wednesday night belongs to ESPN, so the only game we can broadcast is the one by ESPN. So my wife and I are just devastated, but she has a niece who lives right outside of Colorado Springs so we called and said, Do you get the game? And she said, Yes, and we said, This is what you're going to do. You're going to watch that TV and the minute he starts warming up, you call us. She said, Okay. So she calls us. Colorado's just getting killed. It's like ten to nothing. And they call him. He starts warming up, so she calls us. We said, Okay. Put the telephone by the TV, so she did. And for three innings we're listening to this on the telephone. She's got it up as loud as it can go and we listen to it on the TV. He gave up one run in three innings. He did really well.

Colorado, a lot of times, will call up players from Colorado Springs for a week or two weeks. In this case their bullpen was pretty much strapped. They had pitched an awful lot and another player had been hurt so they called him up. They were really only going to use him for that home stand but he did real well so they said, Come on and go with us to Chicago. So that appearance we did see him on TV and we've got that taped, and that was a big thrill for me. Even though it was for only a week, he got up there. He got to see what it was like, and he still has the fire and we'll see what happens.

Cleveland at Milwaukee
Thursday, June 4, 1970

Cleveland	ab	r	h	rbi	Milwaukee	ab	r	h	rbi
Uhlaender, cf	5	1	2	0	Harper, 3b	4	1	2	1
Nettles, 3b	3	1	0	0	Pena, 2b	4	1	1	0
Pinson, rf	5	0	2	0	Krausse, p	0	0	0	0
Horton, 1b	2	2	1	1	Alvis, ph	1	0	0	0
Sims, lf	3	1	2	0	Savage, rf	4	1	2	3
Hinton, lf	0	0	0	0	Walton, lf	4	0	0	0
Fosse, c	5	2	3	4	McNer'y, 1b-c	4	0	1	0
Leon, 2b	3	1	1	2	Allen, cf-2b	4	0	1	0
Heidem'n, ss	5	0	1	0	Kubiak, ss	3	1	1	0
Moore, p	0	0	0	0	Roof, c	1	0	0	0
Hennigan, p	4	0	1	1	Hegan, 1b	2	0	2	0
Higgins, p	0	0	0	0	Peters, p	0	0	0	0
Chance, p	0	0	0	0	Locker, p	0	0	0	0
					O'Dono'hue, p	2	0	0	0
Totals	35	8	13	8	Snyder, ph-cf	2	0	0	0
					Totals	35	4	10	4

Cleveland   2 0 3 0 0 3 0 0 0—8
Milwaukee   1 0 0 1 0 1 1 0 0—4

Cleveland	IP.	H.	R.	ER.	BB.	SO.
Moore	0*	1	1	1	0	0
Hennigan (W. 4-1)...	6.2	7	3	3	2	3
Higgins.................	2	2	0	0	1	2
Chance (Save. 1)	0.1	0	0	0	0	1
Milwaukee	IP.	H.	R.	ER.	BB.	SO.
Peters (L. 0-1)	2†	6	4	4	3	1
Locker	0.2	2	1	1	1	0
O'Donoghue	4.1	4	3	3	2	1
Krausse	2	1	0	0	2	1

*Pitched to one batter in first.
†Pitched to three batters in third.
E—Kubiak. DP—Cleveland 1, Milwaukee 1. LOB—Cleveland 11, Milwaukee 7.
2B—Pinson, Hennigan, Harper 2, Fosse. 3B—Savage. HR—Fosse (7), Savage (3).
SH—Sims. SF—Horton. HBP—by Locker (Nettles). U—Runge, Haller, Odom and
Kunkel. T—3:04. A—8,625.

RAY PETERS

Ray Peters started two games for the Milwaukee Brewers in 1970 but finished his major league career with just
two innings pitched. He gave up seven hits and five walks
while striking out one, and finished with a career ERA of
31.50. He was interviewed October 30, 2001 at his home
in Flower Mound, Texas.

Tell me where you grew up and when you first started playing baseball.

I grew up in Cheektowaga, New York. It's a suburb of Buffalo. It's where
the airport is in Buffalo. That's the town. My father started the Little
League team, I think, when I was ten. Before then we just played from
dawn to dusk. I played everything. I was big for my age. I had to carry
around my birth certificate because I was like six foot when I was thirteen, or something like that. I did the Little League thing and we got
two games away from Williamsport, then I did the Babe Ruth thing. I

went to Bishop Turner High School in Buffalo, and then I got a scholarship to the prep school, Nichols School in Buffalo, so I went there, which was just like night and day academically. It was wonderful. My father's best friend's brother was an umpire who knew the coach at the prep school, and one thing led to another and I went to the prep school and we ended up being undefeated in basketball and baseball and I got one heck of an academic education. I had three no-hitters and a perfect game all in a row. I had scholarship offers all over the place. One day somebody said, Why don't you apply to Harvard and Yale? So I applied to Harvard and Yale and I got into Harvard. My parents worked for the post office. They were mail handlers so I came from a very modest—not a rich—background, a very down-home background.

Were you equally good at baseball and basketball?

No, I was definitely more talented in baseball. I could always throw a baseball.

Was baseball the only sport you played once you reached Harvard?

Yes, I wanted to concentrate. First of all, you're scared to death that you're the one exception that they made and you might be the dumbest kid in the class. You have the misconception that everybody's absolutely brilliant, which wasn't the case. Everybody's smart but they're not all brilliant. Plus, Harvard had like fourteen losing basketball seasons in a row. However, if I had played basketball I would've been able to sit at the end of the bench, not only with one of the guys I played against in high school, but one of my classmates who lived a few hundred feet from me, Al Gore. But I didn't want to do that. I wanted to concentrate on baseball.

Did you choose baseball or did baseball choose you? You were better at baseball and sometimes we like what we're good at.

I definitely had more talent in baseball. I had size and I learned a lot in high school. I could've played basketball, probably at Harvard, but not at a top basketball school. I was not that good. I was decent but I absolutely had excellent talent in baseball, plus I'm a voracious reader and I understood the game. I always loved the game. I know the history of the game. I guess it was like that for my father. He was a baseball player when he was younger. My older brother was not a gifted athlete but a true sports historian, a student of the game. I always understood the game, the nuances. I loved the game.

Did you have a favorite team growing up?

Probably Cleveland. New York City—the New York Yankees—that was 420 miles away. A lot of people west of the Mississippi think that if you're from Buffalo then you have lunch at the Empire State Building. They don't understand the distance. Cleveland was only two hundred miles away. They had the great Cleveland teams, the 1954 World Series, and you had them on the radio. It was great to listen to Mel Allen and Phil Rizzuto and Red Barber doing the Yankee games. We could get those games, but Jimmy Dudley did the games for the Indians. Jimmy Dudley ended up announcing the games for the Seattle Pilots in their one and only season in 1969, which was kind of interesting since later on I was in the Pilots organization.

Did you ever get to go to any of the Cleveland games?

I saw one memorable game, one memorable doubleheader. I think it was 1958, a doubleheader between the Yankees and the Indians in the old stadium down there in Cleveland, that huge stadium. And what I vividly remember was that the Indians were getting clobbered and they brought in Rocky Colavito to pitch because they were so far behind. Rocky Colavito pitched one or two innings in that game. Now, if you fast-forward ten years later, to 1968, I didn't want to go back to Buffalo after playing in the College World Series so I went to live in New York City. I go to a New York Yankees game and Rocky Colavito, who's from the Bronx, I believe, now plays for the Yankees and the Yankees are playing the Indians. I remember vividly Vic Davalillo in center field for the Indians. The Yankees are losing and they must have been short of relievers, so they bring in Colavito to pitch and he gets the win. Rocky Colavito pitched twice in the major leagues and I saw him, as a civilian, a nonpro player at that time, pitch both times. I have to be one of the few nonpros that saw him pitch both times he pitched in the major leagues.

When you're in high school, are you only a pitcher or are you playing other positions?

No, I played first base also.

Were you a good hitter?

I was a switch-hitter, decent hitter. I'm ambidextrous, too. I pitched batting practice left-handed and things like that but they wouldn't let me

193

pitch left-handed in a game, which I regret. I think it was 1957 or 1958 that the Mexico Little League team—Monterrey, I think it was—won the Little League World Series, and they had a pitcher who threw a perfect game and he was ambidextrous. And then their shortstop pitched and won the championship game the next year. That was when I was ten years old and I just figured I could do that. I could throw with either arm. So my brother, who I owe a lot to because he recognized my talent—he just worked with me all the time—and I, we had a Wiffle ball and so I learned how to switch-hit and I switch-threw. I mean, daily. Every day for hours I would do that. So I became a pretty good hitter left-handed, and I did throw batting practice left-handed. I threw batting practice in major league spring training. I used to throw batting practice to Gorman Thomas left-handed, but they wouldn't let me do it in a game. What really ticks me off, thirty years later almost, is that Harvard had a guy about five years ago that, in fact, did pitch in a double-header—one game right-handed and one game left-handed. And they talked about him, but hell, I did that. Bert Campaneris did that. There were a few people who could do it and I was one of them, but they never let me do it in a game.

As a high school pitcher, what are you throwing besides a fastball?

Three pitches. I used to come three-quarters on the fastball. Sometimes I'd come sidearm with a fastball, so fastball, two-seamer, four-seamer. I had a hellacious twelve-to-six over-the-top curveball, and then a slider. I had the repertoire. I really had the repertoire in high school. The best I ever pitched was probably when I was sixteen, seventeen, eighteen. I absolutely, positively could've pitched in the major leagues when I was sixteen, seventeen, and eighteen. After that I was good but I wasn't as consistently good, and I think the body was breaking down from that point forward.

I imagine that there were plenty of scouts around when you were a senior.

Oh yeah. Since I was like fifteen years old. I never saw them, though. My father kept them away, the coaches kept them away, but they were there. It was pretty relentless.

You've got Harvard on one hand and scouts on the other. Were you tempted to turn pro out of high school?

No. It was a no-brainer. Again, this is with a little bit of hindsight, but I never even gave it a second thought. Education is for a lifetime. That's trite but it's true. An education is for a lifetime. Those who last in athletics are the ones that are the freaks, especially pitchers. It's unnatural, if you look at the slow motion. I remember going over to Dr. Kerlan and Jobe's, the guys who were the orthopedic surgeons for Sandy Koufax and performed the surgery on Tommy John. I guess this must've been 1970 or 1971. I had shoulder problems or bursitis or something, and Kerlan had this huge picture of Sandy Koufax in his office, and you could see the unbelievable angle of his arm going back prior to reaching his release point. That's not natural. And from probably age eighteen on, I just wasn't as consistent. I mean, I was still good, don't get me wrong. Obviously I got to the big leagues—I got my cup of coffee—but I just wasn't as good. Because of my size, I'm coordinated but not that coordinated. I only have one piece of film of me pitching and I now look at that and feel like I was lucky to last as long as I did, because I threw against my front foot so it was a very jarring motion. I threw almost entirely with my arm. But you know what? Kinesiologywise, my body doesn't work any other way. You look at the follow-through of tall guys like the Steve Carltons and the Randy Johnsons. I'm very tight and they're very loose. Maybe it's yoga or something, but those who last—really last, especially tall people—are the oddity, not the norm. Those are the freaks because probably the ideal size is like Tom Seaver, about six one and stocky, where you get that leg drive, very compact. It's sort of like golf. I mean, I could hit a golf ball 350 yards, but boy, if I screw it up taking that club head back, if I screwed up a hair with the arc, then I am so way off.

With greater height comes more moving parts and more things can go wrong.

That's absolutely true. If you look at some of these guys now, they're so compact. I've learned a lot. You never realize how much you know until you start to teach people, and batting a ball, hitting a tennis ball, throwing a ball, punching anybody, it's all arm speed. From the point of the coil to where you make contact or let the ball go or hit the ball, it's all the speed. The bat speed from the top to where you hit the ball or the arm speed from where you cock your arm to when you let it go. It's really that simple and people confuse it to hell. It's just a lot easier if you're shorter. It really is. I mean, look at Agassi. It's all mechanics. The tall guys typically burn out quicker. And again, looking back, sports medicine was nowhere near where it is now. When I was complaining about not having arm strength, all they did was take x-rays of my shoulder. I had neck surgery four months ago that I probably could've had thirty years ago. Twenty years ago I find out that one leg is an inch and a half shorter. I wear an inch-and-a-half heel lift. That's no sour grapes. That's just the way it was. Today it's just an entirely different world. That's not going to change anything. I may have lasted one more year and made decent money one year, but, again, to last is the oddity.

You said your parents were mail handlers. Is Harvard giving athletic scholarships at this time?

No, Harvard does not give—still to this day, and I've been extremely active—any athletic scholarships whatsoever. It's all based on need. Harvard accepts the class and then figures out how to pay for it. My parents didn't have any money. I don't think they paid anything. I got student loans and I had jobs where I cleaned the bathroom or I worked in the kitchen. I did that for four years. No, there's no such thing as athletic scholarships.

You played on a strong team in high school and Harvard is without scholarship athletes. Is the level of competition comparable, or is it a noticeable step up to Ivy League baseball?

It is actually a step up because there are more athletes there than you think, it's just that they choose to do other things. We had more all-state athletes at Harvard—a surprising number that played football and baseball—than you would think. Many more never played because they really were there for academics. We had a very good team. We went to the College World Series in 1968. We lost, I think, 2–0 to St John's and I think we lost 2–1 also, in extra innings, to Southern Illinois. Our strong suit was pitching the years I was there. I think they went to the quarterfinals in 1972 and 1974. If I had played my senior year then my catcher would've been Pete Varney, and Pete later played for the White Sox and for the Braves. We would've had a heck of a team. There were a couple other guys on that team that played minor league baseball. We would've had a chance to win the national title. There are plenty of athletes in the Ivy League, it's just that many of them choose not to participate there.

If you had scouts following you in high school, they must've still been following you at Harvard. Your dad's still in Buffalo, so who keeps them away now?

It was up to me. I talked to them. I was drafted four times before I signed, but I was adamant that I was going finish my education. I just said, That's what I'm going to do. I did sign, though, my senior year because our coach, Norm Shepard, retired. I was drafted by an expansion team, plus I did want to make some money so I could help my parents pay some bills off and things like that. I don't know, really, what they actually did offer me out of high school. I mean, I hear it was a hundred thousand dollars and stuff like that, but when the opportunity came along with an expansion team, that was a hell of a shot, and that's the overriding reason why I signed in January of 1969 and didn't play my senior year. I went to spring training for three or four weeks and then came back and finished school and then went on and started my career in June of 1969.

Did you get a decent signing bonus?

No. Nine thousand dollars split over two years so it would reduce the taxes. But hey, every year I didn't sign it was going to be less. Every year I didn't sign, the bonus just went down. 1965 was the year of the first draft, so if you didn't sign out of high school you had to wait until after your sophomore year, I think. Then it was every year thereafter. I was drafted by the Tigers and the A's and in 1968 by the Mets. I'd just got back from the College World Series and went to New York. I didn't want to go back to Buffalo. I knocked on doors and found a job with G. H. Walker and Sons. Mr Walker happens to be the grandfather of our current president. I go work there and he comes down one day into the bowels of the building where I was working as a transfer clerk and he says, Hey, we just drafted you. And I go, What are talking about? Well, he owned part of the Mets that Joan Payson didn't. He said, Go on out to Shea and pitch during the All-Star break. There'll be some other guys we drafted and players who hung around. So I go to Shea Stadium at the 1968 All-Star break and I walk in and there's Gil Hodges smoking Winstons, there's Yogi Berra smoking Camels. I, at the time, smoked. I smoked Lucky Strikes. And I hadn't thrown a ball in six weeks. So I get out there and pitch against other guys who were drafted and stuff like that. I struck out eight in four innings but the consensus was that I hadn't improved since high school. I was throwing okay but I wasn't really on top of the game. Then I look around at who's there, and who did I meet? Nolan Ryan, who is younger than I am, Jerry Koosman, Gary Gentry. These guys were all my age or younger. And the next year they won the World Series.

That's pretty heady stuff to be able to throw at Shea Stadium with all of those guys. You didn't feel like maybe you're late coming to the party since they're your age and are already there? You weren't tempted to sign and finish school in the off-seasons?

It was tough, but no. I mean, I was that close. I was going to finish. And I think maybe down deep I knew that it just wasn't a long-haul thing. Maybe I just convinced myself. Believe me, it was tough, especially out of high school. Even though it was a prep school, they really didn't shelter you from the phone calls from the recruiters from colleges. I mean, I had a hundred colleges calling me. It was just awful for somebody eighteen years old. I didn't know anything. It was very frustrating. But once I got on the plane and I visited Harvard, that was it. I mean, that was like going home. I'd never been on a plane before. You can't do this now, but the Harvard Club of Buffalo sent me over there. I stayed with students. Even in the Harvard interview we didn't talk about sports. We talked about something else. It was just a very warm and wonderful experience. I'm sure my roommates would say, Oh, no, you were going crazy during that time. Yeah, sure, I was tempted.

You said you wanted to help your parents out and I know you have student loans to pay off and that the nine thousand dollars was split over two years, but did you do anything special for yourself when you signed the contract?

No. I did nothing. I paid off student loans.

198

There wasn't anything special about the night that you signed? Nothing to commemorate that you're now a professional ballplayer?

No, no. It was, Okay, I did it, now let's get on with it. I mean, I knew I was going to do it since I was ten years old. I felt I had the talent to do it, it was just a matter of when I was going to do it. But I also always knew that I was intelligent, so I always had that balance. I had only met a few professionals in sports. At that time, as a college graduate, you really feel like a fish out of water. This is 1969. Today you have a lot more college-educated players and everything. Over the years I think there's been eleven or twelve players from Harvard that have played in the major leagues and I really don't know if any one of us got the necessary time in for a pension.

I had great fun when I played professionally, especially with the Latin American ballplayers because I majored in Latin American history and Spanish. I got along great with them. I learned more and more Spanish. It was a great experience. My professional baseball career was only three and a half years but it was definitely a great experience.

You graduate in June of 1969. Where do you go from there?

Well, I went to spring training sometime in February or March. I weighed 225 and they want me down to two hundred pounds, because Ewell Blackwell, in the early 1950s, was my height and weighed about two hundred pounds. So I starved myself. I go to Newark, New York. Earl Torgeson was the manager. Great guy. I think I pitched in two or three games—I have a shutout—and immediately get promoted to Clinton, Iowa.

Newark is rookie ball and Clinton is single A.

Right. I finished the season in Iowa, did okay. Go to instructional league in Phoenix and did fine there and then I go back to Buffalo and I substitute taught. Go back to spring training in February of 1970. Halfway through spring training they decide I'm going to go to Double-A, and they don't have a Double-A team, but there was a split Double-A team with Montreal and so I ended up in Homestead, Florida, for spring training with Montreal. I go to Jacksonville. I pitch one or two games. I have a shutout. Get promoted to Triple-A Portland. My first appearance in Portland I came in in relief and got hammered. They threw you in there when you have a big lead or are losing, which is the right thing to do, so you get your feet wet because it is a new deal. I think the second or third start I had a shutout. I think I had two shutouts out of three, something like that, and then I got promoted to Milwaukee.

So this isn't a September call-up?

Oh, no. No, no. This is June. I go up in June and I pitch against the Indians in County Stadium. In the two games that I pitched I gave up seven hits—four of them broken-bat bloops—five walks, and I struck out Ray Fosse on a curveball and that was it. I truly don't think I got a helluva chance, to tell you the truth. I really didn't see eye to eye with Dave Bristol. Against Detroit, Dick McAuliffe was the leadoff guy and he gets a hit, I walk the next two guys, Elliott Maddox and Al Kaline, then Bristol takes me out and Skip Lockwood comes in. Lockwood struck out Norm Cash, the first batter he faced, but Willie Horton blasted a two-strike pitch into left field for a grand slam home run and I get sent back to the minor leagues.

Let's talk about the game in Cleveland first. You pitch two-plus innings there.

Yeah, two complete against Cleveland and then I honest to God don't remember what happened in the third inning.

199

Who's the catcher?

Phil Roof caught me against the Indians.

You're a rookie. Did you ever shake him off or did you throw exactly what he asked for?

No, I did exactly what he said. I jammed Tony Horton and he gets a blooper to left. Duke Sims hits one off the end of the bat for another single and Ray Fosse bloops another jammed pitch into center. Two of those were broken-bat hits.

The Detroit game makes your ERA skyrocket. Are you with the big club when darkness falls after the game in Detroit?

The next day I'm not. The next day he told me and gave me the plane ticket.

You're on the road. Where does he tell you? Are you in the hotel?

I think he called me in the hotel so I went up to his room and he said something along the lines of, Hey, just go back down and work on your stuff. Something like that. And he gave me a plane ticket, and I was back down on the plane to Portland or wherever Portland was playing. I can't remember where.

Did you finish the season with Portland?

I finish the season with Portland. And I really started to have arm troubles then. One good game, one bad. I think I had two or three shutouts that year, but then on the other hand I'd have some spells where I had a lot of walks and I couldn't get the breaking ball over. Somewhere in the pros I lost my over-the-top, twelve-to-six curveball, which, looking back, means obviously there was something structurally, mechanically wrong, because I had a Jim Palmer, Mike Mussina, real curveball. And I couldn't throw it. It just killed me to throw it. And I had a lot of cortisone. They'd say, Oh, it's just tendinitis, bursitis. That stuff was building up. I had to have those shots a lot. So that's when I threw more sliders and things like that, and tried to come up with an off-speed pitch, but when I had the downer it was a good downer. Probably the last good one I remember was the one I threw Fosse. I struck him out on that good curveball. After that I never really had it. From that point on I have a fastball and a sinker. I finished up the year with Portland, then I went to instructional league in Phoenix and they tried to change me into a reliever. They tried to change me into a sidearmer, almost an underhand reliever, trying to throw sinking fastballs away.

Is that an effort to reconstruct you as a pitcher or is it a move away from what they think is giving you pain?

I think the fact of the matter was that I was just too inconsistent throwing the old way so they wanted to try and see what they could get out of me, in a positive way. I said, I'll try anything. I want to play. So we tried that and I did very well that winter and I'm living in Phoenix and I think I took like six weeks off after instructional league and then here comes spring training 1971. I'm all geared up, and I can't throw the ball ten feet. I'm absolutely in agony.

You said your arm was giving you trouble and you were having problems with your control during the season. Are you surprised or disappointed when September comes and you have teammates being called up late in the year and you're not?

Yeah. If you're telling me, Just go work on it, then why don't you bring me back up?

It's not like the Brewers were in the hunt.

Oh, no. Hell no. But I felt like I was still a prospect, not a suspect. I'm sure you've heard that before. Hey, they want me to go to instructional league.

And it sounds like they're actually trying to provide you with some instruction.

Oh yeah. And I'm happy about that. I've all of a sudden become a short reliever and I'm throwing the ball and getting ground balls and, hey, this is great.

Well, if you've lost the curve and you're down to two pitches, then using you as a reliever makes sense.

Right. Right. I'm fine with that. I had shown them I could really do the job in instructional league and here at spring training 1971 I can't throw

201

the ball ten feet. I go to the doctor and the doctor just shoots me up with cortisone, but after two or three weeks I'm finally starting to come around. I go through spring training. Finally my arm's back. I go through spring training, get sent to Evansville, which is now the Triple-A team for the Brewers, I get a couple innings in there and get traded to the Phillies, which means I go to Eugene.

What was the trade?

Me and Pete Koegel for Johnny Briggs. Pete was my size, except he was a football player to boot. He had like a thirty-two-inch waist. He was a big guy. If his bat speed were quicker he could have been around for a long time. He was a great roomie. At that time I was hoping to play one more season and put some money away. I was on the major league roster the year before so I was making $10,000 a year playing in Portland. I got called up in June, before June fifteenth or June thirtieth, and since I got called up before, I made that $10,000 salary for the entire year. I got paid for the month of September, which was great. And then they sent me a contract, I think, for the minimum salary again, which I think was still $10,000, so I was happy. I said, Hey, if worse comes to worse we can bank some money here and I can go to law school, or something like that.

They trade you and Pete Koegel for Johnny Briggs and you go straight from Evansville to Eugene.

Del Crandall was the manager in Evansville. I had just found the apartment, just signed the lease, just got the phone installed, just got the checking account set up, just got the furniture. You couldn't rent furniture in Evansville. You had to get it from Louisville and have it delivered. I called my wife in Phoenix. She is literally getting in the car, leaving her parents' house to drive to Evansville, when I catch her. This was before cell phones and everything else. I caught her just as she's going out the door. Stop. I just got traded. I'm going back to the Pacific Coast League.

Crandall's the one who tells you that you've been traded.

Right.

How do you feel about it? You don't like Bristol and he's still managing the big club.

I'm thinking this is great. This is a new start. This is wonderful. I think this is great.

So you go out to Eugene.

And just absolutely anything and everything that could go wrong did go wrong. Couldn't catch a break, didn't have good stuff. It was a great time, good people, all that wonderful stuff, but absolutely terrible on the field.

Does it hurt to throw when you're in Eugene? I know you said that everything that could go wrong did go wrong, but did you have pain throwing?

I can remember taking Darvon and seven aspirin before games. And DMSO. That was one of the in-vogue, bad-arm cures during the years that I played.

What is DMSO?

Dimethyl sulfoxide, and it stinks like hell. You rub it on. I believe it was used as a horse liniment back then.

Is there any point in that season when you think you might be called up to the Phillies?

No. No, no. I'm hoping I can make it through the season and get paid. I pitched games into the fifth inning and it'd be tied or I'd be ahead by one and the reliever would come in and just get hammered. Other games I'd get hammered. I think I was 1–9 or 2–10—something like that—but in no way did that represent how I pitched. I didn't pitch that bad, I guarantee you.

    The first game I pitched with Eugene was in Hawaii. We were playing the Islanders and it was the last game of the series, and when you play over in Hawaii you have a curfew on the last game so you can get on a plane and get back to the mainland for another game the next night. We're losing something like ten to nothing in the bottom of the seventh or eighth inning and it's bases loaded and two outs and whoever's pitching for us has had it. I hadn't pitched in a week and a half and I have nothing. I've got absolutely nothing warming up, absolutely zero. And now I'm trying anything. To hell with it. I'm going to go back and throw my old way. I'll try anything. So I get in there and it's like nine to nothing, ten to nothing—something like that—bases loaded, two outs. Steve Whitaker, who was a teammate with the Brewers the year before, left-hand hitter, the next Mickey Mantle, all that stuff, he's up. So John Felske, who manages the Phillies later on, is my catcher at this time. He calls for a curveball. So I just gut it out and throw an overhand curveball, my slow curveball, and Whitaker hits it foul like 450 feet. Kills it. John comes back and says, Another curveball. So it's another twelve-sixer. Nice curveball but there's not enough sharp break. Whitaker hits it foul about five hundred feet this time. So I've got two strikes on him now and he's hit them nine hundred feet.

But before I had come into the game, I remembered how Ken Sanders with the Brewers the year before had taught me how to hide Vaseline. Now, I don't know if I called Felske out or if we had a sign for it or what, but the third pitch I threw was a Vaseline ball, and it acts sort of like a split-finger. That sucker went right down the middle, right at the belt buckle, and just totally fell off, just went straight down. And Whitaker knew what it was. He swung and missed by a foot. Then Felske did the right thing. Just like you heard about how Yogi Berra supposedly used to do with Whitey Ford, he let the ball hit the ground, rubbed the Vaseline off and stepped on the plate for the third out. We come back and score eleven runs or whatever in the next inning or two, another reliever comes in and gets the win. I mean, I had absolutely nothing and it looks like I did a helluva job getting out of a bases-loaded jam, allowing our team to come back and win. Absolutely bizarre. That was the first and last break of any kind I got the rest of the year, but that was the best Vaseline ball I've ever seen in my life. The thing dropped just like you imagine it would do. And Whitaker was so pissed. He knew it, too. Felske just dropped the ball, rubbed it off in the dirt, and stepped on home plate for the third out since the bases were loaded.

One of the great things about 1970 was Jimmie Reese was our batting coach in Portland. Just to listen to the Babe Ruth stories, because he was Babe Ruth's roommate. Just a wonderful guy. We're living in Tucson ten or fifteen years later and I go to a spring training game and I see Jimmie Reese and he remembers me. He comes over and says hi. Same thing with Tommy Lasorda. Some of these guys, like Lasorda, you just absolutely hate as competitors. You just hated to play against those bastards, but he spent, I'll never forget, twenty minutes with my oldest son at spring training when my son was five years old, and to this day my son is one of the biggest Dodger fans. Lasorda sent him an autographed photo for his eighteenth birthday. So Tommy Lasorda, who supposedly broke the record for saying the F word seven hundred times in forty-two seconds, is really a stand-up guy.

It doesn't sound like returning to baseball in 1972 was an option. Had you made up your mind sometime while you were in Eugene? When did you know that your last major league game was your last major league game?

I physically knew it when I was in Eugene. It just isn't working.

Did you know it before then? Did you know it when you had the pain and couldn't throw during spring training of 1971? Or did it take the year in Eugene to realize it?

I think I probably knew it but things could change. You can get lucky. Maybe the pain goes away. Not that I didn't want it, not that I didn't work hard to get there, but down deep I think I knew it. When I went back to Buffalo between 1971 and 1972 I went to see a doctor in Youngstown, Ohio, who specialized in sports medicine—this is really at the beginning of sports-medicine specialization—Dr Vuksta, and worked on some specific arm exercises to build up my shoulder. I just wasn't getting the strength. I just didn't have the strength. So I was hanging on. I mentally knew that I probably wasn't going to make it but I was going to do everything physically that I could to try to do it, and it just didn't happen.

So what happens in 1972?

In 1972 I got a minor league contract from the Phillies. I figured I was done. Actually I was thinking I was going to get released, but I got a minor league contract. So I go to Clearwater and I'm throwing the sinkers and stuff again, and I pitch nine innings and I give up one run, a home run to Andre Thornton, and I get released the last day of spring training by Dallas Green.

In 1971 with the Phillies, with Eugene, I'm trying to go the old way— over the top, three-quarters. I said, Okay, I'm going to go to spring training, if they invite me to spring training in 1972. I'll do whatever they want. I've tried. I've done all the exercises. I'm into DMSO, I'm into Darvon, I'm into greenies, I'm into anything. Let's just see if I can hang on one more year just to put some money away, then I could go to business school or something. I'll be fine. I have a little nest egg. So I pitch nine innings. I certainly didn't anticipate anything. Janis, my wife, is in Phoenix. I had her fly out. I'm doing fine. Everything is going well. I throw one gopher ball in nine innings. I did great. And out of the blue they release me.

Are you thinking you're going back to Eugene?

I'm thinking I'm going back to Eugene.

205

Did you think you had a shot at the Phillies?

No, I didn't have a major league contract with Philadelphia. I had a minor league contract. I think it was for the same amount, $10,000. But here's what, down deep, I think happened. Dummy me, I asked questions. I hear that you can get called up to the big leagues three times and then after that you can't be called up, you have to go to another organization. Where does it say that? How does this work? Where does it say that? Why? I've been talking to a lot of the players. I've been talking to the Latin Americans. Where is it? I'd like to explain this to people. So inadvertently, naïvely, I'm making a mistake.

You're a troublemaker. You're not the guy who violates curfew every night but you're the guy who's making everyone aware of their rights. You're acting like the amateur lawyer in prison.

In my opinion, that's exactly what happened. And since I speak Spanish I got along very well with the Latin Americans. I honestly was just asking questions. People forget that the first players' strike was 1972. The first twelve games of that season were postponed, and I got released the last day of spring training of 1972. How tough is that? I called up everybody. I called up Chuck Tanner because I had pitched a shutout against Hawaii, where he was the manager, the year before. I called up everybody. I said, Screw it. The hell with it. And then it dawned on me. Well, you dumbshit. All I was trying to do was be honest and help somebody and all that came across was that I was a troublemaker. I believe that's exactly what happened.

You can't do anything if you're released the last day of spring training.

No. Absolutely not. It was just bullshit.

You would've been better off getting released in June.

Absolutely.

Did you miss baseball?

Yeah, I did, because I did well. I did well. All right, so it's gone. I tried. I tried for the next month and then my mother got ill. I could've gone down and played in Panama, in the league down there. Tommy Lasorda helped arrange that for me, but my mother got ill with cancer and she passed away during this period of time and I didn't do it. I didn't do it. When is it over? I just decided, we just decided, Okay, that's enough. That is enough. I was very bitter at the time. Tommy Lasorda tried to help me. He got me in contact with scouts and everything else, but at that point in time, could I have substitute taught for three or four months waiting for a phone call to be a fill-in on a Double-A or Triple-A team? No. You know what? There's more to life than that. I have the greatest admiration for people who just hung in there, so don't take this the wrong way. Some of these guys love the game so much but that's all they knew. And I knew there was more to it than just that. But I would have loved to have got beaten on my own terms. I mean, two innings in the big leagues? You start me but you couldn't have called me back up? Yeah, of course I was nervous, but did I have good stuff on those two days? Yes, I did. They only got singles. And then to release me the last day of spring training when I gave up one run? But that's life, and as I've told my boys, life is not fair. The scales of justice aren't balanced and Lady Liberty is blindfolded. That's the breaks. Those are the facts.

Is it fair to say that Dallas Green and Dave Bristol are your two least favorite managers?

I would say that's absolutely true.

Did you have a problem with Bristol besides him using an early hook?

Oh, he was just so totally foreign. At least to me he was. Everyone had to look the same. You couldn't have the high stirrups. You could only wear Adidas or Pumas if the logo on the shoe was blacked out. You're going to look like this. I mean, talk to people about this. He was so regimented. I just didn't think that highly of him, but a lot of people didn't. He had rules for everything. He had Ron Plaza as the DI leading calisthenic drills and Frankie Crosetti, notorious as one of the cheapest guys on the face of the earth, as third-base coach. It was quite a crew. It was quite an eye-opener. They did not overly impress me, but what the heck did I know?

Probably one of the biggest mistakes I made was listening too much to pitching coaches. Why didn't I listen to my arm? Why didn't I listen to my high school coach, who knew? My high school coach, Andy Anderson, was terrific. Just because you're a major league pitcher doesn't mean you know anything about how to teach and how to coach. I mean, I had Bob Lemon, Sal Maglie, Jim Bunning, Bob Tiefenauer, and I don't know who else as pitching coaches at one time or another. You know who helped me the most? Bunning. What the hell could Bunning say? He had the world's worst follow-through and everything else. Everybody else tried to get you to do it their way. It's all the release point and how you get there. Luis Tiant did pirouettes out there. It's where you release the ball and how your body, how your hips, are in relationship with how the ball is released. I don't care how you do it.

When I was coaching Little League, the older kids who were having trouble throwing strikes, I said, Imagine you're in center field, the winning run's on third base, the guy tags up, and you have to throw him out at home plate. What do you do? And instinctively they catch it with their shoulder forward, and then they open up and throw. They do that naturally. That's how I warm pitchers up. Throw long and then come in short. It's psychological. And then when you get on the mound, you're not pitching. You're throwing a guy out from the outfield. It's all in the mind. People make it much more confusing and detailed than it is. It's really kind of simple.

When you pitched your debut against Cleveland and got knocked out in the third, did you get to bat?

No, I never got to bat. I never got to bat.

Did you have a bat?

No, no. You just grabbed somebody's bat. After that, about a month later, I'm in the minors pitching against Phoenix—and this is absolutely true—and I think it's tied or something like that. The bases are loaded and I'm up. I'm looking down at the third-base coach and the count is 3–1 and I look down there and he doesn't give me the take sign. So I said, To hell with it, so I get into my Willie Horton stance and I swing as hard as I could and I hit a grand slam home run. That was Floyd Wicker's bat. Floyd Wicker was a cup-of-coffee player. I don't think he played a whole lot in the big leagues. Nice guy. Hung around for forever, and he never had a grand slam home run, in the minor leagues, anywhere. And I used his bat. He was so pissed at me. Here's a pitcher hitting a grand slam home run. They're all just dying laughing and everything else when I come back to the dugout. That was cool. That was cool.

Did you keep anything from your professional career? Did you come home with any souvenirs?

I got my hat, I got the blue dickie that I wore underneath the uniform shirt, and I got my travel bag, which is a Seattle bag, the minor league bag. You have to remember, they didn't have two nickels to rub together so you didn't have Brewers bags per se. They were Seattle Rainiers bags, so those are the three things that I have. People always say, Where's your uniform? You don't get the uniform. You don't get to keep any of that stuff. I think I have one of my gloves. I had a contract with Rawlings, which was two pair of shoes and one glove a year, and I still have one pair of unused shoes that are all leather—kangaroo, which is outlawed—so I have those in shoe trees.

Do you watch much baseball nowadays?

Very little. I watch the World Series and stuff like that. The strike zone is just absolutely absurd. Most of the announcers still screw up when they tell what the pitch is. My sons are twenty-seven and twenty-four and they grew up in Mesa, Arizona, literally five minutes from where the Cubs have spring training, and so they would come home from school and watch WGN. They grew up watching and listening to Harry Caray on WGN, then watching the Braves games with his son Skip. My older son just got married a few weeks ago and he lives here in the Dallas area and the other son lives in Boston. When we all get together we invariably reminisce about watching the Cubbies and soon it becomes a Harry Caray impersonation contest. We three end up rolling on the floor and my poor daughter-in-law, who's not a jock at all, is sitting there trying to figure out what the hell we're doing. But she'll learn.

Baseball is something I did, my sons did. They weren't exceptional athletes but they truly understand the game. It's the most beautiful game. They understood just from osmosis or whatever. Cal Ripken is slow. How can he do this? Because he knows what pitch is coming. He knows his pitcher has good control. The guy's a right-handed power hitter. He's going to throw him a curveball. Therefore, chances are, he's going to try to pull it and it's a double-play ball so he takes one step to the left. All these subtle nuances that typically you don't get on TV from the play-by-play or color-commentary telecasters. It's like learning soccer for the first time. Once you learn the game it's spatial, and there are a lot more spatial relationships and triangles in baseball. I mean, I'm appalled that nobody knows how to bunt. Nobody knows the basics. I was on a plane with Don Blasingame about five years ago. I was sitting behind him. I think he may still be with the Phillies organization. He was running the minor league instructional stuff, and he was saying the worst thing he faces right now is that all the old coaches are gone. He'll have a job

209

forever because he has to coach the coaches because nobody teaches them the fundamentals.

Because nobody ever won an arbitration hearing with the number of sacrifices they had the year before.

That's right. Hit the cutoff man. Just fundamentals. It's just an absolutely glorious game and what could've been could've been but it wasn't.

Are there any particular pitchers you like to watch?

Maddux. Maddux is just wonderful when he's on. He's just absolutely wonderful. He's just got pinpoint control. He's by far the best to watch. I mean, when I was up there in spring training I got to watch Jim Palmer. I think I charted a game while I was in the bigs where Sam McDowell had a one-hitter against us. I've had the opportunity to either see in person or be on the same field with a lot of great players. I pitched against Al Kaline. My favorite right-hand hitter was Al Kaline and my favorite left-hand hitter was Vada Pinson and I pitched against Vada Pinson, who should be in the Hall of Fame. Vada Pinson should've been Rookie of the Year, but they gave it to Willie McCovey with all those fewer at bats. He gets traded the year that finally the Reds make it. I think he's probably the fastest guy ever from home to first. Three years ago he had the most hits of anybody who's not in the Hall of Fame, nearly twenty-eight hundred. He was a gazelle. Beautiful to watch.

But everything is so damn slow with the commercials and everything. I'd rather go watch minor league games. I mean, I go back to Buffalo and they still draw a million people a year for Triple-A ball. The best thing that happened to Buffalo is they didn't get a major league team. I don't know if you've been to that stadium. That's a beautiful stadium.

I have no regrets. I had my chances. I was extremely fortunate to get paid to play. I occasionally still receive autograph requests from collectors out there. That amazes me. I send them a photo and a letter telling them of some of the players I was close to back then and then I stress how important an education is. If somebody takes the time and effort to send me an index card to autograph they deserve something even better in return.

Detroit at Baltimore
Friday, April 9, 1971

Detroit	ab	r	h	rbi	Baltimore	ab	r	h	rbi
McAuliffe, 2b	4	1	1	0	Buford, lf	3	1	0	0
Kaline, rf	3	1	1	0	Blair, cf	4	0	1	1
Northrup, 1b	4	0	2	2	F. Rob'son, rf	4	1	1	0
Horton, lf	4	0	0	0	Powell, 1b	4	2	2	1
Rodriguez, 3b	4	1	2	2	B. Rob'on, 3b	3	1	1	0
Freehan, c	4	0	1	0	Hendricks, c	2	0	1	0
Stanley, cf	4	1	1	0	Ret'mund, ph	0	0	0	0
Brinkman, ss	4	1	1	0	Etchebar'n, c	0	0	0	0
Niekro, p	3	0	1	1	Johnson, 2b	4	1	2	4
Foor, p	0	0	0	0	Belanger, ss	4	0	0	0
Tim'erman, p	0	0	0	0	Cuellar, p	2	0	0	0
Jones, ph	1	0	0	0	Shopay, p	1	0	0	0
					Hall, p	0	0	0	0
Totals	35	5	10	5	Totals	35	4	10	4

```
Detroit      2 2 0 0 0 1 0 0 0—5
Baltimore    0 0 1 1 0 3 0 1 x—6
```

Detroit	IP.	H.	R.	ER.	BB.	SO.
Niekro (L. 0-1)	7.1	8	6	6	3	4
Foor	0*	0	0	0	1	0
Timmerman	0.2	0	0	0	0	1
Baltimore	IP.	H.	R.	ER.	BB.	SO.
Cuellar	7	8	5	4	3	0
Hall (W. 1-0)	2	2	0	0	0	1

*Pitched to one batter in eighth.

E—Niekro, F. Robinson. DP—Detroit 1, Baltimore 1. LOB—Detroit 6, Baltimore 5. 2B—Powell. 3B—Blair. HR—Rodriguez (1), Powell (1), Johnson (1). U—Chylak, Denkinger, Frantz and Deegan. T—2:29. A—9,442.

JIM FOOR

Jim Foor's major league career spanned three seasons. He pitched one inning for the Detroit Tigers in 1971, another three and two thirds for the Tigers in 1972, and one and one third for the Pittsburgh Pirates in 1973 for a career total of six innings. In those six innings he walked eleven while striking out five. He gave up ten hits and finished with a major league career ERA of 12.00. He was interviewed November 2, 2001 at a Chinese restaurant in Houston, Texas.

Tell me where you were raised.

I'm from St Louis, Missouri, which, from what I hear from most people, is the best baseball town in the United States, or the world for that matter, and I feel very fortunate to have been there. Baseball's a part of daily life in St Louis for many people and it was for me.

Were you a Cardinal fan growing up?

Absolutely. Yes. It's hard not to be, but from the time I was seven I really got into baseball. That's really the first year I played. Since the time I was seven I wanted to be a major league baseball player and I had no distractions in between.

Did you have a favorite player?

Stan Musial is my all-time favorite player. In fact, probably the highlight of my sports career is that I had dinner with Stan Musial one night at an awards presentation. I sat right next to him and that's the absolute biggest thrill I've had in my sports life.

Did he live up to your expectations?

Yes, or exceeded them. He's still known as one of the greatest players on the field and off the field. He lived up to or exceeded that.

Did you get to go to many games as a kid?

Yes, I went to quite a few games. I was playing amateur baseball in the late fifties and early sixties and the 1960s are, I think, considered by many people to be one of the greatest eras in baseball. I was playing amateur baseball at that time, and being in St Louis then, playing baseball in that era, was wonderful. I got to see, routinely, Bob Gibson pitch, Sandy Koufax pitch, Juan Marichal pitch, Ferguson Jenkins pitch, Warren Spahn pitch. They were so frequent I didn't think of them as highlights then. That was just a normal, every-series occurrence, and I look around today and go, How many kids today can go to the ballpark in their hometown and see someone who's going to be in the Hall of Fame as often as I got to?

Did you play other sports as a kid?

Yes. I played football all the way through high school, I played basketball all the way through high school, and I played baseball all the way through high school. I played on the tennis team when I was in the ninth grade because the junior high didn't have a baseball team. I was cocaptain of my tennis team and I was undefeated. I also had a city ranking in tennis when I was fourteen.

Obviously you were a good all-around athlete. Was baseball your best sport or just the one you liked the most?

Actually both. I was a better baseball player than I was at any of those other sports and I liked it more also. When I was ten years old I was fortunate enough to be on a baseball team that won the Missouri-Illinois state championship. When I was twelve I was on the football team that won the Missouri state championship, so I played on some very good teams when I was growing up, and I played with some very good athletes.

Did you play other positions besides pitcher?

I played first base for a long time. In high school I didn't. I just pitched.

Were you the best pitcher on your team in high school?

I would say yes, probably.

What are you throwing in high school besides a fastball?

I threw a fastball and a curve and played with a change-up. I started throwing a curveball in games when I was ten years old. And had a very good one at that age.

Was it a drop-off-the-table curve or did it work side to side?

Both. It had a lot of movement left to right and also up and down. I had a very big curveball and I threw it very hard.

Do you throw overhand or three-quarters?

Probably three-quarters.

Do you have scouts looking at you in high school?

Yes. At any one of my games, starting sometime in my junior year, there were as many as fifty major league scouts at any game. There was another pitcher that pitched in the league that I was in and his name was Jerry Reuss. And he won more than two hundred games in the major leagues, so typically in a game where I pitched against him there were often many scouts.

Were you drafted out of high school?

Yes. I was drafted in 1967 by the Detroit Tigers in the first round. I was the fifteenth overall pick in the draft.

You know you're good, but was that better than you thought you were? Being the number-fifteen pick overall has got to be pretty heady stuff for a high school senior.

When I was a junior I was all-Metropolitan St Louis and as a senior I was an all-Metropolitan pitcher, so within the city I knew that I was one of the best. I don't remember there being an all-state team in Missouri at that time, and when you start looking at the country it's pretty hard for me or anybody else to judge how you compare with somebody in California or New York or wherever. I expected to be drafted just from conversations I'd had with scouts and farm directors.

Did you expect to go in the first round?

After a time I did. There was a *Sporting News* article that came out in early May of 1967 and there was a list of twelve players. Apparently there had been an informal poll of scouts in the country and I was one of the twelve that was listed. If there was any truth to that then I was figuring to be a fairly high draft choice, not knowing where, but high.

Did you have any hope that you might be drafted by the Cardinals or do you even care?

The Cardinals drafted tenth. They drafted Ted Simmons. If the Cardinals would've drafted me I probably would've thought that was great, but at that time I wanted to be a major league player and beggars can't be choosers, so it didn't make that much difference.

Detroit makes you their number-one selection so they have to be offering you a nice signing bonus. Do you even consider going to college?

The way I approached it—along with my parents—the first thing I wanted was to play major league baseball. I had scholarship offers from the University of Missouri, the University of Illinois, and several other places.

I'm sure so. Being a first-round draft pick, there probably aren't too many college programs that wouldn't have rolled out a red carpet for you.

Probably. Yes. The approach was to wait for the draft to see how high I was drafted, to see what they were offering, and to make a decision from there. So going to college was not ruled. In fact, at the first meeting with the Tigers after being drafted I told them that I was going to school regardless of whether I signed or not. It was never, Play baseball or go to school. My intention, at the time, and always has been, was to do both. Or try to do both.

How do you find out you've been drafted? Do they call you?

I got a call on the day of the draft. I can't remember what day of the week it was. I think it was June fifth. I got a call around ten o'clock in the morning, or ten-thirty. I'm guessing that the draft started at eight o'clock or eight-thirty that morning. And I was waiting at the phone. School was out so I got up early and waited by the phone.

Is this the best day of your life so far?

Probably.

How long is it before they come to the house to talk to you?

I think within a week.

And they make you an offer.

They make me an offer. I remember asking for more, but reaching an agreement within a relatively short period of time and that was it.

What did you do with the signing bonus?

Actually I gave it to my dad and he invested it for me.

That's pretty responsible behavior for a high school senior.

Oh yes.

No car? No stereo?

My dad's a smart guy and I knew that.

How long is it after you sign before you report?

Actually the Tigers flew me to Detroit where I attended a series with the Tigers at home. Of course, I wasn't on the field. I wasn't on the roster.

This is number-one-draft-pick treatment, though. Everyone else is on a plane to play rookie ball.

That's pretty much true. I get to go up and work out with the big league team, watch the games, meet the executives and the administrative people and the players and do a lot, so that was pretty nice.

What happens next?

I went to the Lakeland Tigers in Lakeland, Florida. The classification at the time was A baseball. By the old classifications it was probably C baseball. And I played there from the middle of June or later until the end of the season around September first.

How did you do?

I was disappointed. I finished 3–6. We finished in last place. I probably pitched much better than I thought I did because when you go from high school to a professional league—whatever professional level you go to—you're going to be in a higher classification of baseball and there's going to be an adjustment for most anybody.

Did they ask you to stay for instructional league?

I think that was discussed, but I went to school. I went to school in the fall at the University of Missouri in Columbia as I had told them I wanted to. In fact, I told them that I wanted to go four years straight but in the second semester of my freshman year I changed my mind.

Now, when you tell them that you're going to go to school instead of instructional league, what kind of reaction do you get?

At the time I don't remember there being any question about that or any reaction by the Tigers that would be construed as negative. Again, that's my memory. In hindsight I think that probably some people in any major league organization—some people or a few people or at least one person—might not like that.

Because if you're doing anything other than your job then you can't be fully focused on your job.

Those are your words, but I agree with the thought behind them.

So you go to school and then head to spring training?

No. I did not go to spring training. I told them before I signed and after I signed that I was going to school for four years so I went two semesters.

You're not labeled an attitude boy for that?

I don't know that. Again, I never heard anything from any of the Tiger personnel, be that executives, coaches, managers, players, anybody. I'm sure that there was probably at least one person in that organization that didn't think that was real good. But if there was, I don't know who that person was, and if there were many, I don't know who they all were.

So when do you report?

I go to school the second semester and then about the time spring train-ing starts I get kind of itchy to play baseball because I do like to play baseball, and, of course, it's tough to drop out of school at that point. And I didn't do that. I finished that semester, let's say at the beginning of June, and I reported to Lakeland, Florida, where I'd played the previous summer, where they had a mini-summer training for the people who have been in school and now are going to play baseball. The kids who have been drafted who are now going to play baseball. It gives the coaches and the organizational people a chance to work people out, see how they're performing, and assign them to the right level. So I went down there for that and I was down there for seven to ten days and I was sent to Toledo. Was there for one week. Never played and was sent down to Montgom-ery.

Is that confusing?

Yes, a little bit. That didn't make any sense to me.

Did you learn anything later in your career that cleared that up or was that just one of the quirks of baseball?

I think that was one of the quirks of baseball, and I think actually what had happened was that I performed very well against the people who were there, and because of my performance there were some unrealistic expectations. That's a very large jump, which I didn't necessarily know at the time. But I went to Triple-A and Frank Carswell was the manager of the Toledo team that year and I think—and this is speculation on my part—him being a hitter, he probably didn't have any great appreciation for very young pitchers, which I can understand. It's two months into the season and I have very little experience. It would probably be very difficult for any Triple-A manager to jump for joy unless I performed some kind of miracle in their face.

Who's your manager in Montgomery?

Stubby Overmire is the manager in Montgomery. He pitched for the Tigers and several other teams. Little left-handed pitcher who pitched in the forties and maybe a little bit in the fifties. I think he played eight to ten years.

Since he's a pitcher, is he able to help you?

Yes, yes. Stubby was a very quiet man and manager. He didn't say a whole lot. When he said something, you figured you probably better listen because it might be important, because he didn't say a whole lot. He wasn't one of these guys who would come out and go to the bullpen with you and work with you for thirty minutes or something, but through the course of a game, through the season, he'd come over and talk to you about certain things for brief periods. So yes, I think he was very helpful.

Do you finish the year in Montgomery?

I pitched there and finished the year there. And we had a very good ballclub. It was a very successful team. I think we finished second. We had lots of good players, a lot of great guys. Jim Leyland was the catcher on that team.

Could you tell back then that Leyland was a future manager or did he acquire those skills later?

No, he was already on his way. What he used to do—and again, he was only a player—he almost started functioning as an assistant coach. He played, and played most of the time, but he started functioning as a coach. I don't remember how old he was—he was probably around twenty-four—but I quickly saw that he probably wanted to manage.

Do you go back to school after the 1968 season?

I go back to school at the University of Missouri and this time I decide I'm going to go one semester. At the time, school started sometime in September and the fall semester usually finished in the middle of January, which worked perfectly for a baseball career. You could pretty much play until the end of the year unless you got into some long playoffs or got to the major leagues or something like that. School was out in the middle of January and so you got a month off before you went to spring training, so I started going to school one semester a year. And it worked great.

Whose roster are you on when you go to spring training in 1969?

In 1969 I'm on the big league roster. I go to spring training with the big league team and they are the World Champions.

Do they have to put you on the roster in order to protect you from the minor league draft, or is this a vote of confidence based on your performance the previous season?

I suspect it's both. And again, all of those draft rules change quite a bit—who you can draft from other teams and how many years they've played and what level they've played and all that kind of stuff. I probably didn't understand all the rules at that time and I know that I don't understand them now.

Did you think that you had a shot at making the opening-day roster when you went to spring training?

I think I probably did just because I was there. Realistically that wasn't right, but yeah, I probably had a little thought of, Wouldn't it be great if I did? Again, this was the 1968 World Champion Detroit Tigers.

Was it intimidating at all to be in spring training with those guys? Sharing a locker room with Denny McLain and Al Kaline and Mickey Lolich?

I don't remember finding it intimidating. I was just a little bit awestruck. Here's where we want to go. Here's where we've wanted to be since we were seven years old. This is pretty close to getting where we want to be.

You feel like a rookie inside. Are you treated like a rookie?

Oh yeah. Absolutely. I'm a rookie and I'm treated like one and I act like one and smell like one and look like one and I am one, both literally and

221

figuratively. But one of the best things about spring training was my locker was right next to Eddie Mathews. That's a thrill. I'm sitting right next to Eddie Mathews every day. And, of course, growing up in the fifties and sixties, he's one of my favorite players. He's one of the great ones.

How long into spring training is it before you're reassigned? Is it fairly early or is it a close call?

No, I'm probably cut in the first relatively big cut.

Assignment back to the minors is probably a foregone conclusion when you get there.

I'm sure that the Detroit Tiger management, had they come to the conclusion at the end of spring training that I would be on the big league team, I'm sure that all of them would've been surprised at that. Not just one of them but all of them.

Where are you assigned?

I got assigned to the minor league camp and got sent back to Montgomery.

Are you still throwing a fastball and curveball?

Yes. I'm still throwing the same stuff. That was probably the worst single year of my career. I hurt my arm in June or July. Elbow tendinitis.

Is this a sudden injury?

No, this is not a one-pitch deal. It happened over, probably, three starts.

Do you take any time off?

Maybe a little bit but not very much.

But you tell them that you're having problems. You don't keep it to yourself.

I think that I did and I think Stubby knew about it and I think we took the let's-watch-and-see approach. I surely don't blame Stubby.

Oh, I wasn't trying to assign blame. My reason for asking the question is sometimes if you're young you feel nearly invincible. You can either have the hope that the injury will go away, or there can also be the fear of telling someone that you're hurt because you're scared you might lose your place. A lot of people will try to pitch through injuries when they shouldn't.

And that really occurs to everybody who pitches or plays baseball or plays football—When am I hurt and when am I not hurt? Can I slide through or do I need a medical opinion? And usually we don't know for sure until our hindsight tells us.

Do you stay in Montgomery the whole year?

No, when I got hurt the Tigers sent me to Detroit to have their doctors look at me and the prognosis was I had tendinitis—which I did—and I had told them at the time, I said, Please look at my arm and tell me what we can do, but I want no knives and no needles. I was up there for a few days and I basically went home after that, to St Louis.

How early is this?

This is June or July. It's about midseason so I missed about half of that year.

Is this just killing you?

Yes, at times I could not lift my left arm up high enough to comb my hair without crying.

How are you emotionally? How does it feel to be at home in July?

Awful. Just awful. I'm not supposed to be at home in July unless I'm traded to the St Louis Cardinals. I'm not very happy. So I go back to the university, take another semester, and go to spring training. This is now 1970. And when I get to spring training, lo and behold, I still have tendinitis. It was as though it was the day after I had left to go up to see the doctors in Detroit. So I basically rested my arm for seven or eight months and nothing positive had happened. I was rested. At some point I was cut from the big league team. Obviously I couldn't pitch for the major league team. I couldn't pitch for any team.

At the end of spring training I stayed with Lakeland and I was put on a little program to recover. The program was I would pitch for the Lakeland Tigers one inning in a game every four days. I would pitch in a game against the Florida State League teams and we would start with one inning every four days. I didn't start the game but it was like I was on a four-day rotation. But I only pitched one inning. And I would go in and I would pitch an inning, and I would throw the ball as hard as I could and didn't throw any breaking balls. Fortunately for me, those first couple of times were ten- and twelve-pitch innings. Then I would come out of the game. My arm would be killing me and I would put ice on it and then the next three days I would loosen up, and then I would pitch another inning. So I did that for three or four outings and my arm started feeling better. Then I probably had another outing where I was scheduled to pitch two innings in the game. And so I did that and then there may've been one more game and after that I was fine. There was no pain. No anything. I'm throwing breaking balls, throwing fastballs, doing everything I want to do. And I got assigned to the Montgomery team.

So I went to the Montgomery team in probably the middle of May and got into the starting rotation and had a very good year. And the team was very successful. We had several good baseball players on that team, and again we finished second. Lerrin LaGrow was on that team, Bill Gilbreth was on that team, Bob Strampe was on that team, and we were all pitchers who were on the major league roster. Tim Hosley was our catcher. Paul Jata played on that team. Bob Molinaro played on that team. Ike Blessitt played on that team. Several people on that team had at least some time in the major leagues.

But at the end of the season you're still painless.

I'm as good as I've ever been. Absolutely painless. No tendinitis.

Do you go back to school?

I go back to school, take another semester. I majored in chemical engineering. That was my major the first day I went to school and I have a degree in chemical engineering. I went to school over a period of ten years to get a bachelor's degree and I went to the same university and had the same major. The reason I'm telling you that is when I talk to kids who are good high school players or good college players, I tell them, if you want to play baseball you can do that, and if you want to go to school you can do that. You can do both. You don't have to say, I'll do one or the other. You don't have to do that and I think that applies to many things in life. Not everything. Sometimes you may have to choose one or the other, but if you think about it and work it out you can have both of them if you do what it takes.

You go to spring training in 1971 and you're on the major league roster.

And I make the big league team. I had a very good spring, make the big league team. Ted Simmons hit a line drive and hit one of our starting pitchers, Joe Coleman, in the head, so he was out for a while, and looking back I probably took his place. He came back probably ten or twelve days into the season and I went to Triple-A.

Did you get to pitch in the ten or twelve days you were up?

Yes, I had a couple of appearances and didn't set the world on fire.

Do you start the season in Detroit or on the road?

On the road. The first major league game I pitched in was in Yankee Stadium.

You're sitting in the bullpen, they call your name, you loosen up and come in. What's the situation?

It was probably the sixth or seventh inning. I don't remember who started or any particulars about the game. The thing I remember the most is that it was an afternoon game in Yankee Stadium and it was 20 degrees. Now, most of my professional experience had been in Lakeland, Florida, and Montgomery, Alabama, and 20 degrees was somewhat of a shock to me. I had spent some time in Toledo and we'd had snow at games in Toledo, but that's what I remember most about the game.

Do you know who you faced?

For some reason I think it was Bobby Murcer but I don't specifically remember.

How are you when you're in the game? Are you conscious of when you're on the mound?

I'm probably extremely nervous. When you're an athlete and you perform in a game in front of whatever the low crowd can be—I've pitched in games where there were fifty-eight thousand people there—you can go through all sorts of things. You can be unconscious, you can be in the zone, you can be I-don't-know-what-I'm-doing. There are all those sorts of things. I'm nervous, and of course I wasn't in very long and this is the first time I've pitched as a major leaguer in a major league ballpark.

Coleman comes back and you get sent to Triple-A. Do you know he's coming back? Do you know that your name is on the ticket to Triple-A?

No. No, I don't know that. I don't know that.

Who tells you you're going to Triple-A?

Billy Martin, I think. I'm very unhappy that I'm not in the big leagues anymore.

Are you surprised?

Probably a little bit, but I shouldn't have been.

Do you get back with Detroit that year?

226

No. I make three appearances in the first two weeks of the season but don't make it back to the big leagues that year.

Are you surprised, disappointed, that you don't get brought back during September call-ups?

I'm very disappointed not to at least go up after they expand the roster. And I don't recall the circumstances. I would guess that somebody went up when they expanded the roster but I don't remember who and I don't remember thinking, Why did they call him up and not me? That may've happened, but I don't remember it happening.

Are you on the major league roster again in 1972?

In 1972 I'm on the roster again but I don't make the club. I got cut in the second cut out of three.

So it's not a close call but you're still disappointed.

Yes, I'm very disappointed and I go to Triple-A and have a pretty good year. I got called up to the big leagues on July fifteenth, so I was in the big leagues for roughly three months, the last half of the 1972 season.

You pitch in seven games for a total of three and two-thirds innings. You've got to be pitching almost exclusively to left-handed batters.

Right.

You pick up your one and only major league victory in 1972.

We were playing the California Angels in Detroit and I remember Clyde Wright started for the Angels. I don't know who started for us. But we were down 10–2 in the sixth or seventh inning, and I came in to pitch and we scored nine runs to go ahead 11–10 and won the game.

Did you get the ball?

No.

That doesn't seem fair. It seems like you should get the ball for your first major league win. Did you ever get to bat?

No, I never did. Probably the closest I came to getting an at bat was that game. I had the batting helmet on, I went over to find a bat that I thought didn't belong to anybody, and Billy Martin told me to sit down. Actually Al Kaline pinch-hit for me with the bases loaded and two outs and he struck out.

You give up your one and only major league home run that year.

Jim Nettles. Graig Nettles's brother.

Do you remember where?

Tiger Stadium. First-pitch curveball. Pretty good pitch, too. It wasn't a bad pitch.

Tiger Stadium is not the friendliest ballpark to pitchers. Did it barely get out or did he kill it?

There wasn't any doubt about it, but I've hit balls in the stands up there, too.

Are you on the postseason roster that year?

No, I was not on the postseason roster.

Do you have hurt feelings? Are you surprised?

Unhappy. Of course, I was in seven games and pitched three innings in half a season. I felt like I hadn't played in three months so I went to the club and asked them if I could play winter ball. I had decided not to go back to school and they said okay, and I went to Puerto Rico.

Did you ever ask Billy Martin why you weren't being used more often?

No. I think at the time—and I think this was somewhat consistent with what he did over his managerial career—I think that he was much in favor of older, veteran players over younger players. There are other managers like that and there are other managers who are exactly the opposite. He was that way, in my opinion, so the guys that I grew up with in the organization, who were in Triple-A—at the brink, so to speak—maybe we all didn't get the best opportunity that one could get.

That's one of the downsides of playing for a winner.

Right. When you have a winning team you make less changes.

Did you stay around Detroit long enough to attend the League Championship Series?

No. I go to St Louis and get ready for winter ball. I probably went to winter ball during the playoffs. I went to winter ball in very early October.

Who do you play for in winter ball?

I play for the Mayaguez Indios on the west coast of Puerto Rico. We had a relatively poor team. I pitched, under the circumstances, pretty well, but my record was like 3–6 and nobody's ever happy with a 3–6 record, and it's hard to convince anybody that you pitched well with a 3–6 record. I pitched until almost the end of the year, and because the Pirates had traded for me, I was traded in winter ball to the Pirates' winter-ball team.

The Pirates trade for you and Norm McRae. How do you find out about that?

I got a phone call in my hotel room in Puerto Rico. I don't remember the person but it's probably a Pittsburgh official. I was very happy at the time. I thought it was a new opportunity for me.

Where's the Pirates' winter-ball team?

In Santiago, Dominican Republic. And I flew over New Year's Eve. And, of course, Clemente flew out that morning and had the plane crash. He took off from the San Juan Airport, the same place I had left.

That's got to be an absolutely awful time.

It's devastating. It's devastating for the players and the ballclub and the organization, obviously, when you have a Hall of Famer who dies. Anybody who gets killed. We already know that he's one of the greatest players ever, and of course we're not happy with anybody's loss of life, but obviously it's a big blow to the organization.

And you're there about twenty-four hours when the whole place goes into mourning.

Yes. I know I spent the night in Santo Domingo. In fact, they may've told me. I went over there the next day and they probably had that information already. In fact, I think that's the way it happened. I learned it from the guys in Santiago. Dave Ricketts was the manager. He was a coach with the Pirates at the time. So I really got that information from them.

Given the circumstances, do you do anything besides sit in your hotel room for the next several days? Do they continue playing ball?

Yes, we continue to play ball, but the schedule was a little bit different over there. In Puerto Rico we basically played six days a week and had Monday off, but over in the Dominican Republic they told me they had two regular-season games left and then the playoffs. And it seems like we had several off-days in between games. It turned out I was over there for three weeks and during that time we only played four games. To this day I don't quite understand that, but that's the way it was.

Where do you start the 1973 season?

I'm in the big league camp but I'm not on the roster. The major league players were on strike and didn't come to camp until about three weeks later than they normally do, so it was a different spring training, let's put it that way. It was a shortened spring training.

One thing, though, is I felt very welcome over there. I felt like I was a part of the team. Willie Stargell came over and introduced himself to me. He was the ultimate team leader. I can't imagine that there's been anybody that's been a better team leader than him. And he doesn't walk around with a shirt that says, I'm the leader, but he is the leader. He's Pops. Just an incredible man, both on the field and off the field. And if you talk to any other Pirates who played during that era, who played with him, they'll tell you the same thing. He was so dynamic he made you a part of the team, whether you had thrown a pitch yet or not. Or had an at bat. He made you a part of the team and he made you feel like a part of the team. I can tell you ten different stories of things he did for me personally. And not that he didn't do them for other people. He probably did them for other people. He was an incredible leader, a dynamic person, and obviously a great baseball player.

I enjoyed being on that team immediately. I had a good roommate. Richie Hebner was my roommate. We had a good time. I had played against a lot of them and knew a lot of them and made friends very quickly so it was a good experience. I enjoyed being with the Pirates the whole time I was there.

Where do you start the year?

I was cut. I was probably the last pitcher cut, and I went to Charleston, West Virginia. Triple-A in the International League. We won the International League championship in 1973 and I have a diamond ring from that team. The best game I ever pitched was with Charleston. I was in the rotation, and then I was taken out of the rotation and made a closer, a left-handed closer. And then near the end of the season a lot of guys got called up to the Pirates. Bruce Kison was on that team. Dave Parker was on that team, and Ed Ott and Art Howe and Frank Taveras. There were twenty guys on that team who went to the big leagues that year or the next year. So they had taken Bruce and a couple other pitchers and our manager was Joe Morgan, who managed the Red Sox for a couple of years. So he put me back in the rotation and I pitched a game against Richmond, which is the Braves team, and I pitched a one-to-nothing shutout. I gave up nine hits, I struck out none, and I walked none. I gave up one hit every inning, never one before one out, and my team turned at least four double plays. I got a lot of help. And it was probably over in an hour and forty minutes at the most. I probably threw eighty-five pitches.

And you get called up in September.

I get called up about the first week in September. Ramon Hernandez, who was the left-handed closer, had some injury and wasn't going to pitch anymore, so I was called up to take his place, basically. They needed a little more left-handed pitching.

You get into three games for a total of an inning and a third and you don't give up any runs. Are you used, like we talked about before, only against left-handers?

Right. They called me up—they called me at home—and I flew to New York. We were playing the Mets that night.

So you had already gone home from Charleston?

Right. I was in St Louis at the time they called me. Charleston had lost the playoffs so I had already been home for about a week. They called me up and I met them in New York and I remember Seaver pitched that night and pitched a great game and we were behind and so I came in and pitched, probably, the seventh inning. I pitched an inning that night and then we left for Montreal.

So you report to Pittsburgh's spring training in 1974 and you're on the forty-man roster.

Yes, I'm on the forty-man roster. I go to spring training and I get cut.

Early?

Earlier than I thought I would be cut. In most of the organizations I've been with there are usually three big cuts during spring training and I think mine was the second.

And then you're traded to the Royals for Wayne Simpson. Were you surprised by this trade at all?

Yes and no. It seems like when you're traded you ask yourself, Did the other club want me, or did my club want to get rid of me? And you may not know that answer.

So you go over to Kansas City's complex and are immediately assigned to their Triple-A ballclub.

231

Yes. I'm not on the roster and I go to their Triple-A camp and go from there.

And where is their Triple-A team?

In Omaha. Omaha, Nebraska.

And you play all of 1974 in Omaha?

I played the whole year in Omaha. We had a relatively unsuccessful team. And it was a fairly young team. In fact, normally when I played I was the youngest guy on the team or one of the youngest guys on the team, and when I got on this Triple-A team I felt like a veteran.

Is this telling you anything or is it just odd and you notice it?

No, I think it's just that I notice it. Of course, with a lot of hindsight, that's about the way it works out. I'm twenty-five, and if you're twenty-five and in Triple-A you shouldn't expect to be the youngest player on the team.

On the other hand, it's better than being twenty-five and in Double-A.

Yes. Your chances of being the oldest player there are pretty good.

Do you ever see another major league roster in the regular season?

No, I do not get back to the big leagues.

How long do you play before you decide that's enough? Do you get to decide or does an injury decide for you? What are the circumstances of your departure from professional baseball?

Well, with the Royals, or with Omaha, I probably had my best personal season ever, and one thing you find out is even if you personally have a good year but you're on a bad team, it's still not much fun. Because previously, the year before, when I was with Charleston, I probably had an average season—in fact, below average for me—and had more fun because we won eighty-eight games out of 141. We were hammering everybody and it was a whole lot of fun. Of course, we had a very good team.

Are you surprised when Kansas City doesn't call you up at the end of the year?

Yeah, maybe a little bit, yeah. I was surprised because I had a good year and I didn't think they had much left-handed pitching at the time. I think they had two left-handers, Splittorff and Mingori, and Splittorff was starting. And I had a pretty good year in Triple-A. And they weren't the pennant winners so I looked at it like they didn't have anything to lose. But they didn't call me up.

How long do you last with the Royals organization?

Well, I asked to be traded that year.

How do you ask to be traded? Who do you ask? The farm director?

The farm director. They send you a contract and I call them and say that I'm not going to play for this amount of money, so basically I just forced the trade.

And if you say you forced them to trade you I assume that means the trade actually happened.

The Royals traded me to the Cardinals, so I played in Tulsa in 1975. Ken Boyer was the manager. We had a real good team with a lot of good players. John Denny was there. Keith Hernandez was there. The team had a good year and I had a good year, but I left early in order to go back to school.

Now do you go back or is that it?

I went to school the whole year. I'd made up my mind that I was going to go back to school full-time. The Cardinals sent me a contract in the spring and I called them and told them that I was going to school and couldn't report until May the twentieth or twenty-fifth or something and they released me.

But you were expecting them to do that. You weren't surprised that they released you.

I wasn't surprised they did that. I didn't know what they were going to do. I wasn't surprised at that. So I got out of school that semester and I had one more year of school left so I thought, Well, I need a summer job. What can I do for a summer job? Why don't I play professional baseball? So I called the Cubs because they tried to trade for me the year before. I called the farm director, and he said, Well, no. We won't sign you but you might call the farm director of the Oakland A's, so I called them and they said, Come on out to Tucson and try out. So sometime at the end of May—the day after I got out of school—I got on a plane and went to Tucson and I tried out for the team and I signed with the Tucson Toros.

It's kind of amazing that you can show up at the end of May for a tryout and get a Triple-A contract.

Well, it depends on what the need is. They thought I could help them. So I went to Tucson and we had a relatively unsuccessful team. We had a relatively young team and the Pacific Coast League is a much different league. It's a hitter's league, like it's always been. And I found that out. Everybody hits .300. If you hit .300 then you're pretty average in that league. But one of the benefits of going out there was I got to go to Hawaii. I'd never been to Hawaii so that was nice to do. Then we came back from Hawaii and we went to Sacramento. And I don't know if they have Triple-A baseball there anymore but the left-field fence was two hundred feet from home plate. I think there were two guys on Sacramento's team that hit fifty home runs that year. Two hundred feet is like a Little League field. I like to talk about Sacramento because it's a whole new baseball experience. The left fielder throws people out at first base on ground balls. I pitched very well there. We had a three-game series there and I pitched four innings and gave up two home runs, which was awesome. My target there was the ankles. Not the knees but the ankles. I basically threw the ball at home plate.

Now do you leave Tucson on August fifteenth like you did the year before?

Yes, I do. Actually I retire. I announce my retirement. There wasn't much of a media hoopla.

Again, is this a phone call to the farm director?

Yes, this is a phone call to the farm director saying I'm going back to school and I'm leaving about the fifteenth. I'm retiring and thank you for letting me play.

Do you have thoughts about the summer job the next year? I know you're finished with school then but how much do you miss it that first year?

Well, I've always considered myself very fortunate that I probably had withdrawal for two different days and I know that there are other people that have much worse withdrawals than that. Part of that was I had prepared myself a little bit for it—mentally and financially—after the season in Tulsa. So I knew I was going to get to the end, unless something happened.

Actually I got very close to getting to the big leagues with Tucson. You'll probably remember, that was 1976 and that was the year that Charlie Finley tried to trade away all his superstars. He basically tried to unload that whole team. But the commissioner nullified the trades and Finley wouldn't let them play. So we, the Tucson Toros, were in Salt Lake City and the manager got a call after the game and told us, all of us, the team, that we were going to Oakland in the morning. And we were going to be the Oakland A's. We're going to do it Charlie's way. So we packed our bags and we got up at five in the morning and we got in the hotel lobby and we had our bags in our hands and the manager got another call and said forget it. It was a Sunday and there was a scheduled game in Oakland at one o'clock, so we were six hours away from being in the big leagues.

That's almost got to be heartbreaking for the kids who had never been there before.

Probably.

If that had happened, under those circumstances—and I'm not saying you didn't deserve to go—but if it had happened under those circumstances that year, would it have been harder to retire that August?

Oh yeah. I'm sure it would've been. If I could've gone up and actually played—of course I would've evaluated what I'd done—but I probably would've reconsidered things.

It's seems like it would be a lot easier to walk away from Triple-A than it would be the majors. But still, Triple-A is close. It's not like anybody's telling you you can't play.

Nobody told me I couldn't play. And I'm not that far away. But the basic reason that I retired was that I didn't feel like I was going to get another shot at the big leagues, or to make a big league team.

Within the year you'll have your college degree so you had somewhere else to go, which also makes it a little bit easier.

Yeah, I interviewed for engineering jobs. Got a job in Houston so I came down to Houston. Again, had I gotten back to the big leagues that year or the year before I would guess my decision would be totally different. But the basic reason I stopped playing was I got a little tired of the lifestyle, the Triple-A buses and the travel. The number-one reason behind my decision to retire was I didn't think that I was going to get the opportunity to get back to the big leagues. And had I had that opportunity, or thought I had that opportunity, I probably would've made a different decision. In fact, I know I would have.

Do you watch much baseball now?

I probably watched more of the World Series this year than I ever have, or at least in a long time. Now I'm kind of a casual fan of all sports. I pay attention to everything, but not a whole lot of attention to any one sport. I follow the leaders in baseball. I probably look at those every day. I want to know who's got the best batting average and who has the most home runs and RBIs and who has the most wins. I do that as opposed to maybe following a particular team.

Is the game the same? Do you recognize the game when you see it on television? Is it the game that you played, or does it seem different?

I tell you what, now that I'm fifty-two, sometimes when I look at a major league baseball game I think, You know, I did that, but it's been so long ago that you kind of say, Did you?

How important is that Topps baseball card?

Well, since I only have the one it's kind of neat. I can go to the card show and ask them if they have the 1972 Topps card number 257 and they go, Who's on that? and I say, I am.

Cincinnati at Atlanta
Saturday, April 13, 1974

Cincinnati	ab	r	h	rbi	Atlanta	ab	r	h	rbi
Rose, lf	5	0	1	0	Garr, lf	5	0	3	4
Morgan, 2b	3	0	1	0	Office, cf	5	0	1	0
Driessen, 3b	5	0	0	0	Evans, 3b	4	0	0	0
T. Perez, 1b	4	0	1	0	Baker, rf	5	1	2	0
Bench, c	3	1	1	0	Lum, 1b	5	2	2	1
Rett'mund, cf	2	1	1	0	Johnson, 2b	1	3	1	3
Concep'n, ss	4	1	1	3	Foster, 2b	1	0	0	0
Griffey, rf	4	0	1	0	Oates, c	3	1	1	0
Billingham, p	1	0	0	0	M. Perez, ss	4	3	3	2
Hall, p	0	0	0	0	Morton, p	3	0	0	0
Kosco, ph	1	0	1	0	Aker, p	0	0	0	0
Osburn, p	0	0	0	0					
Crowley, ph	1	0	0	0	Totals	36	10	13	10
McQueen, p	0	0	0	0					
Geronimo, ph	1	0	0	0					
Totals	34	3	8	3					

Cincinnati	0	0	0	0	0	0	0	3	0—3
Atlanta	0	3	4	0	3	0	0	0	x—10

Cincinnati	IP.	H.	R.	ER.	BB.	SO.
Billingham (L. 1-1)	2	7	6	6	2	1
Hall	2	1	1	1	0	2
Osburn.................	2	4	3	3	1	0
McQueen....................	2	1	0	0	1	1
Atlanta	IP.	H.	R.	ER.	BB.	SO.
Morton (W. 1-1)	8	8	3	3	4	2
Aker	1	0	0	0	1	1

E—M. Perez (1). 2B—Office (1, off Billingham), Garr (2, off Billingham). 3B—Garr (1, off Osburn). HR—Concepcion (2, off Morton), Johnson (2, off Billingham), M. Perez (1, off Hall), Lum (2, off Osburn). SH—Morton (1, off Billingham). SB—Morgan (3, 2B off Aker/Oates). CS—Morgan (2, 2B by Morton/Oates). U—Jerry Dale, Chris Pelekoudas, Paul Pryor, Bob Engel. T—2:29. A—11,238.

PAT OSBURN

Pat Osburn pitched six games in the National League
as a member of the Cincinnati Reds in 1974, and six
games in the American League as a member of the Milwaukee Brewers in 1975. He yielded thirty hits in his
twenty and two-thirds major league innings, striking out
five and walking thirteen. He finished with a record of
0–1 and a career ERA of 6.53. He was interviewed February 2, 2002 at his home in Bradenton, Florida.

Tell me where you were raised and when you first started playing baseball.

Well, I was born in Murray, Kentucky, and we moved to Florida when I
was eight years old. I grew up playing in a place in Kentucky that actually had a league before Little League. It was called Kourey League, after
a guy named George Kourey, and as I understand it, it was in western
Kentucky and Tennessee and maybe parts of Indiana and Illinois. I remember we would always play an all-star game. My brother is three

years older than me so he went through this first, so I was already familiar with this all-star game in Anna, Illinois. It was a little town, I guess, close to the size of Paducah, where I was living. And they would come across the Ohio River, and they would always play these all-star games. There were like four or five divisions of kids when you played Kourey League. I started when I was six, so probably it was six, seven, eight, and nine, and from there you would probably go into Little League. But by that time we had moved to Clearwater, which is where I grew up, and I played junior high and high school baseball all the way through.

Were you a pitcher from the first day you stepped on the Kourey League field?

Pretty much. I mean, I played other positions, too, but I was pretty much a pitcher.

Are you a pitcher because you've got a good arm, or are you a pitcher because you're left-handed and it's either pitch or play first?

I think probably I'd thrown so much with my brother, and at that age they're looking for a kid that can throw strikes. And I could get the ball over pretty consistently. Initially I think that was probably it, and then it just so happened that I developed and had a pretty strong arm.

Were your parents athletes?

Mother wasn't. I mean, she looked like she could've been an athlete but she never played anything more than high school. She grew up in a real rural community. They didn't have any Little League or anything. We still go back to the little town where she grew up to visit her grave, and there's maybe eight hundred people in the town.

My father grew up in a town called Hazel that was just over the border from Tennessee, and he played sandlot baseball. They would go to Murray, Kentucky, which was maybe seven or eight miles away, and he said they used to watch teams that would come through barnstorming. There was a field there because of Murray State University, and they'd get the best local players and they would play an exhibition game. I don't think he ever was good enough to be picked as one of those guys, but he played on these little pickup teams, Sunday afternoon-type things. So that was his interest. And he was a big St Louis Cardinals fan. I can still remember listening to Harry Caray.

If your dad's a Cardinal fan, are you a Cardinal fan?

Oh yeah. I grew up in the sixties with Boyer and White and Groat and, of course, Bob Gibson, and, a little bit later, Curt Flood. I can remember all those guys because we used to make a trek every two or three years. From Paducah to St Louis was maybe a three- or four-hour drive. We'd stay at the Chase Hotel and Sportsman's Park was maybe ten or fifteen minutes away. We'd get there for a Friday-night game, see a Saturday game, and see a doubleheader on Sunday.

I remember this guy named Bob Hazle that played for Milwaukee. They called him Hurricane Hazle. He had this unbelievable hot streak for like eighty games during the summer of, I think, 1957. That was one of the times we were in St Louis and we were watching Milwaukee. And Sportsman's Park is about 300, maybe 310, to right field, with a high screen, maybe twenty-five or thirty feet high. I bet you he hit six balls off of that screen for doubles in just those four games. And I remember my dad making such a big deal about it. He said, I can't believe they can't get this guy out. It was upsetting him, and I think the Cardinals only won one game out of the four.

But yeah, I grew up a Cardinal fan. Stan Musial was probably my dad's favorite, and probably mine, too, to a degree. But I just liked the Cardinals.

It sounds like baseball's important in your family if that's how you spend your vacations.

Yeah. But when we moved to Florida it became sort of blurred what team I was pulling for because Atlanta was the closest team. The only ballgames I could listen to was Milo Hamilton and the Braves. I followed the Braves even though I wanted the Cardinals to win. I followed the Braves because that was the team I could hear.

When you're in high school, are you only a pitcher?

No, I played first base when I didn't pitch. We had a good program, a good coach there. His name was Doug Mason. He was on the Clearwater Bombers, a fast-pitch softball team, and he had played at the University of Florida on a scholarship so he knew baseball. We probably got taught a lot more fundamentals than other high schools. At other schools the coaches are like the jv football coach or somebody who just brings out the bats and balls, so I think that's why we always had a better, fundamentally sound team. We were probably no more talented than other teams, but we just did the little things better. We always had a good team.

Did you play other sports?

Yeah, I played football in high school. I played basketball in high school.

Did you like baseball the best, or were you best at baseball?

Up until my senior year in football I was being scouted and written about in the papers, and I got scholarship offers from Florida and FSU.

Were you a quarterback?

Yeah, quarterback, but the year before I had seen a guy that played at Sarasota High School. Our team, at the time, was 7–0. Their team was 7–0, and their quarterback was Guy McFeeney, who went on to the University of Florida. At the time, he was the best high school quarterback I had ever seen. I thought, This guy is phenomenal. The next year he signed at the University of Florida and they immediately made him a wide receiver. And I thought to myself, If that guy can't make it as a quarterback, I know what's going to happen if I get there. I'm going to be made a defensive back or a wide receiver or something like that. And, you know, I didn't want to do that. I felt, If I can't play quarterback then I would rather direct my ability towards baseball.

I hurt my knee in football about halfway through my senior year, and had cortisone shots and basically taped it up real tight. It wasn't bad enough to have an operation, they said. And I sort of lost some of my desire then, because when you're not healthy but you're still playing you don't feel like you're on solid ground. Then later on, actually, I ended up tearing the knee the rest of the way when I was a junior at Florida State playing baseball, and I had it operated on then.

Is there a noticeable drop-off in the recruiting process in football when you have the knee injury? Are Florida and Florida State still calling you?

Yeah, Florida and Florida State were still there. They just said, We've been told it's a meniscus, which is a cartilage. It's not anything to do with ligaments or anything, and we'll get our physician to do the operation and you'll be fine. So neither one of them felt like it was a big deal.

Did it heal? This has got to affect you during baseball season.

After it tore the rest of the way, they said it was already partially torn. It didn't bother me pitching so much but I was a left-handed hitter and when I would stride and swing, when I would twist sometimes—and this happened four or five times—my knee would feel like it would lock. Then I would massage it and try to stretch it out. What the cartilage was doing was getting in a position where I couldn't straighten my knee out. Then, if I was pitching, I would have to come out. If I was playing first base, I could kind of go three-quarters speed and still be okay. It'd be sore the next day and then the next day less sore and after a couple of days it'd be fine again.

Do you get as much attention from colleges for your baseball skills as you did for your football?

Less. Believe it or not, the guy at St Pete Junior College, which had a terrible baseball program, said, Well, I can give you your tuition, books, and you can eat your noon meal at the snack bar. But that was my only offer so I thought, Well, I guess I'll go to St Pete Junior College. Then my brother met this guy, Tony Lovecchio, at Rollins, and Tony had seen me as a junior and he remembered me, and then when he met my brother he said, Oh, that's your brother? I remember him. He was really good. And Tony said something to Joe Justice, the coach at Rollins, and they sent a scout over to watch me pitch. And I must've done well that night because out of sort of nowhere they said, We'll give you a scholarship to Rollins.

243

I was probably six one and maybe 170 pounds, so physically I was a fast runner for football, but you could blow me over with a puff. But that next twelve months I grew to about 185 pounds, and I got a lot stronger throwing. We played the University of Florida. We played Miami. Michigan State came down for what they called baseball week, so we played some major schools, but by and large we played Florida Southern, University of Tampa, St Leo, Jacksonville, Stetson—teams like that—so I accumulated a good record. Then, at the end of that year, that was when the Vietnam crisis was and you were seeing people brought home in body bags on TV every night and I had a real feeling of, Hey, I love my country, but I don't want to go over there and end up a casualty. And at the end of my freshman year I had like a 1.85 GPA.

Well, I went to the Cape Cod League to play summer baseball. So I played and I had a good summer in the Cape League, and my mom called me and said, Hey, they just sent it over from Rollins. You've got a 1.85 GPA. Your scholarship will still be there, but if you don't bring your GPA up to a 2.0 after your first quarter, your scholarship will be taken away. Well, it scared me. It didn't scare me that they might take my scholarship away. It scared me because I might be out of school and classified 1A, or whatever the term was. Well, when I was at Rollins we played some junior-college teams for exhibition games. We had played Seminole Junior College and Valencia Junior College and Manatee Junior College and I pitched in two of those games and had done pretty well. I asked my mom, Will you call the guy at St Pete Junior College and the people at Manatee and see if they'll offer me a scholarship? Because I wouldn't have to sit out a year going from a four-year to a two-year. So she called and the guy down at Manatee said, Tell him to come on. I'll give him everything I can give him—housing, books, and tuition. So I came down here then and played. Like I said, my driving force was probably the fact that I was going to be okay from the military. So I played here and transferred from here to Florida State, and then played a year at Florida State and signed after my junior year at Florida State.

Is it correct to assume that since Rollins is catching on to you at the last minute, that there are no pro scouts around?

I was drafted out of high school, believe it or not, by St Louis. There were like 564 boys drafted that year and I was like 520 or something. I remember when the man came in I told him, I want $25,000 to sign, and he looked at me like, Are you kidding? Obviously we never got together. Like I said, I was a little bit of a late bloomer. Not that I wasn't a good player, but I looked, physically, sort of weak. I think people were saying, Yeah, he's a good player, but he doesn't have much power.

Since you're now at a junior college you're eligible to be drafted after your sophomore year. Were you?

Yes, the Seattle Pilots drafted me in the winter draft, and in the summer draft, the Chicago White Sox drafted me.

Did you come close to signing with either of them?

With the winter draft, the Pilots sent me a letter that said, We've drafted you. Nobody ever called me or anything. I never understood that but I was told that a lot of times that happens in the winter. That teams will draft and, based on who they were able to sign, if they didn't think they needed another left-handed pitcher, they'd go, Well, we drafted him but don't even contact him.

Then in the summer the White Sox drafted me and I had a great year at Manatee Junior College. We were one game away from going to the national championship. I actually got beat in that game. I was 11–0 and got beat one to nothing by a team from Georgia for my only loss of the year and we didn't get to go. I would say that we were twice the team they were but it was one of those things. We hit probably six or eight line drives right at people. We have an error and a sacrifice bunt and then like a fourteen-hopper between the shortstop and the second baseman. I can still close my eyes and see it. The shortstop started for it and so did the second baseman and then both of them sort of looked at it. The ball stopped on the outfield grass and the boy came home and we got beat.

I talked with a guy named Jack Sanford. I think he was used to pitch for the San Francisco Giants. He came out and talked to us and I sort of held to my same thing. By that time I knew there was some interest in me and I had just completed my sophomore year and now I felt like I had something to offer. What made me feel even more aggressive about that was I was named first-team junior college all-American, and I was also on an all-star team that went to the Pan American Games. Ron Fraser, who just retired at Miami, was the coach, and I was the only junior-college kid asked to play on that team. I was the number-one pitcher and the number-two pitcher on the team was Steve Rogers. Of course, I didn't know Steve Rogers from Adam then, but he was a kid from Tulsa, and everybody else was at Michigan State or Iowa or Arizona State or someplace like that. And heck, I was the number-one pitcher. I pitched the final game against Cuba. We got beat 2–1 in nine innings. I pitched eight and a third. I got the loss but pitched a good game. So I felt like, Hey, my stock's going up.

You're playing at another level and you're holding your own.

Yeah, so I felt good about that, especially because of the Cuba team. That was before they had a lot of defections. I mean, you had some defections from Cuba but basically everybody was saying, Hey, that was a Triple-A team that you were playing in Cuba, so I thought, I'm in good competition here. So I went to Florida State then, again had a good year, was named all-American at Florida State, ended up 13–2, went to the College World Series. We got beat in the final game, which I started, by Southern Cal. In that game, there was a man on first base, I laid a bunt down the third-base line, a sacrifice, and as I was going towards first base, the ball was between where the cut-out grass was and the chalk. I mean, it was right there. The third baseman came in, grabbed it, and threw. And you know how the ball will sail back. Well, as I'm lunging for first base, the first baseman's coming into me because the ball's sailing into the line. My foot comes down, he hits me, snaps my knee, the rest of that cartilage tears, and I'm out of the game. At that point we were winning one to nothing, but they ended up tying it and it went fifteen innings and we lose 2–1. Dave Kingman was one of their big players. Freddie Lynn was on that team as a freshman. Jim Barr was the winning pitcher for Southern Cal in that game. Brent Strom was on that team. They were pretty loaded.

Who did Florida State have?

The only guy to really make it big was a guy named John Grubb. Mac Scarce, who's probably my best friend from college, got maybe three years in the big leagues as a left-handed reliever. But that was about it. A guy named Gene Amman was a fantastic college pitcher. I didn't throw that hard but Gene threw even less hard than I did. His best fastball was probably eighty-five.

I'm assuming that you were the number-one starter at Florida State if you make the all-American team.

Actually, Gene had a better year than I did. I was 13–2. I had like a 0.82 earned run average. He's 15–0 with like a 0.68 earned run average. That was before aluminum bats, I will point that out. But he was fantastic. Gene won two games in the College World Series without a loss. I won one and then that second game I think I would've won but never had a chance to. That was my second start. We were told that Gene had been voted Most Valuable Player of the College World Series, and that had been the first time ever that the MVP wasn't from the winning team. And believe it or not, Gene didn't make all-American that year.

What are you throwing? You're talking about you didn't have very hard stuff.

Well, I didn't throw real hard. I wouldn't think of myself as a fastball-slider pitcher. I had a pretty good moving fastball away from right-handers. It would run away and sink. And then I would throw a four-seam fastball if I ever wanted to try to come in or up on anybody, so the ball wouldn't tail back over the middle of the plate. Just an assortment. I had a pretty good change-up. I had a pretty good curveball.

But you're a pitcher rather than a thrower even though you're still relatively young.

I would think of myself throwing more of an assortment of pitches than most people who were the college select guys. Like Burt Hooton. Burt

Hooton was in that tournament and he just had two pitches. Man, could he throw hard. They beat us 5–2 to put us in the losers' bracket, and then we came back out of that to beat them, but he pitched against us and people were coming back to the dugout saying, I can't see it. I can't see it.

Do you have to have the assortment of pitches because you don't have a ninety-five-mile-an-hour fastball, or did you have good coaching earlier than most people?

Probably a mixture. I think pitching is on-the-job training, because every day you go out there you may have a little different stuff. And of course it depends on the level of competition. If we were playing Rice University, which didn't have a very good program, you knew they only had two or three guys in their lineup that could hit your fastball. You probably didn't throw a lot of breaking balls or off-speed balls to the six, seven, eight, and nine hitters. You were doing them a favor.

The Reds draft you after your junior year. Do you even consider going back for your senior year? You lose your leverage if you do.

Yeah, but we had had so much success at Florida State. I liked it. I was doing, for me, pretty well in college. I didn't join a fraternity. I just had baseball. I was pretty focused as a junior in college and had pretty good grades. I had done well enough that I felt good about getting my degree. And that was a direction I wanted to continue, regardless of baseball. So when the Reds drafted me, I talked to a gentleman named George Zuraw. I remember him coming out to the field and scouting me as a junior when he was with Pittsburgh. But he came to the house and we talked money and I felt like I was in the driver's seat. I was goofy when I asked for it, but I think I asked for $100,000.

How high did they draft you?

Well, I was number one for the Reds, but in the secondary phase. That was for kids who had been drafted before but had not signed. That was a much smaller pool of kids.

When's the College World Series?

Mid-May.

So you've been home a couple of weeks. Have you had the knee surgery yet?

247

Yeah, and that was the thing. They wanted to have a wait and see. After you come back, we want you to work out your knee this summer. We have six months to sign you, and we'll see what happens. And I could understand that. So I came home to Clearwater, my parents' home there, and started doing pretty regimented, twice-a-day weight lifting. And it was the first time I had lifted weights for my whole body. It was the first time I'd ever seen a Nautilus machine. So I do the bench press, I do all of it. But mainly I did leg extensions. I guess I was there for about eight or ten weeks, and I was coming home every night thinking, Hey, my body is changing. I couldn't believe the difference. Then I started throwing a little bit and I had major strength in my knee, probably more strength than I'd ever had before, because back when I was in high school it was taboo for baseball players, especially pitchers, to lift weights. So I wished that I had lifted weights earlier because after that summer I threw again for George Zuraw and I don't know how much I had picked up, but I had picked up speed. I could tell I was stronger, and I think George could tell I was stronger. He didn't tell me that. I think he's thinking, I wonder why nobody's offered this kid any money before now. Then I signed with him. I didn't get the $100,000, obviously, but I got more than I'd been asking for out of high school and junior college so I felt like I got as good as I could ever expect.

When do you actually sign the contract with the Reds?

Probably in September.

There's nowhere for you to go this season.

No, actually, they send me to instructional league right here in Bradenton, out at McKechnie Field where the Pirates spring train.

So you go to instructional league without having played in their minor league system.

Right. And at that time instructional league was the best players from their A ball, Double-A, and even some Triple-A teams. Hal McRae, actually, was on the team over here in instructional league.

Did you do anything special with your bonus money?

I bought a Dodge Charger.

New?

Oh yeah.

Did you get to pick the color?

Yeah, it was like a metallic, greenish, dark green, sort of brownish green. You know, the whole dumb thing. I think it was like $4,600. Oh yeah, I bought that new car. I had to have that new car.

Are you living with your parents when you're in instructional league?

I was living with my parents in Clearwater and commuting every day, so it was about forty-five minutes each way. We only played about forty games. I end up 6–0, a 0.90 earned run average, and the Reds are competing in the World Series in 1970 and the next spring when they come out with the spring baseball edition of *Sports Illustrated,* they're writing about the Reds and they mention me. They're saying, The next Don Gullett, or something like that. If Pat Osburn can make the leap from instructional league. So again, my confidence is off the ceiling.

Well, you were a college all-American and now you're bigger and stronger than you were before.

249

Yeah.

But you're a nice kid and you're able to get your head through the door.

Yeah, but it was growing. I go to spring training then and they invited me to the major league camp. And even though I had a good spring in major league camp—granted, it was probably only ten or twelve innings, but I did pretty well, I thought—I got sent to Triple-A with Indianapolis. So I thought, Well, I'm starting at the Triple-A level. That's not too bad.

You said "even though," as if you were disappointed being sent to Triple-A. But that's a very high designation for a rookie. You're okay going to Indianapolis, aren't you?

I'm okay. I'm okay with it. But as the season starts in Indianapolis, and it's cold and you've got an old stadium and the locker room's crappy, I'm thinking, Hey, we had better stuff than this at Florida State. I don't see anything so hot about this.

Maybe you would have if you'd played single A or Double-A ball.

Yeah. Probably. But see, I was used to single A in the Florida State League, and that was all the spring training fields so that level was a lot better. So I was disappointed about that but I was not disappointed in the reception I got from the players in Triple-A. It was good in the fact that I didn't know this until later, but kids who came out of college and sort of jumped ahead of somebody who had come out of high school and played two or three years but was still in A or Double-A ball, when you jumped ahead of them, there was some jealousy there, and some envy, but I never had that. They were always nice to me and made me feel part of the team even though most of the guys that were in Triple-A had played maybe three, four, five years of professional ball, and a lot of them had played three or four years in the Reds organization, so they had that camaraderie already. Of course, sometimes familiarity is sort of bad, because there's also jealousies that grow up between those people. But for the most part, I had good teammates to play with. My confidence is still high but I'm seeing that, Hey, just about everybody can do what you can do.

How do you do that year? This is 1971, right?

Yeah, 1971. I had a good year again. I ended up only 8–8, however my earned run average was like 2.60. I came in second place in the league in earned run average to James Rodney Richard. Of course, he had like three times as many strikeouts as I did. But the catcher on the team, Bill Plummer, helped me quite a bit. He was good for anybody, but he was especially good for a young pitcher because he was a good thinker behind the plate.

Had he been at Triple-A before? Does he know the hitters? Is he helping you with pitch selection or is it broader than that?

He just overall helped me, and I think also he had a level of confidence, the way he carried himself, that you felt like, Hey, Plum's going to get it right behind the plate.

You talked about being accepted by the team. Do you remember what other left-handers are on the team in 1971?

A guy named Mel Behney. He was a Michigan Stater. He was a talker, man. His nickname on the Reds was Words. I think of him being a skinny Rodney Dangerfield. Not that he'd be doing one-liners, but he'd talk about something here and then jump over there. He was fun. Actually, I think Ross Grimsley is on the team. He starts on the team and he gets called up very shortly after the season starts, maybe after three or four starts. A guy named Greg Garrett who they had gotten from the Angels the year before is on that team.

Pedro Borbon's on the team. Jim Cosman. He had been up in the major leagues and come back down. He had hurt his arm. He was a good guy to have on the team. He was probably thirty years old then. There was good chemistry on the team, I thought. And the pitching staff made the team. Our hitting was so-so. We didn't have a lot of power. We had a good defensive team. Tony Muser played first base, a good glove guy. A guy named Jimmy Qualls, who had been in the big leagues before, played second base. Darrel Chaney played short, and a guy named Dick Kenworthy played some third base for us. He had been up and down. Plummer is the catcher. He had an arm that was comparable to Bench's.

Do you go back to instructional league after the season?

No, I don't, because they had told me I had probably pitched enough innings—I had pitched about 170 innings that season—and we think you need to take the winter off. Pedro had asked me if I would be interested in coming to the Dominican and playing with his team in Santo Domingo. He sort of scouted as he played, but the Reds sort of thought it would be best if I didn't go. And it's ironic, because I think that's what ended up hurting me. By not going. I went back to FSU and took classes that fall. And remember the summer before, I starting lifting weights? Well, I had a friendship with some of the people that were still there on the baseball team, of course, and got to know a lot of football players. Well, I got access to the football weight room. I get over there and I hurt my shoulder lifting weights. I was too scared to say anything to anybody. I'm doing military presses and I'm feeling really strong this particular day, I guess, and I was lifting and I could just tell something went wrong. I get back to my apartment and the guy next door to me is an FSU alum. He played baseball a year ahead of me and he's doing the same thing. Back to school in the fall. And I said, Mike, get your glove. I've got to throw. And sure enough, I go to throw and I'm like, Oh, God, what have I done? So, I just didn't do anything then. I never went back to the weight room after that. I told my mom and dad about it, and every couple of days now I'd say, Mike, let's throw a little bit. And it was getting gradually better. But I think I would've had a much better chance of staying in the big leagues if it hadn't been for weight lifting that one particular day.

251

Did you ever confess to the Reds?

I don't think I did. I don't think I ever told them.

There's no sense in telling them in 1974. That doesn't really do any good, so if you don't tell them within a month or two you probably never tell them.

Well, it's getting better, like I said. By the time spring training rolls around, I can throw with no pain.

You're throwing with the same motion and the pain is less each time you go out.

Correct. I go to spring training, though, and I can tell I don't have the same snap on the ball. And, like I said, I was never extremely fast to begin with. I bet you I dropped three or four miles an hour. I'm probably throwing in the low eighties. They said, Oh, it's just adhesions, because you haven't thrown since last year. You have to break those adhesions down.

This is a trainer or coach talking from watching you throw, right? You don't ever have a doctor look at it.

Right. None of that.

They're making educated guesses without knowing the whole story.

Yeah. Right. So we break camp. I was in the big league camp again, but after the second cut I'd thrown maybe in two situations and the first time it's like, I remember getting three outs, but they have to be the three hardest hit balls I've ever seen. But they all went at people. I think they could tell then, because we had some intrasquad games, too. I just wasn't getting people out, and the people I was getting out were hitting ropes right at people. So I go to Indianapolis, and believe it or not that year I would throw the ball as hard as I could, and there would be this dull ache in my shoulder. And again, I'm trying to do what they're telling me. You have to throw through these adhesions and break them down. I end up 8–8 again but my earned run average is like 4.50. I go to trying to quick-pitch people, trying to learn how to throw a spitball, trying to do anything to be able to get people out, because every time I would throw my fastball, if it didn't get hit, my arm was hurting when I got the ball back and I just thought, This is what they must mean when they talk about pitching hurt. Because every time I went out there I had pain. I've heard Gibson say that every time he pitched one year it hurt him. He wouldn't even throw in between starts, there was that much discomfort.

But you're not missing starts.

No, not missing any starts. The Reds, to their credit, are staying with me, saying, Hey, we know this kid's going to come back, we just don't know when. The whole year I had maybe four or five well-pitched games, just because I had great control that particular game, or maybe got a couple of double-play balls in crucial situations or something, but I'm not the pitcher I was the year before.

I go back again to Florida State in the off-season because, at that point, I didn't want to play winter ball. I thought, Man, get me away from baseball, so I went back to Florida State again. I go to spring training the next year and, Hey, my arm doesn't hurt. I didn't have the pop back, but there was no pain. And I just sort of picked up a little bit more savvy, maybe, on the mound. I knew more about what my ball was going to do, and just became, I think, a little better pitcher. I think I was 13–7 for the year, made the Triple-A all-star team, and thought, probably, at the end of the season I would get called up when they expanded the roster.

Do you have that thought either of the two previous years? Was Sparky actually increasing the roster in September? The Reds are in pennant races most of these years and a lot of managers don't want to fill out the clubhouse with players they're not going to use.

I felt like, at the end of that season, maybe I'm going to get called up, because I had a really good year. Milt Wilcox is gone. He got traded halfway through that season, to Cleveland, I believe. Ross Grimsley is already in the big leagues. There's only a few guys on that team that I thought it might be their time before me. But I think they took up Borbon, Darrel Chaney, and Bill Plummer, and that was it. And it was one of those things, probably like you said, Sparky's in a pennant drive, and probably going to a World Series, and he doesn't want some young rookie disrupting anything in the clubhouse. So that year was over, and I was glad it was over after 1972.

At the end of 1973, when I made the all-star team, I felt like, Hey, I'm a little better pitcher now, even though I could tell my arm wasn't right. I just couldn't throw the ball as hard. My breaking ball wasn't quite as sharp, but in spring training of 1974 I make the club out of spring training.

253

Was that the best day of your career?

It'd have to be close. I felt like I was on cloud nine, or cloud ten maybe. Sparky had called me in. It was one of those things where I knew it was down to the last two or three days before we were going to break camp. Rumors are floating around. This is going to happen. That's going to happen. I really didn't know if he was calling me in to tell me, Hey, I'm going to send you out to Triple-A, so when he said, Here's how we're going to use you, I was almost to the point of giddy it felt so good. So that was probably one of the highlights, really, when I think about it.

The first game I'm in was in Atlanta. The first pitch I throw, Mike Lum tears out a row of seats in right field. I mean, it's a rope. But I'm thinking, Why in the hell did Bench call that pitch? Bench was sitting right there on the inside corner, and that's right where that ball was going. I'm sure it wasn't right there at knee-high, but it was going to hit his glove. It may've been between the knees and the waist. And he turned on it and, like I said, he hit a rope that was out like that.

When you come into this game, is Cincinnati well behind?

Yeah, it's a mop-up.

So this is when they should be bringing you in.

Yeah. So that takes some of the nervousness away pretty fast, when your first pitch is hit like 360 on a rope, and I end up pitching two innings. Didn't allow another run, and felt pretty good about it.

Shortly after that we have a road trip to Pittsburgh. We'd played maybe fifteen or twenty games. And Tom Hall is on the team. He's not the short man, but he sort of comes in to get one or two men out from the left side. Tom Hall cuts his finger, had to have some stitches, so Sparky comes to me and says, Hey, we're going to use you in Tom's spot until he gets well. I don't see the mound again for like ten days. And it probably just didn't call for me to come in, but I thought, when he came to me and told me that, Hey, I'm going to see some action here, and it didn't work out like that.

The next time I pitch was at home against L.A. The way I remember it I come in with either the bases loaded or a couple of men on to face the left-hander. I think I end up walking him. The next guy up is Garvey and he hits one. It didn't leave quite as fast as Lum's, but it went much further. I think he hit it over the center-field backdrop. It had to be 440 or 450. A grand slam. But again, it's like a mop-up because they're beating us like 8–3. And I think the game ended up like 12–4 or something. It wasn't where the game was on the line because if it was, he probably would've never let me face Garvey. He would've brought in a right-hander, I'm sure.

So I've had two appearances. One's not bad. I only gave up the one run but it's a home run. And then the next time I'm in I give up a grand salami. I remember Rose came up to me after the game. From my standpoint, Rose was a great, great teammate. After that particular game he came by and said, Hey, nice pitching. Boom boom. And I knew that he meant it in a way like, Hey, you're part of the team. Just because you gave up a home run. And then he came back by later, to the cubicle I was in, and he says, Hey, forget about it. You've got to get them the next time you go out there.

My roommate was Clay Carroll. Another nice guy. Clay was like, Hey, don't worry about it. Everybody gives those up. So it was good to be a Red. The Reds had a feeling of team unity, and, Hey, it's going to take all twenty-five guys to win. Now, it wasn't like that with all twenty-five players, but that was the feeling I got from people like Perez and Rose. Not so much with Johnny Bench, although I had some interaction with him because of being the pitcher and catcher, of course. He was much more of an introvert than Pete. Pete was always out there. But I think everybody on that team was for everybody else on that team to do well. So that was a good thing.

I had a couple more appearances but my one sort of shining moment was in St Louis. It all goes back to St Louis. It's in Busch Stadium, not Sportsman's Park, of course, and Gibson is pitching. He gets his three thousandth strikeout that day with Geronimo. Clay Kirby starts, gets hit pretty hard. I think he's given up six runs in the first three and one-third innings. I come in and for the next three and two-thirds innings I either give up no hits or one hit, but no runs. I heard later that Joe Nuxhall said he wished he'd gotten me for the star-of-the-game show, or whatever they called it, but he didn't. Somebody else had hit a home run and I think it was Johnny. And Nuxhall was saying, This is the kind of pitcher I think he could be. He said, It reminds me of the kind of stuff that Claude Osteen has. And I thought, Well, Claude Osteen. He's sort of a soft-tossing left-hander. Picks on the corners. Changes speeds.

After that game, the next time I pitched was in L.A., and I made a pitch to Bill Russell, he hit a one-hopper back to me, and I felt something pull in my groin area. I threw him out at first base and then I thought, Wow, I've never felt that before. So I'm out there on the mound and I'm trying to stretch it out. It seems like I got the next guy out, but I come in in between innings and Larry Shepard, who was the pitching coach, asked me, What's the matter? Are you going to be able to go?

And I said, Yeah, I think I'm okay, and he said, Well, we're going to get somebody else in anyway. It was one of those games, again, that wasn't on the line. L.A. was beating us by three or four runs so it didn't really matter. And I was never put on the disabled list but I couldn't pitch. Every time I would try to throw and push off, I just couldn't do it. There was no strength there. I felt like it was going to pull again. And then they sent me out to Indianapolis. Well, years later, I know now what they did. They couldn't do it. If I would've gone to Marvin Miller then, he would've said, No, they can't send you down. You've got to be put on the disabled list. They can't send an injured player down to the minor leagues. Well, I didn't know that. So I got sent down and I was probably close to a month getting that thing rehabbed. I had some injections in there to try to heal it. I got sent down near the first of July, before July Fourth because I remember when I got to Indianapolis they had this big fireworks thing. I saw the fireworks there. I probably pitched August and September there.

And because you were hurt, you weren't even concerned about whether or not they would call you back up.

At that point I just wanted to get healed. And I had like five starts, and I ended up 2–3. I don't know what my earned run average was, but I was pitching well. I felt like I was pitching close to where I was way back in 1971.

Before the weight lifting.

Yeah, before the weight lifting. Maybe not with the same speed, but certainly with placement, knowing how to set hitters up. And I thought, Maybe there's a chance I'm going to get called back up. Well, at the time, the girl I was married to, and she was never a big proponent of me staying in baseball, she was like, You need to finish school. Let's get out. And I said, You know, if they don't call me up, I'm going to tell them they're going to have to trade me or call me up.

How long had you been married?

Two years. We had a child and I think she was just saying, Hey, you're making like $1,200 a month in the minor leagues for six months. That's not a whole lot of money.

But you're so close to the big leagues. You're Tom Hall cutting his finger away from the majors.

Oh, I agree. Yeah. But you know, I was stupid. I should've told her, You don't understand, but I was frustrated, too. There were a couple of guys up there in the big leagues that I thought I was better than, and I thought, Why don't they bring me back up? I'm healthy now. I'm throwing the ball well. But basically it was like, We don't need to move people around to bring you up because you can mop up better than this other guy can mop up. Looking back I see that probably the best-case scenario for me, ever, would've been fifth starter on a team. And with the Reds I was even lower than that, and they didn't have time to worry about it. Whoever we're going to let mop up doesn't really matter. You couldn't stay healthy so we're going to get somebody else that can stay healthy. But anyway, I go to them with like a week or ten days left in our season, and tell them, Hey, if you don't bring me up or trade me, I'm going to quit. Well, I put myself in a corner, but I quit.

Really?

Well, I drive home from Indianapolis with like a week to go and Indianapolis ends up playing Iowa in the playoffs. We were in first place.

You walk before the season's over.

I walk before the season's over.

Whoa. You've told me about your entire career in baseball and that's pretty much the first instance of rebellion that I've heard. Where does that come from?

I don't know. Her influence, I'm sure. Because I'd always been one to get along with people.

You're the younger brother.

Yeah. Yeah. So, I don't even tell my mom and dad. I show up and my dad just can't believe it. He's just like, You need to call them and tell them that you're coming back. And I said, No, I can't do that, Dad. I've made my bed here. I'm going to have to lay in it. They'll trade me or something. And sure enough, they trade me to Milwaukee that winter, and I'm happy because I'm thinking, I can pitch in Milwaukee.

So you're out of this self-created situation and you're traded to an organization where there's room.

Right. It's a second-division team, and their pitching staff is like average at best. I go to spring training and they're using me as a short man. I bet you I pitched twelve or fifteen outings in spring training with the Brewers. I'm pitching to one lefty or two lefties, and I give up one run in all of spring training. And Ed Sprague, who I knew from the Reds, he tells me, You're a lock. We don't have any left-handers in the bullpen except this guy Rick Austin. He says, You're a lock. We've got to have a lefty. I'm in Boston the day before opening day. We're there. We're going to play the next day. We still had twenty-six players. But Ed said, You're a lock. You're not going anywhere.

Well, there was supposed to be a two-for-one deal with Cleveland. Two of our guys were going to Cleveland for one of theirs. The trade doesn't happen. They have to send out one guy. I get told, later, it's either they send out their fifth or sixth outfielder or they send me out. We have eleven pitchers. They send me out. In hindsight, they made the right decision. The guy they kept was Gorman Thomas.

Anyway, I go to Sacramento, their Triple-A team, and we played in a converted football stadium. Locker rooms worse than you could've imagined. If the town hadn't have been so nice, I think everybody would've quit the team. It was terrible. But we used to love to go on the road, or I did anyway because I hated playing on that field. I think it was 268 to left field. They put up a high fence.

And you're a left-hander.

And I'm a left-hander so I don't like pitching there obviously.

Are you starting or relieving?

I'm doing both, some starting and some relieving. They had no real plan. I had a pretty good year, though. I'm either 8–8 or 7–9 and a pretty good earned run average for that stadium. I think I was in the mid fours. At the end of the year I think that I'm going to get called up, and I do get called up.

Who's the manager in Milwaukee?

Del Crandall. He had been the Triple-A manager at Evansville when I played at Indianapolis, so he had seen me pitch before and that was one of the things they told me when I got traded. Hey, Crandall had seen you pitch at Indianapolis and liked what he saw.

I get called up and it was funny. When I got called up to the Reds I was excited to go to the park every night. I was like pumped about playing baseball. A couple of years later when I get called up to the Brewers, and it's the final month of the season, the thrill is gone. I still wanted to do well when I got out there, but I'm not excited about getting to the park. It's starting to be a job. And I can't tell you what the difference was. It was just that feeling that I'm not excited about playing baseball like I used to be.

Does it have anything to do with playing on a second-division team? Or not having the physical capabilities that you used to?

Yeah, it might be. Yeah.

You do get to start a game.

I get one start, in New York, and it was a comedy of errors.

But it's Yankee Stadium.

No, because that was the year they had to play in Shea.

I'm so sorry.

Yeah.

It would've been really cool to have your one start come in Yankee Stadium.

Yeah, that would've been good.

Was that the one career loss?

Yeah, that was the loss. There was a fly ball to left field. Charlie Moore's playing left field. The field's wet or something. He slips down. I mean, it's a routine fly ball, he slips down, the ball drops in and the guy gets a single. If he'd been running he'd get a double easy, but he's loafing—but he's loafing because it's a routine fly ball. I jam Thurman Munson so bad that he hits a grounder between first and second. A guy named Bob Sheldon who was up from Triple-A was playing second base, and to this day I don't know what he was doing. He doesn't get over to get the ball and I swear it stopped like two feet onto the outfield grass. That's how slow it was going. Another play is a ball to George Scott at first base with men on first and second. Tom Bianco, another Triple-A call-up, is playing third base. I don't know what George is thinking but he throws to third base trying to get the force out. He throws it at Tom and Tom's six feet away from the base so now the bases are loaded. It was a comedy of errors but I sustained the loss for it.

When you start the year with Cincinnati and you're a reliever with this wide variety of pitches, how does Bench know everything you throw? Do you shake him off at all?

Oh yeah. You remember a guy named Bob Robertson with Pittsburgh? Big, burly guy. Hit a lot of home runs. This is in Riverfront. I think I had six major league strikeouts. He's one of them.

I had seen Robertson in a spring training game when the pitcher had him either 0–2 or 1–2, but he had thrown fastballs right by him. And I thought, this guy, he's got to be sitting on a fastball because he hasn't shown that he's done anything. The guy's got to be up for a fastball. Well, the pitcher throws a change-up, and I thought a good change-up. And Robertson hits it like 390 for a home run. And I'm thinking, What does he know that I don't know after this guy just throws two fastballs by him? He's got to be like, Hey, I got to catch up to this fastball.

Anyway, the situation sort of occurs again in Cincinnati. Not that I threw the fastball by him, but I'd gotten strikes with the fastball. And Bench calls for the change-up. I'm going, I remember spring training. I'm not going to throw that change-up. So he puts up curveball. Nope. No curve. Finally he comes back to the fastball like, Not the fastball. He'll kill it. And sure enough, I throw the fastball, and Robertson's looking for an off-speed pitch. Why? I don't know. And he takes one almost right down the middle. Strike three. And I'm thinking, Isn't that funny that this guy would be that kind of hitter, but I guess as you get to know people in the big leagues you get to know that they look for certain pitches. It doesn't matter if they have one strike or two strikes against them. I'm looking for that pitch and if you don't throw it to me, okay, I'll strike out and I'll get you next time. But I thought that was unusual. A big, strong guy like that you usually think of as a good fastball hitter.

Did you ever face a batter and catch yourself thinking about who he is?

That happened to me in spring training pitching to Al Kaline. I had his baseball card since I was eight years old. He'd been a big leaguer ever since he was like nineteen, so he's probably thirty-five or thirty-six, and I thought, Man, I've had this guy's baseball card on my spokes. You know, when you used to put them on with clothespins? But that was the only time I ever thought about it. I faced Hank Aaron in spring training and Reggie Jackson in spring training, but I just saw a batter up there and tried to hit my spot with the right pitch.

How do you get out of baseball? You finish the season with Milwaukee and it's not fun anymore.

I finish that season with Milwaukee and it's not fun anymore. I go back to school. The next spring training is shortened by about three weeks because of the potential strike. And in the two years prior to that I'd always gotten a contract that said, If you make the major league club, you'll make this. If you make the minor league club, you'll make this.

A split contract.

Yeah. During that winter I'd been traded to the Kansas City Royals. Well, I just got a contract that says, Here's what you're going to make in Omaha. I'm thinking, I'm in my seventh year. I'm still in Triple-A. That's seven years in Triple-A. I'm tired of it. I'm not going to. I'm going to finish school. I had one more quarter to graduate. C'est la vie. John Schuerholz was the minor league guy, at that time, with Kansas City. And I called him and I said, I think I'm going to retire. I'm going back to school. He said, Okay, call me if you change your mind, or something like that. So I went to school, finished May fifteenth, May sixteenth. And I called John a week before I'm graduating and I said, I changed my mind. I'd like to play for the summer. He says, I can't give you a job in Omaha now, but I've got an opening in Jacksonville. And I'm thinking, He doesn't know it but I'd rather be in Jacksonville. I'm closer to home. I'd been out in the American Association so many times I knew the bus schedules. So I was glad to be in Jacksonville. I went to Jacksonville, played that summer, did okay. Nothing special. But when I ended that year I knew it was out of my system. And so that was the last year I ever played.

Are you still married when you went to Jacksonville?

Yeah, I'm still married when I went to Jacksonville.

But you quit from lack of desire, not pressure from home.

No. I had my degree then, and I didn't have any more fantasies of winning twenty games and being in the Fall Classic or anything. I knew at that point that the best scenario I could hope for was to be the eighth, ninth, or tenth man on a pitching staff. And if you fought the fight when you were younger, you don't have as much to fight it with now. You need to get out and think about earning some money some other way.

Did you know what you were going to do other than not play ball the following year?

Not definitively. One of the Manatee Junior College supporters had known me and followed my career. He was a pretty good athlete in his own right when he was younger and he called me, because I had come back here because my wife's family was from here. He called and said, I'm going to start a little insurance agency. I can't pay you that much going in but I can pay you as much as you're probably making in the minor leagues every month and you'll have it for the whole year. And that sounded pretty good to me. He said, You'll be the king of nothing right now, but if you make it into something it'll be a pretty good ride. So we started in 1976 and I bought the agency from him fifteen years ago and it worked out good for me.

A pretty good ride?

262

A pretty good ride. I'm comfortable. I never looked back and regretted getting out when I did. I think I got out at a good time. My enthusiasm had maybe not bottomed, but it was down there where it didn't matter to me as much if I did bad. I still had the highs when I did good, but if I didn't do good it was like, Well, okay, let's go to a movie, or let's have a beer or whatever.

So when all the major leaguers hit Florida the following spring you don't have any withdrawal symptoms?

I probably did a little bit, because when you first get out you probably still think, Hey, if things would have been a little bit different, maybe this, maybe that. But now it's been twenty-something years and I can look and say, No, you probably achieved about what your talent would allow you to achieve, and it was time for you to move on. It was a lot of heartache, but that was just the game itself. The fun part was the camaraderie between the players and all the people you got to meet and all that goes on in the clubhouse and on the road and all that stuff. That was fun, and those memories are something that I treasure as much as, or more, than the actual performances.

Do you watch much baseball now?

I watch the playoffs and Series. But to turn on a ballgame and watch it for nine innings is boring to me. Now, I'll go out to spring training. I have tickets to the Pirates' spring training and I'll go out and watch. I'll take my lunch hour over there. Get a sandwich, watch three or four innings, and come back to the office. And that's my fix for baseball. I enjoy seeing that. I enjoy watching it. I see the kids with the Pirates. A couple of years ago there was this left-hander that I thought, That was Pat Osburn about twenty-five years ago. Pretty good stuff. Little short on the fastball, but I saw him for a couple of years in spring training. He had a little cup of coffee with the Pirates, and then I don't know what happened to him. He probably went back down to Triple-A and then he was probably like me. He was probably like, Hey, if I'm not going to make it I'm going to probably get out. But I sort of look at those guys and I know what they're going through and I know what they're feeling and everything, so that's my sort of connection. You know, the guy that steps up there and hits thirty-five home runs, or the guy that can throw ninety-five miles an hour, I don't have any connection with them.

Detroit at New York (AL)
Monday, September 4, 1978

FIRST GAME

Detroit	ab	r	h	rbi		New York	ab	r	h	rbi
LeFlore, lf	2	1	1	0		Rivers, cf	5	1	2	1
Whitaker, 2b	3	0	0	0		Randolph, 2b	4	1	0	0
Staub, dh	4	0	1	1		Munson, c	4	1	1	2
Thompson, 1b	4	0	0	0		Heath, c	0	0	0	0
Kemp, lf	3	0	0	0		Jackson, rf	3	0	0	0
Parrish, c	4	0	1	0		Johnson, ph	0	1	0	0
W'kenfuss, rf	3	0	0	0		Thoms'n, 2b	0	0	0	0
Rodriguez, 3b	3	0	1	0		Chambliss, 1b	4	1	2	3
Trammell, ss	3	0	1	0		Nettles, 3b	4	1	2	1
Wilcox, p	0	0	0	0		Piniella, lf	4	1	2	1
Burnside, p	0	0	0	0		Spencer, dh	3	0	2	0
Tobik, p	0	0	0	0		Sherrill, pr-dh	1	1	0	0
						Dent, ss	4	1	1	1
Totals	29	1	5	1		Guidry, p	0	0	0	0
						Totals	36	9	12	9

Detroit	0	0	0	0	0	1	0	0	0—1
New York	1	0	0	0	0	8	0	0	x—9

Detroit	IP.	H.	R.	ER.	BB.	SO.
Wilcox (L. 12-9)	6.1	8	5	5	0	8
Burnside...........	0.1	3	4	4	2	0
Tobik................	1.1	1	0	0	0	1
New York	IP.	H.	R.	ER.	BB.	SO.
Guidry (W. 20-2)	9	5	1	1	3	8

2B—LeFlore (22, off Guidry). 3B—Nettles (1, off Wilcox), Chambliss (3, off Burnside). HR—Rivers (11, off Wilcox). HBP—Kemp (1, by Guidry). CS—LeFlore (11, 2B by Guidry/Munson). U—George Maloney, Ted Hendry, Greg Kosc, Jerry Neudecker. T—2:19.

SHELDON BURNSIDE

Sheldon Burnside pitched in parts of three major league seasons. He made his debut for the Detroit Tigers in 1978 and threw for the Tigers again in 1979 before finishing with the Cincinnati Reds in 1980. He pitched a career total of thirty major league innings over nineteen games and in that span yielded thirty-eight hits while striking out eighteen and walking eleven. He finished with a record of 2–1 and an ERA of 6.00. He was interviewed October 17, 2001 at his home in Montgomery, Alabama.

Where were you raised and when did you first start playing baseball?

I was born in South Bend, Indiana, but I started playing baseball in Cleveland, Ohio. My parents lived there. My dad had a job setting up warehouses for Premier Company, and when they released him in 1963 he had a clause in his contract that said he could not work anywhere in the United States with a competitor, so at the age of ten I moved to Toronto, Canada, and continued to play baseball up there, just playing sandlot ball for twenty, twenty-five games a year. In Canada, everybody else was playing hockey. The Blue Jays had not gotten there yet.

In Canada they didn't even have high school baseball but I was seen by a bird-dog scout and that's how I was discovered. I was a left-handed pitcher and at the time they asked me to a tryout camp. What I found out later is those camps are set up, primarily, to look at two or three players. Somebody walking off the street and getting signed is so rare. They're set up to take a look at the two or three players they have in mind and that's it. The other hundred are there to field ground balls and stuff like that. But I went to that tryout camp and did very well. I pitched some batting practice. They told me to let it go or whatever, and the very next day I got a call from the Tigers to sign a contract to play with them.

You were ten when you moved to Toronto so I imagine you had played Little League for a couple of years. Are you playing first base as well as pitching?

As a matter of fact I only played first base. I didn't start pitching until I was about fifteen.

Since baseball is not Canada's national pastime and they don't have high school baseball, what's the competition like for that age group?

The competition was definitely not that good. When I was sixteen or seventeen years old, sometimes Buffalo, New York, would come up and we would have a tournament. Of course this was during the time of the Oakland A's and Buffalo had the brand-new stretch-nylon uniforms, and they were good. They were good—don't get me wrong—but there's the old adage about good pitching beats good hitting. If you've got some kind of hoss up there who can throw the ball, you can beat any team. I pitched, and at that time I was starting to come into my own, and we had a couple of good pitchers so we were able to hang with these American teams. But our hitting, our fundamentals weren't strong.

With my eleven-year-old we'll come to the ballpark an hour and a half before the game to take batting practice, infield, more batting practice, throwing, and we'll have three practices plus two games a week. It's so much more involved in the United States than up in Canada. There I grabbed my glove, hopped on my bike, and went to the ballpark and we played a game. We had umpires but it was nothing like they do now. I don't know how it was back then because when I came to the States and played pro ball, everybody was pretty well fit, and here I was. I had a lot of baby fat on me. I never really played baseball. I was blessed with an arm.

If you're a first baseman when you move to Toronto, how do you become a pitcher?

As best as I can recall, when I was fifteen years old we had the best player in the league on our team and he was the pitcher-shortstop. And we didn't play many games so the same pitcher could pitch every game. When we got into the playoffs, however, the games were closer together and I was somebody who could throw strikes so I was kind of the backup pitcher if, for whatever reason, our ace couldn't pitch. He was there for all twenty games in the regular season, but we were in a playoff game and he faltered and it was like a championship game or whatever and they brought me in in relief in the last two innings, and I struck out six in a row to end the game, to end the season, and we won the championship. The next year I was the hot commodity. I was a pitcher. And I was drafted as such. After that one outing I was always a pitcher first and a first baseman second.

267

When you go to the tryout camp and you're not quite in shape, how old are you?

I was seventeen.

Do you have arm strength?

Just from playing sports—tennis, basketball, football.

How about stamina?

Stamina is definitely a problem.

What pitches are you throwing?

Just a fastball and a curveball.

Who teaches you the curveball?

I picked it up myself, just horsing around with other kids when I was twelve and thirteen. I was throwing knuckleballs and everything, and I picked up the curveball.

Did your curve drop off the table or was it more of a side-to-side movement?

I had both. I could throw it like a Steve Carlton, three-quarters, and I could throw it sidearm, strictly left to right, where it would break straight across.

I'm assuming since you have those two curveballs that you change your delivery some, but are you primarily over the top or three-quarters?

Primarily three-quarters.

And then you might drop down against a left-handed batter with the sidearm.

Exactly.

You played all sports except hockey, right?

I did not play hockey. I got in there too late. By ten years old everybody had been skating for six or seven years and I was very far behind so I never really attempted that. But I played tennis, baseball, and basketball. Those were my three main sports. I really didn't play football. I wasn't that contact type of athlete. Even though I'm big—and they wanted me to play football—something about practicing in subzero weather did not appeal to me. Now, the games were probably fun, but the practices in the mud weren't.

Are you equally talented at all sports or are you better at baseball?

At the time I was good at tennis.

Do you play year-round? Are there indoor facilities? Do you have access to them?

Yes. They have indoor facilities. I played inside during the winter. They had high school tennis and I played for the high school team. I never got good enough to play singles but I did play doubles for the team and I guess that was the realization, when I did play singles—I was seventeen and I got beat by a thirteen-year-old—then I realized that this wasn't really my dream, to play tennis. I wasn't that good. I had limitations. I wasn't that quick. And it wasn't a question of looking for another sport to play professionally, or to take to the next level, it's just that tennis wasn't there for me anymore.

It sounds like baseball chose you rather than you chose baseball.

Right. My parents always came to every game but they never pushed me. I was strictly on my own when I went out there and practiced and played. And I think the thing that drove me was the tryout camp. The second thing was I was getting ready to go into college, and at that time, at seventeen or eighteen, I didn't really know what I wanted to do in college. And I didn't know enough to know, Just go to college and after two years you'll probably figure out what you like after you've taken all the courses. I didn't know that so I was kind of paranoid, and here comes this tryout camp in the summer after I graduate from high school and it gave me a great excuse. Once I signed a professional contract I didn't have to go to college.

How does the bird-dog scout find you if there's no high school baseball?

They don't have high school baseball but they do have organized leagues. And the leagues are a little bit different than here. Here you play in a house league for the whole year. At least from ages eight through sixteen.

When you're talking about a house league you're talking about almost neighborhood competition.

Right. So you might have some pitcher that blows away everybody and then at the end of the eighteen-game season they pick an all-star team, and that all-star team plays in a tournament. Subdistrict, district, regional, state, with a two-game elimination. If you're good enough you can play quite a few games. The point I'm trying to make is, up in Canada, if you're good enough, they do away with that house league. They start kind of like an all-star team right at the beginning of the year and they start playing subdistrict games right away so you get the best competition automatically. In my mind, it would be easy for a bird dog to go to those games.

Is any team besides Detroit interested in you?

About three days after I signed, the Expos called me. Of course, the Tigers said, Nobody's interested in you.

Do the Tigers tell you that no one is interested after they offer you the contract but before you sign it?

Yes.

This is a negotiating tactic.

Yes. And I was so naïve I said, Why don't you send me to college first? Pay for my college.

Did they give you that?

No. They said that doesn't exist. You either play ball or you go to school and forget about it. But you have the opportunity of a lifetime, to play pro ball. We wouldn't be sitting down here talking to you unless we thought you had the talent, the potential to be a major league ballplayer.

So they're not offering you much money.

$1,000.

That was their first and final offer and that's what you took.

Well, they gave me an incentive clause, you know, for A ball, Double-A, and Triple-A, and if I made it to the big leagues.

And when is this?

1974. In the summer. But I didn't play until 1975 in Bristol.

You signed a contract but you didn't have anywhere to go? They didn't pack you up and send you to rookie ball?

No sir.

What did you do for six months?

Work, the same thing I did after every minor league season. After every minor league season you came home and you worked because you only made $500 a month, and you had to pay your expenses and your room and board. They paid for a hotel and they gave you $6.50 meal money a day, but, you know, you had to find a job after the minor leagues, so I worked until March. And I worked out, because I realized, Hey, I better get in the best shape possible because I'm going down to Lakeland, Florida, with Americans that have played this game all year long, and here I am a Canadian playing twenty-three, twenty-four games a year. I better do everything I can to get ready.

But you can't play organized baseball legitimately until you get to spring training because you're a professional once you sign that contract.

I kept playing. No one knew about it so I just kept playing sandlot ball.

You sign the professional contract and they lowball you.

They don't lowball me. I'm just a free agent in Canada who's got an arm. The ball moves and I've got a curveball and I'm six five and I'm about 220 then. I'm just big, tall, and throw the ball hard.

How fast was your fastball?

When I was throwing well the tops was ninety. Where I really got my arm was we used to line up snowballs right in a row with a fort that we'd make out of snow and we just had drag-out, hour-long snowball fights.

Were you pretty accurate with the snowball?

I was awesome.

Did you ever hurt anybody?

We used to take snowballs and douse them in water. Then we used to hide behind a house, and, on a four-lane road, fire them and try to hit the sides of trucks and all that. What used to really get good was when you could catch a truck when the guy had his window down a little bit. Then you'd aim for the window and see if you could nail him.

You've got to be a pretty easy target in return. You're a tall boy and you can only duck down so low, right?

At that point in my life I was just a normal kid. It's the chance of a lifetime to go down to the States and play ball.

I would've signed the contract, too, but I'm not a six-five left-hander who can throw ninety miles an hour.

The most fun was when you have negotiations when you led the league in complete games and ERA and wins and they say it's because you've never got to the big leagues. I've been signing everything for the last three years and I have a good year and they're like, No. Sorry. You're the first one that's ever held out signing a contract. Here I am, a twenty-two-year-old sitting in a leather chair, you know, and the team president's there and the marketing director's there.

Was the day you signed your professional contract the best day of your life to that point?

I did sign the contract, and that was a high for my parents, but I never told my teammates and we kept playing for like ten more games. Then after the end of the season we had a team party and they made me MVP of the team, and that's when I told them. That was the best day of my life to that point, but the MVP was something I'll never forget. That was big.

How do you get to Lakeland? Do you fly? Do you drive? Do they buy your ticket?

I flew. They bought my ticket. The Detroit Tigers bought my ticket. You take a taxi or a regular limo bus takes you to the park.

Are there a whole bunch of guys about your age looking around trying to figure out what the hell they're supposed to be doing?

The first-year players, yes. It was very nice. They have Tiger Town and they have a dormitory and a dining hall. They had all the practice fields all right there. It was almost like a college campus. And they had probably 150, 250 kids from seventeen to twenty-five.

Are you nervous? Just happy to be there? Are you intimidated? Where are you when you get out of that taxi?

It was exciting. I was ready to go and ready to find out how good I am. I signed the contract in July and August and there was all this waiting. All these workouts and all these weights and sit-ups, push-ups, throwing in the gym. Here I am. Let's see what I have.

Are you in the best shape of your life when you showed up in Lakeland?

At that time I thought I was. But after a week I realized I wasn't. The first couple of days I couldn't even get out of bed they ran me so much. I didn't realized what "in shape" was all about.

How long are you in Lakeland?

Through spring training. After spring training they didn't have a spot for me, even though all through spring training I didn't give up an earned run. I pitched about fifteen innings, struck out about twenty batters, had a great spring training, but they couldn't find a spot for me on their A club because it was already predetermined at the start of spring training or whatever. But they didn't want to send me home to Toronto to wait until the rookie-ball league started up in June, so they kept a twenty-year-old kid in Lakeland, Florida, just to practice with the team. Then I have to undress and sit in the stands or do whatever—they didn't really care—and when they were on the road I couldn't accompany the team so I would just sit in Lakeland, Florida.

Is this encouraging because they didn't send you home or is it frustrating because you're not part of a team?

It was encouraging that they did not send me home but after a while it was frustrating because, you know, it was two and a half or three months just sitting around pitching batting practice, working out with the team and not playing.

But when June comes you go to rookie ball.

I play rookie ball in Bristol, Tennessee, or Bristol, Virginia. It's a town that sits right on the border.

Do you stay with them the whole season?

I was the opening-day pitcher and stayed with them the whole year.

Was it a good year?

I had a very bad start. The first three games I was hit pretty hard. I was demoted to the bullpen. I really just did not have my heart in the game. I was having too much fun, so to speak.

What do you do for fun in Bristol?

Party. Drink beer. Hang with the guys. Just not staying focused. But the day I'll never forget—what woke me up—was there was a short bus ride to a neighboring town—Kingston, I think—and I had missed the bus. I was in the mall doing something. I think I was playing pinball. But time got away from me, and by the time I hopped in my car, when I got to the ballpark the bus had left. So, of course, I zoomed on and I actually beat the bus to the park, but that didn't matter. The manager was so upset with me. He said, What are you doing? And I said, Well, I beat ya'll here. Time got away from me. He said, I don't want to hear it. Get in the bullpen. I stayed in the bullpen until about the sixth inning and he got me to warm up, brought me into the game, and he handed me the ball and looked at me and he said, Listen to me right now, son. Either you throw the hell out of this ball right now or you're on the first plane back to Canada. That's what he told me on the mound. So he walked off the mound and the catcher—you know, pitchers and catchers are always best friends—he said, Okay, Shelly, let's go get 'em. First guy up? Knock 'im down. So the first pitch I threw behind his back about three feet and the next pitch I nailed him in the ribs.

274

Were you trying to hit him on the first pitch?

Oh yeah, but I missed him. I threw too hard. Second pitch I nailed him and after that I pitched good in that outing, got back in the starting rotation. I was like 1–4 when I got taken out of the starting rotation and I ended up 4–6. I lost a couple of close games but pitched very well. Got left-handers out consistently. I don't think a left-hander got a hit off me all year and I guess the word was the coach had talked to one of the players at a team party after the season and that player came up to me and said, You know what the coach said about you, Shelly? I said, What? He said you have a chance to make it. So I was twenty years old with my heart racing, and I went home to Toronto. I had a losing record, my ERA wasn't that bad, but I had something to look forward to the next year.

Are you still throwing fastball and curveball?

Fastball, curve. No location. I had no idea about location yet. I was still just trying to throw as hard as I could.

You come back to spring training in 1976. Where do you go when camp breaks?

Lakeland, Florida. I stay in Lakeland for A ball.

How does that year go?

The year goes very well. I start off hot—6–3, ERA in the twos, and I was the first player promoted to Double-A.

And where's the Double-A club?

Montgomery, Alabama.

And when does this happen?

Around June.

About a month and a half, two months into the season. That's a pretty quick bump.

I'm on the move.

Obviously you're still a starter at this point. Do you finish the year in Montgomery?

I finish the year in Montgomery. I ended up, I think, 6–4. Had a good year. The team won the championship. My first game in Double-A I got hit pretty hard and lost that game. The next game I pitched was here in Montgomery and I threw a seven-inning no-hitter against the same team.

This was the second game of a doubleheader?

Right. My last out was Eddie Murray. I popped him up on a curveball.

Who on that team makes the majors?

Lance Parrish. Jason Thompson was there for a little bit and then he was sent up to Triple-A. Steve Kemp. Jack Morris came up later. I think he was a late signee out of college. Our shortstop got hurt when we were coming towards the playoffs, and we brought up this seventeen-year-old kid just signed out of high school. He had played one month or a month and a half of professional ball when he was brought up to our team and he was told, Just field. We don't care if you hit. We just need a shortstop. And that was Alan Trammell. We had a lot of good players on that team.

Lance Parrish is the regular catcher, I assume. When you're in the minors, is Parrish calling the pitches or do the pitches come from the bench?

The catcher calls the pitches.

Is he good at calling a ballgame?

Oh, yes. He's learning. This is Double-A. In high school he was a third baseman. He had never really caught. The Tigers made him a catcher. Les Moss was the manager. He would set up the pitching machine. Lance Parrish was the only member of our Double-A team that had two-a-day practices. In Montgomery, Alabama, in the summer, he would be out there at eight o'clock in the morning for two or three hours working on catching fundamentals and hitting. When they had a bucket of balls it wouldn't be a bucket of balls. They'd have a trash barrel of balls and Les and Lance Parrish would work together. And that was Les's job, to make Lance into a catcher. Les Moss was a catcher in the big leagues.

Is that why Lance Parrish is at Double-A? Because Les Moss is there?

One of the reasons. Plus he played A ball or rookie ball and he was the number-one draft pick for Detroit so he was going to be on an accelerated scale.

You're playing in the old stadium up on the hill above where Hank Williams is buried, right?

That's right. We even had a Canadian come visit us and that's the one thing he wanted to see, was Hank Williams' grave.

Where do you go after the 1976 season?

This time I was asked to go to instructional league in St Petersburg, so I played there until December.

What are you working on?

My motion, my pick-off moves, change-up, that sort of thing. I was trying to learn a different pitch, pick-offs, how to pivot, things like that.

Do you go back to Montgomery after spring training in 1977?

I go back to Montgomery. I was disappointed because I thought I'd proved myself in Montgomery, but spring training kind of did me in. I don't know if they had a spot for me or whether it was predetermined but I didn't have a good spring training. I pitched against Triple-A hitters and they hit me hard. I didn't do well, so they sent me back to Montgomery.

How about the season?

1977 has its ups and downs. I had ten wins and twelve losses, led the league in complete games. I lost three games 1–0. I lost one game 2–0, lost two games 3–2. My mother passed away during the summer. The only bright spot of that year was I met Cindy. That was about the only bright spot. I met her the week before my mother passed away from cancer.

How do you meet your future wife?

I caught her on the rebound. She broke up with her boyfriend and needed a place to go that night and her girlfriend said, Let's go to the ballpark. I hear there's a team down there and it's fun to watch. There's a lot of guys down there.

Does your future wife like baseball at this time?

Never saw a baseball game in her life.

If she's going down there with her friend to watch a bunch of guys then she's got to be pretty close to the field.

She was there before the start of the game. She had on a one-piece red jumpsuit that fit nicely. And a bright red jumpsuit like that kind of stands out in stands that are confederate gray. So everybody looked up and asked, Who's the blonde?

I'm thinking that you're probably not the only ballplayer who noticed her.

That is precisely right.

Do you draw straws? Is it rocks, paper, scissors? How do win the lottery for the right to approach your future wife?

I was in the bullpen because I was a starter. You hang out in the dugout a little bit, then you go to the bullpen and you talk to the pitchers and everything. And you can actually go up underneath the Montgomery stands almost and see the bullpen. The stands open up. And she, during the game, came out towards the bullpen—there's no fence or anything—and is looking at a scorecard, and our backs are turned to her and then one of us looks around and sees her. No straws or nothing. I jumped up and I was the first one over there.

So at this time you not only have a good curveball with two separate motions but you're also quick. You've got a good first move.

It was the best first move I ever made in my life.

I'm sure that you and your wife have discussed this. Were you the one that she had picked out?

I don't think she had picked out anybody. She was trying to see the names and where they were from and who they were. She was just looking around. She enjoyed life. She enjoyed talking to people. She enjoyed meeting new people. She was not shy. On the contrary, I think I was.

278

Did you get fined for talking to her during the game?

No, they didn't see me. I waited until we were out in the field and our coach went down to the dugout and he couldn't see around the dugout wall. If he was at third base he could see in the bullpen and know if I got up and disappeared.

How much would the fine have been if you'd been caught?

Probably twenty dollars, twenty-five dollars. At that point in my career I'd just gotten a raise and I was making $750 a month.

What's your living situation? How many players go in on an apartment?

My first year, in Bristol, we had four people in a four-bedroom trailer. By the time you get to Montgomery you're usually down to a three-bedroom apartment with three guys. It all depends on what kind of apartment complex you get into. There's low end and there's high end. The guys who got the big signing bonus could afford the extra $150 a month for the high end, whereas I was on the low end.

How was the organization when your mother passed away? How much time did they give you away from the team?

They gave me a week. She had cancer so she had been sick for a while and they let me go home for a week while she was still conscious and could understand where she was. Did I miss a start? No. I was a starter so it was pretty convenient. They were good. It was okay. At that time Detroit probably had one of the best minor league systems in the major leagues. If you played for Detroit in the minor leagues at that point you had a lot of respect. Baltimore had a lot of respect. They treated their players fairly. They may not have paid them a lot but they treated them fairly and you had a chance to make the big leagues, where some other teams, like Texas or something, they usually got their players somewhere else. They never utilized their people up through the minor leagues, developed them, spent money on them.

Is Les Moss still the manager in 1977?

No. Eddie Brinkman was the manager. He was a real good shortstop and he was there mainly because of Alan Trammell and Lou Whitaker. That's the first time they paired those two up.

With Moss gone, is Parrish gone as well?

Parrish is up to Triple-A and that's where Moss is, too.

Do you, your teammates, know that Trammell and Whitaker are special? Do we know that they're together? Batman and Robin? Peanut butter and jelly?

Yes. Trammell is so talented. He makes every play. He's Mr Automatic. And Whitaker was a third baseman in rookie ball and they made him into a second baseman. He was just a great athlete. Great hands at the plate.

You rarely hear one name mentioned without the other. Did they get along okay?

Perfectly. They roomed together from day one in Double-A.

Does it really matter if teammates get along?

They were beautiful, but on the other side of the coin, the organization knew when some people did not get along, or some players—and that's just like in everyday life. In business they would be sat down and talked with and if they didn't correct their behavior they wouldn't be there anymore. And that happens sometimes.

Regardless of performance? I mean, if you're batting .400 and hitting fifty home runs a year they don't really care if you get along with anybody else or not, do they?

Yes they do, and they get sat down and talked with, but if you hit that much and you do that well—I'm just talking from a minor league standpoint—then you're up to the next level anyway. You're up there. You're part of your peers. Some minor league ballplayers, first-round draft choices, will walk into a clubhouse like, I'm the man and I know it, and you're just helping me get to where I need to be.

Do we have, for lack of a better term, enforcers on a ballclub to keep those kind of players in line? Is that something that Les Moss or Brinkman would handle or are there designated players who decide that the draft choice needs a dose of humility?

Mostly it's done by the manager, but you have experienced people, at least with Detroit, who have been in the minor leagues for a number of years that would be kind of like tutors to young players. And they knew that was their role and they accepted that role, because they were getting the high end of the dollar in minor league pay. And they were probably married, and they were happy to have a job doing what they wanted and where they could possibly go to that next level as a coach. You always had an elder statesman for a catcher. You always had some pitcher who had been around the league and in the minors for a while. You probably had a backup infielder that had been around.

Do the guys who act as tutors advance to the majors as coaches?

Oh yes. That's the good old boys. That's the Bruce Kimms, the Jerry Manuels. It's everybody in coaching.

Do you make the forty-man roster for spring training in 1978?

Forty-man roster. Big times.

Is this the best day of your professional life so far?

So far, yeah. Yeah, it's pretty good. Wearing the white uniform is big time. Running out there and feeling like a part of the team even though you've got a long way to go.

How does it go?

It was uneventful. I don't think I even pitched. I might've pitched one inning.

If you're not pitching, are you worrying about being cut?

No, I'm not.

You knew that you'd be cut. You knew you weren't going to Detroit with the big club.

Right. There was no way. I knew. The reason why you're on the forty-man roster is because you have to be protected. If you're not protected by the major league club, then another club can pick you up for practically nothing. And they didn't want to do that because I'd shown promise.

How many years before this goes into effect?

Three years. After three years they have to make a decision to either put you on the roster or leave you out there and any team can pick you up, and if they pick you up they have to move you up to the next level. Which, in my case, would be Triple-A.

So that's why you're not pitching. You're not going to Detroit but they're protecting you. You're slated for Evansville and it will take a very unexpected event for you to end up anywhere but Evansville.

I probably need about four good breaks—like Milt Wilcox's leg, John Hiller's wrist. Four good breaks.

Are you in Evansville all year?

That's right, all year long. Half as a starter and then Eddie Glynn got called up to the major leagues in July. I was not dominating as a starter. I was probably 6–4, something like that, and Les Moss, who was the manager at that time, came up to me and said, Shelly, we need a left-handed reliever out of the pen. The best, the fastest way to the big leagues is to be a left-handed reliever.

This is the first time you've been a reliever since Bristol, right?

This is the first time I've been a reliever since Bristol. I relieved a little bit in Bristol because I was intimidated. I just couldn't get focused. Other than that I'd always been a starter. Lakeland, Montgomery, and then Evansville up until that July.

Do you have any fear when he calls you into the office?

Oh yeah. Anytime you have to go into the manager's office, you're either getting released, reassigned, whatever.

When he tells you it's the fastest way to the majors, how do you take it?

At the time I feel it's a demotion. I feel like I'm starting to falter, because when you're in the minor league system you have to have momentum. You can't be stagnant. Even though I was 10–12 in Montgomery, I had a good year. I pitched well. I got beat one to nothing, two to nothing, but I was pitching well. I was completing games. I kept the team in games, so I had that momentum. When you get to Triple-A and you're almost there, all of a sudden you start to level off and then, at the time, being a reliever, I'm thinking I'm starting to go down in my career.

How do you do as a reliever?

I do great. I was 7–0 with three saves. I did very well. Just lucky as hell, I guess. I don't know.

Is that 7–0 record all good news or are you a little disappointed that you did so well because that might make it harder for you to go back and be a starter? Or are you just happy you're doing well?

I'm happy I'm doing well, but in the back of my mind I want to be a starter. But I'll do this now until I get my chance to start again.

And September first you get called up.

September first, I get called up.

And you go straight to the team.

Yes. Straight to the team. I think they were in Kansas City, and then from there we played in Yankee Stadium.

Who else gets called up then?

Jack Morris.

So you and Jack Morris and some other guys get plane tickets to Kansas City, and you're bouncing off the roof of the plane because you're headed to the big leagues. You get there, get your uniform, and the fountains are going in the stadium in Kansas City. Did you get a high uniform number? Did you get any choice as to what your number is?

At that time, yeah, it was a high number. You're very humble when you get brought up because a) I'm a free agent, b) I'm from Canada, c) I got $1,000 for a bonus. Now, the guys who got the $150,000 bonus, yeah, they negotiate. They say, Is it okay if you have this number? But somebody like me, everything is decided for you and you smile.

But they fly you to Kansas City, you've got a major league uniform, you've got a locker, somebody's moving your bags for you, and you're staying in really nice hotels.

First-class hotels.

After the September call-up, since you're shoving an extra twelve to fifteen guys into the locker room, are all the rookies lockering next to each other?

Yes.

So you go up, join the team, and you're sitting in the bullpen. When's the first time you get called to loosen up?

Yankee Stadium.

Are they calling you on the phone or are they motioning from the dugout?

Phone.

Are you nervous when the phone rings? Do they tell you before the game that if they need a long reliever then you're going to be the guy?

No.

So when the phone rings you have no idea who it's for.

That is correct. What you've got to remember now is I'm a left-handed reliever. You'd have to be an idiot not to think you're going to have a chance to pitch in Yankee Stadium, because that's why everybody wants to have a left-handed reliever—to beat the Yankees.

You know that flying into LaGuardia?

Yes. I have an excellent chance to pitch. They want to see what I can do.

Do you remember who started that night?

I think it was Milt Wilcox.

Does he get rocked early?

It's about the fourth or fifth inning, but he gets rocked.

Are you the first guy in?

I'm the first guy in.

And Detroit's behind.

We're behind by about two runs, I think. It was close, and this is the year the New York Yankees are on a roll and they catch Boston on the last day and then they win it in a one-game playoff.

This is Bucky's year.

This is Bucky's year.

So you come in, and I'm guessing that the first guy you pitched to is a left-hander.

Mickey Rivers.

Is this the start of an inning or the middle of an inning?

One out.

Anybody on base?

Bucky Dent. We've got a photograph of my first pitch and you can see Bucky Dent on first. A lawyer from New York, about a month later, sent me the negative and said, I just want to let you know this was your first pitch of your major league career.

That was nice. Is Lance Parrish the catcher?

I don't think it was Parrish. It was Milt May.

Do you remember anything from the pregame meeting about how to pitch Mickey Rivers, or are you just following Milt May's signals?

At this time, forty-man roster, call-up in September, and we're out of the division race. We're not even close, I don't think. They didn't have a meeting, I'm pretty sure, but basically I was just going with what the catcher said. I didn't know any of the hitters. They might have sat down and talked with the starters about the hitters but the relievers that were called up, or pitchers like me, didn't have that meeting. Now, the next year they did. We all sat down and talked about each hitter.

You get Mickey Rivers out.

The first pitch was a ball, second pitch was a fastball on his hands that he popped up, so I got the first hitter out.

Are you a little less nervous after you get your first out?

I do recall that I could not feel my legs. Honestly, I could not feel my legs. There was just nothing there. I knew I had to push off and drive, but I could not feel my legs.

How long do you last?

Just a third of an inning. I never finished the inning. Thurman Munson got the first base hit off me. I walked Cliff Johnson, then I think I walked another batter and that loaded the bases. I do remember breaking Chris Chambliss's bat in half where the barrel went to third base and he hit a two-bouncer past Jason Thompson and it went down the line for a triple.

Chris Chambliss hit a triple?

Chris Chambliss hit a bases-loaded triple off me with the barrel of the bat down the third-base line. It ended up they scored four runs off me in a third of an inning. You work your butt off for four years and finally get a chance to pitch in the big leagues against major league hitters and I give up four runs in one third of an inning. There were a couple of walks and a couple of close pitches. You hear that from every person who had a cup of coffee in the big leagues, but it was rough. There were two broken bats and a close call on the pitch to Cliff Johnson. It was just one of those things. Welcome to the big leagues. Welcome to the Yankees, where they make things happen. In the minors, if I threw that same pitch to Chris Chambliss, it wouldn't have made it out of the infield, but because they're so much bigger and stronger they're able to do that kind of stuff. So welcome to the big leagues. Four runs. I went to the dugout. Ralph Houk was the manager.

Was he the one that comes to get you?

Yeah. He says, you know, Hang in there, big guy. They didn't hit you hard.

Was this the first visit?

The first visit and I'm out of there.

But you know you're gone. You know he's not coming to talk to you.

Nah. He said, They didn't hit you hard. And they didn't. Three of the hits were through the infield.

You can't really throw your glove or anything because you're a rookie.

No. You're very humble. I sit on the bench like you're supposed to.

You don't go into the clubhouse.

No, no. You sit down on the bench and you wait. You wait at least until that inning's done. Then you can go to the clubhouse if you want to, but you never leave with the reliever who just relieved you still out there. You wait until he finishes. That's the unwritten rule.

Did you stay on the bench the rest of the game?

I probably did. I don't know. It's Yankee Stadium and I may not be here very much longer.

You get pats on the shoulder.

Yeah, because with Detroit, the team's made up primarily of minor league ballplayers that came up through the Detroit Tigers system. Alan Trammell and Lou Whitaker, who I'd played with, are giving me the Hang in there, Shelly. The nice thing about Detroit was that we were a family.

What's that night like? Do you get on the phone? Do you go to a movie to get your mind off it? What do you do?

It's just hard. I don't remember exactly but I went out to dinner with a few guys. They said, Come on out, because that's what you do after a ballgame. You do have a spread but it's not really the best food in the world. You go out and they just say, Hang in there, Shelly, and, You'll get your chance again. Everybody's supportive. It was nice with Detroit. I can't say enough about how much of a family it was, and how everybody pulled for each other. Whatever you might have heard where people wanted you to do bad so they could get the chance, it never was like that in Detroit. We felt, in the minor leagues, that if the team won, then everybody would go up. Everybody would go up. The worst thing that could happen was to be on a losing team. And I was very fortunate. We won the championship two years in a row in Double-A. In Triple-A we were right down to the wire, the last game of the year, and lost the championship. Winning takes care of all those mental problems and things that might fester on a losing club, you know, where some players are just out for themselves. It was nice with Detroit.

   When we got back to Detroit, instead of staying in a hotel room by myself, Lance Parrish let me stay with him at his apartment.

When do you get to pitch again?

Detroit. The Yankees again. And that was probably the best outing I had. I pitched three and a third innings, struck out three or four people. Struck Reggie out twice.

Is this about a week later?

Yeah.

Was that the next time you got up in the bullpen?

287

No, there's other times, but basically it's more just to stay loose and get your work in. Every day or every other day you go to get up. As far as having a chance to pitch in a game, that was the only time.

And you strike out Reggie Jackson twice.

Once looking, and the next time I threw a 3–2 fastball. I challenged him down the middle and he missed it, so that was kind of cool.

So you feel a lot better.

Oh yeah. I'm here. I can do this. Now I can feel my legs. I'm ready. I'm pumped. Let's do it. It felt good. I did well. I threw all my pitches, you know. Lou Piniella and all the boys. I got them out. This game we were losing again. We were down, I think, by four runs, so I was kind of mop-up. And these Yankees are professionals. How much were they trying? The game wasn't on the line. They might've just been taking their swings and getting out of there. But on the other side of the coin, when I pitched against the Yankees the first time, they took Jackson out. They didn't let Jackson face me because I was a rookie in his major league debut. Here's a guy who could be throwing ninety-five miles an hour hurting my star player. Take him out. And they pinch-hit Cliff Johnson for Reggie that game. It's like, You're not going to let me face this left-hander, are you? You don't know who he is. He could kill me.

You finish the year with Detroit. Do you go to winter ball in the off-season?

We went to Puerto Rico. Mayaguez. That's when Cindy and I got married. Some of the best times of my life. We eloped with Lance Parrish and his wife. We got married in St Thomas.

So Parrish is down playing with Mayaguez as well.

Yeah, that was great. Lance and Jack Morris. Somehow I guess Mayaguez and Detroit had a thing. They do that. They send three or four players that they want and recommend. They say, Shelly, you need some off-season conditioning. You go down to Puerto Rico. It's the best out of the three winter leagues. And it was better than working, because it was either go down to Puerto Rico or go home to Canada and work and make some money. And they paid good money down there. Cash.

That was the best time. I had a real good year down there. I think I was 10–2. They invited me to play in the Caribbean World Series. Our team didn't win the championship but they usually pick up two pitchers or something to go to the Series and I had such a good year. They were in San Juan that year. They got me a first-class suite and they paid for Cindy to fly up and for one game I got paid like eight grand.

So Lance Parrish is living with his fiancée somewhere and you're living with your fiancée somewhere.

In the same apartment complex, right next to each other.

And you decide to go to St Thomas and get married.

We had a three-day break. You had more days off in Puerto Rico, in winter ball, which was nice. You had at least one day off a week.

Who decides that since you have three days off it'd be a good time to get married?

Lance. Lance wanted to get married, and he wanted us to come with him to be the witnesses.

Why St Thomas?

Everybody gets married in St Thomas. Cruise ships go in to St Thomas and you get married in St Thomas. A lot of people get married in St Thomas. It's just the four of us. We take a little two-prop plane over there. We were engaged but we had no wedding date planned at all, so before we take off, I just asked Cindy, Why don't we do it, too?

She has a twin sister who got married just three months before and her parents had to put all the money out for that. I didn't want to have to go through that whole routine. I just didn't want a lot of attention. I didn't want to have any part of that so I said, What the heck? Let's get married.

And you got married on what day?

December first, 1978. And our marriage license has their new name on it and their marriage license has Cindy's maiden name because they got married first. So basically when Lance got married, I got his first autograph, or second one. He signed his own marriage license first.

Are you on the forty-man roster in 1979?

Yes.

Do you think you've got a good shot at making the club this time?

After being 14–5 in the minors. I won something like twenty-five games that year, including winter ball. I knew I had a good chance. But, you know, like anything, at this point, Detroit had so many rookies that it depended on how you did in spring training.

And Les Moss has moved up to manage Detroit this year.

Ralph Houk retired and they appointed Les Moss as the manager and everybody loved that move. He knew all of us.

Do you break camp with the big club?

It was between me and Jack Morris as to who would make the club. We both worked hard at it. He would have a good outing and I would have a good outing. And Les came up to me the day I was supposed to pitch against Boston. He came up to me before the game, because I was kind of the nervous type, and said, Shelly, I just want you to know right now, before you go out there, that you made the club, so just go out there and pitch. I went out there against Freddie Lynn and all the boys and I pitched five innings, struck out like eight. I was just on cloud nine. That's when I felt my legs but I didn't feel my feet touching the ground because I was on a high. I beat out Jack Morris for the roster spot. Jack got sent down to the minors and I made the big leagues and broke with the team in 1979. Twenty-four man. Then I knew I belonged. That's when I knew I was there. It was just a matter of pitching.

Do you get a lower number?

Oh yeah. 42. Did they ask me what number I wanted? No. I don't care. I wasn't big on numbers.

You pitch in ten games and throw a total of twenty-one innings, so at some point you get sent down.

Yeah.

Is Les still the manager?

Les had a raw deal. Unfortunately, that's life. When the team doesn't do well, the manager is blamed. But Les was well respected. Well respected in baseball. A well-respected manager who knew how to use a pitching staff. What happened—and it was just one of those deals—in the spring that year, in April, Detroit had terrible weather. We had like ten rainouts or snowouts. We weren't playing at all. Throwing on the sidelines or throwing inside a hallway or something to try to get work just wasn't the same. And with all these rookies we had. Trammell and Whitaker were second year or third year. Lance Parrish and Kemp and Jason Thompson. Everybody was saying this was Detroit's year and we got off to a real bad start. We got rained out and snowed out so much that we never got it in gear, and when we started to lose and the pitching staff stunk—I stunk, everybody stunk—sometime in May, they called it Ash Wednesday or something, they sent like six of us down to the minors. Six guys. That's very rare. They sent us down, made a couple of trades, and then about a week later they got rid of Les Moss and hired Sparky Anderson. They didn't stay with Les and I don't think anybody could've managed with as many rainouts as we had in the month of April. We never played and it was just a raw deal. I always felt bad about that. I always thought that if I had pitched better—because I know that Les stuck his neck out for me to make the team—that if I had pitched better, a) I would've been in the big leagues, and b) he would've been managing the team.

How quick do you have to report?

It's funny. When you go up to the big leagues, from Triple-A to the big leagues, you've got twenty-four hours. When you get sent down, you've got three days.

You get sent down to Evansville?

Well, yes and no. I went to Evansville and we unpacked our car, got an apartment, got our furniture and everything, and then I went to the ballpark. And they said, Whoa. Hold up, Shelly. We don't know what's going on but don't unpack. I said, I've already unpacked. And they said, Hold on, because something's going on. So I sat in the stands for a couple of days and then found out I was being loaned to the Indianapolis Indians, the Triple-A club for Cincinnati.

Is that legal?

Yeah, they do that. They loan players.

291

But you don't want to be loaned. People like to play with their best toys. You can play with the toys I don't want to play with.

Right. Exactly. The next day after I got loaned, Champ Summers was traded from Cincinnati to Detroit, and that's the way it was for the rest of the year. June, July, August. We were in Evansville for three days when I got sent to Indianapolis. We were eating steak for breakfast and steak for lunch because we had gone grocery shopping. Then we gave the rest of the food away when we left. And I'm seeing the writing on the wall.

You're in the stands waiting and they actually say, You're being loaned to Indianapolis? So you're on your way to Indianapolis before the trade actually occurs.

The trade didn't actually occur officially until September or October, after the World Series.

So you're the notorious player to be named later?

I was the player to be named later. I was just loaned to them for the rest of the season. Champ Summers was traded for a player to be named back in May. I think what it was was the Cincinnati Reds weren't sure about me, so they wanted to have their own manager look at me for a month, two months, three months. They liked what they saw. They tried to bring me up but I was claimed on waivers. I had to go through waivers because it was after the trading deadline, and somebody stopped me from going up.

Are you upset?

I'm upset because I'm losing a family. I'm leaving Detroit.

When do you know that you're gone? That this loan is permanent?

After the World Series.

Not until then.

Not until then.

It doesn't seem like there would be, especially at a Triple-A level, a lot of incentive to take a loaned player. They're having to move their own players aside.

Why would another Triple-A team have an interest in giving you work unless they were going to keep you?

An agreement between Cincinnati and Detroit. Cincinnati and Detroit kind of worked together then. They're no threat to each other because they're American League and National League, so they do things like that. You know, I was a left-handed reliever. I had good stuff. I had good numbers. They didn't have a problem using me. And later on I found out that in this particular case they just wanted to have a real close look at me, to see if I was worth a Champ Summers, because Champ Summers went on to play for Detroit and had a couple of good years. I pitched strictly relief, strictly left-handers only. That's what I did for four months.

You're not happy. You still want to be a starter.

I want to be a starter. I proved it in minor league ball. I proved it in winter ball playing against major league talent in Puerto Rico. I was 10–2 down there. I want to be a starter.

This sounds like a real screwy kind of purgatory.

Purgatory. Limbo. I was depressed. But grow up. Get over it. You've still got a chance to make it to the big leagues. | 293

After the World Series, the trade is announced and you're the player to be named later, and you now belong to Cincinnati and you're not surprised. What do you do that winter?

Yeah, Mayaguez actively seeks me and I pencil my own contract. I get paid tons of money, can fly back and forth. They pay to bring my wife down. Living the luxury. A Fiat to drive. This is the closest thing to the big leagues. This is better than the big leagues. This is first-class. People come up to me and say, Mr Burnside.

And you start for them.

Starting, again, for the second year.

But all good things must end. Are you on the forty-man roster with Cincinnati?

Forty-man roster for Cincinnati.

Did you make the team?

No, I didn't break with them.

Do you get cut early or late?

Late. The last day before camp breaks.

Are you surprised? Are you mad?

I just take the lumps. You've got to. I remember the time I got sent up with Detroit and sat on the bench in April with it raining and everything, so at least I'm going somewhere where I can work. I'm working. I'll get a chance to pitch instead of sitting on the bench for ten days.

How do you find out that you've been cut when you think you've got a shot at making the team? Cincinnati's not a very good ballclub this year.

That's true. McNamara. McNamara called me into the office and said, We're going to go with these people right now. You go down there and get your work. You'll be up here. No problem. Don't worry. Keep your head up high, Shelly, and you'll be all right. And that's what I did.

So you go back to Indianapolis. How long are you there before they bring you up?

Not too long at all. A month maybe. A month and a half.

Do you remember what happened that would make room for you?

No, I'm not sure. I was the first one brought up that year. And I was in the big leagues probably for a month, two months. It's funny. The whole time I'm just pitching to left-handers. Bring me in, bring me out. And then McNamara comes in and he brings me in to relieve, my first National League game and we're playing the Expos, and he brings me up to face Gary Carter.

Who's a right-handed hitter.

Right-handed hitter. And after all that time in the minor leagues with Indianapolis where I pitched exclusively to left-handed hitters, period. To the point where it was one hitter and out. One hitter and out.

You assume that this is what you're going to do in the majors, that this is Cincinnati's plan from Day One. So you pitch to Gary Carter.

And I get him to 3–2. I throw three fastballs and he fouls every one off. I throw a curveball and he hits it out of the park.

But from then on you pitch great. You get in seven games, you pitch four and two-thirds innings—they obviously go back to the lefty-lefty strategy—you've already given up the home run to Carter and you finish with an ERA of 1.93. If you've got a 1.93 ERA, then you don't allow another run. Why don't you stay?

Joe Price, I think, got hot in Triple-A so they brought him up. I mean, they really were high on Joe Price and I got sent down. It was a lefty-lefty swap. I stayed in the minors. I was young. Didn't know how to handle some things and I got depressed. Got down. I did not have a very good year in Indianapolis. I turned it on the last month but there was a span of about two months where I was getting hit pretty hard. Everything I was throwing up there was getting hit. My ERA got up to five, I think. I think I got it down to under four by the time I left Indy, and got called back up in September when they expanded the roster.

Did you pitch at all in September?

Once, I think. Maybe once. And that's when I wanted to pitch so bad just so other teams could see me pitch. But they never pitched me.

You go to spring training in 1981.

I go to spring training in 1981, but I've been taken off the forty-man roster.

There's a photograph of you by Walter Iooss in your baseball room that ran in Sports Illustrated. *How do you end up in* Sports Illustrated *if you're not on the forty-man roster?*

I was invited to spring training as a nonroster player, and I thought I might have an outside shot. Some people do get to stay. I had a couple of spring training games and pitched well. As a matter of fact, one game I threw six innings against St Louis and I threw a no-hitter. There was a gale blowing—a lot of wind—but nobody got a hit off me in six innings. Two days after that game I got sent down to the minor league training camp. Then I pitched there until the day before the last day of spring training and they announced over the loudspeaker system in the minor league complex, Will Sheldon Burnside come to the office? And Sheldon Bender was there, and he said, We're giving you your release. You're just not going to fit into our plans. So I left. I ran into my Triple-A coach from the year before and he said, Shelly, I'm sorry. I tried to get them to release you. They knew they were going to release you. I tried to get them to do it earlier so you could hook up with another team but they wouldn't. They wanted to keep you just in case somebody got hurt. I'm sorry. So I said, Thanks a lot. I packed my bags. Cindy's five months pregnant. I went to the White Sox camp just to throw on the side. That was when the White Sox were picking up every left-hander in America. I think they were trying to get a monopoly on them. I threw on the side. They said, Shelly, you look good, but right now it's just too late. Get back with us maybe in June. There may be a spot open. But it's too late. We're breaking camp. So I drove home to Montgomery and hung it up. I said, That's it. Cindy's five months pregnant. I had saved up about twenty, twenty-five thousand dollars. Bought a house for $46,000 here in Montgomery on the east side of town and got a job.

The *Sports Illustrated* came out the following year, in 1982. I'm working at Lowe's selling lumber and my father-in-law calls me up and says, Shelly, did you take a look at *Sports Illustrated?* This is a year after I'm out of baseball. I say, No. He says, Your picture's in it. I said, It ain't funny. Kiss my ass. He says, No, no. He comes to work and there it is. He opens up the magazine and there I am with Tom Seaver and everything. I'm not on the cover but I get a full-page spread in *Sports Illustrated* and I'm not even playing baseball.

You've been out of baseball for about eleven and a half months. Did you remember the guy taking the picture?

Yes, that's why I look goofy like that. Relaxing with my feet, doing leg raises. Yeah, I remember. But they didn't print anything that year. And that was the year I got released.

So the last professional baseball team you played for was the Cincinnati Reds. You didn't play in the minors after that.

That's correct. In September I played for Cincinnati and then in spring training they released me. They sent me down to the minor league complex for a week, or two weeks, but I didn't break camp. That was the last time I played. Until I turned forty.

What happened then?

I play in an over-forty league they have here, in Montgomery-Birmingham.

How's that going?

I'm a starter.

New York at Detroit (AL)
Friday, September 7, 1979

New York	ab	r	h	rbi	Detroit	ab	r	h	rbi
Randolph, 2b	3	0	0	0	LeFlore, cf	4	1	2	2
Murcer, cf	4	0	1	0	Whitaker, 2b	3	2	2	2
Piniella, lf	4	0	0	0	Kemp, lf	4	0	0	0
Jackson, rf	3	0	0	0	Summers, dh	3	1	2	1
Scott, dh	2	0	0	0	Thompson, 1b	4	0	1	1
G'mble, ph-dh	2	0	1	0	Morales, rf	4	0	1	0
Chambliss, 1b	4	0	1	0	Parrish, c	3	1	0	0
Stanley, 3b	3	0	0	0	Rodriguez, 3b	4	1	1	0
Dent, ss	3	0	2	0	Trammell, ss	3	0	0	0
Gulden, c	2	0	0	0	Robbins, p	0	0	0	0
Narron, c	1	0	1	0	Billingham, p	0	0	0	0
Clay, p	0	0	0	0					
Kaat, p	0	0	0	0	Totals	32	6	9	6
Slagle, p	0	0	0	0					
Totals	31	0	6	0					

New York	0	0	0	0	0	0	0	0	0—0	
Detroit	2	1	0	0	1	2	0	0	x—6	

New York	IP.	H.	R.	ER.	BB.	SO.
Clay (L. 1-7)	2	5	3	3	1	1
Kaat............	4	4	3	3	2	2
Slagle................	2	0	0	0	0	2
Detroit	IP.	H.	R.	ER.	BB.	SO.
Robbins	2.2	2	0	0	2	0
Billingham (W. 10-6)	6.1	6	0	0	2	3

E—Clay (1). 2B—Thompson (14, off Clay), LeFlore 2 (19, off Clay, off Kaat), Morales (21, off Kaat). 3B—Whitaker (7, off Clay). HR—Whitaker (3, off Clay). CS—Summers (5, 2B by Kaat/Gulden). U—Marty Springstead, Larry McCoy, Joe Brinkman, Vic Voltaggio. T—2:20. A—28,943.

ROGER SLAGLE

Roger Slagle pitched in one major league game for the
New York Yankees in 1979. He lasted two innings, giving up no hits, no walks, and no runs while striking out
two. He was interviewed October 18, 2001 at his home
in White House, Tennessee.

Where did you grow up and when did you first start playing baseball?

I was brought up in Larned, Kansas, and I started playing baseball in
Little League. Actually it was before Little League. We were probably
seven or eight years old. There were two teams in town, the Midgets and
the Dwarfs. I think I played for the Dwarfs. We just played like two
games in the summer and that was it. We played each other and had
little bitty wool uniforms like the old Yankees, and they were hot.

We had an old man named Wayne Howell that coached. He had a
ballpark right across the street from his house and we'd go out and he'd

hit us balls. He was retired and he'd play with us all day long if we wanted, and really gave us a great sense of baseball. All of the kids just kind of hung around together and we had an unbelievably good team. From a town of like five thousand people we were playing all-star teams from towns of fifteen and twenty thousand and just whooping the fire out of all of them, so it was a great beginning for baseball.

Were you a pitcher from the beginning?

No, I was a second baseman because I was kind of short, but then I hit a growth spurt. Then I was center fielder and played first base because I was taller and had a lot of speed. When I started throwing I was real wild. I threw harder than anybody but I had no clue as to where it was going. But they worked with me. We had another kid, a left-hander who was real good named Wesley Lewis. His family eventually moved to California and he was supposed to be a fairly good draft pick. I think the Padres drafted him but he got drafted by the Army also and tore up his knee on an obstacle course and I never did hear what happened to him after that.

So when do you start pitching?

I really started getting into it when I was eleven and twelve. We moved up to the thirteen- and fourteen-year-old league and I had started throwing a curveball and tore some muscles in my arm trying to throw it. I had no business throwing it, but I didn't have anybody to tell me any different. The other kids were doing it so I decided to do it. I guess we played until I was fifteen and then we didn't have a team anymore. It was a small town. I would play in an occasional softball game and not really do much, but finally a semipro baseball team came through when I was seventeen. They had a tournament over in a town about twenty miles away and they were missing a team to finish it out so they asked the local fast-pitch softball team to play in it. I knew one of the guys and he knew I could pitch and they needed a pitcher and they asked me to pitch against these semipro guys, but I hadn't thrown a ball in a couple of years and it was really stupid to come out and just air it out without throwing in so long. I wasn't in shape but it's when I knew I could compete against guys like that, because I came in in relief and I struck out the first nine pretty much all on fastballs. Then I ran out of gas and they blistered me.

You didn't have a high school team?

No, we didn't have a high school team. We tried to get one up but they said it would hurt the track program. We had about six guys out for track my senior year. I went to college when I was seventeen. I went on a basketball scholarship to Hutchinson Junior College but we got up an American Legion team in my hometown that summer. I was just coming off surgery on both my knees and my right foot at the same time. I grew too fast. I had Osgood-Schlatter disease. I had some bone spurs and stuff that needed to be taken care of so I just got it all knocked at once. So when I started pitching my legs weren't as strong as they should be and I threw but I really wasn't as effective as I wanted to be. Anyway, through that I got discovered and after my sophomore year playing basketball I signed with the University of Kansas to play baseball.

So you didn't play baseball in junior college either.

No, we didn't have a team there. After I left they got up a team.

What else did you play besides baseball and basketball? Obviously you were a good basketball player if you were a scholarship athlete.

I played football some. I was the quarterback and kicker and defensive back in high school and was asked to play in junior college when the quarterback got hurt, but I was tall and thin and just coming off of knee surgery. I wasn't going to play football.

But you were good at every sport you played.

I was good at every sport I played, yeah. At one point in time I was offered a scholarship in six different sports—football, basketball, golf, tennis, cross-country, and track. I was very fast. I was one of the tops in the state in the hundred-yard dash. In tennis, one of the guys that I knew in high school, from our town, got second in the state, but I could play with him and beat him on occasion and he was a year older than me. I played in two rec-league tournaments and I won those but baseball was really what I wanted to do. I felt that was my best shot to play professionally.

Were either of your parents athletic? Where did all this talent come from?

My father was captain of the track team but back then you didn't really play many sports because you had to work. It was a farming community. My mom was extremely fast. She was tall. Both of my parents are five

301

ten and I guess I got a lot of it from my mom, but nobody really played sports so I don't know how good either of them were. Maybe I was lucky or a freak. I don't know.

You said that your mom was fast but she didn't play sports. How do you know that your mom is fast?

Well, it took me until I was thirteen before I could outrun her. She'd say come home and I'd run or do something and I was the fastest kid in town and she'd get out and kind of chase me down, just kind of goofing off. My parents did what parents were supposed to do. They were there for everything that I did and my sister did and they worked hard.

Did you have a favorite team or favorite player when you were growing up?

The Cardinals were always my favorite team. Bob Gibson was probably my favorite pitcher. Lou Brock. Stan Musial was my first favorite because he was a pitcher turned outfielder. He could hit. He could do it all.

Other than thinking it was your best shot at the pros, was there something else that made you choose baseball over the other sports?

I played everything so I was just enjoying whatever was in season. I really enjoyed playing and I think that's the one thing kids do wrong nowadays. They choose too early. All sports will help you in some form. My kids play everything and try not to specialize. Of course, they're still young. As I got up to choose between basketball and baseball I could tell from the competition that I excelled in baseball. In basketball I had to work and I wasn't dominant on the court like I was when I was pitching. I could throw harder than anybody else. People would come up and say, Where have you been? Nobody throws like that. But I don't think that did my arm any good, either. As my career went on I did damage by throwing like that.

But it's American Legion ball when you start getting noticed.

Yes, coaches had seen me, and then after my sophomore year when I finished basketball and I knew I was going to play baseball, I got onto the local semipro team in Hutchinson—the Hutchinson Broncs. They brought in a lot of good college players and got them together as a group. It was a really good league. I think they called it the Victory League. The national tournament is held in Wichita, Kansas, every year, and all the teams from Alaska come down and it's just really, really good baseball. It's like an all-star thing with some of the best players from college. And I just tried out—they asked me to try out—and made the team. The first year or two they didn't pitch me much against really tough teams, you know, but I set records for the lowest ERA and I was averaging close to two strikeouts an inning. They would mix me in against a good team every now and then, but they didn't overexpose me.

When I was playing American Legion we made the state tournament and the Kansas coach, Floyd Temple, saw me and offered me a scholarship. I guess I signed too soon. I really would've liked to have gone to Louisiana State or Arizona State or something like that. I know I could've had a chance at LSU because a lot of guys that I played with were from there, but I just signed too soon.

But if it's something you want to do I can certainly understand why you'd accept the first offer.

Well, like I said, I was from Kansas and I didn't know. I was kind of naïve. You just kind of go with the flow and they were the first team that showed an interest. I didn't even check. They hadn't had a winning team in forever.

You're relatively inexperienced at this time. You didn't play high school ball and you didn't play juco ball. This is primarily natural talent showing through.

I learned how to throw what was called a forkball then by looking at a program. I saw the grip and I threw it the first time and there was just an unbelievable break. This was in Legion ball when I started tinkering with it. And the next pitch flew over the backstop, so I tinkered with it a little more because I had big hands and could split my fingers a long ways. I just kind of tinkered with it and got it to where it would work so I became a fastball-forkball pitcher. I threw a big curve but it wasn't consistent. I couldn't rely on it. I didn't really throw anything else because I didn't know how. I never had a pitching coach to teach me anything.

So when you show up at Kansas for your junior year you have a fastball, a forkball, and if someone puts a gun to your head and asks you what your third pitch is, you can say curveball.

Yeah, pretty much.

Does your fastball have movement or is it just real hard?

A little of both. I had learned to throw a two-seam and a four-seam so I knew how to make it sink and rise. They said I was throwing around ninety-seven so I was throwing a lot harder than anybody back at that time, so I didn't really have to have a third pitch, especially if the forkball was working. I didn't hardly give up any hits then.

So you weren't throwing it towards the middle of the plate and watching it move.

I tried to hit spots, but some days, you know, it just isn't there. Like I said, my Little League coach taught me how to pitch. I was pretty good for eleven and twelve, growing up. I knew what the gist of the game was. It was just a matter of execution. Some days you could and some days you couldn't. As a kid, some days you're sharp and some days you're terrible.

Do you play two years at Kansas?

I played my junior year, then I had surgery on my shoulder and won a medical hardship for the next year so I could have another season of eligibility.

What'd you do to it?

I tore up my bicipetal tendon. It comes off the back of your arm and fits in a groove in the bone and I'd worn that bone out. They'd keep popping it in but it got to where I couldn't throw between starts because once it popped and got numb I didn't have any strength. I couldn't pinch your hand if I squeezed as hard as I could. I just lost the grip and the ball would just take off. After that happened I knew I had to have the surgery and when they got in there they found those muscles that I had torn trying to throw a curveball when I was twelve. The doctor tried to mess with that and just screwed my shoulder up. He said, You probably won't play anymore.

So by the time you're twenty-one you've had surgery on what?

A foot, both knees, and my shoulder.

So you take a year off.

Well, I was trying to throw. I tried to make the comeback but I had a lot of scar tissue, I guess, and during that summer I went back to Hutchinson and was trying to play again and was throwing and my arm just snapped. I mean, it just popped and all of a sudden I had my fastball back again and I felt good. It was like I broke those adhesions loose. When I'd pitch a game before that I couldn't stay loose. I would warm up, go into the game, but then I would have to play catch between innings just to stay loose enough to go back out. So I was throwing for two and a half to three hours straight when I would pitch, but I had such good endurance that it never phased me that I was probably throwing three or four hundred balls a game.

How do you do your final year at Kansas?

We did well. I was like 7–3 with a 1.19 ERA. I made first team All Big-8 and, I guess, honorable mention all-American. The Yankees drafted me and I didn't know they'd ever watched me play. I'd been drafted before by Philadelphia, but that was right when I had surgery and they didn't want to sign me. I'd also been drafted in the secondary phase by San Diego and I made a mistake by not signing with them. I took some advice from people I thought knew baseball. It's more complex than you really think. I should've signed with them. I would've got a lot more money. I knew I would be drafted again because of the year I had but when I graduated I had no bargaining power. By then I was twenty-two. I didn't know what to tell San Diego. They said, Tell us an amount, and hell, I didn't know what to say. I didn't want to overprice myself and I didn't want to be too cheap and nobody seemed to have any answers for me. They didn't really make an offer. They said, Tell us what it'll take, and I said, Hell, I don't know. You tell me something. And they kind of hemmed and hawed around until finally I said, Well, forget it. I'll take my chances in the draft.

Now, what are the people who are telling you not to sign thinking? What logic are they using?

They just thought I would be better off waiting for the next draft because they thought I would be a higher draft pick. What they didn't realize is I had no bargaining power. I went to school for five years and it was either sign or go do something else so I ended up taking the Yankees' offer and I was kind of unhappy about it, but I was getting to play ball.

305

So how much did the Yankees give you?

I got the incentive bonus and, I think, $1,500. And I know I could've had twenty or twenty-five thousand if I'd have signed with San Diego when I wanted.

You sign with the Yankees in June of 1976 and you sign for a lot less than you think you're worth, but on the other hand you're now a professional athlete. Are you happy?

I'm happy. I'm excited. It's a new phase. I just figured, Well, I'll go show them. The way I looked at it, it was my fault. I listened to people and I made the decision to not sign so it wasn't anything to sulk about. Ultimately it doesn't matter. You want to get to the big leagues and I was going to go show them what I could do.

When the Yankees are offering you $1,500 and the incentive bonus, do they mention your shoulder surgery during the discussions or negotiations?

No, they just basically said, Here's the offer. Take it or leave it. They knew that I'd had the shoulder surgery but I'd come back from that, and they had evidently watched me pitch, I just didn't know it. They knew I had good velocity and a real good split-finger. The main thing, I guess, too, was that I was a good athlete. I was very good at fielding my position, I could pinch-run, and I could hit some, too. I got to DH a little bit in college but I needed a lot more work on it than what I got. When you don't play and get to bat you lose a lot.

You get drafted in early June. When did you sign?

I signed pretty quick. I think it was the middle of June and I was already sent out to meet the team in St Petersburg.

Do they buy you a plane ticket?

Yeah, they paid for all of that.

Do they tell you that somebody's going to pick you up at the airport?

No, I think I caught a cab to the hotel and I met the coach and some of the players. It was kind of mid-morning when I got there. The white guys told me what not to let the Dominicans call me so I learned a little

Spanish real quick. I didn't think a whole lot of it. And they asked me if I wanted to stay at the room for the night because I was tired. I hadn't had any sleep for the prior twenty-four hours trying to get stuff packed and ready but I had that nervous energy, so I said I'll go meet my teammates and see what's going on and kind of get started.

What classification is this?

It's Class A.

Do you stay with this team for the rest of the year?

Yeah.

Do they start using you immediately?

I pitched that night. I was running sprints in the outfield and they yelled at me and said they'd had a big fight the night before and a couple of guys were suspended and whatever and they said that I might be in relief if the guy got in trouble. I came in in the fifth and it was kind of funny because I looked around the infield and I was the only guy who spoke English. They said, Your catcher will come out and ask you if you're tired because that's about all the English he knows. Well, I got into a little bit of trouble the second inning I was out there, and sure enough he comes out and he says, Are you tired? And I looked around and everybody in the dugout's laughing. And I said, Hell, no, I'm not tired. So he went back behind there and I did real well. I threw five innings and only gave up three hits and got a win. No runs. And I just kind of went on from there. I didn't give up an earned run in my first twenty-eight innings, I think.

Now, how are you communicating with the catcher? He might know these hitters but it's your first day. He doesn't have a clue what you can throw, does he?

Well, it was weird. Orlando Pena was our pitching coach and he spoke fluent Spanish and he was real excited that I was coming because I threw the forkball and that was his big pitch and nobody else in the organization threw it. The catcher caught me warming up—a few pitches—and he saw what I threw, and I knew what I wanted to throw, so then if he called something and I didn't want to throw it, then I made sure he knew it. My catcher was Juan Espino and he ended up having a pretty good career going through with Toronto and New York, and maybe another team.

You finish out the year in A ball. Do you hang around for instructional league?

They want me in instructional league. I wanted to get my car and I barely had time to fly back to Kansas, get my car, and come back down. Instructional league was in Sarasota.

Was instructional league instructional? Do you learn anything?

Yeah. Basically they just wanted me to throw some more. They wanted me to mess with relieving a little bit because I threw the split-finger and Bruce Sutter was coming on. We worked all over the field, just getting used to all the plays that they run and a few other things. They wanted me to work on a slider a little bit. And I did real well. I might've lost a game but my earned run average was under one point five. I always had a low earned run average. Then the next year I went to West Haven, Connecticut, which was Double-A, and I led the league in earned run average.

Are you still a starter?

Yeah. I was like 10–9 as a starter. We had a really good team. I think we finished forty-plus games over .500.

Are you in Double-A the whole year?

Yeah. And after the playoffs I go back to instructional league again and do about the same things, but they wanted me to start relieving.

How do you feel about that?

I didn't really care. If it was faster to get to the big leagues I wanted to do it. That's all I cared about. And I knew that the Yankees weren't using their minor league system. By then I could see that it was free agency all the way. They didn't use us.

Whose roster are you on for spring training in 1978?

They sent me back to Double-A. West Haven. And I was pretty upset about it. I wasn't vocal about it. I wasn't ranting or raving but over the years I had kept track of a lot of stuff and I thought I had done better than anybody they took and I thought I should've been promoted instead of going back to West Haven. Anyway, I pitched opening night and everybody in the Yankees' major leagues, Triple-A, Double-A, and A—we all throw shutouts. Don Gullett in the big leagues, Jim Beattie in Triple-A, me in Double-A, and I think it was Chris Welsh in A ball. Every one of us pitched a shutout on opening day, and two or three days later all of us are up. I went up to Triple-A, Beattie went up to the big leagues, and Chris took my spot.

At the time it was bad because I was in West Haven, Connecticut, and our Triple-A was in Tacoma. I'd just bought a new car and had to leave it there for all of my buddies to tear up. But I had a real good year in Triple-A. I led the league in ERA again, was 13–8, 14–8, something like that. We won again. I think there was a year or two in there that all Yankee teams won everything from the majors down to A ball. We just had dominant teams. I guess what made us so good was we had really good clubhouse camaraderie. You know, on a lot of teams pitchers don't hang out with regulars. We didn't have any of that. We all got along great. We all knew we weren't going anywhere. We knew we were stuck so we might as well have fun, play some good ball, and kick some butt. We enjoyed each other's company and I guess that was the best part. We all just had fun.

Did you ever wish that you'd be traded from the Yankees?

Not the first few years. You don't really know. We were working our way up the ladder. Each year we made a progression so we didn't really start thinking about it until after my Triple-A year in Tacoma. The Yankees said they called and called trying to find me because they wanted me to come up but they never called. All they had to do was call my parents. I left and went down to California with my roommate—he lived there—and I ended up staying. I thought, It'll be good warm weather, good to work out. So anyway, they tried to tell me that and I said, Well, that doesn't make sense to me, that you tried to call. My parents never got a call so you didn't try that hard. So that made me kind of start wondering, and then the next year I hurt my arm at an off-season job. I tore a tendon in my elbow and had a broken collarbone from kind of roughhousing.

Was this two different events?

Yeah, two different incidents.

So you don't go to instructional and you don't go to winter ball.

Well, they wouldn't let us play winter ball. I was set up to go play with a pretty good team in Puerto Rico but because of what happened to Jim Beattie and Gil Patterson—good pitchers we had who hurt their arms—no pitchers could go to winter ball. I took a job for five dollars an hour in a damn factory. That's how I got hurt. I was carrying a heavy form and it just slipped out of the guy's hands and it was like 250 pounds and it just frayed that tendon. Pulled it right off the bone.

I liked playing for the Yankees. I liked the people there and all but that's when I was kind of getting into, What the hell am I doing here? I went to spring training and couldn't throw so spring training was a waste. I stayed behind in A ball until I got in shape, then went to Columbus. The Triple-A team had moved from Tacoma to Columbus.

But once you were able to throw you went up to Columbus.

Yeah, and did not have a good year. It was AstroTurf. I think I was 1–8 on our home field. The only game I won was a shutout. I was like 7–2 on the road, on natural grass, because I got to where I was throwing a lot of ground balls. I don't know. I just didn't do well. But when the season was over I got called up to New York because I wasn't good enough to make the rotation for the Triple-A playoffs. I was on the forty-man roster and they had to do something with me. And they figured, Well, the best thing to do is to just call him up and when the playoffs are over we'll call the rest of the guys up. So that's when I came up and got my one shot at pitching in the majors.

How do find out you're going to the big leagues?

They tell the coaches and they tell you at the ballpark. Me and Brian Doyle were going up together.

Do you know what it's about when the manager calls you in?

No, at the time I really didn't because I really wasn't sure what we were all doing. I figured I'd be going along to the playoffs and he said, They want you and Brian to go up to New York. The plane's leaving in the morning. We got there on a Sunday. I think we were playing Kansas City. I don't know who was pitching but I got up and threw in the third inning, the fourth inning, sixth, seventh. Hell, I pitched a whole ballgame in the bullpen. I was so pumped when I got up to throw that after I had warmed up four or five times, hell, I was shot. And then they finally told me that I was going in if it went into the tenth inning, and thank God Oscar Gamble hit a home run in the bottom of the ninth to win it because I would've gone out there and gotten absolutely annihilated.

Now, do they tell you before the game that you're the long reliever that day?

No, we weren't really in a pennant race that year, and I knew they would get me in at some point in time, but when I wasn't sure. If certain outs weren't made then I probably would've gone in that first day, but it just didn't work out that way.

When do you actually get in a game?

We were in Detroit, and by then I had kind of gotten into the flow a little bit. I don't really know how many days I was there before I pitched. I had been with all of those guys in spring training for a few years so it wasn't like I was overawed. I mean, I knew them and they were friends of mine and it was just a good experience. I was real good friends with Goose Gossage. And Sparky Lyle and Graig Nettles were real good to us. They kind of watched out for the younger kids. And I had pitched in the Mayor's Trophy game in New York. I just drove down from West Haven and pitched and then drove back to West Haven. When we were in the playoffs against Kansas City I was in instructional league. I got called up—me and another guy—to throw batting practice. They flew us to Kansas City.

That must've been pretty cool.

Yeah, it was nice. And so I got that experience so I was pretty comfortable being there with everybody.

But you make your major league debut in Detroit in Tiger Stadium. Do you remember who started the game?

Kenny Clay pitched for us. Jack Billingham pitched for them.

Did Clay get hit hard?

No, it was just one of those games where he struggled a little bit. Steinbrenner was on him pretty hard—off and on—and it was messing with Kenny's head. Kenny had great stuff. He was a good pitcher and probably should have made it, but for some reason he was in Steinbrenner's doghouse. I don't know what it was. It seemed like when he could've used some encouraging words he was being blasted.

So what inning do you go in?

I guess it was the seventh. I pitched the seventh and eighth. I knew I was going in while I was warming up and I was talking to Goose. The people there were great. That's one thing I remember. They were right there on top of us. It wasn't our first day there and you get to talking to people in the stands and I would go out and when other guys were warming up I would protect them from foul balls. People knew that it was going to be my first game and, man, they were really nice. It was a great experience for me. And then to go out and pitch. And I did really well. I threw two innings and got everybody out and struck out two.

Do you remember who you pitched to?

The first batter was Steve Kemp. I got behind him 3–1 and I just threw a batting-practice fastball in there. I didn't want to throw a real fastball because I knew that, as aggressive as he was, he would just kill it. I knew he was aggressive and I was hoping he would take the bait and he did. He tried to jerk it and he pulled a weak grounder to first and I ran over and covered and Chambliss threw me the ball and that kind of really got all the jitters out. Although I really wasn't nervous. In fact, when I went in to pitch, Gossage asked me if there was anybody that I needed to know how to pitch to and I said, Yeah, Billingham, just kind of cutting up and messing around, because I knew he wouldn't bat anyway. So we just kind of laughed and I went out and got my warm-up. I was throwing to Brad Gulden. He was my catcher in the minors so I knew him and he knew me. The next batter was Champ Summers and I struck him out. By then I was throwing a screwball so I got left-handers better than right-handers. I had no trouble with left-handers and I got him fishing. Then the last guy was Jason Thompson. And all three guys were having great years. I'm facing three big left-handers. And Thompson foul tips one that catches poor Brad Gulden in the crotch and they have to carry him off the field. He was hurting bad so Jerry Narron, who was also one of my catchers, came in, so that was comfortable. I think Jason hits a grounder to short or something like that, and Fred Stanley throws him out.

In the next inning Jerry Morales led off and hit the ball to short, too. Then I threw three nasty pitches to Lance Parrish—an outside fastball right on the corner, then a sidearmed forkball that just bottomed out, and he stood back and looked for a second, and then I threw a slider right on the outside corner and struck him out. That pitch was perfect. He just kind of shook his head and walked back. Then Aurelio Rodriguez hit a rocket to Reggie, a line drive to right field that Reggie caught for the last out. I didn't fool him at all.

So except for the fact that the Yankees don't come from behind and win, you have about as good a major league debut as somebody could ask for.

Yeah, two perfect innings and really pitched well. I felt good about it.

But you don't pitch for the rest of the year.

Well, that's where Rick Anderson comes in. After the playoffs were over, they call him up and they don't have room on the roster for him and he had such a good year. I mean, he was like 14–3 with twenty saves and a 1.59 ERA. I mean, he had an ungodly year. So they take me off the roster and put him on but they keep me up there to throw batting practice. And then that's when the incident came in Cleveland where they said Billy Martin paid Rick Anderson to hit somebody. We were at Cleveland and we just got the crap beat out of us. They accused Billy of paying pitchers to hit people. I don't know how it came about but it was kind of a shitty deal. What he did is he gave the three guys $100 to go out and have an evening on the town. They had just got whacked around in their major league debut. Hell, you'd like to go out and kind of have a few beers and shake it off and that's all it was. It was really way overblown.

First of all, a manager doesn't have to pay somebody, especially a rookie, to plunk somebody. Billy Martin could tell Rick Anderson to go out there and hit the next guy and Rick Anderson would go out there and do it.

Oh yeah. And Billy was an aggressive manager. I think it was all a matter of Steinbrenner wanting to find a way to get rid of Billy. It was one of those years. I think that was the year Goose missed a lot of time because he broke his thumb in a fight with Cliff Johnson in the locker room. It was just one of those damn years where everybody was bitching at each other and they weren't playing well. I think they won in 1977 and 1978 and now here's 1979 and they were third in the division at best. I don't know if that was Billy's last year or not but there was a lot of crap going on.

As a rookie, are you underneath the radar? You see what's going on but you're completely out of it, right?

Well, I was in some of the stuff. We had a day off in Boston and Goose called me up and said, Let's go out and do something, so we did. I think Yastrzemski's going for his three thousandth hit. I'm still on the roster but it's been a while since I've pitched. We've all been drinking and having a big time and Billy gets word that Goose was bad-mouthing Art Fowler, which he wasn't. They were on Goose for cussing in the locker room and he said, Hey, that's our place. It ain't no damn nursery. And Art said something to Goose and so he said, Hell, you ain't nothing but Billy's bobo anyway. You ain't teaching anybody shit. You're just Billy's drinking buddy. Well, then Billy gets mad and he comes up and he wants to fight Goose and Goose says, I don't want to fight you. And this is back at the hotel and Billy's wanting me to leave and I'm just standing there in the hallway like, Oh shit, you know? I'm Goose's friend but Billy's the manager and I'm thinking, What the hell do I do? I'm about ready to shit. Finally they talk it out and Billy leaves. Everybody was drunk. It was our day off. So the next day Billy calls me into his office, wanting to apologize for the incident and wanting to make sure I didn't feel bad and all, and I said, No, everything's fine, and he says, By the way, did I leave my sunglasses in your room? And I said, Billy, we weren't in my room.

But I really liked playing for Billy because he didn't play favorites, and I liked that. I wouldn't want to play any other way. He was a fighter. But I liked everybody I played for pretty much. That was a class organization. We were the only team to have pitching coaches at every level. Everybody else had a roving instructor so if you were having trouble and the guy wasn't going to be there for a month you were in deep shit. We had somebody there. We filmed some of our games so you could see what you were doing and whether you were doing anything wrong. Of course, I wish I could've been with somebody else because I know I would've got a shot at playing in the big leagues, but it still was a good experience. The friends I made. I don't think it would've been as enjoyable playing with anybody else just because of the situation. We all knew we weren't going anywhere, but then it was the New York Yankees. If you were going to be on a team, that's the team to be on. When you think of baseball, that's the New York Yankees. In spring training the Yankees would bring in Mickey Mantle, Whitey Ford. Of course, Yogi was already there. I mean, hell, what place has people like that coming in the locker room and staying with you for a couple of weeks? Whitey would help the pitchers. He's just a great guy, and Yogi's probably the most loved man in baseball. I mean, there's nobody that says anything bad about Yogi. I just really enjoyed it.

Are you on the forty-man roster in 1980?

Yeah. I knew that I kind of got shit on a little bit but it didn't bother me. Hell, I got to play. I was in a big league game. I was fixing to get over the arm woes, or so I thought. I was feeling good. And then they want me to relieve in 1980. I come out the first six games in relief but I throw as many innings as any starter. I have three three-inning relief appearances. I get a save the first time, then a no-decision, then they decide they want me to start a game. So I go from pitching every two or three days to once a week. I said, Hell, I want to throw, but they didn't want me to throw because I'm still maybe getting in a game.

But I finally do pitch in Rochester, New York, and it's rainy and after that surgery, God, it just ate my arm up. I knew it was going to be a bad day when I strike out the first guy on a forkball—and I mean the bottom fell out—and the batter turned to walk off and the umpire called it a ball and I just said, Oh shit, it's gonna be one of them days. And it was. I just got ripped. I gave up like six runs in three or four innings. It was painful to pitch. I was hurting and they knew it so they decided they were going to send me down to Double-A to warm weather and I said, No, you don't understand. It was the rain. It was cold. I'm fine. But what they really wanted to do was bring somebody else up and I was starting to not be in their plans anymore. So I went down to Nashville. It was supposed to be a couple of weeks and it ended up being two months.

I was leading the league in pitching. I've got a one-point-eight ERA, forty strikeouts, and three walks. I'm just really dominating and having a great time and they call me up to Triple-A. And I had caught pinkeye from one of the guys on the team. He'd used my towel, and I got it. Well, I go up and they didn't put me in the first game because I look like I've been jilted and crying. So I go out and pitch the next night and it was twilight and hard to see anyway. I came in the inning before and said, Hell, if a guy hits one at my head, I'm dead, because I can't even see it back from the catcher. The first guy next inning hits me right between the eyes. Almost killed me. If it had been an inch lower it would've killed me. It felt like someone stuck a shotgun to my head and pulled the trigger. Boy, it was loud. I went down. I've got pictures of it. I put my glove to my face but you can see the blood running down my arm. And the ball's got a cut in it just like a horseshoe, the same shape as my nose where it went in. It just crushed everything. I don't know how I didn't lose my left eye. I was conscious the whole time and I could see my teammates coming over. My shortstop got sick. I thought, Oh shit. What do I look like? The trainer came out. He was an old Vietnam MASH doctor and he just grabbed my nose and squished it and I could feel it and he broke something off and I said, Don't touch me no more. But he stopped the bleeding and I went to the hospital and a plastic surgeon came in and straightened my nose out the best he could and stitched me up. It took thirty stitches or something, just a real short area. And I figured I'd be ready to go in a couple of weeks but I had spots in my cornea and they wouldn't let me pitch anymore for the rest of the year and that's kind of the start of the downfall because they didn't want to protect me anymore on the forty-man roster. I'm damaged goods.

In 1981 I came back and did great. I was leading the league in complete games. I was like 9–5. I left a game after six innings with a two-run lead but I knew when I left that game I had hurt my arm. It was painful. It was against Cal Ripken and them when he was at Double-A. I started out in Triple-A but then they said, We know what you can do. We want to see what everybody else can do. I went down but I could see what was going on. I did real well the first half of the season, then tore my rotator cuff and sat out the rest of the year. Came back the next year. They didn't want to do surgery. I pitched sixteen innings in spring training, never gave up a run, but they sent me back to Nashville so I said, This is it. I'm through. Came back the first game and I think about the third batter I tore it again. I think I pitched in about five or six games but I couldn't throw. They put me on the disabled list and I was pretty much the pitching coach for the rest of the year. I'd always try to help the pitchers with their mechanics and all because I had a knack for it. We had a really good team and a bunch of really good young pitchers. Hoyt Wilhelm was our pitching coach but he was out a lot. He had gout or something where even the weight of sheets would send fire through your body. And he was getting older. But I really learned a lot from Hoyt. He really taught me how to pitch control. It's like shooting a gun. He'd say, You set your target and if you're off, if you're low and outside all the time, then instead of looking at the glove, look at the catcher's shoulder. Set your sights a little different. And I never had trouble with control from then on. I was blessed with good pitching coaches. Pat Dobson was another of our pitching coaches in Nashville and he really made it enjoyable. If I had to be sent down then at least I was in a great city. That's when Nashville was first getting teams and, hell, we were drawing twenty thousand people. It was really a great experience to be here. I was disappointed but at the same time I was enjoying myself, playing ball, hoping somebody would see me and I'd get a shot. Then when I tore my rotator cuff again I knew it was over with. I knew that was the end of it.

Do you have any regrets?

Well, I wish I had signed with San Diego so I could see how I would've done in more than one game, because I think I would've done well. It was a great experience. I got to be around some very famous people. Great ballplayers and great people, too. I still, to this day, stay in touch with Goose.

Did you keep memorabilia from your career?

I didn't keep the ball that I pitched with in the big league game. As I was walking off the field there was a kid right on top of the dugout, little kid, maybe three years old—I'd seen him when I came in before—and it was the end of the game and he was just really having a big time with his mom and dad, so when I came off and saw him there I just rolled the ball across the top of the dugout to him. I thought, I'll get more of these. I never dreamed, after that, that I would never pitch in another game so I gave him the ball. But I've got signed balls by Mickey Mantle and Whitey Ford and Yogi and Reggie and from some of my friends. And I've got some balls like the '84 Padres when they won. A couple of my room-mates, Tim Lollar and Chris Welsh, were pitching for them. Other than that it's just some games where I struck out a lot or had a real good game or something like that.

Do you watch much baseball now?

Mostly the playoffs. Until it gets near the end and records are being chased I'm not that interested in it unless it's somebody that I really like.

Do you cheer for any particular team?

I cheer for the Yankees. I cheered for Seattle this year, too. And I liked Oakland and the Cardinals. If they're playing good ball, then I like watching it. I don't like sloppy ball. One thing that I am disappointed in now is the people that they allow to pitch in the big leagues. The lack of talent. They're not ready. There's been too much expansion. I mean, when you call up a kid from Double-A and he's not even a .500 pitcher and has a high ERA, I mean, what are they thinking of? They think they're going to get big league hitters out? Hell, there's no wonder they got home run records being broken. The talent is down, I think. And there are smaller ballparks. To me, it's kind of making a mockery of the old records that stood for so long. It's a shame it's that way because I really don't think some of these guys are any better. It's just diluted pitching and smaller ballparks. And possibly a livelier ball.

But I got to do something that you dream about as a kid, so I can't complain about any of that. Maybe if I had taken better care of myself, or listened, maybe I would've prevented some of the injuries, but all that's hindsight. When you're young you think that nothing can hurt you or stop you, and hell, you're not going to listen to everything that's going on.

Philadelphia at Montreal.
Sunday, October 5, 1980

Philadelphia	ab	r	h	rbi	Montreal	ab	r	h	rbi
Rose, 1b	2	0	2	0	White, rf-cf	5	1	1	3
McCa'r, pr-1b	3	2	1	2	Bernazard, 2b	4	1	2	2
Brusstar, p	1	0	0	0	Cromartie, 1b	2	0	0	0
Aguayo, ss	5	0	2	1	Raines, lf	3	0	0	0
Isales, rf	4	1	1	1	Dawson, cf	3	1	1	1
G. Vukovich, lf	3	0	1	1	Pate, rf	2	0	0	0
Lerch, p	1	0	0	0	Wallach, lf-1b	5	0	1	1
Gross, 1b	1	0	0	0	Mills, 3b	3	0	2	0
Virgil, c	5	1	1	0	Scott, pr	0	0	0	0
Dernier, cf	5	1	2	0	Macha, 3b-c	1	0	0	0
J. Vukov'h, 3b	5	0	1	1	Manuel, ss	4	0	0	0
Loviglio, 2b	4	1	0	0	Hutton, ph	1	0	0	0
Davis, p	2	1	1	0	Ramos, c	3	1	2	0
Unser, ph	1	0	1	0	LeFlore, pr	0	1	0	0
Smith, pr-lf	1	0	0	0	Speier, 3b	1	1	1	0
					Ratzer, p	1	0	0	0
Totals	43	7	13	6	Carter, ph	0	0	0	0
					D'Acquisto, p	0	0	0	0
					Tamargo, ph	0	1	0	0
					Dues, p	0	0	0	0
					Parrish, ph	0	0	0	1
					Lea, p	0	0	0	0
					Montanez, ph	1	1	1	0
					Totals	39	8	11	8

Philadelphia	0	0	2	3	0	0	0	0	0	2—7
Montreal	2	0	0	0	0	2	0	1	0	3—8

Philadelphia	IP.	H.	R.	ER.	BB.	SO.
Davis	5	4	2	2	4	4
Lerch...........	3	4	3	3	2	0
Brusstar (L. 2-2)	1.2	3	3	3	0	0
Montreal	IP.	H.	R.	ER.	BB.	SO.
Ratzer	4	9	5	5	2	0
D'Acquisto	2	1	0	0	0	1
Dues	2	0	0	0	0	0
Lea (W. 7-5)	2	3	2	1	1	1

E—Bernazard 2 (10). 2B—McCarver (1, off Ratzer), Unser (6, off D'Acquisto), Virgil (1, off Lea), Dawson (41, off Davis), Ramos (2, off Lerch). HR—White (7, off Brusstar). SB—Dernier (3, 2B Ratzer/Ramos), Aguayo (1, 2B off Ratzer/Ramoss), Smith (33, 2B base off Lea/Macha), Bernazard 2 (9, 2B base off Davis/Virgil 2), Scott (63, 2B off Lerch/Virgil), LeFlore 2 (97, 2B off Lerch/Virgil, 3B off Lerch/Virgil). CS—Smith (13, 3B by D'Acquisto/Ramos). IBB—Smith (2, by Lea). A— 30,104 .

STEVE RATZER

Steve Ratzer pitched in thirteen games for the Montreal Expos over the 1980 and 1981 seasons. His major league debut, a start against the Philadelphia Phillies, occurred on the last day of the 1980 season. He gave up thirty-two hits over twenty-one and one-third innings while walking nine and striking out four. He finished with a record of 1–1 and a career ERA of 7.17. He was interviewed February 4, 2002 at a picnic table in front of Wal-Mart in Lakeland, Florida.

Tell me where you grew up and when you first started playing baseball.

I was born in Paterson, New Jersey, but that's because my father sent my mother home to have each of the children. I never lived there. About 1960 my father bought a house on Long Island—Jericho, Long Island—and that's where I first played baseball.

I remember the first baseball game I ever played. I don't remember the game but I remember one thing that happened, because I had never played organized baseball. I remember they put me out in center field in the last inning of the game just to see if I could catch or throw. I'd always thrown with my dad. My dad was a ballplayer. And I remember running. And today it's like the Willie Mays catch to me, because I was eight years old. I still remember catching it over my shoulder. Now, whether I really caught it over my shoulder, I don't know, but I made that catch and after that I played every inning of every Little League game.

Are you younger than the rest of the players at that time?

Yeah. I was like eight years old and I was playing Little League already, which was like ten to twelve. Most of the kids were older.

I've talked to very few professional ballplayers who ever played the outfield in Little League.

I was eight years old and this was the first time I ever went out there. I mentioned my dad. My dad was a great ballplayer. He went to Eastern District High School, but he had to support his mom. He was offered a contract with the Dodgers—this is what he told me—he passed away a long time ago, but this is what he told me back then. Because he was supporting his mom at the time, he couldn't go.

What position did your dad play?

Third base. That's what he told me. I never saw him play baseball. I just had a catch with him all the time and he had a great arm.

Did he want you to be a baseball player?

Absolutely.

And you shared that dream?

I loved baseball. I've always liked baseball.

When you were a kid, that's what you wanted to do when you grew up.

Always. I was a Mickey Mantle fan. He was the greatest person in the world. I don't have a lot of heroes. My dad was one of my heroes, but if

322

there was anyone that I looked up to it would be Mickey Mantle. Now, a lot of stories have come out and things like that, but I respected Mickey Mantle for what he went through. I read every book about Mickey Mantle back then. He was just my hero. He was The Mick, and I wanted to be like him. I didn't care about anybody else.

I wound up, when I was in college, becoming very close friends with Eddie Ford, Whitey's son, staying over at their house in Lake Success a couple of times and never seeing Mickey, knowing he was in the house. But then in my final season of professional baseball, in 1983, I met Mickey Mantle. I was with the Denver Bears. I think we might've been the Zephyrs by that point, I'm not really sure. But we were in Oklahoma City and Mickey was the first-pitch celebrity. And I waited until he walked out, and then I walked out along with him and just talked to him for about five minutes.

He was bigger than life. I'll never forget his smile. He had a great smile. That Oklahoma drawl, or whatever you want to call it. I appreciated him taking five minutes of his life to spend with me. It was a different experience for me than I had ever had, because I had never had other heroes. And I met him, and I talked to him, and he was a real guy. And I shook his hand and his hand was like super, super big and strong and thick. This was I don't know how many years after he played baseball, but I wanted him to go up there and hit. I wanted some of these young kids that I was playing with to see Mickey go up there and hit a ball over the right-field stands, because in my thoughts he could still do it.

How long does it take for them to move you from the Little League outfield to the pitcher's mound?

A week. My first practice they saw how I could throw and I was pitching.

What position did you play on the days you weren't pitching?

Shortstop or third base. I was never really a good hitter, though. I mean, I was a good hitter in Little League. I hit .390 in high school against pretty weak opposition in New York City.

Are you the best player on your Little League team?

Yeah. Absolutely.

Are you playing other sports?

Basketball. I loved basketball. First of all, I was slow. I was never a fast runner, but I could shoot, just like most pitchers can shoot. I had a good outside shot. I liked to assist. I played point guard. I grew up in New York City. Street ball. We didn't have a lot of baseball fields, so if I wasn't playing baseball I was playing basketball. I loved the workout, because when you play basketball serious for a couple of hours, it's a serious, serious workout, and I liked that about it.

Are you noticeably better at baseball than you are at basketball?

Absolutely. I liked playing basketball, I think, better than playing base-ball. I liked pitching as much as playing basketball, but I liked playing basketball as much as I liked playing baseball because there's just so much action all the time. Maybe you can see it. I'm a little bit hyper.

When do you first start getting noticed by recruiters and scouts?

It didn't happen until my senior year in high school. I didn't pitch a lot until my senior year in high school and the reason is, in New York City, you only play a twelve-game season. You play two games a week for six weeks, and if you have one great pitcher, nobody else ever pitches. So Jeff Freid was our top pitcher when I was in high school, and he was a senior when I was a junior. He pitched all the time. I went into my senior year in high school, I think, 8–1 in the previous two seasons, and that was only because he had a shoulder injury once, and he got the flu a couple of times, so I had to pitch. The only game I lost in high school I pitched all ten innings against Flushing High School and I lost 2–1 on a passed ball.

But your senior year, you're the Jeff Freid.

Absolutely.

And you're pitching almost every game, and if your only high school loss is against Flushing your junior year, then you go undefeated your senior year.

Right. I was 11–0 my senior year.

Are colleges and pros both coming to games that year?

Pros a little bit. Not a whole lot. Colleges? Substantial. I had a bunch of scholarship offers. In the last game in high school I pitched a no-hitter in Yankee Stadium for the championship of New York City.

Was that the best day of your life to that point?

That was probably the best day of my life in my life. We won 2–0 against George Washington, which is where Manny Ramirez and many other major league players went to high school. We won 2–0 and after that there were thirty-five scholarship letters within a week. I traveled a little bit and had some fun traveling and seeing what college I wanted to go to and that type of thing. My mom was sick with cancer. She was going to pass away within a couple of years. We knew that. So I wound up choosing St John's and going to St John's because it was home. I lived at home and she did pass away during my sophomore year.

Is there a baseball history at St John's, or is it purely a decision to stay close to home and your mom?

St John's is a good baseball school. Mike Proly was before me, and, of course, Frank Viola and John Franco came after me. St John's just had a good, solid baseball program, good educational program. They also went to Florida and trained at major league spring training sites every other season, so I knew I'd get some exposure there. But what made it happen for St John's was Jack Kaiser, who was the baseball coach at the time. He became the athletic director and then I think he became the ECAC commissioner. A quality man. He's just a great man. I saw him in September last year. I played in a golf tournament for my college pitching coach, Howie Gershberg, who's sick with cancer right now. I was the guest speaker because Viola had to go see his daughter swim in Minnesota or something like that, and Franco was still playing.

Are you at St John's all four years?

Yes.

Are you getting attention from the pro scouts?

Absolutely.

The rule, at the time, is they can't draft you until your junior year.

Right. Junior year. They started talking to me but they always said I couldn't throw hard enough.

What are your pitches when you arrive on campus?

Fastball, curveball. I always had great control.

Are you coming over the top?

Yeah, and I threw sidearm and I twisted my body and I did everything I could. I was a sinker-slider pitcher mostly.

You were a pitcher, not a thrower.

Exactly. I was a pitcher. I was a pitcher. Today I can still hit spots.

Did you have these skills in high school?

I had them in high school. I think I walked six guys my senior year in high school. I didn't walk people unless I was pitching around them.

When you get to St John's, are you immediately the number-one starter?

Mike Proly was the number-one starter. Marty Dwonarksi was the number-two starter. He was a left-hander and threw really well. And they really didn't have a number-three starter. But the first game of my freshman year we were playing the police. The police have a really good team and these guys didn't want to pitch against them because they were good. I pitched a no-hitter. Won two to nothing. So that's two no-hitters in a row, with taking the summer and traveling around the United States with my best friend in between. We just traveled around. I didn't throw a baseball. I got to practice, practiced for a week, and pitched in this ballgame against the PBA and pitched a no-hitter. And after that I pitched every four or five days in college. If I hadn't done well, this whole thing could be real different. I mean, they threw me out there and said, Pitch. It could've been very different. I moved past a lot of pitchers that had spent two and three years establishing themselves at St John's just to get the opportunity, but I pitched well that game and that was it.

Do you get drafted after your junior year?

Nope. Didn't get drafted after my senior year either.

Are you disappointed the first time?

No, not disappointed. I was going to finish college. I knew I wasn't going to be a high draft pick so I was going to finish college without a doubt. I had aspirations but I knew that I was not this flamethrower that was going to light the world on fire when I got the chance to play professional baseball.

But you're not drafted after your senior year either.

Right. Very disappointing. Tremendously disappointing. I led the nation in ERA my junior year.

Are you surprised as well?

Yeah. Disappointed and surprised. I was on the USA baseball team. I led the nation in ERA. I don't know my exact figures but I think I was 42–10 in college. I still have the record for the most wins ever at St John's. Disappointed and surprised, yeah. I didn't expect to go high, but I expected somebody to draft me, somebody to take a shot.

Do any of the scouts who have been following you contact you after the draft to explain?

Three teams called me the day after the draft—the Expos, the Tigers, and the Yankees.

Do they all tell you the same thing?

No, they all tell me a different story. The Yankees said, We want you to go to Double-A. We think you can contribute at the Double-A level, but we don't know whether or not you'll make it to next spring training. We think you're a Double-A pitcher. We think you're a Double-A pitcher now and you may never be better than a Double-A pitcher.

And this does not make you feel special.

No, it doesn't. So the Tigers say to me, We're going to send you down to Lakeland, and we'll see how you do. We think you're a good A ball pitcher. You're going to have to show us what you can do. There might be an opportunity for you. I said, Okay. And the Expos called me up. Tom Giordano was the scout who called me. He ended up being the head scout for the Baltimore Orioles. He said, We're going to send you to rookie ball. We're not going to give you a bonus. You're going to go to rookie ball, and if you're the best pitcher in rookie ball you'll get to A ball. And if you're the best pitcher in A ball you'll go to Double-A, and if you're the best pitcher in Double-A you'll go to Triple-A, and if you're the best pitcher in Triple-A you'll pitch in the major leagues. I said, Okay.

Nobody's offering you a bonus and the monthly salary is comparable.

$600 a month, something like that. I think the Yankees said $800.

What about the Expos organization made you go with them?

The message, and the fact that they sucked. My dream was always to pitch in the major leagues. If I'm going to pitch in the major leagues, probably the best opportunity for me is going to be with a team that's as bad as the Montreal Expos. I just knew that the Expos were not a great baseball team. They told me that if I produced at each level that I would move. I can't ask for more than honesty, and they were honest. They were all honest, but two of them said, There's no future, and one of them said, Do well and you'll move through the system. Okay. Then I'll just have to prove that you're all wrong.

How soon after the draft do you sign?

Two or three days.

Where do they send you?

They sent me right to Lethbridge, Alberta, Canada. I think it's ninety miles from Calgary. I flew to Calgary, landed in Calgary, and they're paging me at the airport. Pick up the red courtesy phone. I'll never forget those words, because I picked up the red courtesy phone and they said, You're on the next flight back to New York. You need to call home. Your father's had a heart attack. You need to go home.

I signed the contract with Tom Giordano at the airport with my father. The plane took off and my father fell down and died. I didn't know he had died. About halfway through the flight back I felt something happen to me, and I knew that he had died, but nobody had told me that yet. They told me he had a heart attack. And I got back to New York and buried my father. I spent a week mourning, then flew back to Lethbridge. There's one small part of my life with the Expos that I wasn't happy with, but to this day I feel they were a class organization. They did what they said they would do, and the way they handled that whole situation, they could not have shown more class. Absolutely could not have shown more class. The Expos were owned by the Bronfman family at the time. Mel Didier was the director of the minor leagues. Pat Daugherty was one of the coaches up there and Lance Nichols was the manager. They could not have been more supportive or understanding of the whole situation. Fabulous. They even found me a place to live while I was in New York so I would have a place to live when I got back to Lethbridge. I didn't have to look for a place to live. They don't do that. I roomed with Andre Dawson, and we became very good friends. It was wonderful.

In hindsight do you make a connection between signing the contract, becoming a professional baseball player, and that being your father's dream?

Absolutely. Without any question.

In a sense he's been fulfilled.

Without any question. Without any doubt in my mind. I don't go through it anymore, but I went through that millions of times, that this was my dad's dream, this is what he wanted. I don't think there are too many who knew my dad that wouldn't have understood that. I mean, he was an executive vice-president of a big company called National Shirt Shops, which no longer exists. They went out of business about a year after he passed. This was a different era. He would leave work—which was unheard of in those days—to come watch my high school baseball games. Unheard of in those days.

Do you have siblings?

Yeah. I have a brother and a sister.

Younger? Older?

Both younger.

How much sense of family do you take with you to rookie ball, having a younger brother and sister, and both of your parents having passed away? You're really on your own.

I was twenty-one, my sister was twenty. My brother was fifteen.

What about your brother?

329

We still struggle today, because I left to go play baseball.

Were you supposed to come home and run the house until he graduated?

I was supposed to come home and take care of him and teach him about life, in his mind. My dad had remarried. He married the woman who had introduced my mother to him back in the forties. Two years after mom died, he married Frieda.

So your brother lives with his stepmother and finishes high school, but he thinks he's your responsibility, not Frieda's.

Absolutely. You're exactly right.

And you were starting your life.

I was out and about and pursuing my baseball career and kind of very close-minded about where I was going.

What does "close-minded about where you were going" mean?

Monomaniacal. I was focused on what I was going to do with my life and my career and didn't have time for my little brother. Didn't have the time that he expected me to have.

That sounds more like his words than yours.

Yeah, they are.

I mean, you're twenty-one years old and you've just signed a professional base-ball contract.

I'm living the dream.

I'm not trying to paint you with a stereotype brush, but professional athletes are not generally known for their selflessness.

I agree.

You're twenty-one, which is a pretty selfish age to start with, and you're start-ing in rookie ball trying to achieve your dream and your father's dream.

Right, but I didn't make time for my brother.

Did you come home during the off-season?

I didn't come home to my brother. I got a separate place, a different place. Didn't spend a whole lot of time with him. And these are my words. I was not there for him as his father, or as his older sibling teaching him about life. I'm not mad at myself for it. He's mad at me for it. He'll never get over it. We don't have a great relationship.

When I finally got to the major leagues, when the season ended—I lived in Colorado at the time—I drove through Buffalo where he was going to college, stopped by to see him, and he didn't have time for me. I was going to stay there as long as I needed to. My season was over. I was going to go to winter ball but I had a month before I had to go and he just didn't have the time of day for me. So I got back in my van and drove to Colorado. I learned from that.

That's payback.

Yeah, it is. But that's human nature, I think. And again, I'm not mad at him for not making time for me. I wish we had a better relationship today. But I make no effort. He made some effort for a while, and I didn't respond. I can't say there was a real reason. I love my brother. He lives down in Boca Raton and has a very comfortable life. My brother's a good guy. He's one of the good guys.

You referred to baseball players as not being selfless, and you're really right about that. You can still be a nice person and a good person, and I don't think I've ever been looked at as a bad person, or not a nice person. On my gravestone I hope they just write, Good guy.

How's Andre Dawson as a roommate?

Fabulous. One of the finest men that I've ever known in my life.

Would you say he's a clean person or a messy person?

Clean.

Were you clean or messy?

Clean. We could not have gotten along better. We lived with an older couple and we'd wake up every day and breakfast was prepared. We were living in their basement and we'd wake up and there'd be breakfast and we'd go out and we wouldn't do a whole lot during the day, and we'd come back and there'd be sandwiches before the game. And after the game there would be sandwiches and notes for us. It was an old couple that just took care of us. It was wonderful. I don't think we paid them but $100 a month or something. Now, you're talking almost thirty years ago, but they were just happy to have us, have nice young men living in their home.

How do you do in rookie ball?

Andre won the Most Valuable Player in rookie ball and I won the Cy Young Award. We probably went through eighty ballplayers that season. Six people from that team made it to spring training the following year, so we saw about seventy-four people released.

When a guy gets called into the manager's office, do you know that that guy's gone?

Yeah.

How do you react to a situation like that? A teammate being released? Does it depend on how well you know him, or is that just a situation that you physically want to be away from because there's not much more to say than, Hey, good luck?

Well, it depends on who you are. A lot of the players would make sure they got out of the clubhouse before this guy got out because some guys go crazy. I'm from New York. I've always wanted to do the right thing. I don't know if that's New York or if that's just Steve Ratzer.

It isn't New York.

Okay. Maybe it was my parents. I always wanted to give the guy a pat on the back and say, Hey man, don't give up. You're eighteen years old, or you're nineteen years old. Don't give up just because it didn't work here. And I wasn't afraid of the guy that was going to take the bat and break the lockers. He wasn't mad at me. I didn't beat him out. He didn't play well. That's why he's going home. If you played well, they kept you around. Not a whole lot of guys play well in rookie ball. There are a lot of seventeen-, eighteen-year-old kids that are facing pitchers like me. Maybe that's a bit arrogant, but I'm twenty-one years old. I went through four years of college. They've never seen a curveball.

Anything with a wrinkle and they have problems.

I would throw a curveball and they would literally fall down, and it would be right over the middle of the plate. They could hit any fastball I threw up there unless I spotted it. So I think it's the person. Like I said, a lot of the guys would try and get out of there. What was interesting was, off of that team, four of us were flown to Montreal at the end of the rookie ball season. Andre, Andrew Dye, Art Miles, who was the number-one draft pick, and me.

I don't think I've ever heard of Art Miles.

No, you never heard of him. I don't think he ever got out of A ball. He was from Texas and he really struggled. I don't think he hit .200 that year.

They flew us out and let us spend a week with the major league team. Batting practice, hanging out in the clubhouse, just to give us a feel, because we were the four people that they thought, off of that team, might have a chance. Obviously one was a draft pick. Andrew was a number-four pick. I think Andre was like a twelfth-round pick. And that was special. That was fun.

What were you thinking while you were up there? Were you impressed by the level of talent?

I thought that I was as good as them at that point. And I had to. I had to think I was good enough at that point. I was already twenty-one, twenty-two years old. I was good. I watched them. And they threw harder than me, most of them, but I wasn't impressed. I didn't want to be impressed. Maybe I convinced myself not to be impressed. But there was nobody that showed me a whole lot.

What do you do after the season?

I go back to New York, work for Macy's, get my own place. I worked for Macy's as a computer programmer. That's what I studied at St John's, computer science. That was before PCs were invented.

When you're filling out the job application at Macy's, do you tell them you've got to be at spring training in four months?

I lied. I told them I wasn't going to leave. I did a bad thing.

I wasn't trying to indict.

I don't have a problem with the question. I'm just telling you that I lied and I don't like admitting that I lied because I don't lie. But I had a computer degree. I had a 4.0 in computer science in college. Anybody will hire me.

How do you manage a 4.0 in computer science and graduate in four years while you're playing baseball full-time? That's pretty rare.

Well, my 4.0 was in computer science. My cumulative was like a 3.2.

Still, being the number-one starter and graduating in four years with those kind of grades is pretty impressive. College athletes don't graduate in four years.

Not now. I think we did then. I think we did. At St John's, that was important. There were a couple of easy courses—theology courses—that you knew you were going to pass. I found theology real easy, and I got like 780 on my SATs in math. I have an aptitude for math. I have a mathematical, logical mind. And computers are all logic. I found that all I had to do was think it through and I could do it.

334

It wasn't like you were locked away in your dorm room surrounded by books.

I never studied. I had an aptitude and I didn't have to study a lot to do well.

So you go to Florida in the spring of 1976.

They took me to major league camp just as an invitee. The four of us, again, from the rookie ball team, so I knew somebody. And I did not pitch in any of the major league games. I pitched in the intrasquad games. That was Gary Carter's first season in the big leagues. He was a right fielder, I think. I got to throw a lot of batting practice, and I was glad to throw batting practice. I got the exposure, my name on my uniform. That was kind of cool. Then I went to A ball.

Were you disappointed with that assignment?

No, because they told me. I was not disappointed at all.

You're moving up a prescribed ladder.

I know that, and that's what they told me, and they were true to it.

Where does Andre go?

He goes with me. For a week.

It must've been a good week.

He had a pretty good week. By the end of that season he was in the big leagues. I don't even know if he lasted a week. It might've been two games. I think he had four home runs or something crazy like that.

Where is A ball?

West Palm Beach, Florida. Which was great. This was when we trained in Daytona. We trained in Daytona and then went to West Palm for A ball. I played the whole season there. Had an average season, I think. I started, probably, two games, and relieved in most of the others. I think I was about 8–8.

At the end of the season, are you disappointed that you've relieved more than you've started? Do you see it as a demotion, or are you just happy to be making progress?

The thing I was disappointed in was that I didn't make progress, that I wasn't the best pitcher in A ball by the end of that season. There were better pitchers in the league, there were better pitchers on my team. I was frustrated.

A lot of guys got released that season, too. Guys were all over the place. I remember one guy was John Scoras. He used to cry into his newspaper every day that he wasn't hitting .300. All-American guy and every day he would read the newspaper and sit there. We shared an apartment, and he would sit there and just bawl. He had hit like .400 in the Pioneer League the year before. He wound up getting released, but he had broken all the records. Everything that Andre did the year before, he did better. And then he came to A ball and couldn't hit a breaking pitch, a better breaking pitch.

I was disappointed. I went home and worked tremendously, tremendously hard, physically getting myself in shape, getting my head right, getting myself in the best physical condition because I knew if I didn't have a good spring I was going to get released.

Is this running? Is this lifting? Is this throwing?

I never lifted weights. It was running, exercising, stretching, throwing. Throwing a lot.

And you already have the repertoire from way back.

Right. I knew how to pitch, but I didn't perform, so I wanted to get as sharp as I could. So in 1977 I go to spring training and pitched in some intrasquad major league games and pitched very, very well. I had a tremendous spring. Saved my career, and was sure that I made the Double-A team. And the last day of spring training they sent me to A ball. Felipe Alou was my manager.

Are you upset? Surprised? All of these?

I'm glad I'm still playing, but I know that I've got it. I mean, I don't think I gave up a run in spring training. I was hot. I knew I was throwing the ball as well as I've ever thrown it.

So you're like, Fine, I know I won't be here long.

I won't be here long, and I wasn't. I was there about a month. And Felipe told me, You're my man out of the bullpen. You're my closer. That's the way it is. And I think I saved twelve games in a month. Went right up to Double-A. Gave up seven runs in Double-A in three months and finished the season in Triple-A.

Where's Double-A?

Quebec City. Beautiful city. I loved Quebec City. I like culture, and there's a lot of culture. I like wine. Quebec is a great place.

And Triple-A was where?

Denver.

So you go from A ball at the beginning of the season all the way up to Triple-A.

And winning the championship. Pitching in two of the championship games and winning one.

Does the Triple-A manager use you in relief as well?

Two starts. I was only there a week of the regular season and then the playoffs. Two starts in the regular season, one start in the playoffs, and one relief appearance in the playoffs.

Where are you for spring training of 1978?

Major league camp.

Forty-man roster?

No.

So Triple-A is your hope. Where do you end up?

Triple-A. I start in Triple-A in 1978. I had a good season. I think I was 7–9, or something like that. It wasn't a bad season. A five-something ERA in Denver, which was one of the better ones on the team. I was really learning how to pitch at that level because I had just come up for those two weeks the season before. The old adage was—and this is what you always heard—was that if you can get out of Double-A, you're good enough to play in the big leagues. Well, I got out of Double-A. I made a whole season in Triple-A and pitched pretty well that season. And I was invited to winter ball.

You said, "learning how to pitch at that level." That's not a literal sea-level reference, that's a Triple-A reference.

Absolutely. Double-A guys, you can make mistakes with. With Triple-A guys, if you make mistakes you get whiplash.

Do you consciously pitch differently at altitude?

Absolutely.

Do you try to throw more sinkers?

More sinkers, less sliders. You try and jam hitters more. You don't want them to get extended. At Mile High it was still a poke to right field, but I hit balls out in batting practice to left field, and I couldn't hit so I knew that it would fly. Right-handed hitters you pitched off the plate outside, or off the plate inside, but there was nothing that I was giving them to hit.

So you would pitch differently to the same hitter depending on whether or not you were home or away.

Without a doubt. Without any question whatsoever. No question. I remember a guy named Mike Calise with the Springfield Redbirds hit a ball off of me into the second deck at Mile High Stadium, and I just didn't think that anybody could ever reach it. I tipped my hat. I went, Holy shit. I'd never seen a ball hit that far in my life. He was a power-hitting first baseman and he had probably fifty home runs that year, and he got all of that one. He got every bit of that.

So I went to winter ball, played in Venezuela. I played with the Phillies team. Ruben Amaro was there, Tony Taylor.

How do you end up with them?

They saw me pitch in Oklahoma City. Their Triple-A team was in Oklahoma City and they wanted me. I went down there and did very, very well. We won the Caribbean Series.

Is the money comparable between Triple-A and winter ball?

Oh, no. I'm making a lot more down there. Two, three thousand dollars a month down there. Triple-A I was probably making about twelve hundred, fourteen hundred a month. It was a way to make a living playing baseball. And I speak Spanish.

And it keeps you from lying to Macy's.

You got it. And it was furthering my career, I thought. I went down there and pitched well. I went down there for two seasons, to Venezuela. I went down there after the 1979 season as well.

For the same Phillies team?

Yeah. Aguilas del Zulia. It's the team in Maracaibo. I had a great experience down there. Drank a lot of Polar, which is their beer, and a lot of Brugal, which is their rum. I really, really enjoyed it—the culture, again. Came back in 1979. I started a lot in 1979. I had a good season. Jack McKeon was my manager. He was an interesting sort of guy. He had already managed the Kansas City Royals before that. Kind of a slob. He needed a place to live and I had been living in Denver for three years at that point so I helped him get a place and my friend had to replace the carpeting where McKeon lived because he used to put out his cigars on the carpet. But that was Jack. He was a good manager. He knew the game. Told you what you wanted to hear instead of the way it was, and I've always struggled with that in life. I'm a guy that says it the way it is. I wear my feelings on my sleeve and he kept telling me that I was going to go up and do this and do that, and it wasn't going to happen. I wasn't even considered. Played winter ball again and then in 1980 I go back to Triple-A.

Are you starting to get a certain level of frustration?

I'm getting to a level where I know that I belong in the major leagues because I'm better than some other people that I'm seeing going in front of me, but I have not performed at the level that they had told me I needed to perform. I needed to be the best at each level and I wasn't the best at Triple-A yet. So that winter in winter ball, and going into spring training, I was committed, to myself, to be the best pitcher in Triple-A. The best. And leave them no choice. And I was. I think I was 15–4.

Starter?

I was a starter most of the year. I started out as a reliever. Billy Gardner was my manager. Just a great guy, but obviously when you have a great year you think your manager is the greatest guy in the world. 15–4, ERA in the threes in Denver. Just a tremendous year, and I got called up to the major leagues. I got there and sat around for a month.

You get called up on September first, but you don't make your debut until October fifth.

It was the last day of the season.

Where are you?

In Montreal against the Phillies.

How much notice did you get?

Five minutes.

Really?

Oh yeah. I didn't know I was pitching until I got to the ballpark. We had lost the pennant to the Phillies the night before so everybody went and got drunk and had a bunch of fun and came to the park hungover.

Were you one of the ones who had gone out the night before?

No, no, no, no, no. I thought I might pitch. I wasn't going to screw it up.

When the Expos lose the game on October fourth, you know there's a strong possibility that you're going to pitch on the fifth.

I was the only guy that hadn't pitched. I didn't know I was going to start, but I knew I might pitch. So I warm up, I feel good. They announce me, I'm all excited, I'm in the big leagues. Bobby Ramos is my catcher. I throw a sinker low and away to Pete Rose. He's my first batter. Perfect pitch. My perfect sinker, about eighty-six, eighty-seven miles an hour. Right on the outside corner. Like I was in midseason form. Umpire calls it a strike. Pete Rose turns around and looks at Bobby Ramos and says, Man, he's got a helluva sinker. Bobby calls time out, comes out to the mound, and says, Hey, man. Pete Rose just told me you had a helluva sinker. I said, Cool. Let's throw it again.

Oh, no.

Yeah. Did he set me up or what? So we throw the exact same pitch and Pete Rose hit it right between short and third for one of his five million base hits and I thought, What a stupid ass you are.

They hit me pretty good. They hit me pretty hard that day. Not ridiculous, but I gave up my share of singles and didn't strike out anybody. I remember that.

You give up five runs in four innings but you don't lose the game.

Mark Davis was the opposing pitcher. He'd been called up also. I don't think he had pitched the whole month either, and he pitched kind of the same way I did. Didn't lose. Gave up five runs. After a month off I wasn't really that unhappy with my performance. I always gave up a lot of hits. Didn't walk anybody. Got a lot of double plays. That was just the way I pitched. I was a sinker-slider pitcher. You give up hits when you're a sinker-slider pitcher.

3Check Out Receipt

Main - Elkhart Public Library (Main)
574-522-2665
www.myepl.org
Thursday, July 05, 2012 5:41:16 PM

Item: 33060010359479
Title: Cup of coffee : the very shor
areers of eighteen major league pitche
Due: 7/26/2012

Item: 33060012530493
Title: A great teammate : the legen
Mickey Mantle
Due: 7/26/2012

Total Items: 2

Check out our 2012 Summer Reading progr
!

Let's go back to when you get called up a month before. Do you remember how you found out you were going up?

Jim Fanning. He was the general manager.

He calls you in Denver?

No, he was in Denver. Called me in the office along with four or five others and told me I was going to the big leagues.

And Andre's there and you know some of the other guys from spring training and being at Triple-A.

And we were the best minor league team, maybe, in the history of the minor leagues, so a lot of us went up to the big leagues. So I wasn't uncomfortable at all.

You don't feel like you belong but you're not a stranger either.

You have to make yourself belong. You don't just belong. They're going to find out whether or not you have the mettle to be there. There are a lot of arrogant—more than cocky, arrogant—ballplayers. And some of them just don't want you to be there.

341

Do any of the guys just called up get to play?

Oh yeah, they were getting in. Tim Raines was getting in. Jerry Manuel would play a little bit at second base. Bobby Ramos came up with me. Tim Raines came up with me, Tim Wallach, Jerry Manuel. Hal Dues came up with me.

Is Dick Williams accommodating at all?

I hated Dick Williams.

You look at his picture and he comes across a little gruff.

That's what he was. He was exactly what his picture looked like. In 1981—and I'm skipping the best I ever pitched, which was winter ball of 1980—in 1981 when I became a Montreal Expo for real—I made the team out of spring training—Dick Williams called me in his office. And I already knew I had made the team because of my relationship with coaches and different people. I already knew that I was on the team. I'd only given up two runs in twenty-eight innings in spring training. There's nothing you can do. I had to make the team. I was 15–4 the year before. Most Valuable Player in the Caribbean Series in winter ball. Dick Williams looked at me and said, I don't really want you on the team, but you left me no choice. So you're on the team. He said, If it was up to me, I'd have somebody else on the team.

It sounds like he doesn't like anybody.

He rolled out the red carpet for Tim Raines. Literally rolled out a red carpet for Tim Raines. In the clubhouse.

Not being sarcastic.

Not being sarcastic. Rolled out a red carpet for Tim Raines.

Why? How?

I don't know why. I mean, I think Tim won a game. I don't remember where it was but I remember Dick Williams literally, physically rolling out a red carpet for Tim Raines.

And is everyone in the clubhouse just shaking their head?

Yeah. Dick Williams, you know? There were certain players that he was congenial and nice to, and most of the other players didn't like him. Like you said, he is what his picture looked like. I'm the tenth pitcher on a ten-pitcher squad, the twenty-fifth player on a twenty-five-man team. You don't tell me that you don't want me on your team. Now I'm a manager of people. I've had five hundred employees at a time. There are certain things you leave unsaid.

Sure. If he doesn't want you there he should keep it to himself.

Or trade me. Trade me. The Phillies wanted me. I mean, I knew kind of what was going on.

You said that you had relationships with some of the coaches. Is there anybody working for Williams that you do get along with?

I got along with all the coaches. They believed in me and thought, without saying it—I guess you just know it sometimes—felt I deserved a better shot. I think Galen Cisco felt that way. He was my pitching coach.

How long are you up there in 1981? You pitch in twelve games so it sounds like you were used a lot.

I was used because we were losing. I have never pitched in a major league game where my team was winning. I never did.

You were the mop-up guy.

I was the guy who went in when we were getting our ass kicked. I have never thrown a pitch in a major league game where my team was winning. I never did, and obviously I never will.

But you did win a game.

They pinch-hit for me. Rowland Office pinch-hit for me against the Phillies and we scored a run and I think we won 3–2, something like that.

That's not a mop-up game.

I wasn't always in mop-up situations, but I never threw a pitch when we were ahead, to save a game or protect a lead.

So how long were you there?

I'm going to guess two months. I was there until about two or three days before the strike when they traded Ellis Valentine, who was on the disabled list, for Jeff Reardon. Jeff Reardon took my locker, took my number, took my apartment, and will probably go to the Hall of Fame. And I understand somebody wanting Jeff Reardon to pitch instead of Steve Ratzer. I'm not mad at Jeff Reardon. I was happy for him. I mean, he threw the ball a lot better than I ever threw the ball.

Williams is still the manager that year and this is right before the strike so you're not on strike.

They sent me to the minor leagues.

So the good news is you're getting paid.

Minor league salary, but I was getting paid. I might've even stayed on my major league salary. I don't remember.

Who tells you that you're being sent down?

Dick Williams.

Does he seem happy about it?

He was happy to get Jeff Reardon. He said, I want you to know that we traded Ellis Valentine for Jeff Reardon and we're going to send you back to Denver. Maybe someday you'll get back here. And I looked at him and I said, Maybe you should've given me a fucking chance to save a ballgame. And I walked out of the office.

How far down the hallway do you get before you realize that you won't be playing on the Expos as long as Dick Williams is manager? Can you tell him what you want to tell him because you're not risking anything?

Well, I also don't want to be a prick. He said, Well, I wish you the best of luck, shook my hand, and I walked out of the office. You don't want to burn a bridge with a major league manager. Even if you should, you still don't want to. At least I don't want to. And I wanted to pitch for the Expos. I wanted to go back.

But you said to him, If you'd have given me a fucking chance. I mean, we've talked about your singular focus, your drive. You used the term monomaniacal at one point. But this is the first time I've heard an I-fight-authority statement come from you.

For sure.

This is about as disrespectful as you get.

No, I've been more disrespectful, but knowing of my situation and knowing that all I ever really wanted to be was a ballplayer, I don't want to burn any bridges.

But you don't think you were risking anything by talking to Williams that way.

I was going to be the best pitcher at Triple-A. I could still pitch at Triple-A. And I knew that there were major league teams interested in Steve Ratzer. So I think I risked a little bit of my position with Dick Williams, but I didn't have any standing with him anyway, so it was okay.

Do you say what you say out of complete honesty because that's what comes out of your mouth, or is there any forethought to it? Is there an agenda?

No, it was from my gut. It was from my gut. It was impulsive. Totally impulsive. I knew that I could be the stopper on that team and I could help them succeed.

September first, players are brought into the manager's office in Denver and they're being called up to the majors and you're not one of them, but you're not surprised.

No. Not at all. What I was surprised about was that somebody else didn't call me up. I went down there and I pitched very well. My team won the league championship and I was one of the leaders on the team in winning the championship.

So you're surprised that somebody didn't trade for you.

Right.

And your baseball hopes and dreams in September of 1981 are that somebody would trade for you.

Yeah, and it happened.

When?

December. I got traded to the Mets.

Who do the Mets give up?

Frank Taveras, their starting shortstop. One for one. I was excited. I was in winter ball. Felipe said, This is great. Are you excited? I said, Absolutely.

So you report to the Mets in 1982.

I was non-roster with the Mets, but I was in spring training day one.

Who's the manager?

George Bamberger.

The Mets are pretty bad that year.

They're really bad. Tremendous Triple-A potential, though. The young kids they had were the Darlings, the Terrells, the Ownbeys. Strawberry was coming up. Dwight Gooden was just breaking in. Unbelievable.

So are you assigned to Tidewater?

Tidewater, yes. I was the Rolaids Minor League Fireman of the Year. I led the team in wins, saves, percentage, strikeouts. Every pitching category. I got like eleven plaques.

And you're waiting for the manager to call you in.

The whole season. They call me up and I win the Mayor's Trophy game against the Yankees. They call me up to pitch in the Mayor's Trophy game and I pitch like four innings and win against the Yankees, and I'm sitting there going, What are they waiting for?

They had seen you in spring training. They can read the newspaper and the reports coming up every day.

And when I left spring training, Bamberger called me in personally, one on one, and said, You're going to be back with the Mets.

Are you getting a bald spot from scratching your head?

The Mets sucked. I'm twenty-eight or twenty-nine years old. They're bringing up the Darlings, the Terrells, the Ownbeys. These guys throw ninety, ninety-five miles an hour but they don't know how to pitch. They're bringing them up, giving them some exposure. They don't need Steve Ratzer. What do they need a twenty-nine-year-old reliever for? They're not going to be good for another four or five years. They're not going to challenge for another four or five years. Top minor league pitcher, average-at-best, mediocre major league pitcher. They probably don't need me so I probably went to the wrong team. I got traded to the wrong team. But why isn't somebody else interested?

I finish 1982, go back to the Dominican. I love it down there. Play winter ball. And come back and the Mets invite me to spring training. And I'm a very well paid minor leaguer at this point. And I didn't report the first day of spring training. I come back from winter ball and didn't really know if I was going to play baseball anymore.

And this is why you're late to spring training?

Yeah. I didn't like the contract and I was not happy with my scenario with the Mets. If I didn't get there the year before, they're never bringing me up. So I don't show up. I called and I spoke with Frank Cashen. I said, This contract's a joke. And all I'm going to do is come down there and throw batting practice for four weeks and go back to Triple-A and be a good Triple-A pitcher.

Is it a cut in pay, or do they just not offer you a raise?

It was the same contract, I think. About four grand a month or something. It wasn't a lot of money. I deserved more. I said, There's no opportunity for me with the Mets if I didn't get there last year. He said, What do you want to do? We want you to be part of our organization. Maybe when you're done playing you can be part of the organization. He was very nice, but candid with me that, Yeah, you're right. You're not going to pitch for us in the big leagues. I said, If I'm going to pitch in the minor leagues, I want to live in my house. He said, Where do you live? I said, Well, my house is in Denver. I own a house in Denver. I'd like to live in my house. He said, Well, I don't know if the White Sox are going to be interested in you. I said, Well, why don't you give me ten minutes. So I called Dave Dombrowski with the White Sox and said, The Mets are willing to trade me, and I need an opportunity to pitch in the major leagues and I was thinking that you might be interested. Two minutes later, literally two minutes later, Tony LaRussa calls me. He's the manager of the White Sox and he says, How fast can you get down here? I said, I'm leaving in two hours, Tony.

Where are you?

I'm in upstate New York. Lake Louise Marie, in a house that my dad had bought, just kind of vacationing.

Trying to get your head straight.

347

Right. That's it. Exactly. And I packed my stuff and drove down to Sarasota to train with the White Sox.

Who did they give up?

Nothing. A player to be named later.

That was pretty nice on Cashen's part.

It was nice on his part. I'm not mad at the Mets. If there's anything that I'm frustrated with, I'm frustrated with my goal. Talking about being a monomaniac. My goal was to pitch in the big leagues. If my goal was to pitch in a World Series, or to pitch in an All-Star game, I truly believe, even though I never threw a pitch ninety miles an hour in my life, that I would've done it.

Do you think subconsciously you might've had some kind of letdown once you made the majors because that was your goal? That doesn't mean that you're not working as hard and doing everything you're supposed to do, but maybe the itch wasn't as strong.

348   I don't know. I think the itch was as strong, but it's kind of hard to pitch when you know, when they put you in the game, that your manager doesn't have faith in you and doesn't really care whether you succeed or not. In today's world that's the harsh reality of life, but back then I still had these idealistic views. I want Dick Williams to think I'm a great relief pitcher and let me pitch.

What if you had been a little bit more rebellious, took a bigger chance off the field? Like telling Dick Williams that you wish you'd had a chance before he sent you down to Denver?

I went to spring training with the Mets with a full beard and long hair. I was going to be mean. Jesus Alou, in winter ball, said to me, Make yourself mean, because you don't pitch mean. You don't present yourself as mean. You're a mean pitcher. Everybody knows that about you. When you have to hit them, you got to do what you got to do. You do it. But make yourself look mean. That was rebellious for me. That was big. That was big.

And you still got sent to Tidewater.

And then I shaved. And cut my hair and pitched great in Tidewater.

So you join the White Sox in Sarasota.

I went down to Sarasota and have the spring of my life. I pitched, literally, every other day, an inning or two. Close to thirty innings. I give up
two or three runs. I'm positive that I've made the team. And I did. The
day before we break they make room on the roster for me. They trade
Steve Mura to the Oakland Athletics to make a roster spot for Steve
Ratzer. I did it. I'm back. Mura's excited about getting a chance to go
pitch, because even though he had a guaranteed contract, he was going
to be sent to the minor leagues. This happened at like ten o'clock in the
morning. He flies to Arizona, they do a physical on him. By eight o'clock
at night he's back in Florida and has a bad shoulder. Guaranteed contract. Bad shoulder. I'm going back to the minor leagues. I got in my car
and I drove to Denver. I'm done. I can't do it anymore. This is bullshit.
And Tony and Dave Dombrowski, together, said, You're going to be back
with us. I said, This is bullshit. This is bullshit. Pay the guy and put me
on the team because I'm going to contribute. We're going to win the
fricking pennant this year and I'm going to contribute. And they did.
They wound up winning the division. I said, And I'm going to contribute. And Tony said, You're right. You're right. You're right. Dave's saying,
You're right. You deserve it. You belong here. But our hands are tied.
There's nothing we can do, because he's got a guaranteed contract. I'm
pissed. This is probably as mad as I've ever been in baseball.

Toughest drive ever?

Yeah.

Were you by yourself?

I was with my ex-wife, and my daughter.

*With your daughter in the car there's only so much control you can lose, but you
have to be fuming.*

Yeah. It was tough. I remember pulling over and running for three or
four miles, then getting back in the car and driving. Soaking. Dripping
sweat. Getting to Colorado and going out to the golf course, using one
of their drivers and just hitting buckets and buckets of golf balls because
I was just mad. I was mad at the world. And I was there about two weeks

349

and the general manager of the Denver Bears, Jim Burris, called me up and he said, What are you doing? Now, I had pitched for the Denver Bears at the end of 1977, 1978, 1979, 1980, the end of 1981. I'm their all-time pitcher, or whatever. They have an all-time Bears team and I'm the all-time right-handed pitcher, me and Ryne Duren. So he says, What are you doing? Nothing. And I don't know that I really want to do anything or really care to do anything. I'm just kind of pissed off right now. I need to get a job and start supporting my family.

Did you tell LaRussa and Dombrowski that you weren't going to report?

No, I just didn't report. I got in my car and drove. They didn't know where I went.

But Denver's their Triple-A club, so you go where you're supposed to go except you don't make it to the ballpark.

Well, the team's still in Florida. I mean, I just left. They start a week later. They're about five games into their season and they're like 0–5 when Burris calls me up and goes, What are you doing? Nothing. Got a job? No. He goes, I'll pay you five thousand dollars a month and the White Sox will pay you five thousand dollars a month. You need to come work for us. I said, Okay. Ten thousand dollars a month in the minor leagues? I'll play baseball for a few months. Why not? So I go back and I play, starting without any hope of ever playing in the major leagues, and all of a sudden I'm pitching great. And we're winning. And now all of a sudden they're watching me again, they're talking about me going back to the big leagues and things like that. Meanwhile the White Sox are winning their division. They don't need any help. Either way was okay. I'm making a good living now and that kind of thing.

Living in your own house, seeing your daughter.

Living in my house, spending time with my daughter and my family. Just before the end of the season I go on a sixteen-day road trip. I come back from the sixteen-day road trip and she didn't know who I was. I called up Jim Burris and I said, Jim, I'm done. There are more important things than baseball.

Does anybody try to talk you out of it?

He said, We've got the Little World Series next week. I said, So? He said, Well, I'd like you to fulfill your contract for just another couple of weeks. Finish the season and pitch in the Little World Series. I said, Out of respect for you, I'll do that. So I did. I pitched. I finished that season, went back home, spent about a month with my daughter, and got a job. That was it.

Did you have any withdrawal symptoms the next season?

No. None. I was going to be successful in my new restaurant career, and I became successful fairly quickly with that. Spending time at home. I took all the money that I had made and we invested it in something that didn't work, so within two years I was just about broke. I was making a good living in the restaurant business but I had no savings left. I had saved quite a bit of money through winter ball. I was a celebrity in winter ball. Last month they invited me down there, to the Dominican, to throw out the first ball on the twentieth anniversary of our championship. So we went down there for five days and wined and dined. I was on the front page of the sports section.

That's got to be nice.

It was great. It was great. My wife had never been a part of my life with baseball. We've only been married two years. She's a crazy sports fan and she'd never experienced anything like this. She knew I had played in the major leagues but she never realized the adulation. I can't go anywhere down there, even today, without most people knowing who I am, in this country that's really become a different country than when I was there twenty years ago. It was Third World twenty years ago. Now they have fast food and Outback.

Did you keep anything from your career? Do you have the ball from the no-hitter that you pitched in Yankee Stadium?

Absolutely. I have the one from high school. I have the ball from my win against the Phillies. I have that ball.

That's a fairly rare thing. They stop the game any time a batter gets his first hit but they don't have that for a pitcher for his first win or first save.

Gary Carter handed it to me. I still have some hats but I don't have any uniforms. I have my Mizuno glove with my name stitched in it.

Do you have any regrets?

351

Am I content with my major league career? Probably not. But I don't have regrets. I am tremendously proud of what I accomplished in baseball. I could've been a lot more successful. I should've been a lot more successful. As I said, part of the problem was me, because I said this is how far I want to go. When I went to winter ball, I said, We're going to win the championship. And we won the championship when they hadn't won in fifty years. And I'm going to be the man. In the nine-game championship series, I pitched eight innings in the seventh game, until the seventeenth inning, and we won 2–1. Then Pascual Perez beat Mario Soto two to nothing in the eighth game. And then in the last game I pitched from the fifth inning to the fifteenth inning on one day's rest, and we won 2–1 when Jerry Augustine walked Harry Spilman with the bases loaded in the fifteenth inning. I wasn't going to lose. And that's what I took to the mound with me when my team was ahead or tied. I very seldom lost out because that was my edge. That was what I took that made me better. And I never had that opportunity in the majors. They call it *orgullo,* which is "guts" in Spanish. That's what Steve was about. I wish they had. It'd be a different conversation today.

Baltimore at Seattle
Tuesday, July 30, 1991

Baltimore	ab	r	h	rbi	Seattle	ab	r	h	rbi
Devereaux, cf	5	1	2	0	Briley, lf	4	1	2	0
Hulett, dh	5	0	1	0	Reynolds, 2b	2	1	0	0
C. Ripken, ss	4	1	2	1	Griffey Jr., cf	4	1	1	4
Evans, rf	3	0	1	0	O'Brien, 1b	4	1	1	0
Milligan, 1b	3	0	1	1	Davis, dh	4	1	2	1
Segui, lf	4	0	0	0	Buhner, rf	4	1	1	0
Gomez, 3b	3	0	0	0	Cochrane, 3b	3	0	0	0
Hoiles, c	3	0	1	0	Sch'fer, ph-3b	1	0	1	2
Orsulak, ph	1	0	0	0	Bradley, c	4	1	1	0
Melvin, c	0	0	0	0	Valle, c	0	0	0	0
Bell, 2b	4	0	1	0	Vizquel, ss	4	1	1	1
Smith, p	0	0	0	0	Krueger, p	0	0	0	0
Poole, p	0	0	0	0	Swift, p	0	0	0	0
Jones, p	0	0	0	0	Murphy, p	0	0	0	0
Olson, p	0	0	0	0					
					Totals	34	8	10	8
Totals	35	2	9	2					

Baltimore	1	0	1	0	0	0	0	0	0—2	
Seattle	0	6	0	0	0	0	0	2	x—8	

Baltimore	IP.	H.	R.	ER.	BB.	SO.
Smith (L. 5-3)	1.2	6	6	6	2	0
Poole......	3.1	1	0	0	0	6
Jones...	2	0	0	0	0	2
Olson	1	3	2	2	0	1
Seattle	IP.	H.	R.	ER.	BB.	SO.
Krueger (W. 9-3)	6.1	8	2	2	2	3
Swift	1.2	1	0	0	0	1
Murphy	1	0	0	0	0	2

E—Reynolds (12). PB—Bradley (1). 2B—Bell (3, off Krueger), Hulett (4, off Krueger), Bradley (5, off Smith), Buhner (8, off Olson). 3B—O'Brien (3, off Smith). HR—C. Ripken (22, off Krueger), Griffey Jr. (12, off Smith). SF—Milligan (2, off Krueger). U—Larry McCoy, Durwood Merrill, Tim McClelland, Don Denkinger. T—2:43. A—18,725.

STACY JONES

Stacy Jones appeared in four games, starting one, for the
Baltimore Orioles in 1991. In 1996 he appeared in two
games, both in relief, for the Chicago White Sox. He
pitched a total of thirteen innings in the major leagues,
yielding eleven hits and six walks while striking out
eleven, and finished with a career ERA of 3.46. He was
interviewed October 21, 2001 at his home in Attalla, Alabama.

Tell me about where you were raised and when you first started playing base-
ball.

I was raised at the foot of the mountain down here in the woods. There
was nobody who really lived around us too much. We had to go down to
that little school that you passed. That's where we went to school. Me
and one of my best friends, who played, actually, with the Phillies for six

years, we'd ride our bicycles down there every day. And we would play what you would call sandlot ball. What's funny about that little group, every one of us played college baseball and two of us played professional baseball. We played serious ball.

Most guys that I talk to knew they were good because they were a head taller and ten miles an hour faster. How long did it take to find out you were good since all of these other guys obviously have talent as well?

Well, I actually got cut from a team when I was fifteen. I was fifteen and got cut from a fourteen- and fifteen-year-old team because I couldn't run fast. Like I say, I wasn't that great to begin with. I guess you could call me a late bloomer. I had height. I was skinny as a pole. I was about six foot and weighed 120, 130 pounds at that time. And then between my sophomore and junior year, I grew six inches. I didn't gain that much weight. I was like six foot five and 155, 160 pounds. And then between that and my senior year I started adding a little weight and that's when everything kind of took off.

We played baseball all the time. I was always pretty good in sandlot ball but I never really got real good until later on my senior year. Nobody ever really said, Well, you can go to college here, or You're going to be the next Steve Shields. Nobody ever did that. Steve was the big dog back then.

Did you play basketball? Six five and 160 pounds sounds like a basketball player.

I played basketball. I actually had some scholarship offers in basketball. My high school basketball coach called me in the office one day and he said, Would you like to play college basketball? And I said, No, I'm playing baseball. And he said, You're going to play college baseball? How do you know that? And I said, I just know. And nobody had ever come to me and asked me, Are you going to play professional ball? Nobody had ever asked me to play college ball. I wasn't that good at that time. This was between my junior and senior year of basketball, so baseball hadn't even hit yet in my senior year. I knew it. I don't know how to explain it but I knew that's what I was going to do.

As for finally somebody coming around? It took until to the very end of my senior year for some colleges to start coming around. My coach would say, There's a scout from Jacksonville here. There's a scout from UAB. And then in the state playoffs, coaches from UAB, coaches from Alabama, coaches from Auburn, coaches from Mississippi State, Florida,

356

and Georgia, all of them started coming. So basically it was the scouts that saw me and said, You need to look at this kid. I was about six five, 180 when I was a senior.

So now they start showing up at the doorstep or calling. They're kind of driving us nuts, a little bit. And I told Dad, I'd like to go to a big school. Dad wanted me to go to UAB. He liked Harry Walker at UAB. I was a big Alabama fan. Everybody in my family was an Alabama fan. Barry Shollenberger was the coach there. We went down to the University of Alabama and they were playing the number-one team in the nation, Miami. They played them in a three-game series and that day, I think, they were playing them in the last game of the series. And they beat them two out of three. Miami wound up winning the national championship that year. But I sat at the ballgame and I didn't meet any players. Not a one. I sat up there with my high school coach, Larry Foster, and my father. And we were there for three hours and when the game was over with, Shollenberger came up and talked to us and we went to Shoney's. I never saw the field, I never saw the clubhouse, I never met a player, never saw the University. We went straight to Shoney's. We sat down for about an hour, ate, and then he pulled the papers out and wanted me to sign. I brought them home and they were on my refrigerator for years.

The next weekend I went down to Auburn. Now, I'm a country fellow. I like country stuff. I met all the players, went through every bit of the facilities. The coaches were real nice. They took me out to the country, you know, where you'd go out if you wanted to go hunting or fishing. You could get away. That was an outlet. I could get away from school, I could get away from baseball, I could get away from girls, I could get away from home. I could go and do that. So that's the direction I took, with Hal Baird. He recruited me. I was the first in-state player Hal Baird had ever recruited. My freshman year there was me and Gregg Olson. Gregg's still playing now. He was also drafted by the Orioles. He was the number-four overall pick and I was the fifty-fourth overall pick. We wound up signing with the Orioles together.

Is it just the college scouts that are watching you your senior year of high school? Do you get drafted that year?

There were several of them. There was a scout with the Mets. There was a guy with another organization that said, What would it take to sign you? Well, you're a high school kid. You don't know. And the parents get involved. And I've seen it too many times where the high school coach says, It'll take six figures. It'll take six figures. I'm not saying Larry Foster did that, but that's what I heard was said. It'll take six figures to sign this

357

kid. He's got a full scholarship to go to Auburn. He's got a full scholarship to go here, to go there. It'll take six figures. So I didn't get drafted.

Was that discouraging at all?

Not really.

Because you knew what the situation was and you had a place to go.

That's exactly right. If I could do it all over again, I would've probably gone to a junior college first, in the sense of school-wise. Coming from a small town and stepping into a major university was a big shock for me. I'm away from Mom and Dad. And school wasn't a priority. Hey, I'm out here having fun.

What pitches are you throwing in high school?

Fastball and slider. That was it.

Both of them over the top?

358   Three-quarters.

Did you have a favorite team growing up?

Yeah, the Dodgers. Steve Garvey, Ron Cey. That group. Player-wise I liked George Brett. Him and Steve Garvey.

What position did you play in high school on days you weren't pitching?

I DHed. I DHed or I played first. Now, I hit ninth in the order, but I led the team in hitting. I couldn't hit a breaking ball. If you throw me anything with a wrinkle in it I'm going down. So they look at the batting order and figure, Hey, he's batting ninth. He can't hit. We'll throw him fastballs. My high school coach played for the Royals and the White Sox organizations. We've had five players play professional ball out of Etowah High School and there's probably seventy or eighty players that played college ball out of that high school. Around here it's the mecca of high school baseball.

When you get to Auburn are you a starter?

No, I was out of the bullpen. I got to pitch a little bit, and as the year kind of progressed I moved into a starting role. I started the second game of the SEC tournament over the juniors and seniors. And also over Gregg Olson who, like I said, would end up being the overall number-four pick in the nation. I started gaining a lot of weight and muscle. We were on a weight program and I went from 180 to 230 in a full year. And my velocity went from eighty-one, eighty-two in high school to eighty-eight, eighty-nine, ninety in college.

Have you got natural movement on the fastball? Are you throwing it towards the center of the plate and letting it move on its own?

That's funny that you're asking me that. At that time I was a power pitcher. Here, hit what I've got. Later on, as my career went along and after I got injured, I learned that there's movement involved. You know, everybody talked about movement, having the ball sink and cut. Now, I did have the ball cut and it would sink but it wasn't something I knew how to do. I didn't know how to control it. As a power pitcher, if you don't go through it real well and it comes off one side of your finger, it'll cut. If it comes off the other side of your finger, it'll sink. And I didn't know how to control that. When I had my first surgery in 1991, rather than throwing ninety to ninety-four, now I'm throwing eighty-five, eighty-six, eighty-seven, and I'm getting hit. I've got to learn how to do something, so I learned how to manipulate the ball then. And when my velocity came back, I was able to implement both of those. The power part and the finesse.

Are the coaches at Auburn trying to get you to work on a third pitch?

In high school I was a fastball-slider, and when I got to Auburn they said, We need to invent another one. So we went to a split-finger. And that was an off-speed pitch rather than everything going ninety miles an hour. We mixed in that split-finger and that's going eighty-one, eighty-three miles an hour. And that's a big difference. All you're doing is trying to get them a little bit out front. Mess with their timing. Really and truly you get people out one of three ways—forwards and backwards, in and out, and up and down. I didn't have that back and forth yet until I started working with the split-finger. And it took a long time to master that.

Are you drafted after your junior year at Auburn?

Yeah, that's when I left school. Didn't leave on a good note with Hal Baird. He said I did something that I didn't do, and I'll swear to this day that I didn't do it. It was the last home game. We were playing a Division II school and all the scouts were there. They wanted to see Gregg throw, and all the guys that might possibly get drafted. And Gregg went in in the seventh inning, and Coach Baird said, All right, Gregg, you've got two innings and Stacy, you've got the last inning. And I went down there and warmed up and Gregg struck out five of the six batters he faced, and he said, Gregg's going back out. It didn't bother me that I wasn't going to pitch. I knew that I was going to start the first game in the SEC tournament.

There was a bucket sitting there, and I had just got through warming up and he told me to sit down and stop throwing. And I flipped the ball and it missed the bucket. It went over in the little hedge grove down the line, and I walked over there and got it out of the bush and put it in the bucket and I'm standing there. And I see him. He's walking down to me. Hal Baird's walking down to me. He calls me and I meet him halfway and he starts airing me out that I threw the ball in the parking lot. Somebody had told him that I threw the ball in the parking lot, that I was mad. I don't know if he was actually told that, or actually assumed that I had got mad. So he's telling me that I'd never pitch for him ever again. So the first game of the SEC tournament we play Mississippi State and he starts a freshman. I'm the quote unquote number-one starter. Gregg's a closer. He starts a freshman, Mississippi State jumps up on us ten to nothing in the first three or four innings, then Gregg comes in, holds them, and we score six or seven runs, and then I finally got to pitch the eighth and the ninth. We didn't give up any more runs, but I didn't ever start again for him. And that's why I left.

So you knew before the draft that you weren't going back to play baseball at Auburn.

That's exactly right.

And in June of 1988 both you and Gregg are drafted.

Yeah, he was my roommate. That was the year that the Orioles had started out oh-and-twenty-something and Frank Robinson was fired. That was the year. It didn't matter where I was going, I knew I was going. I was pretty frustrated with school because I wanted to go play summer ball. Two years in a row I had the opportunity to go to the Alaska League and Coach Baird talked me about of it. I had the opportunity to go up there.

I had the opportunity to go up to the Cape Cod League both summers, and Coach Baird talked to my parents and said it wouldn't be a good idea because we need to get a fresh start on next year school-wise.

I'm not going to lie to you. I wasn't the best student in the world, but I felt trapped. There was nothing I could do. I guess when I stayed in school for the summer I didn't do great because I was frustrated that I didn't get to go. All I did in the summertime was work out with the football players. That didn't bother me. I enjoyed the working-out part but I didn't like the whole scenery of being locked down there in the summer. I went to school every quarter from 1985 until I left in June of 1988. I understood doing that after my freshman year, but not after my sophomore year.

My sophomore year was the year of the Olympics, preparing for the Olympics. They were going to pick the Olympic team. And I loved baseball so much and this one thing, if you remember anything about me, I wanted to play for my country so bad. And Coach Baird tried to talk me out of going to Millington, Tennessee, to try out for the Olympic team. My roommate, Gregg, was invited. He was an automatic invite from Ron Fraser. I think Ron Polk was also involved with it. And I wanted to play so bad for that team. Not only because my roommate was going, but I felt like I could play on that team. So I told my mom and dad, I'm going to Millington, Tennessee. I'm going to try out for the Olympic team. And they were behind me. So I called and made reservations. I think you had to even send some money in, I'm not sure. And I went in and told Coach Baird, I said, I'm going to try out for the Olympic team. And he sat there in the chair and leaned forward and he said, I don't want to bust your bubble, but you're not going to make it. And I said, Why not? This is the Olympic team. It's tryouts. He said, Son, that team's already been picked. I said, No, it's not. They're having tryouts. I didn't want to believe him.

So I went up there and Fraser's assistant coach was there running it. And there were a lot of coaches there and a lot of kids that had just come out of high school and junior college that didn't have very many skills at all. And I'm sitting there. I throw two innings, you know, and there was a kid from California who was invited, and he threw a palmball. I can't remember his name, but he threw a palmball and that's all he had. He probably didn't throw eighty miles an hour. And they asked him to stay. And here I am throwing ninety, ninety-two, ninety-three miles an hour and the coaches are talking, Hey man, you've got a chance. And when I left there I thought, I've got a chance. But I never got another phone call. Then I knew Coach Baird was telling me the truth. I watched Gregg pitch against Cuba. I was in Gregg's wedding with Jim Abbott and he

361

was actually on that team. I wanted to be a part of that and that's something I never got to do.

But if you don't go, you don't know.

I would've always regretted it. And I never regretted going but now I know. It was kind of an elite thing. But that's what I always wanted to do. If I could go back and take my nine years of playing professional ball and my thirty-one days in the big leagues and throw them away and play in the Olympics, that's what I'd do.

Gregg gets drafted in the first round in 1988 and you get drafted in the third round. That's pretty good money.

I wound up getting $40,000 and an extra $7,500 for school. And I think Gregg wound up getting a little over $100,000, $150,000, somewhere around there. I'm not sure exactly what he got because I never asked him.

Was $40,000 their first offer?

No. Their first offer came in about $15,000.

That's a low offer for a third-round pick. You knew you weren't going back to Auburn. Did they know it?

They didn't know it.

So you were able to negotiate with them some.

Yeah. I was at the apartment down in Auburn. The scout, Lamar North, called and he said, I'm over here at the hotel. We're going to meet and I'll make you an offer. My dad drove down. We went to the hotel, sat down in the chair, and he talked for a little bit. He said, We're interested in signing you. We want to sign you. We want to sign you or we wouldn't have drafted you. I'm going to make you an offer and if it's not good enough you can back to school. And it was $15,000. I was expecting $40,000 or $50,000 right off the bat and then we'd go from there. And my dad said, Well, to be honest with you, I really appreciate your offer but you're going to have to come up with more money than that. I was excited. That signing bonus didn't matter to me. I wanted to get a little bit but I also wanted to start playing. And at that time, when you're in those shoes, you think, Oh my gosh, we're telling them no. They're leaving and they're going to write me off. And actually, before we left that hotel they got up to $20,000 or $25,000, and we left in good faith.

Two or three days later they called me back and it was kind of a back-and-forth and we sat up there in that living room and me and Dad talked and he said, Son, you can get a whole lot more if you'll just be patient. And I said, Daddy, I want to go play. Because that's really and truly all I wanted to do. When you compete you don't think about money. And I was ready to go compete. Dad said, Well, if you're happy with that. The $7,500 was the incentive bonus. It was $1,000 for Double-A, $1,500 for Triple-A, and $5,000 for the majors.

Is signing the contract and becoming a professional baseball player the best day of your life to that point?

Yeah. Yeah. That was the happiest day of my life.

Did you do anything special with your bonus?

I bought a car.

What kind of car?

It was that black Beretta sitting right out there. Brand new. It had seventeen miles on it. Looking back, I wish I'd done a whole lot different. Invested it. But that's what I spent it on. I wound up buying that car.

It takes you a couple of weeks to get the numbers right so when do you sign the contract?

It was about the middle part of June. It didn't take us ten days, because I was ready to sign.

How long does it take after you sign the contract before you're either in the car or on a plane going to rookie ball?

Three days. I actually didn't go to rookie ball. I went to extended spring, but it was a rookie-ball camp. Spring training was in Florida. This rookie league was right outside of Bethesda, Maryland. It was at St Mary's. I went there and stayed two weeks.

Did you drive up there or fly up there?

363

Flew.

They send you a plane ticket and you go over to Birmingham to fly out and you land somewhere in Maryland.

My parents dropped me off in Birmingham and I actually flew into Hagerstown and we went out to the college and they were all happy to have me. At that time I was the highest pick that had signed. I actually met two or three bigwigs then. I met Cal Ripken Senior. He came in for a day or two and I thought that was the biggest thing that had ever happened in my life.

Were you slated to be a starter?

Yeah, I was going to be a starter, and I was looking forward to it, but here's kind of the downside of rookie ball. They said, We expect you to be a starter in the big leagues in about four years. And I'm thinking, My God, it's going to take me four years to get there.

You were hoping for sooner.

Oh yeah. I'm going now and I'm expecting maybe next spring I'm going to be in the big leagues.

In hindsight, they might've been underestimating the four years. A lot of clubs have a minimum number of minor league innings they want their prospects to throw before coming up, so four years could be a fast track even though that's not the way you took it.

No, that's not the way I took it. I was taking it like they were saying I wasn't that good yet. Now I know. They draft you on projection, not where you're at now. They're projecting you in one year, two years, three years, not where you're at now.

They're drafting six five, 230, with a fastball in the low nineties.

Oh yeah. That's exactly what they're drafting, and you don't realize that. I mean, it's a business. That's the side that most people don't understand. Like right now, I'll go to the office and they'll start talking about the playoffs and this and that. They don't realize the business side of it. It is a business. It's not a game. It's just like any commodity you sell. It's a business. They're in the entertainment business, and that's all they're in. And that's the side I didn't understand until later on.

Do you spend the full year in rookie ball?

I went to Erie, Pennsylvania. Now, that was New York–Penn League, high rookie ball. Elmira, Batavia, Waterloo. Those teams. I'm starting and I did real well. Now, my record didn't show it. I was like 4–3, or 3–3 or something, but my ERA was like one something. And I thought, This is wonderful. I'm doing pretty good. I knew every time I went out I was going to do that well. You just have that feeling, that confidence. And then I moved up to the highest A ball club in Hagerstown, Maryland, and actually went to the playoffs with them and that ended the year.

Do you go to instructional league in the off-season?

Instructional league down in West Palm Beach, Florida, and that's where my eyes kind of lit up and I understood that it was more of a business.

They call it instructional league. What kind of instruction did you receive down there? Are you working on developing your pitches?

I was actually working on another pitch, which was my split-finger, and improving my slider. Now, my slider was good, but I needed to improve it where it was more consistent. And that's, basically, all baseball is. If you've got the ability, it doesn't mean you're going to make it unless you're consistent. You can go out there and throw the nastiest slider in the world, but your next one might be terrible and then it gets hit for a home run. You have to be consistent, and that's what I went down for. To develop another pitch, to get a little more associated with the organization, and actually improve that slider. The more innings, the more confidence you build, pretty much means the better command you have of your pitches.

My problem, really and truly, wasn't a problem that a lot of people have. I had too good of control, and that doesn't sound like it makes sense but it really does. If you're around the plate too much, then you get hit. Now your walks per strikeout looks great but your hits per inning goes up, so if you look at nine innings and you average walking four or five, your hits per inning will go down because you're going to be erratic around the plate and the hitter's not going to feel as comfortable stepping in. But as your walks go down, your hits per inning goes up, and that was my problem. I was too much around the plate. I had to learn to actually throw out of the strike zone, and actually had to learn how to knock someone down.

365

Had you not had to brush someone back or plunk somebody in college ball?

In high school I was asked to hit one person. I was a freshman.

Had one of your guys been hit?

No, they were running the score up. Larry Foster, my high school coach, played several years of professional ball. He knew, and at that time I didn't. You don't want to embarrass somebody on the baseball field. Well, they were running the score up. The score was like eighteen or nineteen to one and they're still stealing second, they're stealing third. They're just running up and down. And he sent me in just to hit somebody. I was out on the mound, he walked out onto the field, and he said, I want you to hit him. He walked out to the mound and he used some words he shouldn't have used. The batter was big, maybe six four or five, and here I was five ten, maybe six feet, and I didn't weigh 120 pounds. And I go through my delivery and I throw it at him. And I miss him. Catcher throws the ball back and I throw at him again. And now he knows that I'm throwing at him. He steps out of the box and looks at his coach and says, If he hits me, I'm going to get him.

The catcher knows what's going on, right?

The catcher's supposed to catch him before he gets to me. He knows what's going on.

What do you do with the third pitch?

I miss him again. He actually moves forward, because if you're trying to hit somebody you throw it behind them and they back into it. This time he moved forward and I missed behind him. And he steps out of the box again and says the same words, I'm going to get him. And the coach says, Go get him if he hits you. So on my fourth one I miss him again. He goes forward and I miss him. He throws his bat down and stands there and walks down the line, and he's yelling at me. I'm a freshman. My high school coach walks out and he says, Son, you don't have the balls to play this game. Go get your ass on the bench. And I went over to the bench and I sat down. That was my first experience ever being told to hit somebody.

Now, in college I hit a guy on purpose, and he's a good friend of mine. His name's Roger Miller. We played against each other when I was seventeen or eighteen. He wound up going to Georgia and I went to

Auburn. And they were beating us pretty bad in a three-game series. Coach walks out to the mound and says, I want you to hit him. He actually said, I want you to hit Roger. Roger was having a phenomenal series. He's like eight for eleven and two home runs. Here it's my turn and now I've got to hit my buddy. We talked before the game and after the game. Well, I hit him. He's walking down to first and the ball rolls down that way. I go to pick it up and he's mad and I walk by and I say, Are you all right? My coach came out and took me out and aerated me out. He said, Don't you ever ask him how he feels after you hit him. Because it was an intentional thing. He said, You've got to learn the game.

Now, it's a psychological part of the game. And as the years went along, after I got into professional ball, they pretty much put that in you, that it's money out of your pocket if you don't have that intimidation factor. So I didn't have that problem from there on, hitting somebody.

You have an excellent ERA in rookie ball and you're moving up and by the off-season you're in instructional league. Do you maintain your confidence there?

When I was in instructional league, the Orioles, the Montreal Expos, the Atlanta Braves, and the Minnesota Twins were down there, and I actually got to see Randy Johnson and Willie Banks—he was a real high draft pick—and the game was a business then. It was run as a business. You're going here, you're going there. And we were playing the Expos in a game and Larry Walker had messed his leg up during the year. I had no idea who Larry Walker was. He was with the Expos at the time. And he led off every inning with an at bat, and he struck out four out of five times and now we're in the sixth inning and I'm pitching against Larry Walker. Boom. He hits one three-quarters of the way up the light pole, and stands there. Watches it. And then he slowly goes around the bases. Little did I know, he had just had surgery on that knee and he couldn't run and that's why he was getting his at bats in. Well, I was pissed. I mean, I was really pissed. The next guy up, I plunked him because Walker didn't run in front of him. I was mad. They're yelling at me out of the dugout—Richie Lewis who had played at Florida State was hollering at me, and I know Richie. All of them were yelling at me, You son of a bitch. Well, in instructional league rules, if you get hit you just stay in there and hit again. Or if you walk you stay in there and hit again. So I had to face that guy I just plunked again.

You go down to spring training in 1989.

367

I was hoping to go to major league camp in spring training of 1989. In 1988, during the year, we flew to Rochester. The major league team was playing the Triple-A team in an exhibition. They invited up Gregg Olson, me, Arthur Rhodes, who's now with Seattle, and another pitcher. We were all invited to go pitch for the big league team against the Triple-A team. Well, Gregg got lit up. And I threw my two innings and didn't give up but one hit and I struck out like four or five, so that kind of boosted my confidence and I was expecting to go to spring training with the big league club. My agent was trying to get me into big league camp but it never happened. I actually went into camp way overweight. I had a great winter, I guess you'd say. Didn't get myself in shape and then when I arrived in spring training Doug Melvin, who was the minor league general manager, called me in and said, We want you to lose about twenty, twenty-five pounds. And I pretty much lost the weight but I was hoping to go to either Double-A or Triple-A and they sent me to A ball again. And I struggled. I got tendinitis in my elbow and they wound up sending me home for the last two months of the season. Didn't want to hurt it anymore.

Since you were hurt the last two months of the season, do you have any clue where they're going to assign you when you report to spring training in 1990?

No. They actually told me I was going back to A ball, which I did. I went back to A ball and I started a little bit, and then they said, We're going to make you a closer. And they did. They put me in the bullpen.

What was the reasoning behind this move? Or did they bother to explain it?

Well, I'm kind of a power pitcher. They wanted to change my role a little bit because I was so violent in my delivery. They wanted to take some stress off of it and get me more outings.

How did you feel about the move?

It didn't bother me at all. I was going to get to play every day then. That's the way I looked at it. It was more of a relief-closer role, because we didn't have a set closer in A ball. They're not going to do that. And then when I moved up to Double-A during the middle of the year, I actually didn't do real bad numbers-wise but my win-loss record was 0–5. If you give up a run in the bullpen you're going to get a loss.

Do you make the forty-man roster in 1991?

Nope. I go to spring training, have a good spring training. They told me I was going to be a closer. I go to Double-A. I was a closer and actually did real well. I didn't start out as the closer. I started out in middle relief. Here's where it actually all started. The manager, Jerry Narron—he's the manager of the Texas Rangers now—he called me into his office and he said, he asked me, Are you going to play in the big leagues? And I looked at him and didn't answer and he walked off. Just turned around and walked off. And it just kind of stumped me. And it was about a week later, he's walking by me and he says, Stacy, are you going to play in the big leagues? And I look at him and pause, and he turns and walks off again. Well, it wasn't five or ten minutes later that Jerry asked me to come in the office, and I went in and sat down and he says, Are you going to play in the big leagues? And at this time I was doing real well. I'm in Double-A. I said, Jerry, you're asking me a question. And he interrupted me. He says, You don't know. He said, That's your problem. And I said, What do you mean? He said, That's your problem. He says, Do you think Anthony Telford will play in the big leagues? I said, Yeah. He said, Do you think David Segui will play in the big leagues? I said, Yeah. He'll play in the big leagues. Do you think Arthur Rhodes will play in the big leagues? Yeah. Ricky Gutierrez? Yeah. He said, But you don't know. He said, Watch how they handle themselves, on the field and off the field. Everything they do. They know they're going to succeed. He said, That's the mentality you got to have.

So when I left his office I was just thinking, Maybe he's right. I'd always had a goal but I never really truly believed it. So I started living my life a little different. I quit drinking. I quit going out at night. I wasn't married at the time. I started fixing my own meals and taking them to the park instead of eating a sandwich from Burger King. I started running more. I started doing a whole lot more exercising, preparing for the games. Paying attention to who we were playing and who's coming up. Who's actually going to face who later on in the game and how well that person's doing. I started learning a little more about the game. Well, I got called up to Triple-A. It wasn't long after he talked to me that I got called up and I went there and I moved straight to the closing role and was doing real well. That was in 1991. They were like, Jonesy's going to the big leagues. You're going to the big leagues. And I was really doing real well. Then I got a phone call. I was in Columbus, Ohio, playing the Yankees' Triple-A club. And Greg Biagini, our manager, called me down and he said, You're going to the big leagues. Congratulations.

Come to find out it was me and Mike Mussina and Jim Poole. It was a big deal because they sent down Jeff Ballard, Jeff Robinson, and Paul Kilgus. It was a big deal because they were sending up three guys and now you're paying three guys who have been on the major league roster for three years. You're paying them something around $1.7 million to pitch at Triple-A and you're sending up two guys, me and Mike Mussina, who have never pitched in the big leagues, and Poole who had pitched a little bit in the big leagues with the Dodgers. Basically they figured that this year was written off on July thirty-first. We're not going to make the play-offs. Let's move forward towards making a decision for the next year.

Who's the manager, Robinson or Oates?

Johnny Oates.

So they've already fired Frank Robinson.

Yeah. We fly straight to Seattle.

You hadn't even made the forty-man roster at this point. Do you know any of the guys on the team?

The only ones I knew were Gregg Olson and Bob Milacki, because in spring training Gregg would ask me to go play golf, and me and Gregg and Bob would go play golf together. And that was it except for some of the guys who had gone up and down while I was in Triple-A. That's the only ones I knew.

Having Gregg there had to be a positive.

He found out I got called up and he was in the Seattle clubhouse waiting on me. I walked in the door and, emotionally, it felt wonderful. Now, it hadn't hit me yet because I hadn't even been in a stadium that much. I didn't even want to go watch the Orioles when I was in Frederick and even in Hagerstown, because the first time I walked on the field I wanted to be in uniform. As it happened it was in Seattle because we went there first.

They were playing the national anthem when I finally got my uniform on. Walked out in the dugout, they were playing the national anthem, stood next to Johnny Oates, and he said, What do you think? I said, I've just left Columbus, Ohio. A few years later I found out he couldn't figure out why I said I'd left Columbus, Ohio. What I meant was, they had AstroTurf there and they had AstroTurf here. It didn't bother me. So I went down from the dugout after the first half inning and went to the bullpen.

Roy Smith started that game and just got pounded. Well, Jim Poole went in first, pitched two innings, didn't give up a hit. Pitched great. Jonesy, get up and throw a little bit. Well, I'm throwing. I'm thinking, I'll just get the kinks out a little bit. I'm throwing. Didn't really throw any away. And then all of a sudden our half of the inning was over with and we're in the top of the seventh and I'm still throwing and Elrod Hendricks is catching me. He's the bullpen catcher. He tells me, You're in. And I'm like, You got to be kidding me. I'm going in this game. I'd talked to my parents and a few other people earlier, and this game's on ESPN. And it didn't bother me. I'm still warming up. I'm not loose yet. I got in the game. Went right out there. Threw my two innings. Didn't give up a hit. Struck out two. The first batter was Dave Cochrane. I struck him out. Two nice innings and I'm done. And then it hit me. Man, that was on ESPN. My parents got to watch. Everybody at home saw me. Anyway, it hit me. I called Dad on the phone. I was under the stands. I couldn't get out on one phone so I'm up underneath the stands on a pay phone. Game's over with, everybody's gone home, and I started crying, because I'm here, Dad. He said, Did you sign your contract? I said, I did. I'll never be back in the minor leagues again. And I went to crying. Dad's crying. I think I talked to him for fifteen, twenty minutes. I talked to him, my mom, my brothers, my grandmother.

Is that the highlight?

Yeah. That was it. That's what I'd always worked for. And it was an obsession to me, because I knew what I wanted and I finally knew how to get there. Now I'm here. What's next? How do you stay? That was what was missing, but it didn't matter. I was there. I didn't know how to act. I'm here. Do I act like a ten-year veteran or do I move out of everybody's way not to talk to anybody?

That was the only game we played in Seattle that trip and we flew out of there and went to Chicago. And I remember my locker in Chicago was two lockers down from Cal Ripken Jr. And that was a man I had idolized pretty much, because he played every day. He was the man. And I remember sitting there, and I'm putting the uniform on and I'm thinking, I'm here. And I'm looking down watching what he's doing, and he's putting his shoe on. He's putting his shoe on. God, he's putting his shoe on. He's somebody like you and me but he was somebody I've idolized and he's doing the same thing I'm doing and I'm sitting next to him. Now, I'm not making what he's making. And I started thinking about, Man, he's making two million dollars a year. And he wound up being the MVP that year, in 1991. He was having a phenomenal year and I'm sitting

371

here and I'm with him. And it was the same way when we got to Balti-more. He was two lockers down. I think Gregg Olson was next to me on the left and I think Ben McDonald was right on my right, and then Cal Ripken. And he would sit in his chair and he would have all this mail. There would be bags and bags of mail. Fan mail. And I remember he would stay in the clubhouse until twelve o'clock or one o'clock at night before he'd go home, and he'd be one of the first people to get there. Now I realize why. He loved it that much. Plus he didn't want to have to walk outside the gate because somebody was going to bother him. I wanted to go out to the parking lot and yell out, I'm going to my car.

For me it was a great experience, but it only lasted seventeen or eigh-teen days. I pitched in four or five games. I can't remember. But I had one bad game. I started against Texas and that's the only time I really got nervous going out on the field. Ever.

Was that in Arlington or Memorial?

No, it was Memorial. It was a doubleheader and the first game went into extra innings. We used six pitchers. Now my parents have flown up to watch me play. They saw me pitch against Chicago. Did all right against them. Now I know I'm starting the second game, and I'm nervous as hell. My mom and dad are supposed to fly out and they were asking me if I was going to start. I knew I was starting but I was already so nervous, the night before I had diarrhea, fever. It had got to me. So I got up that morning and took them to the airport and then came home. And I got in a traffic jam and I sat in the traffic jam on that interstate around Balti-more and it took me until around ten-thirty or eleven o'clock to get back. My nerves are so shot. It really hit me then. I go to the first game. I get to the game a little early and they're like, What are you doing here? You're starting the second game. Go do something. Well, this is what I enjoy doing so I came to the field.

The first game went extra innings. We used six pitchers. I start warm-ing up and there's a rain delay before the second game and it's just a mess. And I pitched four innings and gave up five runs. It was the worst I'd done in years. I didn't have a clue where the ball was going. Every pitch was a dilemma. I was fighting myself. And then when the game was over Johnny Oates called me into the office. We ended up using six pitchers in that game. Some guys threw twice. We used everybody on the staff. He said, I'm going to make you a promise. You'll be back in the big leagues September the first. Now, this is August eighteenth or some-thing. And I was happy. I'm going back to the big leagues. I'm going down to Triple-A but I'm going to come back to the big leagues. And he made that promise. And I was in there with Roland Hemond, Johnny Oates, and Doug Melvin. I'm sitting in the chair and I'm in my uniform still. He said, I promise you. It's nothing against the way you pitch. I like the way you pitch. You will be back here September the first.

I went home to Rochester and blew my shoulder out August the twenty-fifth. Had to have labrum and rotator cuff surgery. I wound up getting shots. Went to Baltimore September the fourth and saw a doctor there. And he said, You need to take some time off. They said, How's your arm feel? I said fine. I'd go out there and throw in the outfield and it was killing me. I wanted to be activated.

I guess it was 1997 when I saw Johnny Oates the next time. Johnny Oates said, I've never made another promise to a player, because I couldn't keep that one. He said, I use you every day as an example that I made a promise to a player that I shouldn't have. Because you never know all the things that can happen. He told me that in 1997 in spring training when I was with the White Sox, that he's never made that promise to anybody else.

He sent you down in mid-August. Had they been holding on to extra pitchers because they knew the doubleheader was coming up?

They had to have somebody to start the next day so they sent me down and called Jose Mesa back up. We flip-flopped. And it didn't bother me.

When you blow your shoulder out, do you feel it on one pitch?

No, I never felt it. I went back down and they said, We're going to make a starter out of you, because the whole year I had been in middle relief or closing so I wasn't used to throwing that many pitches. So when I went back to Rochester they put me in the starting role. Actually threw a couple of times out of the bullpen and then it was, Hey, you're going to start. It's my second start of the year, one against the Texas Rangers and now this one against Syracuse. I threw seven innings, gave up two hits, and the two hits were solo home runs to Cory Snyder. And I lost 3–2. I woke up the next morning and couldn't pick my arm up. I never felt it. And I tore my labrum.

You have surgery.

I didn't really understand what it was until they were going to send me to instructional league and they called me on the phone and I said, My arm's still bothering me. Because I had started trying to throw. So they set it up for me to go see Dr Andrews down in Birmingham. He took a couple of looks at me and he said, You've got problems. They did an MRI and I had a torn labrum. So he called them on the phone and I wound up having the surgery, go to spring training the next year late. I end up getting there somewhere around April or May. I missed all of spring training. It bothered me because Andrews said I'd probably never be the same again. He said, You might not ever be at the level you were at. You're going to lose velocity, you're going to lose strength, you're going to lose resilience coming back. And that bothered me. Now somebody's finally telling me for the first time that I couldn't do something, and I was going to prove him wrong. It took two years to get past the pain.

Where were you for the second half of 1992?

I went to A ball, pitched two months there. Did real well. They sent me to Double-A. I pitched real good there for the last month. Sent me to Triple-A and finished out the last week up there, and did pretty well. And that ended the year.

But it's hurting the whole time. Is it soreness? Is it something you think you can work through?

It was something I had to go through. Scar tissue had built up. An MRI showed that there was scar tissue. I just had to break it up. Granted, now I was on a five-day rotation. The year before I probably only threw sixty or seventy innings at the most. Now I've started 1992 and I've thrown a hundred and something innings, more than I've thrown in the last two years, three years. And I'm on rehab. I pitched good. I had to learn how to pitch. When I got to Triple-A I pitched one or two games at the end of that season, and it bothered me. It started hurting me. I got up on a cold night and I told Jerry, My arm's bothering me. And he said, You're going to have to pitch through some pain, or something of that nature, and I said, I'm serious. My arm's bothering me. So they were going to send me to instructional league and then they said, Hey, he's thrown more innings now than he's thrown in two years combined and he's rehabbing. So they said, Go on home. Rest. Do active workouts.

So I wound up coming home and I got married during that time. She flew down to Florida and we got married during the 1992 season. It was wonderful, that part. I had somebody to go through it with me. And, well, going into spring training the next year I was hurting again. So I called them on the phone and I said, Look, I'm having problems with my arm, trying to get going. Here it's January and it's bothering me.

They said, Go see Andrews. So I went and saw Andrews and he gave me a cortisone shot. Scar tissue's built up. It's understandable. So I go to spring training and just pitch terrible. Arm's killing me. They send me back to A ball and I just struggled. One day it felt good, the next day it's just bad. It'd take me five or six days to get over it. And they called me in the office, and I was pretty frustrated, so I kind of took it out on everybody else. Even like on a bus trip home, guys left trash and stuff on the bus. I was older, and I aired everybody on the bus out. Sorry bunch of slobs. Clean up after your mess. Stuff like that. Well, it wasn't two or three days later the manager called me and he said, Doug Melvin wants to speak to you. So he called me on the phone and he said, Look, we understand what you've gone through. You've done everything we've asked, but we just don't feel like your arm's going to get any better so we're going to release you. And it kind of fell apart then. I started crying. He said, If there's anything I can ever do for you, you feel free to call me. And they don't normally do that. Usually you're out the door. He knew how much I wanted it. That it was the only thing I ever dreamed of. He mentioned something about coaching and I said, No, I'm going somewhere else. Somebody will give me a chance. And I got released and I came home.

When I got home, my wife was there for me. We're living with her parents and I would go and throw in Lincoln, Alabama. And I finally got fed up with my agent. I didn't feel like my agent was doing anything so I got a phone book down and I got the phone number for every major league team and I called every one of them. I asked to speak to the minor league director. And I wound up getting a phone call back from the Giants, and I went and played for the Giants in Shreveport, Louisiana. My first game there I got kicked out for throwing at somebody. I gave up three or four runs and I was frustrated so I knocked somebody down and they kicked me out. Went in the dugout and sat down. They said, No, you're going to have to go inside, so I went inside. The pitching coach, Steve Kline, comes in and he says, Thattaboy. You've got balls. And I said, I did bad. He said, It's your first outing. You're with the Giants. We wouldn't have signed you if we didn't want you. And he said, I've been here for about four years, and I've never had anybody come in and get thrown out their first day.

We were getting blown out when I went in and it kind of got worse when I was in there so I plunked somebody. We went on a winning streak. I don't say that started something, but it kind of got some ideas into the other players. This is the way you play the game. Because they had never been there before and here's this ex–major league player that's only got eighteen days coming in here and busting around and hitting somebody and getting thrown out. But we wound up making the play-offs and I got invited back. I went to spring training and had a pretty good spring. Got sent back to Double-A as a closer. Had thirty-five saves. Made the Double-A all-star team. Got to play here, got to go to Mexico and play the Mexican League all-stars. And then the strike hit. Dusty Baker came in town and that was a link for me, kind of being able to associate with him a little bit. To the point where if I do well in front of him, there's a chance I'll go to spring training. And I did. He invited me to spring training.

They sent me to winter ball down in Culican, down in Mexico. And I went down there for the winter, enjoyed it, did pretty well, came home for Christmas to see my wife and kids. They weren't going to let me come home. The manager didn't like the Giants players being there. He didn't get to pick and choose who he wanted to come down. So I went and talked to the manager and said, Can I go home and see my kids for Christmas? He said, Yeah, but don't tell anybody. Don't tell a soul I let you go. So I went. Got my ticket, flew home, spent three days, flew back. Then it was, You left the team. You didn't tell anybody. So they kicked me out. He did. He told the Giants I had left without telling anybody, so it didn't go over real well but he was wanting me out of there. He wanted to bring some other people in for the playoffs. That was the reason why.

Then what happens?

Spring training 1995. We don't have normal spring training. I'm supposed to be a non-roster invitee to spring training. Well, they call me on the phone in February and say, We want you to come anyway. We're going to invite so many. Little did I know that it was to be a replacement player. So I get there and all these Triple-A people were called in and we're practicing and the strike's still going on. Some of the players from big league camp are going to meetings. The front office calls me in and asks me to be a replacement player. And I said no, and they got mad. Now, this is a business. I told them. I said, I know this is a business. I've got time invested. I can't lose that. Plus, I don't want to be known as a replacement player. And Mr Hyatt, the minor league director, and the other front-office people are pushing me to become a replacement player. And Keith Bodie, who was the manager of the Triple-A team, and I didn't get along because I did not do it. He's a strictly front-office coach. We didn't mesh real well since I didn't become a replacement player.

In baseball you can be put in situations where you cannot come out on top. You can be sent in with the bases loaded and nobody out and expect to get out of it, but you're not going to do it every time. Or you can be put in a situation where there's nobody on and nobody out, you start the inning, give up a base hit, coach comes out there and says, Pitch around this guy. We don't want to get hurt. I pitch around the guy—this happened against the Salt Lake City Buzz—so now it's first and second and he takes me out and puts another guy in that doesn't have any business being in Triple-A but he's a replacement player and they promised it to him. He comes in, gives up a double, my two runs score. That's the way you can damage somebody. If you don't like them, you're able to do that in the management position. So I wound up getting released and I finally let Keith Bodie have it. Now, that's the first time I'd ever let anybody have it. But I let him know how I felt. About the organization, about him, and the way they did me about being a replacement player. So I get back to Phoenix, Arizona, and I go into the front office, trying to get reimbursed for my housing. This isn't two and a half, three weeks into the season and I'd had to put up six months' rent for an apartment. That's the least I could get. And they're supposed to reimburse you. They said, We're not doing it. I called my wife and said, I'm going over there. She said, Don't do it. You're going to get blackballed. You're going to have a bad name. I said, Those son-of-a-bitches have done this to me. I'm going over there to get my reimbursement. So I go over there and I'm sitting in front of this young fellow. He's a gofer for Hyatt. And this young fellow's standing there and I said, I've come to get reimbursed for my apartment. He talked a little bit and then he goes in to tell Sabian, the general manager, and Sabian says, We're not entitled to reimburse that. And I said, By God you are. It's in the bylaws. If we're losing our deposit you're supposed to take care of that. I lost like fifteen hundred dollars for the deposit and first month's rent. Now I've got to pay, on my own, the next six months. So I told him, If you don't go back there and get my damn money now, I'm going to break this computer. He goes back and I never see him again.

Sabian comes around the corner about thirty minutes later, hoping I'd left, and he walks out and there I am and it startles him. And he said, Stacy, we're not going to reimburse you. You didn't honor your commitment because you didn't become a replacement player.

I said, If I ever play against the Giants, you can bet your butt that Barry Bonds is going to eat one. He said, Hey now. We can't go that route. I said, Then you get my check. You're taking money out of my family's wallet. I said, I've got a wife and two kids and you're doing this to me. I'll take it out of your organization if I get that chance. No, he said, let's don't feel that way. I said, Well, you just watch if I get back. Anyway, they released me and I wound up going over to a coach that was my Double-A coach, and he was with the Brewers at the time, and I signed with them.

And that's 1995.

That's right. I signed with El Paso and pitched there for about two months and then went to Triple-A in New Orleans. Now, the Brewers are Bud Selig's old team. He owned the Brewers. And the only people going up and down from the big leagues are replacement players so now I'm right back in the same scenario. I did real well. I didn't get called up and it didn't bother me at all. But I went back to big league spring training with them in 1996. I went to New Orleans, didn't do real well, and got released from them.

I went to Birmingham. I just walked up and said, Can I have a tryout? They said, Who are you? So I told them, and I threw on the side and they offered me a contract and I signed it. It was a split contract between there and Triple-A. I did real well and got called up to Triple-A. This is in 1996. I got called up to Triple-A, did real well there, and then went to the big leagues in the September call-up after I'd been home two weeks. I was on the tractor out there and my wife, at the time, had brought me a pizza, and we were on the porch eating, and she said, Stacy, are you ever going to give it up? And it kind of hurt my feelings. She had been with me this whole time and never said anything about quitting. She said, You had such a good year this year in Birmingham and in Nash-ville. I was 3–1 with twenty-six saves with a one-something ERA. She said, If you're not going to make it with a year like you had this year, then you're not going to make it. And it hurt my feelings.

Anyway, I got back on the tractor. I was pulling dirt around the porch down there and that night we got a phone call from Chicago. Be on a plane in the morning. First they said, Have you been throwing? I said, Yeah, I've been throwing. Of course, I hadn't. They said, Well, be on a plane in the morning. I flew to Chicago and I was in uniform the next day. I actually got to pitch in, I think, two games at the end of the 1996 season. And that was a thrill. I'm back. I proved the doctor wrong, I proved my ex-wife wrong. A lot of people didn't think I'd ever make it back and I made it back. I was back. Here I am. This is where I belong. And I felt like I belonged because I knew Frank Thomas. He played with me at Auburn. I knew a few others during the course of the years, moving up and down. I'm back. Then I go to spring training the next year and I blow my elbow out. Tommy John surgery.

Did that happen on one pitch?

One pitch. It felt like the muscle pulled off the bone.

Fastball or breaking ball?

Just a fastball. And that's where this whole business part of the game comes in again. They wouldn't give me an MRI. They said I had tendinitis. And this went all the way to July. I tried to throw and it was hurting. I'd take a shot, take anti-inflammatories, exercise, rehab, and I'm begging for an MRI. Look, I'm hurting and I'm tired of hurting. I've got to find out what's wrong. So during the All-Star break—we had two days—I called my agent and I said, Get me an appointment with Dr Andrews. So he called and got me an appointment. I saw Andrews and in five minutes he said, You've damaged your ligament. And from the last week of spring training to July, I've been hurting.

What team were you with?

I was in Triple-A Nashville. I was there traveling with them. We're going to Buffalo, we're going to Des Moines, Iowa, we're going to New Orleans. We're going everywhere and I'm with them.

So you didn't get any major league service credit while being injured.

No. No. Like I said, I was there working, rehabbing, exercising, traveling. The coach told me, We've got to have you, we've got to have you. And I was supposed to be his closer. And they told me during the beginning of spring training that if the numbers worked out right, then they were going to trade Roberto Hernandez. And since I was a closer the last year with twenty-six saves, if they trade Roberto Hernandez I would go up and try to work into that role. And that's why they were so patient, from the end of spring training to July. And I wound up leaving a little upset that they wouldn't give me an MRI to find out what actually was wrong. If I'd have been on the major league roster they would've done the MRI the next day.

When do you know that your last major league game is your last major league game?

I never gave it up.

There's got to be some point, though, doesn't there? I mean, you're not planning on going back now. But it's not when Andrews says, Ligament surgery.

No. My wife said, You made it back from one, you can make it back from this one. Don't let them say that this is over. So I have the surgery and I start rehabbing and rehabbing, and I'm getting paid workman's comp. I'm going on and on and on and it's just not there. One day I'll throw and it swells. And it takes me two or three weeks to get over that. Then I start lobbing again and then I get on the mound and start throwing real hard and it blows up again. The ligament just isn't taking that well. So I kept seeing Andrews and they said, When are you going to get out of here? And I said, I'm trying. I'm trying. It finally got to the point where I said, It isn't going to come back. Let's start our own business. Let's get into sporting goods. I'm going to give it up. And at that point my wife and I weren't doing real well.

The Rangers, Doug Melvin and them, asked me if I'd like to be a pitching coach. I flew out there and I turned down the job because of marital problems and I didn't want to leave my kids. And if I left I was pretty sure we'd have been through a divorce. In hindsight, I probably should've taken it. We might be still married. I guess going through the divorce ended it for me, that dream. Because there's no way that I could ever leave my kids, at all. It took me a while to get used to that. That I'll never pitch again in a uniform.

When did the White Sox release you?

They released me at the end of the year. They had the obligation to pay me throughout the regular part of the contract, from October to October. From that point it took like two years but they were still paying workman's comp and I finally said, I'm done. I said, Dr Andrews, let's get this thing over with. Let's get them to finish paying the bills and get me out of workman's comp so I can actually go do something. And that was it. I had had enough.

With going through the divorce and everything, how bad is the frustration of not getting back into a uniform?

It was bad. I think that really and truly was the reason I wound up getting a divorce. I couldn't handle it, because all I had lived for was getting prepared to go to spring training, or getting prepared during the winter for college, getting prepared for high school. That's all I thought of, and now I'm like, What am I going to do now? And she would say, Why don't you go work for somebody? Well, how do you do that? I don't have any skills. Yeah, I went to college but what am I going to do? Here I am thirty-two years old and I don't have any work skills. Where do I go?

And she was like, Well, just apply somewhere. I wanted my own. I'd always been able to control my own destiny. I wanted to start my own business. It was too risky for her, so there was conflict. We were around each other twenty-four hours a day. I was at home. She was here.

That was the first time you had lived together without the knowledge that you were going to be gone in a few months.

That's right. That's right. Everything had been I'm about to go to spring training or I'm coming back from spring training. Everything had been stable and now I didn't have any stability at all. Emotionally I didn't know what to do. Let's put it like this. I wasn't a man. Because I was scared. And that tore me down. You have this image, if you live in a small town like I do. When are you going pro? When are you going pro? There's the next pro baseball player. Now I'm walking down there and I'm not a baseball player. I didn't have an identity so I was living off what I was in the past.

But you're still young.

But I'm still young. But I'm living off the past, that I was a ballplayer, and everybody would talk to me about baseball, and I didn't know what to tell them. I didn't know. I couldn't say, Well, I'm giving it up, because I didn't want that image to be gone. That broke my marriage. It broke it in the sense that I didn't concentrate on my marriage. I took everything to her pretty much. Laid it out on her. Took it out on her, let's just put it that way. Took it out on her when I should've said, That part of my life is over with. Baseball's over with and I'm going to lead my family in this direction. I went to this divorce care at the church and it set me kind of straight. And it wasn't that biblical all the time. It was about, Hey, we're going through an identity crisis of being alone and being something that we weren't before, and it helped me more ways than just going through marriage counseling. It helped me get past baseball, and nobody knew that.

We were in a group where there was like nine or ten people going through divorce care, and everybody had bones in their closet. And I had bones in my closet, but I was able to open up and tell them, Hey, this broke my marriage. I'm not that person anymore. What am I going to do? When I tore my elbow, I kind of knew it then, that it was over with, but it took me until six months after my divorce to finally say, All right, it's time to get up in the morning and get to work. You've got two kids to worry about.

How long ago was six months after your divorce?

I've been divorced about a year now. The year 2000, we were going to spend that together. We talked about being together, but we split up. I went to my family January eleventh, so we haven't spent one night together in a year and ten months. So six months, I guess, is June of the year 2000. So I've been pretty much sane for a little over a year.

When you get up every morning you have to have an objective as to what you're going to do, where everything's planned out and it's all there in front of you. But I didn't have any direction to go. Or I had many directions to go. Do I go back to school? Do I start my own business? Do I go become a pitching coach? Do I go work for somebody else? Does my wife work? All these things my wife had taken care of during our whole marriage and I didn't realize how much she did. Now I'm supposed to do it, and I didn't. I didn't know how to handle it.

When you're in the divorce care at the church, and you're opening up about all of this, do these people in the group know that you're a former major league pitcher?

Yes, and I wasn't the only athlete in there. A friend of mine was in there. He played at the University of Alabama. Big, well-known football player. He was going through a divorce and has actually been put in jail a few times because he couldn't handle it. One time in his life a guy stuck a gun in his mouth, was going to kill him. And here he is, a big, strong football player and he couldn't do anything about it. His manhood was pretty much taken away. He went half crazy.

He's not used to feeling helpless. And there you are as helpless as you can be.

Oh yeah. Everything. From family, to not having a job, to where do I go now.

Are these people able to give you the sympathy that everyone else in the group gets or do they hold on to the stereotype of a rich and spoiled major league pitcher sitting on a pile of money?

Number one, I made it clear right off the bat at the first meeting: I never made very much money. The most money I ever made in one year from professional baseball was about $40,000.

Do they believe you?

I don't think they really believed it, but I never made very much money. The perception out in the city of Attalla, everybody thinks you've got all this money. Somebody even made the suggestion to my ex-mother-in-law that I paid for this road to get paved from a mile and a quarter down there all the way to my daddy's. That's the perception people get, that we have all this money, and we don't. Only an elite few.

You've got thirty-one days of major league service, which means, pension-wise, you're vested into retirement but you'll have to wait until you're forty-five to draw your two dollars a week.

Well, there's a thing to it. If you don't have so much time in, you have to take it out. You can put it in an IRA or you can put it into something else. And I had to. I had to roll it into an individual IRA account. I had $2,500. That's all I had after nine years of service. $2,500. One of the problems with professional sports—baseball and basketball and football—is that everything's structured where you don't make anything until you get there. I mean, you get by. My first contract I made $700 a month. Five of us lived in the apartment in order to get by.

You've got several players now making ten million dollars a year. If you took a team's minor league system and added all of their paychecks together, you're not going to come close to that. And they're getting players a dime a dozen from Puerto Rico, Dominican Republic, Venezuela. They're signing for a plane ticket just to get over here. You've got guys in high school that sign for a thousand dollars because they were drafted and weren't smart enough to go to college. They play one year and they're done. Now they can't go play college ball because they were a professional. They're done on that part.

But, in a sense, the guys who wash out after a year are better off than the ones who last six or seven years, because they're twenty years old and there are a lot of twenty-year-olds just starting out and looking for work. It's a different situation being thirty and looking for work.

There's a big difference. When I said, I'm done, the only thing I had was marketing. I marketed myself for years, because that's all you're doing. You're basically promoting yourself through how well you do. But you can't take that and say, Well, I'm going down to the firm and I'm going to get a job. That doesn't work. In the real world it's, What can you do for me? How are you going to make me money? Well, if you don't have the people skills, if you don't have those social skills, then you're really screwed if you've been playing for ten years. I kind of got lucky there on that part.

I've got a wonderful job. I don't make a killing but I get by and I enjoy it. First job I took was the one I had to have because I was going through that divorce. I went to work for Buffalo Rock merchandising Pepsi. Going in grocery stores and putting them on the shelf for them. Going in the supply room and taking them out and putting them on the shelf. I'd get up to leave at four-thirty every morning. I lived here by myself. Work for ten, eleven, twelve hours, come home, do it again the next day. I'd never done that before. I had to, because I had to pay child support, I had to pay my ex-wife for the house. Fortunately my dad helped me out. I didn't have the money. She took everything. She took it out of the bank. She took everything. The only thing I had was the house and she had half of that. If it wasn't for my dad I'd be so financially broke right now it wouldn't be funny.

So I was loading Pepsis in grocery stores and then I got an opportunity to learn how to run a business. I was working with kids' baseball. I was working with this man's son and I said something about getting up and going to work and he said, How would you like to come work for me? I said, Doing what? He ran a feed store. And he said, I want you to run the store for me. It's a co-op where you have feed and hay and fertilizer, seeds, all kinds of things to do with farmers. And I told my father, Look, he's giving me the opportunity to learn how to run a business. I'm going to jump on it. My dad said, You're crazy. Stay where you are with Buffalo Rock. They're telling you can be in top management quick. But it's not like you're hired and go straight up. It'd take me three or four years and then I'd be up there as a spokesperson, locally, telling people about Pepsi and going to events. But I saw the co-op as an opportunity. So I did that for about eight months and there was a man who came in one day. He's been coming in. He said, Would you be interested in working for Goldkist? I said, Doing what? He said, Working with farmers. And I said, I don't know anything about it. He said, We'll teach you. I said, What do I do? He said, Have me a résumé tomorrow. Make sure you put everything you can about farming on there. So I did it and then went for an interview and I didn't know a doodly question about chickens, and they didn't ask me any. They asked me questions about how do I deal with the public, how do I deal with another person. Leading questions. Being interested in that person. And that's what I basically do. I work with farmers on how to make money. And it kind of goes right along with marketing yourself and that's why I love it. I don't have a time frame where I have to get up in the morning. I do my job, I come home. I don't punch a clock. I have a job to do, I do it, and I do it to the best of my ability, and hopefully one day I'll run that company. Now I'm in charge of thirty farms that's got eighty-three houses and I'm in charge of nearly two million birds every eight weeks. Their health, management issues, everything to do with farming. That's what I do now.

Do you watch much baseball?

No.

Is it tough to watch it?

Yes. Everybody at the office asks me to get tickets to go to Atlanta. One day they gave some tickets away and I actually won two tickets to go. I don't have any interest in going over there and sitting and watching baseball. Now, I do have an interest in people that I see on ESPN that are friends, and I hope they do well. Marvin Benard and Calvin Murray, Mike Mussina. I probably played with or against one-third of all the major league players who are in the big leagues now, and I know them personally, but I have no desire to go watch them play. That part of my life is over with. I envy them but I don't envy their lifestyle anymore. That's what I was addicted to.

Do you have any regrets about your career?

Playing-wise, no, because I did everything I could to make it. Rehab and all that. I don't want to go through that pain anymore. That physical pain, the emotional pain. It was an emotional roller coaster because one day you're doing good, the next day you're doing bad. I don't miss it. I wake up every morning now and I have an objective. I feel good. But when I was playing, like I said, it interfered with my family. I took it out on her and the kids and everybody else because that was my only outlet. So that emotional part, no. I don't miss playing at all.

I miss competing. I love to compete. It's not about money when you play. Everybody says, It's all about money. No, it's not about money. You roll that ball out there for the World Series and tell them that there's no money involved, and they're still going to play their damnedest to win. It's instilled in those players. It doesn't matter if you play basketball, football, or baseball. It's about coming out on top. And that's the reason why they're competitors.

Now, I played with some where it was money, but they didn't stay in the game very long. It was money to them, a little. It was a way to get by and make a living. Those guys didn't stay in it long because they didn't strive to be better. They didn't work out as much. They didn't train as hard.

I watched games on TV and took notes because I knew I was going to pitch against them. You sit there and watch ESPN and say, Here's how to get this guy out. Here's how you get Tony Gwynn out. Here's how you get Paul Molitor out. And I watched TV in the hotel room on the road, me and Ken Shamburg, my best friend. He played with me in the Orioles organization, and he played in the Brewers system, too. He was a position player. And we would sit and watch TV, and he would watch the pitchers and we would talk about them and I'd take notes because I was going to face those guys and I didn't want to go in there blind. And that's why I'm saying I thought about it twenty-four hours a day.

If you were awake, that's what you thought about. How can I do better? What did I do wrong in the last game? What can I do better? How can I make this pitch? Do I need to add another pitch to my repertoire? That was on your mind. That emotional part, that stressful part. You can grow old quick. I don't miss it. I really don't. And if anybody says they do, they have regrets because of the fact they didn't make it. That's a hard thing to really actually say. I miss competing, but I don't miss it. If you'd asked me that a year and a half ago, I'd have gone and played.

Detroit at Seattle
Saturday, April 29, 1995

Detroit	ab	r	h	rbi		Seattle	ab	r	h	rbi
Curtis, cf	4	1	1	1		Amaral, lf	3	0	1	1
Fletch'r, 2b-ss	4	0	1	0		Diaz, lf-cf	2	1	1	3
Pemberton, lf	4	0	1	0		Fermin, ss	5	2	2	0
Fielder, 1b	4	0	2	0		Griffey Jr., cf	4	1	2	2
Fryman, 3b	4	0	0	0		Bragg, ph-lf	1	0	0	0
Samuel, dh	2	0	0	0		Buhner, rf	5	1	1	0
Bautista, rf	3	0	2	0		E. Marti'z, dh	3	2	1	1
Gomez, ss	2	0	0	0		Blowers, 3b	4	0	1	2
Higginson, ph	1	0	0	0		Strange, 3b	0	0	0	0
Penn, 2b	1	0	0	0		T. Marti'z, 1b	3	2	3	1
Tingley, c	2	0	0	0		Wilson, c	3	1	1	0
Wells, p	0	0	0	0		Kreuter, c	0	0	0	0
Boever, p	0	0	0	0		Sojo, 2b	4	1	1	1
Whiteside, p	0	0	0	0		Fleming, p	0	0	0	0
Bohanon, p	0	0	0	0		Converse, p	0	0	0	0
Totals	31	1	7	1		Totals	37	11	14	11

Detroit	1	0	0	0	0	0	0	0	0—1
Seattle	1	0	0	1	1	1	7	0	x—11

Detroit	IP.	H.	R.	ER.	BB.	SO.
Wells (L. 0-1)	6	7	4	4	0	1
Boever	0	5	5	5	0	0
Whiteside	1	2	2	2	2	0
Bohanon	1	0	0	0	0	1
Seattle	IP.	H.	R.	ER.	BB.	SO.
Fleming (W. 1-0)	5	3	1	1	3	1
Converse (Save. 1)	4	4	0	0	1	1

E—Penn (1), Amaral (1). 2B—Pemberton (2, off Fleming), Fermin (1, off Wells), Griffey Jr. (1, off Wells), T. Martinez (1, off Wells), Amaral (1, off Wells), Buhner (1, off Whiteside), Blowers (1, off Whiteside). HR—Curtis (1, off Fleming), E. Martinez (1, off Wells), Griffey Jr. (2, off Wells), Diaz (1, off Boever). SF—T. Martinez (1, off Whiteside). IBB—E. Martinez (1, by Whiteside). U—Jim Schaly, Matt Bohn, Jim Uremovich, John Higgins. T—2:44. A—27,264.

SEAN WHITESIDE

Sean Whiteside pitched three and two-thirds innings for the Detroit Tigers in 1995. In that stretch he gave up seven hits, walked four, and struck out two. He finished with a major league career ERA of 14.73. He was interviewed October 16, 2001 at his home in Haleyville, Alabama.

Tell me where you grew up and when you first started playing baseball.

I grew up in Haleyville, Alabama, which is where I live now. That's where I lived most of my young life and that's where I started playing baseball. I started when I was seven years old, as far as organized baseball, and then I played here until I was a sophomore in high school when my parents moved to North Carolina and that's where I finished my high school ball.

Were you nervous about moving to North Carolina after you'd lived in Haleyville all your life?

Yeah, it was tough, because I had developed so many relationships around here and I had a lot of friends and teammates here growing up, and so I had to go up there and make new friends. It probably was the best thing for me in the long run because when I was younger I was very shy. I was just real quiet and it was hard for me to meet people and things like that, and that was probably the best thing about moving to North Carolina. It probably opened me up to the rest of the world, so to speak.

Did you play baseball in North Carolina as soon as you got up there?

Yeah, and I also played basketball. I was a pretty good basketball player. We moved up there at the end of the summer, after the baseball season, so I started playing basketball and that's how I met most of my friends there.

Were your baseball and basketball skills comparable at the time you moved?

Well, I made it to the big leagues in baseball so obviously my basketball skills weren't quite there but I was looked at by some teams. No big schools or anything like that. Basketball up there is a different breed. That was another thing. It taught me a little bit of humility because around Haleyville we were always winning, and when I moved up there we had a little bit stiffer competition. The competition in both sports up there was better than it was here.

Did you like one sport more than the other? Did you choose baseball or did baseball choose you?

Baseball kind of chose me because, I'll be honest with you, I loved basketball as much as I did baseball. I liked, basically, all sports. I didn't play football when I moved up there because, when I moved up there, their brand of football wasn't what it is in Alabama. I saw that I was going to be bigger than some of my linemen, because I was used to playing quarterback, and I would've been a tackling dummy.

But you played all three sports while you were here in Haleyville?

I played on the B team in basketball and in baseball I started out on the JV, pitched a couple of games, and moved to the varsity. I actually moved to varsity when I was in the eighth grade.

Did you play any other positions besides pitcher?

Oh yeah. I actually made the all-state team in North Carolina as an infielder-outfielder. And I was actually drafted by the Brewers out of high school as a first baseman-outfielder.

What kind of pitches are you throwing in high school?

I threw a fastball and a hard curve. I would just strictly overpower them. That was what I was trying to do.

Who taught you to throw a curveball?

Well, my coach here in Haleyville was a pretty good baseball player. He actually played at some point in his career with the Birmingham Barons and had an opportunity to go to spring training with the San Francisco Giants, but when he underwent the physical they found an irregular heartbeat so they put a catheter in his arm, and of course it was his throwing arm, and they somehow messed up an artery so his arm was no good after that.

  He was a good baseball man. He knew the game. He was a hard man, but he knew the game. He was one who really taught me a lot. And, of course, my father and my brother as well. My brother, who's ten years older than I am, was a three-sport athlete. My dad was a pretty good baseball player when he was in high school. He got looked at by the Kansas City Athletics. He had a great breaking ball but he didn't throw hard enough. They're the ones who really taught me the pitches. As far as fine-tuning and stuff, my coach did.

Is your curveball a side-to-side sweeper or more of a top-to-bottom curve?

I would call it a slurve. It was a hard curve that would come down and in on a right-handed batter.

Does your fastball have a lot of velocity or does it have some movement to it?

Both.

Can you put it where you want it or do you have to throw it towards the center of the plate and let it move?

I was throwing to the center and letting it move. That was one of my fortes as far as my pitching, the movement on my fastball.

And you're drafted at the end of your senior year of high school.

I got drafted on June fifth, 1989, by the Milwaukee Brewers in the twentieth round.

How do you feel about being drafted?

Well, excited for one thing, of course. It's every kid's dream that's played baseball.

Is this the best day of your life so far?

So far. So far. It was expected because scouts were always at my high school games my senior year, but it wasn't expected in some regard because a lot of them knew that I was not going to sign out of high school. I was mature enough mentally but not physically. I was six four and weighed 163 soaking wet.

That does show maturity, to be eighteen years old and know you're not ready even though a major league organization drafts you.

392   I can see your reasoning, but I knew that I needed to get stronger. I had had trouble in high school with my shoulder a little bit, and that's why I played more in the field and made all-state that way. I wanted, basically, to get a little bit of college under my belt, too, and I knew that this was going to be an opportunity for me to get a scholarship and get a little bit of college, and also mature physically. If I had to do it all over again I probably would've gone to a junior college.

Would you have considered signing if you'd been drafted higher?

The scout really wasn't going to try and push to sign me. He just wanted to get me recognized, so to speak, by his people and his organization. And the cross-checker that they have came down and watched me during Legion ball. And he said, Sign the kid. Try to sign the kid. So they made me an offer. It wasn't a bad offer. $25,000 for the twentieth round in 1989 was decent money. But, you know, I just wasn't ready. Plus $25,000 isn't that great of a sum. My parents had always been able to take care of me, but it was a good sum of money, don't get me wrong.

But if you get stronger you might be drafted higher later and get more.

That's also what I was thinking.

Did you have a favorite team when you were growing up?

The Dodgers. My dad was a Brooklyn Dodgers fan and it carried over to when they moved to L.A. and everything, and of course my brother was and I was.

Did you have a favorite player?

Steve Garvey was one of my favorite players. Pedro Guerrero. You never could throw it hard enough for him. And he wasn't going to walk. He was one of my favorite players. As far as pitchers go, probably Bob Welch. And, of course, Steve Carlton.

Why "of course Steve Carlton"? He never played for the Dodgers.

He did things his own way and in a way I kind of admire it.

What if the Dodgers had drafted you and offered you $25,000 at the end of high school?

It would've been a lot harder decision, let's put it that way.

So what colleges are talking to you? All of them?

Not all of them. North Carolina. I went on a visit there. I didn't like it right from the get go. It didn't feel like home. It was a little too aloof for my taste, to be frank. Don't get me wrong, it's a super university, but I could just tell. And I went on a visit to Wake Forest and I also went to North Carolina State. UNC-Charlotte and a lot of the smaller schools. UNC-Asheville. Not any other ACC schools besides Wake Forest, North Carolina, and NC State.

Basically the big four schools in North Carolina other than Duke.

My grades weren't good enough for Duke, I can tell you that. I wasn't stupid by any means. I scored decent on the ACT. I took it one time and scored high enough. I guess when I moved to North Carolina from here I just couldn't get into the school thing. It was just one of those deals where I put classes on the back burner a little bit.

You choose UNC-Charlotte. How did your first year go?

My freshman year was a great year.

Are you still pitching and playing in the field?

I played a little bit in the field, mostly defensively, but after the fall season my coach and I decided that pitching was what I really needed to concentrate on.

Is it because you're not hitting as well as you did in high school?

The breaking balls are a little bit meaner in college. I couldn't make the adjustment. And I was left-handed throwing about eighty-three on the Raygun, which is about eighty-eight on the Juggs, and I just felt like a left-hander throwing that hard at eighteen...and he felt the same way. It was a wise decision. If I could get stronger and fine-tune some things, my chances of playing after college would be greater.

When you talk about getting stronger, are you just growing into your body? What are you actively doing in order to get stronger?

Growing into my body, of course, and lifting. Coach had me doing all kinds of agility drills during the off-season. Strengthening the legs and things of that nature. The coach that I had in college was a sadist. He was tough. But it's like I tell everybody, if I ever played for a coach that I liked he wasn't worth a shit. The coaches that push you, that make you go beyond your means, are usually pissing you off 90 percent of the time. Some do it in a yelling way and some don't. He chose the yelling way.

What kind of coaching staff does UNCC have? Do they have a pitching coach as well as a head coach?

The pitching coach was a grad assistant. My head coach was Gary Robinson and my pitching coach was Jeff Edmonds, and he played at North Carolina.

Are you trying to develop another pitch?

I'm trying to develop a change-up, and of course I'm working on the other two pitches as well.

With the change-up, are you doing anything besides changing your grip on the ball and keeping the same motion?

I did everything I could. It just didn't come easy for me. That's one thing I wish I'd learned when I was in high school. And that's what I'm teaching my nephews, and if my son decides he wants to play baseball, the next pitch he's going to learn after a fastball is a change-up. That's what I was working on. That and, of course, refining the other two.

So by your sophomore year you're strictly a pitcher.

Right. And I was pitiful.

Were you in the rotation?

I was the number-one starter. See, I had a helluva freshman year. I was about three innings short or I probably would've got rookie of the year in the conference. I had strikeouts galore, a great ERA. That was the Sun Belt Conference. Then the next year we entered the Metro and I was just pitiful. And it wasn't because my skills had diminished. It was the old sophomore jinx. I'd done so well the first year. I didn't bounce back like you're supposed to after you have a shitty start. You need to forget about it and move on. That was probably my main problem throughout my career. I was always too hard on myself, but I just had a pitiful year. I think I still hold the record for most decisions in a season. I was 5–10. But I pitched a lot and that helped me. My sophomore year did help me.

In what way did you benefit?

Arm strength for one thing, and just learning how to set up hitters. I'd never really been taught that. I didn't really have to set up hitters until I got to the Sun Belt Conference. It was like the number-three conference in the nation when I signed. They had South Alabama and South Florida and Jacksonville. Not your big-name schools by any means, but they've got a lot of baseball players in Florida. I played in that conference and then jumped to the Metro but we still played pretty much the same teams. I forget who all we dropped. I think we dropped South Florida and Jacksonville. There wasn't stiffer competition in the Metro by any means.

How was your junior year?

395

My junior year went pretty well, until the end. After my sophomore year my head coach left and it was almost December so they didn't have time to find a new head coach, really, that would've been worth their wait. So they gave the job to the ex–pitching coach who'd since graduated. They gave it to him for a year.

So your former pitching coach is now the head coach and you start off well.

Start off well. Of course, the recruiting that year was pitiful. We didn't have any good recruits. I think our number-three starter was a walk-on. And nothing against walk-ons, but we just had a lot of young kids and didn't have any other pitching, so to speak. So basically, when I started, I was out there for the duration. And it wore on me. I got tired. Hell, my first start on January thirty-first I threw 135 pitches. That was one of the things, like I said earlier, if I had it to do all over again I'd have signed to play juco. I was out there for the duration. I was going to pitch.

If the season starts at the end of January and lasts until the beginning of May, how many games is that?

Seventy.

How often are you pitching?

I'm pitching every fourth day, let's say. I can't remember how many innings. And a lot of times they would have us throw on the second day after a start, and instead of throwing in the bullpen we would throw an inning in a game just to get some work. So I pitched in a lot of games and it wore on me. And also, I was hardheaded in some sense. I wasn't going to tell them if my arm was aching. I wanted to pitch. This was my junior year and I was looking to get drafted. Scouts had been talking to me even after my sophomore season. And I was hardheaded. I wouldn't tell them I was hurting.

Is it anything more than soreness from overpitching?

Yeah. I got hurt around the first part of May.

What happened?

Well, to set it up, I pitched at Southern Miss on a Sunday and pitched nine innings. I struck out eleven and Southern Miss, at the time, had some hitters. They were known as the hitting team in the league. They were a fastball-hitting team and I probably threw sixty-forty fastballs to slurves. I stayed in there the whole time and threw 140 pitches. I pitched the whole game and threw too many pitches. Then my next start was against Virginia Tech and I was facing Brad Clontz who ended up pitching for the Braves so there were a lot of scouts there. Well, I was a dumb-ass and didn't tell them I was hurting, but of course at the time he was a prospect and I was a prospect and there were thirty scouts in the stands. Probably every cross-checker with the exception of five teams was there. So there were a bunch of scouts in the stands and it was cold, nasty weather, one of those cold fronts that comes through in May. And I was warming up and my arm just didn't feel right but I still went in. First inning I got hit around a little bit. I didn't have anything on my fastball. In the second inning, the second slider I threw I thought my arm fell off. Pow! That was it.

Where was the pain?

In my elbow. And I thought I had snapped it. Just on the inside where a lot of those guys are getting Tommy John surgery. Right there. And it just popped up on me, and I had tingling down my fingers and every-thing else. It wasn't just a dull aching pain. It happened on one pitch. I threw one more pitch, a fastball about fifty feet. It barely made it to the dirt so I waved my coach out there and that was it. I didn't pitch the rest of the college season.

Is it still tingling after you come out?

It's not right. I went straight to the doctor.

What's the medical prognosis?

I strained it pretty good. I think they call it the medial collateral. They did an MRI and I had a little small tear in it, nothing major. Something that could be repaired with rehab, so I didn't pitch the last month of baseball season.

What's your emotional state? Are you scared that you won't be drafted in June?

My emotional state was not good, obviously. I mean, hell, this is my dream and I'm sitting here thinking, Oh shit, I'm never going to get to play again.

Are you blaming yourself?

In a sense, yes, and blaming the coach, to be honest. But looking back now, there's a lot of people you can blame but the ultimate blame lies with yourself. I was pissed off at the world. Then, towards the end of the season, I went down to the Metro tournament with the team, didn't suit up or anything like that, and they run an article in the New Orleans paper saying that I was slated for arm surgery. And I wasn't going to have surgery.

Does the writer just assume that if you're hurt enough to leave in the middle of a game and can't suit up for the conference tournament then it's got to be bad enough for surgery?

The reporter didn't follow up with me. He didn't ask anybody. He took it from a second source that wasn't even one of our spokespeople. There was a pitcher who pitched for Tulane at the time and he had to have arm surgery so they kind of threw me into the mix. They said I had bone spurs. Hell, nobody even asked. And the scouts were calling and I was telling them what it was. I was throwing. I just wasn't well enough to pitch. Of course, that article runs and then I'm really pissed off.

398

Do the phone calls taper off?

Oh yeah. I kind of found out, secondhand, that that rumor may've been started by my old coach who had left to go scout for the Giants.

Was he doing that to throw everybody else off so he can draft you for the Giants?

That's the rumor that I heard. But you never know what to believe. That's one of those things. People ask me, Do you miss the game? Well, hell yeah, I miss the game, but do I miss the bullshit? No. And it was there. Trust me. At every level. Even in college it was there. But yeah, ultimately that's what he was getting to. He was trying to steal me. At the start of the season I was projected to go in the first four rounds. I'm left-handed, I'm throwing harder now, I've put on about twenty pounds, I'm averaging about eighty-five on the Raygun. And the reason I keep referring to the Raygun is that's all we had in Charlotte so that's about eighty-eight or eighty-nine. And still have a long way to go as far as getting stronger.

What's draft day like?

The day before was really the telltale day. The same scout that drafted me out of high school called me and asked me about my arm, and another scout—I think he was with the Royals—called and asked me if I was going to have to have arm surgery. In the meantime I had pitched simulated games for the Mariners' scout and my old college coach with the Giants and threw fine. Finally they started calling me the day before and that's where I came to hear about my old college coach saying that stuff.

Well, draft day comes and the first ten rounds go by and there's no phone call so I went to go see a movie to get my mind off of it.

Who went with you?

Just my parents and my girlfriend at the time. Of course, my parents are close to distraught, too. And when we get back, my buddy told me that the Tigers had called. Mike Mirabelli was the scout. Super guy. Probably one of the nicest men I've ever met. He coached at NC State for a while. He called while I was gone.

So you call him back.

And he told me that the Tigers had drafted me in the eleventh round.

That's not too bad for somebody who's just popped his elbow.

Oh yeah. See, they signed me thinking they were still going to have to do some surgery or extended rehab. And I knew I was still on the hurt side. But they still drafted me. They felt that strong about me.

So in June of 1992 you're drafted in the eleventh round by the Tigers, but given the circumstances, is the day the Brewers drafted you after high school a happier day?

Yeah, because it was more of a relief the second time around, that I was still going to get that opportunity. I could've gone back and played college my senior year, but we had a new coach coming in and I didn't really want to mess with that. Then it turns out they win the conference championship that year.

How many days does it take Mirabelli to come by with a piece of paper?

Well, they have to be in contact with you within a week. If you're not contacted within a week you're then considered a free agent. He came by after three days and that's where we sat down and negotiated.

Is "negotiation" the right word?

Yeah, we negotiated a little bit. They were trying for a lower signing bonus and then school, but school's a helluva lot cheaper than the signing bonus was, so that's where me and my parents came back and said, We'll take care of school. Give us the dollars. Because after taxes you're not going to get shit.

Did you both get what you wanted?

It was just mutual, really. I told him to just dump that school and give me another five and let's go. I knew I wasn't going to get that great of an amount. Of course, we had to leave the room while he called his man, but he came back and said, Yeah, we'll do that.

How long after the contract is it before you report to rookie ball?

400 | I guess it was about a week. They let me get all my stuff in order. I go to Niagara Falls, New York, for short-season A ball. I went out and got me a brand new car.

Is that what you did with the signing bonus?

No, my parents got me the car with the agreement that I'd help out, which, of course, I never had to. They never asked me to. I was a little spoiled in that regard.

What kind of car was it?

That same Ford Explorer that's sitting out in the driveway that I need to sell.

It's a short season so you're going to be up there about two months. What do you take with you?

Basically my clothes and my glove and that's it. I didn't carry any type of amenities. First of all, we had to stay in this dorm at Niagara Falls University for like two weeks. They had like a two-week minicamp there.

After that they decide to send some guys to rookie ball and some stay at Niagara Falls and I ended up staying with the Niagara team.

Is the Niagara team a bunch of green guys who have signed their first professional contract within the last month?

There's those guys and then there's probably thirty percent of the guys who played short-season A ball the year before, but for the most part it's high school kids and college signees.

You said you'd been throwing simulated games before the draft. Do you ever let loose during the minicamp? Do you feel like you had to let loose? Do you tell anybody about the injury when you get there?

They knew everything. They knew everything. They had me under watch from day one. I told them I was almost full strength in my bullpen throwing and they said, Well, we're backing you back down to half strength. We want you throwing fifty percent. We want you to take your time.

That's got to make you feel better.

Oh yeah. But I was concerned because I did not want to go to Bristol. I did not want to go down there.

Why not?

It's rookie ball. It's a lot of high school kids and I knew I was better than a lot of high school kids. Plus short-season A, even though it's short-season A, sounds better than rookie ball.

Do you ever get up to full strength up there?

Oh yeah. I ended up getting pitcher of the year up there. They used me in relief for the first two to three weeks of the season and then I started letting it loose when I became a starter.

Had you ever thrown relief other than throwing an inning in between starts?

No, I was always a starter.

But this is okay because it's rehab.

Yeah. I ended up striking out a bunch of guys in my first three or four outings. The first ten innings I only gave up one hit. I struck out a bunch of guys and didn't walk that many, probably like ten-to-one strikeouts-to-walks, and then they start me. I'm still on a limited-pitch basis but I end up starting and get a bunch of strikeouts. I was 8–2 in the wins and losses.

So when the season's over where do you go?

I head back home to Cordele, Georgia, and stay there with my parents for ten days, then head to Florida for instructional league.

Are you in love at this point?

Yeah.

And where is she?

She is still in Lexington, North Carolina.

Do you see her at all during this break?

I stopped by for two or three days and then I had to head down.

Is she understanding and excited for you and all that?

So to speak.

Is "instructional league" a misnomer or are they actually instructing?

There's a little bit of instruction. It's more like a spring training. They are working with you on some things, like fine-tuning your mechanics or fine-tuning your pitches. They get you some innings, get you consistent. Then, of course, some of the guys who were just raw as hell they were just trying to build from the ground up.

Do you go back to school after instructional league?

No, I'm too late to enroll. Basically I just worked out in North Carolina and stayed with my fiancée at the time until it was time for spring training. Actually I went down about two weeks early. I threw pretty well down there and ended up breaking camp and going to Fayetteville, North Carolina.

Is this single A?

Yes. It wasn't where I wanted to go but it was still a step up. I wanted to go to Lakeland and the Florida State League because it was a little bit stronger league than the South Atlantic League at the time. But I did go up there as the number-one starter.

How did that season go?

Started out rough and ended rough. I ended up getting reinjured. This time it was my shoulder. We thought it was tendinitis all along. It was sore, and I couldn't get it loose, and finally it just broke down on me and I went back to instructional league at the end of the season to be evaluated.

Did you learn anything other than the fact you have a sore shoulder?

I had a lot of tests run. I had a lot of clunking in my shoulder so I went to Detroit and the doctor looked at it and he thought it was a labrum problem—something that was pretty major—and decided to go ahead and cut me.

I know you have a choice about whether you get cut on or not, but what kind of choice is it?

Well, I had rehabbed it all season long and I had taken every damn anti-inflammatory there was out there and I was to the point of, Let's do something and get it right.

Were you scared at all?

Oh yeah, because going in, with the labrum and all, hell, who knows if you're going to come back or not.

So how does surgery go?

It turns out good. I did have some tears in my shoulder but it was on the underside of my cuff, so the labrum was fine. It was a little loose, but fine. And they shaved all that stuff, cleaned all the junk out, patted me on my ass, and sent me on my way. I went to Georgia this time because I wasn't going to be able to work and my fiancée was living with her parents in Myrtle Beach, South Carolina, during the winter because she had graduated. I was going to have to rehab my shoulder and all that.

Can you do that in Cordele, Georgia?

Well, I had to drive to Macon to do it, but I did rehab all winter long. I got to see the fiancée sparingly at best and went down to Lakeland early again—this time according to their wishes—to get looked at. I was there about a week ahead of the pitchers and catchers and everything checks out good. I wasn't allowed to throw in the bullpen until I went down there so it's all flat, level throwing. So I went down there and really didn't throw that much beforehand because they didn't want me to, so I didn't really start throwing until I went to spring training.

Do you get up to full speed while you're down there? Do you have to stay behind when everybody else breaks camp?

I was full speed my last two times out, and I was in the reliever role and I broke camp with Lakeland.

That would've made you happy the year before. Does it make you happy now?

I knew I wasn't going back to Fayetteville, let's put it that way. But I was sad in a sense because of a couple of guys that I played with in Fayetteville—two of my closer friends that I had kind of developed relationships with—went to Double-A. I still had some friends from Fayetteville who were in Lakeland but I wanted to be in Double-A.

But with your rehab and all it's pretty understandable. And this is the first time that your primary role is as a reliever. What kind of year do you have?

I had a good year, a good year. I moved up after about a month and a half in Lakeland. I moved up to Trenton and Double-A and have a good season there.

What do you do after the season? Do you go home? Visit the folks? Visit the fiancée?

The fiancée is out of the picture now.

Is this "absence does not make the heart grow fonder" or do you just have two different lives now?

Two different lives. She thought I needed to get along with my real life and I agreed with her. She wasn't much of a baseball fan, plus the time apart didn't help matters, either.

Does real life and a baseball life share anything in common? Because even in the off-season you're just kind of pretending, aren't you?

It's not a real life. Yeah, there's no comparison, really. The baseball life is totally different from what I'm experiencing now. It's totally different. She thought that I needed to concentrate more on finishing my degree and getting a real job and going home. And like I said, she wasn't much of a baseball fan, and I think she even was kind of disheartened when I bounced back from my surgery because she wanted to spend more time with me.

Well, that's understandable.

The baseball life is totally different and she wasn't prepared for it.

So where do you go after Trenton?

I stop off in Georgia and go to instructional league for the third time.

This is the end of 1994, before 1995, which is the year that you get called up to the Tigers. Are you still throwing the fastball, slurve, and an occasional change-up?

I'm throwing a little bit more of an overhand curve now along with my fastball, and, being a reliever, you have to show them a third pitch so I would show them a change-up.

How does the slurve become an overhand curve?

My curveball was a little flat, so we tried to put a little more drop on it.

Does the sore arm or the surgery change the dimensions of your pitch and you had to find a new one, or is this more of an adjustment?

I'm just making an adjustment. I didn't change my arm slot or anything. I just made an adjustment on how I threw it. And I did real well with it. I was successful with it.

Is that what you worked on during this instructional league?

Yeah, that and command. One of the things I always really struggled with was command. But I'm working on that and getting a closer look by the big boys up top.

Let's define "command." If I'm a bowler and I turn my wrist a certain way and throw it between this arrow and that arrow, then I want the ball to go the same spot every time. Is that what we're talking about?

Yeah, with my fastball moving so much, they wanted me to learn to harness the movement—kind of like Maddux and those guys—and also get to where I'm hitting spots with my breaking ball a little bit better, because right now they're looking at me as a closer.

We're talking about controlling your pitches within the strike zone.

Right. I'm throwing strikes. I'm trying to get to where I can put them where I want to.

Do you make the forty-man roster in 1995?

Yeah, I make the forty-man roster.

Can you keep your teeth in your mouth or is your grin bigger than that?

Oh, I was excited. It was a big day for me. That was probably my second highlight—getting the call saying I'd been placed on the forty-man roster.

So you go to pitcher-and-catcher camp in late February and you're there with, among others, David Wells, Jose Lima, C.J. Nitkowski, Mike Henneman, and Joe Boever. Are you overwhelmed?

Yes. Hell, I'm twenty-three years old when I report, and I've gone from arm surgery and rehab one November to being on the forty-man the next November. But this is the year of the strike, and that's another thing. I had to sit on my thumbs from the first two months of what normally would've been spring training. I'm sitting here in Haleyville, Alabama, waiting for the damn strike to end, and also attending players' union meetings. I attended two of those.

You go to the union meetings because you're on the forty-man roster, even though you had never pitched a major league inning.

Right. During the strike before, the union let the guys who'd never played—the guys who weren't on the twenty-five-man roster—they let them go to spring training. But this year they asked everybody to sit out.

Of course, I'm not going to cross the damn line.

But you have to be sitting in those union meetings thinking, I'll do anything they want me to do. Let's just start this season while they still love me.

Right.

You're twenty-four years old and you're a rookie when you eventually show up for pitcher-and-catcher camp. When you see David Wells do you call him David or Boomer or Mr Wells?

I called him Boomer. He's probably one of the easiest guys to approach. The first day I report I unload all my shit—or I just set my bag down and they unload it—and go outside to throw a little bit because I haven't thrown in two days because I was traveling. And here I am with my pitching coach, Ralph Truel, to the right of me. He had been down in instructional league the year before and he had played a large part in me getting put on the roster. I think he's with the Red Sox now. He's standing to the right of me while I'm playing catch with Mike Henneman. So, you know, of course I'm nervous.

All of the clubhouse people are treating you nice, moving your gear and all. 407
How are the players treating you?

Basically like your first year at college. They're not really giving you that much attention because, I mean, they're thinking your ass is going to be sent back down in a matter of days anyway. The rookies sat with the rookies in the locker room. If I was the manager in any kind of atmosphere like that I'd have it veteran-rookie-veteran-rookie just to keep that from happening. But that's not how it was for us. Pitchers stayed with pitchers and position players stayed with position players.

So if you're all lockering together—all the rookie pitchers—you can pretty much look around and figure that somebody on either side of you is going to be sent down.

Yeah, it's a matter of time.

Do you get cut?

No, I broke camp with them.

Where's the season opener?

The season opener was in California. Anaheim.

Do you have a place to live in Detroit?

No, not yet. I had a friend, Sean Bergman—he's still playing a little bit these days—we'd made arrangements to get an apartment together.

So your belongings go to Detroit and you go to California with the team. Where do you fly out of if you're in Lakeland?

We went to Tampa.

Is this a charter?

Yeah.

So everybody on there is a member of the Detroit organization or a member of the press covering Detroit. And this is cool.

Oh yeah. You've got Lou Whitaker in the background, yelling, This ain't no college ball no more.

And Alan Trammell's still on the team that year.

Yeah. Super guy.

So you get to Anaheim and you check into the team hotel, and you take a bus to the stadium and you put on the Tigers uniform for the first time for a regular-season major league game and trot out to the bullpen.

Yep. And it was indescribable. It was just one of those things like, Damn. You can't believe it.

When do you first get to pitch?

In Seattle.

This is the same trip.

The same trip. Mike Moore was our opening-day starter and I think it was the season opener in Seattle when Boomer started. We only played one game in Anaheim. They flew us all the way to Anaheim for one game because, with the strike, that was how the schedule hit. And Boomer got shellacked. Griffey hit about a 450-footer off of him into the upper deck. There are fireworks going off, and here I am warming up in the bullpen.

What inning is this?

I believe it was the seventh.

What's the score?

11–2. Somewhere in that range.

Does the bullpen phone actually ring?

No, they gave my sign, which is glove lefty because I threw about three-quarters.

Who's watching the dugout from the bullpen to see who's supposed to get up?

Everybody, because when you're behind that much you know somebody's going to get in.

Is this the first time that they've given your sign to get up and throw?

Yeah.

Is anybody else throwing?

No.

So you know you're going in.

Yeah. I threw my first warm-up pitch about fifty-five feet. It rolled all the way behind the catcher. They had to stop the game to get the damn ball and I'm three feet away from the fans giving me hell. I don't necessarily have butterflies but there's so much adrenaline going that you don't really have all your wits about you.

Are any of your pitches working when you're still in the bullpen?

Yeah. I'm good.

What's the situation when you come in?

I had runners on first and second with less than two outs and my first hitter was Ken Griffey Jr.

Oh my Lord. This is either a dream or a nightmare come true.

You couldn't have pulled a needle out of my ass. And I remember this to this day. I'm looking in from the bullpen to see who the next hitter's going to be because they tell me I've got the next hitter, and it's Griffey on deck. I can remember running in and just glancing over and he's looking in the dugout to see if they wanted to pinch-hit for him, and they made him hit. Lou Piniella made him hit. And I popped him up.

At this moment, when you come in, can you remember how they told you how to pitch to Griffey?

No. I was going by my catcher, Ron Tingley. He was a veteran.

Are you going to throw the pitch he calls regardless of what he calls for?

Yeah, he had caught me a lot in spring training so he knew what I had.

And you depend on him for placement, pitch selection, everything?

Yeah.

And I guess you do a pretty good job if Griffey pops up.

The first pitch was a fastball on the outside for a ball, and the next pitch was not one of my best curveballs that he popped up. He popped out to first base.

Was that Cecil Fielder?

Yeah, sure was. And I take a deep breath and then I'm facing Mr Buhner, who promptly slaps one off the wall. First pitch. And it was a good pitch but they had pitched him away the whole game and he made the adjustment on me.

So it was an outside fastball?

Yep. And he jerked it to left field. A line drive off the wall for a double that scored two.

You've still got a zero ERA because those aren't your runners.

Yeah, but I end up walking the next guy. I think it was Edgar Martinez. I ended up walking him and I was kind of erratic then and my pitching coach came out and calmed me down because I was getting a little bit too quick. I wasn't sticking with my routine. And then Blowers, I think it was, hit a double down the line. It was a weak ground ball. One of those that if it was two feet more towards third then it would've been a ground ball, inning over. So they ended up scoring that one run and then I got the next guy to pop out.

So after that game you've got two and two-thirds innings left in your major league career. Where does that happen?

At home against Cleveland.

Similar situation?

First and second with no outs.

Are you behind?

Yes.

Late in the game?

About the fifth. We were down by four, I believe.

How long is this after Seattle?

It was actually about a week later. We finished out the series in Seattle, then we flew back and I pitched like the third day of that series.

Who do you face?

Lofton, Baerga, Winfield, Murray, Thome, Belle. It's my second appearance in the big leagues. If anybody asks me about my ERA, I just say,

Look, my first two appearances were against the number-one and -two hitting teams in the American League that year. I faced the meat of the order with runners on and no outs.

Did they tag you?

I pitched well the first inning. They only ended up scoring one of the two runs on base. The next inning I came in and did fine.

How'd you do against Thome?

The first pitch I about took his head off. He crowds the plate against left-handers anyway and he had hit a seed off of me in spring training and I wasn't going to let him get the outside part of the plate on me again.

I think of all the people in baseball that I wouldn't want rushing the mound on me, it's Jim Thome.

Oh, well, I didn't try to hit him. I was trying to get him inside. Actually I got him out, walked Winfield, and struck out Belle. I got out of that inning unscathed. I think I walked four total. I walked two in Seattle and two in the Cleveland game.

So you give up runs in the third inning you pitch, which'll account for the two thirds. Which means they actually come and take you out.

Yeah.

You gave up one home run in the majors. Is that this inning?

Yep. I helped Mr Eddie Murray get to the 500 Club. A hanging change-up. A three-run shot.

When he hit it, did you know it was gone?

No, it barely got out. It was in left center, which is not a long way, by any means. Not in Detroit. And it barely cleared the fence. I thought it might be a double. And that's when they came and got me, after that.

Who came and got you?

412

Sparky.

The pitching coach comes out to talk and Sparky comes out to make the change so when he comes out of the dugout you know you're gone. Does he hold his hand out for the ball?

Yeah. He pats me on my ass and sends me back to the dugout.

Does he say, Thank you, Sean, or anything?

No. I will tell you this much, though. There was a disputed call right before Murray came up. I walked Lofton and got an out and then there was a weak fly ball that Baerga hit. Hell, he and I battled it out for like eight pitches. He kept fouling me off, then he hit a weak fly ball to right field and Bobby Higginson was playing right at the time, and he dove. And he caught the ball, or so he claimed. I'm sure Bobby would tell the truth, and he said he caught the ball and then he doubled Lofton up, you know? But the umpire said he trapped it. Sparky came out there for that so he was still hot. He came out to get the ball from me and was eating the second base umpire's ass up. He still was pissed off at the call. And I'd thrown a few pitches because these guys weren't easy outs, by no means. Hell, Lofton was fighting every pitch off and so I'd thrown quite a few pitches. And the game was relatively still in reach. We'd scored a run or two to put it within reach and then Mr Murray expanded the lead on me. So Sparky was pissed off about that and I was, too, but I was a rookie. I didn't say anything to the umpire but Trammell was raising hell at him. Everybody was getting on him so that slap on the ass was more like, You did a good job. It wasn't like he was disappointed in how I did.

You don't get in another game. That's it.

That's it.

How much longer are you with the team before you get sent down?

I'm with the team for eight more days, twenty-one days total.

Are you asked to loosen up in the bullpen during those eight days?

Yeah, I got up twice but both times the pitcher ended up getting out of the inning.

So you're not thinking, Oh, they haven't used me in eight days. This isn't good.

No. I got up and was warming up twice.

How do you find out that you're being sent down?

We were in Arlington, and my brother drove out to see me. His father-in-law drove out, my parents are there, and my sister. And Sparky calls me in and tells me that they're sending me down. This is after the game, before we fly out. They have an off-day the next day. They're flying to Baltimore. So me and Ben Blomdahl, another rookie pitcher, fly back to Detroit.

You both get sent down at the same time?

Yes, except he went to Triple-A and I went to Double-A.

Are they making room for somebody?

No. That year they broke camp with three extra players and they had to trim it down.

The roster had been increased because they were scared people would get hurt because not everybody was in shape because of the strike.

Yes. Ben and I leaving brought them down to twenty-four, but Lou Whitaker was coming off the DL and that brought them back up to twenty-five.

Are you conscious of the fact that they'll be trimming the roster by such and such a date?

Oh yeah.

Did you think it was going to be you?

No, I didn't think it was going to be me. I still had confidence in how I was pitching. I just thought I needed a little bit more time. I'd been brought in to two situations and the first one we were getting the hell beat out of us. Now, the second one's a different story. I think it's a sin to start a rookie in the middle of an inning with runners on. Unless, and now that I think back about it, they were trying to train me to be

Henneman's replacement. That's what I was doing when I was relieving that year in Double-A. See, I never played a day in Triple-A. I went Double-A, the big leagues, and back to Double-A.

Did they have a closer in place at Triple-A so they sent you to Double-A so you could be the closer there?

Right.

Is Double-A in Trenton again?

Jacksonville. They had moved. I went down there and didn't get to pitch like I thought I should. It was May so they'd been into the season for a month and a half, and the manager already had his favorites. He was told to get me my innings but I didn't get them and I was pissed. I mean, the two guys that were getting all the innings in the spots where I was supposed to be were scabs. And nothing against them, but in my eyes they were guys who were just hanging on by a wing and a prayer anyway. They ended up releasing all of them within a month except for these two guys because they were doing a good job. They were good Double-A pitchers—don't get me wrong—but one of them was twenty-seven and never got past Double-A and the other one was even starting to flirt with a knuckleball. But they were getting some innings because winning was all the manager was concerned about. And he gave some shitty reports. I know that for a fact, because my pitching coach told me he was giving me some shitty reports. They called me and asked me what was going on.

You finish out the year in Jacksonville. Are you upset that you're not brought up in September?

I had a little bit of tendinitis, and then at the end of the year I think he had pretty much buried all my chances of getting a call-up. They had put me on the DL. They weren't going to throw me because they didn't want to risk aggravating my arm. And at the end of the season, Jacksonville was in the playoffs and they needed a position player to come up so they threw me on the DL. If I'd have had any kind of sense I would've sued their ass off. But c'est la vie.

I flew up to Detroit. Before I got taken off the forty-man they had me looked at. I played catch there and did the testing—the computer tracking like they do for golf swings and things like that—so I still felt like a chance was there, and drove back and get taken off the forty-man at the end of the year.

What's your frame of mind?

To get back on it. I came in with a good attitude, busted my ass. I worked out with the Triple-A team for part of spring training and then ended up on Double-A again.

With the same manager?

Yeah. I struck out seventeen in twenty innings of spring training. I had my shit back. I was pumped up and everything else.

But there's nobody you can go to to say, This isn't the guy I need to be playing for?

Right. It's enough pressure to go out there and perform but it's another thing to know if you screw up that you're going to get buried because you're not one of his favorites. And I don't think it was ever a thing like personalities or anything else, he just wanted to win at all costs. He wasn't a good developmental manager. He was trying to win.

Did his managerial career progress?

No, he's no longer a manager as far as I know. Detroit fired him the year we're talking about. But I'm not getting to pitch at all so I called my agent and told him to ask for a trade or a release or something. I wasn't happy at all. So he called them up and told them I wanted a trade or a release and they didn't want to do either and I said, Well, then send me back down to Lakeland where I can pitch. And they did. I did not like my manager and I don't care if you quote me. Plummer's his name. He played as a backup to Johnny Bench in Cincinnati. I just didn't agree with his coaching philosophy, but I never really had it out with him until right towards the end. And I never really confronted him then.

Was he upset that you'd asked to be sent down?

I don't think he really gave a shit. He was more focused on winning than anything else, but he was also covering his butt. But the head of player development came down and talked to me and he asked, What's it going to take to make you happy? And I said, Give me some damn innings. Hell, I hadn't thrown in fourteen days. My arm was healthy and I'd pitched well the time before. So I went down and pitched in Lakeland. I didn't stay up in Jacksonville long. I wasn't going to waste another year. I ended up in Lakeland in May, I believe it was, and ended up starting. I led the team in innings that year—of course, I should have—and ended up having a decent ERA and decent win-loss record. When I got sent down, Dave Anderson was the manager at Lakeland. He played for the Dodgers for a few years and the Giants. He asked me when I'd pitched last, and when I said fourteen days, he said, Whitey, are you shitting me? You know, that type deal. I was known by Whitey now. Everybody called me Whitey. So I got my innings in there and pitched well. And by the end of the year, Jacksonville is being managed by Larry Parrish and Larry Parrish was my first manager in professional baseball. I would consider us friends. Plummer's out of the picture and they call me up and I end up getting to pitch in the playoffs. We won Southern League that year and I pitched a couple of games in the playoffs.

As a reliever?

As a reliever. And I did my job. Right now, though, my velocity was down a little bit. Not that much. But they knew I still wasn't real pleased with how I'd been treated and got Rule 5'ed. They only protected me on the Double-A roster that year, and I got Rule 5'ed by Seattle so I went to Seattle's spring training the next year. I'm assigned to Triple-A and have a good spring training, but the fire's not as strong. My season was erratic, at best, with Double-A in Memphis.

Did you start the year in Memphis?

Yes, and I finished the year in Memphis. I pitched decent at times but never really consistent. After I played in the big leagues my arm just never really felt right, and I don't know what it was. I don't know if I didn't keep working it out like I did when I rehabbed it, but I had been rehabbing every day with a physical therapist and nobody's going to be able to do what they do—with the machines and all—on a daily basis. But I just kind of fell off after that and as my skills started to diminish, so did the fire.

Is 1997 the end of it?

Well, I end up finishing the year with the Memphis Chicks, and got Rule 5'ed by the Yankees so I went to spring training with the Yankees. And I said it the other day, If I'd have started with the Yankees I'd still be with the Yankees. It's a business-type atmosphere in a sense, but you also got treated well. Not that we were abused by any means, but hell, as a minor leaguer in the Yankees' system, you're treated as well as some of the other big league teams are. The instructors knew what they were doing. Some teams are known for developing players and some aren't, and it's all because of their instructors. That's why the Yankees are so damn good—they've got great instructors. And they've got that winning attitude, too. Hell, you drive up and you see all of the World's Championship things in Tampa. It's just a different atmosphere. And I pitched pretty good there in spring training, but then El Duque signed and the domino effect hit and I didn't throw for the last five days and I knew it was coming.

Were you on the Triple-A roster?

Yeah. In spring training I pitched Triple-A and Double-A. And I pitched pretty good. My velocity wasn't where it was, and everything else, but I'm still pitching pretty good. I'd developed a pretty good change-up by this point, but when El Duque signed and the domino effect started I got bumped down to Double-A. It's not that I wouldn't have gone back to Double-A. I would've loved to have gone to Double-A, but they probably knew that I was shooting to make that Triple-A team and I got released the last day of spring training. Which kind of pissed me off in a sense, because they could've released me a little earlier so I could've had a little bit of time to catch on with somebody else. And I called up Ralph Truel who's with the Red Sox now, and I could've stuck around and kept playing, but the money wasn't there. I was married at that time.

Where was she when you got released?

She was here in Haleyville.

And you're in Tampa. So you pick up the phone.

And I call her and I said, Well, I got cut. But I had been kind of telling her to expect it. The last four days I could just see it. It doesn't take much to see that you're not going to be the one around when camp breaks. It was the only time I'd ever been released. And it was the final one. But my arm wasn't there.

When you were preparing her, did you talk about what you would do if it happened? That you might want to try and catch on with another organization?

418

Yeah, we talked about it. And she just told me, basically, to do whatever I wanted to do, whatever would make me happy.

What did you do?

Well, I came back, kept working out, kept calling some teams. Got responses like, It was still early in the season, they were set. By then, the fire was about out. After I got home for a little while, I thought about it. I was twenty-seven years old and I could keep playing and try to hook on, or I could start a family. Start a normal life, so to speak. I had a pretty good job offer and I chose just to move on with it. It was a hard decision. Hell, I broke down when I made the decision, but it was kind of a relief, too.

Did it feel like the right decision the next day?

Yeah, it did.

Have you had any major yearnings since? Does opening day do anything to you?

No, but like I told you earlier, I was always tougher on myself than I should've been. I wish that I'd been able to slough it off more. Because I took it to heart. Boy, I couldn't sleep if I pitched like shit one day. And I'd think about it the next day and the next day and that's not the mentality that you need to have to be a successful pitcher.

Do you have any regrets?

I guess the main regret that I have is not being a little bit tougher mentally. I wasn't weak in the sense that I was afraid of hitters, but I let shit get to me too much. And I still do today to a certain extent, but I've got a lot different attitude now. But that's just age. Granted I'm only four years older now, but four years is a long time. I wish I'd have just had a little bit more laid-back attitude.

Do you watch much baseball on television or go to any games?

I haven't been to a minor league game since. I went to one big league game. I watch just a little bit on TV. I follow my friends. I did develop some friendships and I keep up with them. Lima and I used to call each other *majone,* which is "brownnoser." Higgy—Bobby Higginson—and

419

I roomed together our first year of pro ball. He was a twelfth-round pick and we played together in Niagara Falls and knew each other all through the minors. Same thing with Brian Moehler. I played with him in Lakeland and he came up to Double-A. And I played with Tony Clark for two years so I just basically follow those guys, see how they're doing.

You've got some things that nobody can ever take away from you.

Oh yeah, and besides the baseball part, the shenanigans off the field, too. I mean, hell, I've seen so much stuff and been a part of so much stuff. Not necessarily partying or anything like that, but we did some crazy stuff.

It's still a bunch of boys no matter how old they are.

Oh, hell yeah. And playing a game for a living, you're being kids. It was fun. It was. And it still feels good.

BILL PIERRO lives in Brooklyn, New York. He has two children, Bill Jr, a high school Earth Sciences teacher, and Denise, an emergency room worker at Maimonides Hospital.

REVEREND WILLIAM H. GREASON and his wife Willie O. live in Birmingham, Alabama where he has been the pastor of Bethel Baptist Church for thirty-one years.

Joan and **TED WIEAND** have been married for forty-eight years. They have three sons, two daughters, eight grandsons, three granddaughters and one great-grandson. Ted plays golf poorly, and likes to hunt and fish.

JOE STANKA is "thankful that God has blessed him with a wonderful wife of more than fifty years, four fantastic children, a great son-in-law and daughter-in-law, ten special grandchildren and two extra special great-grandchildren." Most of his family live nearby in southeast Texas where Joe has been "happy in retirement" since 1995.

Kathy and **FRED BRUCKBAUER** have been married for forty-three years. They have four children, Terry, Deb, Sandy and Amy, and twelve grandchildren. Fred is now retired in Naples, Florida after thirty-four years with John Deere Company. His hobbies include fishing, hunting, golf, traveling and following baseball, especially the Minnesota Twins.

421

CECIL BUTLER lives with two dogs and two cats in the woods northwest of Atlanta. He spends a great deal of his time with "the woman he goes with." Cecil has two grandchildren and two great-grandchildren, enjoys hunting and fishing, and grows his own vegetables. His beer of choice is Michelob Light.

LARRY YELLEN thanks his wife, Sybil, and his two brothers, Marty and Jay, for continuing to encourage him to become a math teacher at the middle or high school level. Larry is looking forward to his daughter, Stacey, giving birth to his first grandchild in January, 2003. Her due date just happens to be his sixtieth birthday—January 4th. He is also very proud of his son, Michael, for achieving just about everything he ever wished for him.

ARNOLD UMBACH lives with wife Bobbie in Auburn, Alabama. They will celebrate their fortieth wedding anniversary in 2003. They have two grown sons, Arnold III (Trip) and Heath, and three grandsons, Swede, Warren and Dow. Arnold has been practicing law with the same firm for thirty years. He likes to hunt, fish and raise cows.

MIKE JUREWICZ lives in the Twin Cities of Minnesota with his "wonderful" wife, Michelle, their children Ryan and Ashley, and dog Misty. His daughters Jennifer and Juliet are both married and Mike has two granddaughters, Alexandra and Amanda. He is looking forward to retirement so he can devote all his time to his wife and the kids who play baseball in neighborhood parks.

FRED RATH is a real estate developer specializing in the construction and management of apartments in Tampa, Florida, where he resides with his wife Joan. They have two children, Tiffany and Fred II.

RAY PETERS and his wife Janis have been married for thirty-two years, exchanging vows on the only off-day of the 1970 Portland season. They have two sons, R.J. and Brad, and a daughter-in-law, Terra. An executive specializing real estate for financial institutions, Ray enjoys golf, reading and collecting 1960s spy novels. He lives near Dallas, Texas.

422

JIM FOOR has been married to his wife Sandy, "the owner and general manager of the family," for ten years. He has four stepchildren, Melanie, Tal, Olivia, and Phillip, and works as an engineer in Houston, Texas for Kellogg, Brown and Root. After many years of coaching youth athletics, Jim now spends his free time playing tennis, golf and kayaking in Maine.

PAT OSBURN lives with his wife and five children in Bradenton, Florida. He's been in the insurance business for the past twenty years, and his hobbies include golf, jogging and raising golden retrievers.

SHELDON BURNSIDE lives and works in Montgomery, Alabama.

ROGER SLAGLE lives with his wife Sherry, a middle school teacher, in White House, Tennessee. He works as a steel erector with his brother-in-law and a stepson, Trey Coker. Another stepson, Cory, plays college football, while his other two children, Jacie, and Tyler, are also heavily involved in school athletics. Roger enjoys a weekly Sunday morning golf game, and attending the games of children.

STEVE RATZER lives in Lakeland, Florida with his wife Carolee Gathany-Ratzer. He works with Crawford Ker's Winghouse restaurants and coaches boys' fourteen and under baseball with the Lakeland Blaze.

STACY JONES loves his children, Sheridan, ten, and Emma Grace, four.

SEAN WHITESIDE lives in Haleyville, Alabama with his wife Celeste, and their son John Benford Whiteside. He enjoys golf and spending time with his family.

ROB TRUCKS lives with his spouse, Karan Rinaldo, in Long Island City, New York. Born on Roberto Clemente's twenty-seventh birthday, he is a lifelong Pittsburgh Pirates fan with one previous interview collection, *The Pleasure of Influence* (Purdue University Press, 2002), to his credit. He is currently working on an oral family history centering on his great-uncle, Virgil "Fire" Trucks.

423

Thanks to the ballplayers and their families; Karan Rinaldo; Wayne and Emily Trucks; Beth, Richard, Courtney and Caroline Shea; Steve Trucks; Marilyn Rinaldo; John and Emilie Marvosa; and Tony Rinaldo.

Additional thanks to Will Georgantas; Chris Chambers; Michael Smith; Mel Behney; Will, Jessica, Emma June and Sadie Kimbrough; Taylor and Betty Phillips; Geoff, Nikki, Zoe and Amanda Schmidt; Jeff and Tina Young; Will Blythe; Bryan DiSalvatore; Richard Giles; Inman Majors; and Valerie Vogrin.

ACKNOWLEDGEMENT: The conversation with Bill Greason previously appeared in *The Distillery*.

428

PHOTOGRAPHS

cover photo by John Marvosa

page 19, courtesy of Bill Pierro

page 33, courtesy of Bill Greason

page 43, courtesy of Ted Wieand

page 53, courtesy of Joe Stanka

page 79, courtesy of Fred Bruckbauer

page 93, courtesy of Cecil Butler

page 105, courtesy of Larry Yellen

page 121, courtesy of Arnie Umbach

page 137, courtesy of Mike Jurewicz

page 169, courtesy of the Chicago White Sox

page 191, courtesy of Ray Peters

page 213, courtesy of the Detroit Tigers

page 239, courtesy of Pat Osburn

page 265, courtesy of the Detroit Tigers

page 299, courtesy of Roger Slagle

page 321, courtesy of the Montreal Expos

page 355, courtesy of Stacy Jones

page 389, courtesy of Sean Whiteside